FOR HOME AND COUNTRY

THE CENTENNIAL HISTORY OF THE WOMEN'S INSTITUTES IN ONTARIO

FOR HOME AND COUNTRY

THE CENTENNIAL HISTORY OF THE WOMEN'S INSTITUTES IN ONTARIO

L I N D A M . A M B R O S E

With Appreciation

The initial assistance of Paul Bator and the Ontario Heritage Foundation and the award of its research grant were invaluable. It gave the book committee and the provincial Board the impetus needed. The helpful assistance of Special Collections and Library Development, University of Guelph Library, the Ontario Agricultural Museum and the Boston Mills Press were essential.

DONATIONS OF $1,000 OR MORE

Bank of Montreal
Eastern Area Women's Institute
Dufferin North District Women's Institute
Prince Edward District Women's Institute
Mountsberg Women's Institute
Selwyn Women's Institute
Jane O. Croft

OTHER CORPORATE DONATIONS

Matsushita Electric of Canada Limited
Royal Bank of Canada

THANKS ALSO

To the book committee, the FWIO office staff, the many proofreaders and our supportive membership.
To the many other Women's Institute areas, districts, branches and individuals who contributed to the FWIO book expenses.

OVERLEAF: *FWIO Quilt, 1949* — UG, FWIO Collection

7382 Wellington Road 30, RR 5, Guelph, Ontario N1H 6J2 519-836-3078

CANADIAN CATALOGUING IN PUBLICATION DATA

Ambrose, Linda McGuire, 1960–
For home and country: the centennial history of
the Women's Institutes in Ontario

Includes bibliographical references and index.
ISBN 1-55046-190-7

1. Federated Women's Institutes of Ontario – History
2. Women's institutes – Ontario – History. I. Title

HQ1909.05A42 1996 305.4'06'0713 C96-931963-0

PRODUCED BY THE BOSTON MILLS PRESS
(A division of Stoddart Publishing Co. Limited)
132 Main Street, Erin, Ontario N0B 1T0

Design by Gillian Stead
Printed in Canada

Maps compiled by Janine Roelens-Grant, Bev Coutts and Betty Caston Veitch
Cartographer Marie Puddister

To the members of the Ontario Women's Institutes

Mrs. John McCullough, 1949 Secretary, Bernice Noblitt, FWIO President, and Helen McKercher, Director, Home Economics Branch, wave as they stand by a large FWIO ensignia at the 25th annual Officers' Conference, 1973.
— UG, FWIO Collection, *Home and Country*, summer 1973

CONTENTS

FOREWORD

This is a book that was just waiting to be written. Here in its pages are revealed the faces, the characters, the audacity and the inventiveness of a century of women and their work in rural communities across Ontario. Here is the story of a small idea whose seeds were planted, grew and flourished until they touched the lives of millions of women.

On a cold February night in 1897, in the Southern Ontario village of Stoney Creek, the first Women's Institute in the world held its inaugural meeting. No one present that night could have dreamed that this fledgling organization would pioneer in the field of women's issues, the strengthening of family life and the enrichment of rural communities, not only in their own province, but across Canada and internationally.

In 1990, the Women's Institutes of Ontario began making plans to pay tribute to those members who had nurtured their organization and helped it to grow. To date no definitive book had been written about this organization which would tell the story, in human terms, of the accomplishments of individual, "ordinary" members and how they went about changing things.

At the suggestion of Jane Croft, a member of the Board of Directors of the Federated Women's Institutes of Ontario, a motion was passed in 1991 authorizing the printing of a history book as part of the centennial celebrations to be planned for 1997. Thanks to the persistence, fundraising skills and promotion of the idea, and the beginning of the documentation for this project by this one enthusiastic woman, we are all able to share in the very real history of what has become an influential organization across Canada and worldwide.

Very early, a decision was made to tell the story in narrative form, in "storybook" tradition. The Federated Women' Institutes of Ontario Book Committee, comprised of Margaret Atkins, Jane Croft and Lynn Campbell of the Ontario Agricultural Museum, wrote the "terms of reference" for the project, and with the help of Janette Jardine, selected Dr. Linda Ambrose from forty-three applicants. In Dr. Ambrose were embodied the writing skills, the research background, the human touch and the wonderful sense of humour that leaps off these pages, not only to enlighten but to entertain. Through records and personal interviews in every corner of the province, Dr. Ambrose has woven her story. Through it she has provided, for women, for historians and for students of Women's Studies, a rare and valuable resource.

To everyone connected with the production of this book, we owe a tremendous debt of gratitude. From the vision and efforts of Jane Croft to the printed manuscript of Dr. Ambrose, the Women's Institute history in Ontario comes alive. Enjoy and absorb its pages and its pictures from cover to cover, as I have.

Peggy Knapp,
FWIO President,
1989–1991

Springbrook WI, circa 1901. — *Springbrook WI Tweedsmuir History*

PREFACE

What is the Women's Institute? This is a question that I have been asked countless times over the past few years. When friends, acquaintances and university colleagues learned about my research project to write a history book for the Women's Institutes of Ontario, many of them posed that question. Usually it was asked in casual conversation, and I found myself trying to give an answer that was short and to the point.

"It's a group for rural women," I heard myself say, "an educational group that has performed a lot of community work in rural areas throughout the province." Trying to understand, the inquirers would probe further, asking, "A community group, like a service club, you mean?" A service club? "Well, yes and no. They have performed many acts of service, and raised a lot of money, but fundraising is not really the focus of the group." The questioners persisted, asking, "So, what is the focus then?" I tried to clarify. "From the start, the group has always had a strong educational focus, a group for women to learn things. It has even been called the 'university for rural women.'" There, I thought smugly, that's a good answer. "Learning what?" my curious friends wanted to know. "Initially, the group focussed on domestic science, or home economics as it was later called. You know, cooking and sewing and quilting and canning and things like that. Think of the displays at a rural fall fair. The WI is always there." "Ahh, so it's a group that celebrates those very traditional forms of 'women's work,' to keep them in the kitchen, eh?"

"Oh, no, it's more than that!" I protested. "Many women point to the WI as the group that first empowered them to speak in public, learn parliamentary procedure, or get involved with efforts to lobby the government for change. For many members, it was life-changing. They had never thought of themselves as public activists before they joined the WI. This is a group that has really empowered a number of women in new ways."

"A group devoted to empowering women, you say. Well then, how is this group connected to the women's movement?" a CBC interviewer once asked me. Oh boy, my answer to that one would have to be very carefully framed. I had met a few WI members who were proud to identify with the women's movement, and even to call themselves feminists. But I had met many more who adamantly denounced modern feminism as they understood it. They were quick to deny any connection between their group and other more strident women's organizations. To them, feminism was an "f-word," not one they would ever use. "Is it a feminist group? No. Well . . . maybe . . . that depends on your definition of feminism."

What is the Women's Institute? It seems a simple question at first. But the more I thought about it, the harder it seemed to be to find a satisfactory answer, especially a short one. This book represents an attempt to respond to that question with a longer answer. What is the WI? How has it changed over the years? Does it differ from place to place?

There is no simple answer, because this group has many different faces and many different voices. To begin to answer that question, I dug in to the existing research. I searched the libraries and archives for government records, collections of correspondence and policy manuals.

I went further, reading the other histories that have been published about the WI to celebrate its significant anniversaries. The Ontario Women's Institutes had already published three of these, to celebrate forty, fifty and seventy-five years of existence. These books were very helpful, especially in tracing the provincial level of the organization, and its connection with the provincial Department of Agriculture. The books had a tone of celebration to them, predictably painting a very positive picture of the WI's accomplishments and leaders. The tremendous growth of the organization and the inspiration provided by outstanding leaders was unmistakable. The official histories had only

VIPs of the WI, 1979.
LEFT TO RIGHT: *Mrs. Russell Campbell, Officer's Conference Secretary Treasurer; Mrs. Earl Morden, Erland Lee Home Secretary Treasurer; Mrs. Clarence Diamond, President FWIO; Mrs. Clifford Ritchie, Treasurer FWIO; Mrs. John Brown, Public Relations Officer; Mrs. Jeanetta Sager, Secretary; Mrs. Fred Howe, Curator.*
— UG, FWIO Collection, *Home and Country*, winter 1980

good things to say, and they predicted steady and uninhibited growth for the future. More of the same to come, they seemed to say. Yet the past twenty-five years have not been ones of steady growth, and there had to be some explanation for why that was so.

With each government report or official history, one nagging question kept coming to mind. Why did women join these groups? What was the appeal? There wasn't much in the official reports about life at the branch level. The official records were very clear about initiatives and directives coming down from Toronto or Guelph, and it was engaging to read about groups of women linking up with women from other provinces at national conventions, and since 1933, even crossing the ocean to be part of the international arm of the organization, long before world travel was within reach of most rural women. Yet clearly a lot of what was in those official reports and provincial summaries was the experience of only the most privileged few who could afford the time and money to travel. What about the others? What about the majority of members? Why did women look forward so intensely to their once-a-month meeting with the neighbour women? Why were they attracted to a group with so much structure and protocol to respect? What was this organization really like at its most local level?

It was clear from early on in this project that the members themselves would be needed to help me form more complete answers to my questions. After all, they had experienced the history I wanted to explore. I decided to send out a survey to the branches to ask for their help. In early 1993, I mailed a questionnaire to the nine hundred branches on the current mailing list from the provincial office of the Federated Women's Institutes of Ontario.

Researchers suggest that a ten-percent response to a mailed survey is a very respectable return and one from which valid conclusions can be drawn. Anticipating the branch responses, I went out and bought two boxes of one hundred file folders, continued my library research, and checked my mailbox every day. After a few weeks, the replies began. First there were one or two, then two or three, and later that summer, up to thirty-five a week. The response was overwhelming. In the fall of 1993, with funding support from the FWIO and the Social Science and Humanities Research Council of Canada Postdoctoral Fellowships program, I moved my project into an office at the University of Guelph history department, and called in volunteers to help open, sort and file the mail. Eventually, it amounted to more than six hundred responses, and occupied five banker's boxes of file space. WI members proved that they were very happy to be asked for their input into the history book project. The avalanche of mail eventually slowed to a trickle, and at last count, more than six hundred branches wrote back, bringing the response rate to well over sixty percent! So much for the ten-percent response rate.

As part of the questionnaire, each branch was asked whether any of their members could provide more information about the history of the Women's Institute. Almost every branch happily provided a list of willing souls. Then one day a member of Osnabruck Centre branch near Cornwall telephoned. "Do you ever travel to meet with branch members?" A trip was arranged, and after a few hectic days of interviewing in June 1993, I was hooked. This was a very valuable way to gather information. It was clear that oral history would have to be a big part of this project. I completed more than one hundred hours of interviews with Institute members across the province. Most often, I spoke to women in groups. This arrangement was partly for convenience, since I could hear more voices that way, but there were other reasons for the group interview format. Many of the women who talked on tape (and there were well over six hundred of them) were hesitant to participate in an interview at first. They felt that their experiences were too ordinary, too uneventful, too plain to warrant a historian's attention. Yet once they began to answer my simple questions — how they came to join the WI, what their meetings were about back then, who they saw at meetings, what they talked about, what they learned, what they did for their community — the women became very animated. They talked and laughed and cried together as they recalled the wonderful times they had shared in their WI groups, and wondered about what the future might hold for this movement. The taped interviews provide a permanent record of the fond memories, and the predictions and concerns that members shared with me. Oh, the stories! Stories of pranks played on fellow members, stories of finding their way in the city at conventions, stories of warmth and good humour. Some of them I can't tell, because members made me promise not to.

But WI members are more than just good storytellers. They also keep excellent records. They opened those local records to me, their carefully preserved minute books, scrapbooks, and Tweedsmuir history books. They brought out photographs of their groups in action, pictures of themselves, most with much younger faces, enrolled in short courses. The women are proud of these record collections, and many of the members consider themselves (or more accurately, are considered by other people) to be authorities and experts on local history and genealogy. The countless hours I spent at members' kitchen tables, poring over their books and hearing even more stories and more interesting bits of local branch history, were invaluable. What I found recorded there was a world of women's culture, a portrait of rural life that academic historians (most with urban backgrounds) have never explored.

I soon began to understand why women treasured their Women's Institute groups. There was a common theme to the projects they had taken on, a common sense of local pride and accomplishment in defining a project, pushing up sleeves to lobby for and work on it, and finally to see the thing achieved. Many are the photographs and newspaper articles that mark a special occasion in the life of a branch. How many celebration cakes have been cut to mark branch anniversaries across this province? How many times has the local hall been decorated in the Institute colours of blue and gold? How many poems have been composed to celebrate a member or mark a milestone? How many times has the local press acknowledged the essential contributions that the WI made to life in that community? How many local politicians have said the same thing, often with reference to women in their own families who played key roles in making their communities better?

Coming away from those local records, there could be no doubt about the importance of the WI in rural Ontario history. It was not

To co-ordinate the activities and build a sense of anticipation for the upcoming celebrations, the FWIO appointed a Centennial Committee well in advance of the 1997 anniversary. The five members are pictured here. LEFT TO RIGHT: *Lorianne Schmidt, Margaret Zoeller, Katharine Garwood, Pat Salter and Helen Duffield.*
— FWIO Centennial Committee

something that the official records in Toronto or Guelph could convey. This was not something that a focus on the prominent leaders or founders could really capture. This was a phenomenon that was very local in nature, very specific to the small community or concession road from which each branch drew its members. Yet this same local pride was duplicated again and again across this vast province. Branch after branch had its stories of local history to tell, its beautifully kept books, its members eager to introduce me to the Women's Institute in that place.

When the members themselves were asked the question "what is the Women's Institute?" they gave a variety of answers. Sometimes they disagreed with one another when pressed to explain their responses. "Is it a service club?" I asked. "Clearly this is a women-only group, so is it a feminist group?" "This is supposed to be an educational group," I suggested, "so what have you learned from the Institute?" "Did you depend on the WI to teach you how to cook and sew?" Some members were adamant. "I certainly did! I knew nothing about housekeeping at all when I got married," they asserted. Others were not so sure. "To be honest, I already knew most of that," they confessed. "My mother had taught me." "Well, then," I wanted to know, "why did you keep on going to the WI, if you didn't get that much out of it?" "Oh well, now, I didn't say I got nothing out of it. You asked me what I learned. I don't think of WI as an educational group primarily. For me it has always been a social time." But then another member would interject. "Now wait a minute, don't give her the wrong impression. The WI has always been more than just a social club, or tea and cookies and a bunch of women sitting around visiting."

The members themselves were having just as much trouble coming to consensus on their answer to my simple question as I was. Of course, some of them directed me to the Handbook, to read the official definition of the movement. "Well, it is really summed up in our motto," another member would interject. "'For Home and Country,' that says it all."

The Women's Institute has been many different things to different people. These recurring discussions called to mind a familiar fable,

The Convention '97 Committee, charged with co-ordinating the WI celebrations in Hamilton in June 1997, drew on the expertise of representatives from across the province. The following members served: Peggy Knapp, Christine Reaburn, Peggy Mcleod, Katherine McNaughton, Betty Ann Mollard, Mary Janes, Joan Law, Joan Playle, Jerinne Porteous, Ruth Halbert, Rosine Findley, Marilyn Sharp, Leone Foerter, Kay Taylor and Margaret Munro. — Peggy Knapp

"The Blind Men and the Elephant." In the story, several blind men experience an elephant for the first time, and depending on their sense of touch to inform them, each one approaches the animal and takes hold of a different part of the elephant's anatomy. The one who touches the trunk is convinced that the elephant is like a snake, while his friend who feels the leg described the creature like a tree. Another who comes in contact with the side of the animal is sure it is like a brick wall, and the fourth, who grabs the tail, thinks that the elephant is like a rope.

Describing the Women's Institute is just like that. Everyone who has come in contact with the WI has her or his own impressions of it. To some, it is the educational vehicle they depended upon, to others, it's a group committed to political activism. To some, it's where they gained self-confidence in public speaking; to others, it's a friendly cup of tea once a month with the neighbours. For some, it's the group that cared enough to restore the local community cemetery, or the ladies who made a quilt for the family who had the house fire. To the historians, it may be either the brainchild of Adelaide Hoodless and the domestic science movement, or the creation of a provincial government attempting to keep rural voters happy with programs designed to improve rural life.

In the story of the elephant, a heated argument breaks out among the blind men about who is right in his perception of the beast. The wise king intervenes to set the record straight. "Each one of you is right in his view," he pronounced, "and yet, each of you is also wrong." He explains that in order to really understand the elephant, they had to combine their answers and get the bigger picture. The same analogy holds for the Women's Institutes. To understand the Women's Institutes, and especially the history of the WI, as many different angles as possible must be described.

What is and what was the Women's Institute in Ontario? You may be surprised at some parts of the answer. But after all, one hundred years is a long time and the WI has changed many times over the years. As you look to the future, remember that you have to hear from all parts to get the complete picture. Happy birthday, WI!

Adelaide Hunter Hoodless, one of the official founders of the Women's Institutes, turned her family tragedy into a crusade for domestic science education. She is pictured here with her three eldest children, circa. 1886, before the birth of John Harold, the one who died in infancy.

— Adelaide Hunter Hoodless Homestead

CHAPTER ONE

Organizing Women: The Early Founders to 1904

When John Harold Hoodless died in August 1889, at the age of fourteen months, his mother was heartbroken. Doctors in Hamilton, Ontario, concluded that the child had died from "summer complaint," an intestinal ailment that was common among young children at that time, caused by drinking impure milk. Shocked at her loss, and even more at her ignorance of domestic hygiene, this woman took her family tragedy beyond the point of personal grief. She realized that if she, as a careful parent and an educated person, was ignorant of basic domestic science knowledge, then there must be thousands more women like her. Adelaide Hoodless, the bereaved mother, turned personal tragedy into a public movement. Most accounts of the history of the Women's Institutes (WI) of Ontario begin with the experience of this grieving woman.

Adelaide Hoodless's role in the founding of the organization has been told and retold by Institute members so many times that it has grown into well-known and well-loved folklore. She is highly venerated among women around the world; Women's Institute members from all across the globe make pilgrimages to her birthplace near St. George in Brant County. A poem written in 1916 by Mrs. J.B. Shrigley, a Women's Institute member from Dorset, in the Muskoka region of Northern Ontario, is a typical expression of the high regard members hold for Mrs. Hoodless.

All praise to her who oped the door,
Who called the women of today
To take their place and their stand
To guard the home and native land —
Not from the foe who comes with swords,
The greedy, world-destroying hordes;
But those who lurk within the fold
And banish peace still as of old.

Yes, hers shall be a household name
Who laboured not for worldly fame,
But nobly answered to the call
Which makes for good — the good of all;
No jewel'd crown was ever placed
On worthier brow, where time had traced
With gentle hand the lines of care,
Which loving thought had pencilled there.

At the time of Addie Hunter's birth, the family lived in this farmhouse in Brant County near St. George, Ontario. Mrs. Hunter had been recently widowed, but the family could still afford to provide higher education for several of the children. — UG, FWIO Collection

The Hunters' home was comfortable and modest. This view of the family parlour shows one of the bedrooms in what is now a historic site restored by the Federated Women's Institutes of Canada. — UG, FWIO Collection

The name of Hoodless long will live,
A guiding star to those who give
Their best of life, their thought, their care,
The burdens of their kind to share.
Then may we falter not nor stray,
But onward press in wisdom's way.
And all united, firm and true,
To stand and wait, or dare and do.
Long may our institutions stand
To bless the home and native land;
Aye, stand undaunted in his might
For Home and Country, God and Right.[1]

Who was this inspiring woman, whose very name has become a household word among Women's Institute members? Adelaide Sophia Hunter was born on February 27, 1857, in a farmhouse in Brant County on the Blue Lake Road near St. George, Ontario. She was the last child born to Jane Hamilton Hunter, whose husband David Hunter had died just months before the birth. Addie Hunter grew up in the small community where she attended the "German School," the rural schoolhouse just a mile and a half down the road from her family farm. Although we do not know the details of her family's economic status, it is clear that, despite her father's premature death, the Hunters had some financial security, for the family could afford to send her older brothers to college. Addie herself attended a ladies college in Cainsville while she lived with her older married sister, Lizzie. The Hunter family had connections with some very prominent citizens, which helps to explain how Adelaide met her future husband, John Hoodless. He was acquainted with Benjamin Charlton, a former mayor of Hamilton, whose brother Seth Charlton was married to Adelaide's sister Lizzie. Through friends and family, John and Addie were introduced to one another and began a courtship.

On September 14, 1881, when Adelaide Hunter was twenty-four, she married John Hoodless of Hamilton and joined a very prosperous Hamilton business family. As her biographer remarked, "From Addie's point of view, John was a marvelous catch. Not only was he young and popular, a solid citizen and up-and-coming pillar of the community, he was financially well off."[2] The young couple soon began their family, and four children were born in quick succession: Edna Clarkson, born July 7, 1882; Joseph Bernard, born December 10, 1884; Muriel Adelaide, born July 27, 1886;

and John Harold, born June 23, 1888. In the summer of 1889 Adelaide Hunter Hoodless was a busy young mother; married for eight years, she had four children under the age of seven. Then tragedy struck.

The obituary on August 10 in the local newspaper, *The Hamilton Daily Spectator*, was short and concise: "Hoodless — at 55 East avenue south, John Harold, youngest son of John and Adelaide Hoodless, aged 14 months. Funeral at 4 o'clock p.m. Saturday. Friends will please accept this intimation."[3] The Hoodless baby was buried that summer, and "the Domestic Crusader" was born.[4]

After her baby's death, Adelaide Hoodless devoted herself to a new cause: promoting domestic science education. The young Mrs. Hoodless was angry and disappointed that her own education had left her so ill-equipped to run a household without tragic consequences. "She believed the educational system in force in Ontario at that time to be absolutely wrong. She did not approve, at all, of educating boys and girls along the same lines, when their life work was so vastly different. . . . Mrs. Hoodless said girls should be educated to fit them properly for that sphere of life for which they were destined . . . 'home-making.'"[5] She became a spokesperson for a movement that worked to have women trained in the practical science of running a household according to scientific principles, first opening a cooking school in Hamilton in 1894. Later on, she played an important role in raising funds and promoting a school for domestic science on the Guelph campus of the Ontario Agricultural College (OAC). Hoodless was also effective in encouraging the Montreal tobacco magnate, William Macdonald, to donate the funds for building the Macdonald Institute, which opened its doors in 1903. Although she once taught an ethics course there and had written a textbook on domestic science, the school at Guelph soon came to be dominated by other instructors with more solid academic credentials. After her early efforts at fundraising, Adelaide Hoodless still promoted the school but was not really an active participant in it. Although she is generally credited with founding the Women's Institute movement, a recent bio-

OBITUARY

— *The Hamilton Daily Spectator*, Aug. 10, 1889

DIED

Hoodless — At 55 East avenue south. John Harold, youngest son of John and Adelaide Hoodless, aged 14 months. Funeral at 4 o'clock p.m. Saturday. Friends will please accept this intimation.

Adelaide Hunter Hoodless joined an established Hamilton business family when she married John Hoodless. This was their library in the family home, Eastcourt, in Hamilton, Ontario, where they lived after the death of their youngest son. — UG, Adelaide Hoodless Collection

Addie Hunter, shown here as a young woman, married well when she became Mrs. John Hoodless of Hamilton.

— UG, Adelaide Hoodless Collection

graphy by Cheryl MacDonald argues that Adelaide's direct involvement in the WI was limited to public events such as the all important founding meeting.[6]

On February 19, 1897, Adelaide Hoodless addressed a meeting of one hundred and one women in a town hall meeting in Stoney Creek, Ontario. She was there to promote the idea of forming rural women's groups, to be known as the Women's Institutes. It was a stormy winter night in that little town on the Niagara Escarpment, but the crowd received Mrs. Hoodless and her ideas very warmly. Here was the mother who had lost her child eight years earlier, appealing to other women to learn what she had not known and to spare themselves similar tragedies. Hoodless told the women in Stoney Creek that it was time to concentrate on rural living from the women's point of view, to elevate the job of homemaking to the same level as that of farming. What the women needed, she proposed, was a special women's group, a group that could meet together to learn how to improve their homemaking through a study of domestic science.

Adelaide's arguments found a receptive audience that night for a variety of reasons. At the end of the nineteenth century, most women from rural homes were ready to support Hoodless's appeal to invest in the rural household. At a time when much attention was being paid to techniques in scientific farming and strategies for curbing rural depopulation, it made sense to women that equal attention should be paid to the farmers' household and living quarters. Why should more attention, money and concern be lavished on the farm livestock than on the farm family? According to her son, Bernard Hoodless, Adelaide was not afraid to criticize the existing educational system. He recalled an exchange between his mother and a professor of bacteriology from the OAC in 1896. "I remember mother attacking him on the failure to do anything for farm women and children while great efforts were being made to disseminate information on the care and breeding of livestock."[7]

Farmers had access to such information through groups called Farmer's Institutes, which had existed since 1884 under the auspices of the provincial Department of Agriculture. There is in fact a close connection between the Farmer's Institutes and the Women's Institutes, because the person who helped to facilitate the WI organizational meeting in Stoney Creek where Hoodless made her historic speech was a member of the Farmers' Institute. His name was Erland Lee, and he is officially recognized, along with Adelaide Hoodless, as a cofounder of the first Women's Institute.

The meeting of February 19, 1897, was actually the third time that Erland Lee had heard one of Mrs. Hoodless's powerful talks. On the first occasion, he heard her speak at an agricultural conference at the Ontario Agricultural College in Guelph in 1896, where she "told the almost entirely male audience that they were more concerned about the health of their animals than about the health of their children, and that they fed their pigs and cattle more scientifically than they fed their families."[8] Lee was intrigued by what he heard.

Mr. Lee was part of the planning committee for the upcoming annual meeting of the South Wentworth Farmers' Institute to be held in February 1897. Remembering Adelaide

Hoodless as a very effective speaker, he suggested that the group contact her to address the evening session of their meeting, when both men and women would be present. The suggestion was not welcomed by his fellow members. The idea of a female lecturer was too radical for some of the local farmers, and they advised him to choose the speaker very carefully. The final decision was left to Lee, however, and he proceeded with his original idea of inviting Mrs. Hoodless.

Adelaide gladly accepted the invitation. And so it was that Lee heard her speak a second time; this time to his own Farmers' Institute group. Hoodless's talk was not a direct proposal for the establishment of a Women's Institute, but rather a reiteration of her pet theme, "The Value and Need of Domestic Science and Sewing in Our Public Schools." However, in collaboration with Lee, a new proposal took shape. She suggested in her talk that perhaps domestic science education for rural women could best be accomplished through an organization that paralleled the existing Farmers' Institutes for men. After she had finished speaking, Lee inquired how many of the women present that night at the Farmers' Institute meeting would be interested in meeting again to follow up on the idea of organizing an Institute strictly for women. When all thirty-five females present showed interest, Lee invited Hoodless to return to Stoney Creek the following week to make her case.

Squire's Hall, the site of the famous organizational meeting of February 19, 1897, was a community hall in Stoney Creek, Ontario. Adelaide Hoodless returned to Stoney Creek to propose the establishment of a separate women's chapter of the Farmers' Institute of South Wentworth. — Erland Lee (Museum) Home

Thus, the famous founding meeting was scheduled for February 19. "During the week Mr. and Mrs. Lee were busy people," according to the *Stoney Creek Tweedsmuir History*. They spent the next few days "endeavouring to arouse the enthusiasm of the women and also encouraging them to attend the meeting with the result that when Mrs. Hoodless arrived in Stoney Creek, February 19, 1897, she found awaiting her in Squire's Hall, 101 women and one man. Needless to say, that man was Mr. Lee and he kindly acted as chairman for the evening."[9]

For the third time, Erland Lee heard Adelaide Hoodless speak out of her conviction, born of her grief, that "women's work, homecraft and mothercraft, was much more important than men's since it dealt with the home and the care of the loved ones who dwelt therein."[10] These rural homemakers were about to create what would become the largest international rural

THIS IS THE SITE OF
SQUIRES HALL
STONEY CREEK
WHERE WAS FORMED
THE
FIRST
WOMEN'S INSTITUTE
IN THE WORLD

Erland Lee and his wife, Janet Chisholm Lee, worked hard to publicize the lectures that Adelaide Hoodless delivered in Stoney Creek because they were committed to the idea that rural organizations were of benefit to both men and women.
— UG, FWIO Collection

women's movement ever established. Looking back on this founding meeting, one of the charter members, Jennie Morden, remarked in 1976, "Women's Lib is not so new. The Institute always had it."[11] Hoodless's third talk was a reiteration of her impassioned appeal to establish domestic science education, but this time it was accompanied with a specific proposal geared to rural women. The audience voted that night to "organize a Department of Domestic Economy, in affiliation with the Farmers' Institutes, to be called The Women's Department of the Farmers' Institute of South Wentworth." The first Women's Institute in the world was thus created. (The name of the group was later changed to the Women's Institute of Saltfleet, and then changed again to the Stoney Creek Women's Institute, when other Institutes were formed in the township.[12] The first branch still exists, and since 1978 it has been known as "Stoney Creek Charter Women's Institute.")[13]

Hoodless and Lee found that their audience on that first night was ready for just such an organization. In order to understand the readiness of those women, one has to consider developments that had occurred before 1897. By the end of the century, women's organizations had already been popular and well established in urban Ontario for several decades. A social reform movement calling for improved living conditions and new public roles for women was afoot, and Hoodless's experience of losing her baby due to unsanitary conditions was just the kind of problem that motivated women of the time to take public action. Hoodless was a very energetic woman and more typical of social reformers in the 1880s and 1890s than one might imagine. As an urban, upper-class woman with time for leisure and for volunteer work, she was part of a network of like-minded women who were committed to social reform. Over the years, she had connections with several groups working for reform, including the Young Women's Christian Association, the National Council of Women, and later, the Victorian Order of Nurses. Most of those efforts, however, were limited to urban settings.

While Adelaide Hoodless and her counterparts were busy with urban reform, other important developments were occurring in agricultural organizations, and Erland Lee was part of them. As a graduate of the Ontario Agricultural College and an active member of the Farmers' Institute, Lee was the type of person who was at that time heralded as a model farmer and an exemplary rural citizen. Educated farmers such as he were committed to implementing scientific principles in their work and to educating their neighbours and friends in order to spread the ideas of scientific agriculture. To make that possible, the Farmers' Institute was committed to bringing expert agriculturalists to local chapters of their group in order to communicate the latest research, and approaches to it, to the ordinary farmer. Because higher education in agriculture was not accessible to most farmers, lecturers were hired by the Superintendent of the Farmers' Institute to bring their expertise to the farmers. When Erland Lee saw the potential for expanding the Farmers' Institute model to include women, his perception was not widely shared by his male peers. There was one person, however, who shared his enthusiasm, and that was his wife.

Janet Chisholm Lee was certainly a key figure in the launching of the WIs, though she has never been given status as an official founder of the organization. She did, however, exert a tremendous influence in the early days of the movement. Janet Chisholm married Erland Lee in 1889, giving up her career as an educator in the new kindergarten movement in order to do so. When discussions about a Women's Institute were being launched, she worked with her husband to recruit women to attend the organizational meeting. She was instrumental, together with Erland and other friends, in shaping some of the key features of the new group, and she helped to draw up the constitution of the organization. The fact that the final copy of that document was drafted on Janet Lee's dining-room table is a well-known part of that story. The walnut table that she brought from her grandfather's home in Ancaster is on permanent display in the Erland Lee (Museum) Home, just outside Stoney Creek. The Lee Home, now owned and operated by the Federated Women's Institutes of Ontario as a historic site, is a distinctive landmark atop the Niagara Escarpment, overlooking the town of Stoney Creek and the city of Hamilton, that serves to highlight both the Lees' involvement and to preserve an important part of the history of the Women's Institutes of Ontario. Thus, the story of the founding of the WI is a fuller tale than simply that of the grieving mother, Adelaide Hoodless. The organization also owes its start to Erland and Janet Lee.

Other individuals also helped the fledgling WI movement to emerge and to survive. Among them were the charter members of the Saltfleet Women's Institute. The women who agreed to put their money down and take a membership in the first WI group are certainly of great historical significance, for without the members, there could be no WI. The membership of that first branch included some very notable community members, among them the seven who agreed to serve as the executive members: Mrs. E.D. Smith of Winona as president, Mrs. J.J. Dean of Fruitland as vice-president, Miss M. Nash of Stoney Creek as secretary, Mrs. J.H. McNeilly, of Fruitland as treasurer, and three directors, including Mrs. F.M. Carpenter of Fruitland, Mrs. E. Lee of Stoney Creek, and Mrs. C. De Witt of Tapleytown. Adelaide Hoodless was chosen as honorary president, though after her initial address her direct involvement was limited to a few special visits.

The members themselves were the real backbone of the new Institute. The first president, Mrs. E.D. Smith, was described by her daughter Verna as a woman who "was always deeply concerned with everything that lightened the drudgery and long hours of toil of the farmer's wife." Yet when Christina Smith was approached in 1897 to accept the office of president of the new organization, she struggled with her own conscience. Although she was eager to see the group established, because she was committed to the idea that

Erland and Janet Lee's home was a comfortable white farmhouse featuring distinctive gingerbread trim. According to the history books, "A lad named Moore, as a fourteen-year-old carpenter apprentice, carved from the home-grown lumber the verge boards running along the gables and front porch. His original pattern resembles a paper chain of maple leaves. It took him all one summer to do the intricate and artistic carving which is admired by all viewers of the house."

— *Ontario Women's Institute Story*; UG, FWIO Collection

In Memory of
ERLAND LEE and his wife JANET
who pioneered the first Women's Institute
-now world wide-
at Stoney Creek, February 19th, 1897
and to commemorate their home with table
on which the Constitution was drawn up.
Erected by the District of
South Wentworth Women's Institute

With the designation of the Lees' home as a historic site, their roles in the founding of the Institute are commemorated. A plaque erected in 1961 outside their home by the Wentworth South WI reads as above.

— *Ontario Women's Institute Story*

FIRST WOMEN'S INSTITUTE 1897

The world's first Women's Institute was organized at Squire's Hall, Stoney Creek, in 1897. Erland Lee, a founder of the Farmers' Institute, assisted by his wife, arranged the meeting. About 100 women from the Saltfleet Township district attended and were persuaded by Mrs. Adelaide Hoodless to form an organization of their own to improve their skills in the arts of homemaking and child care. Here, in the Lee home, Mr. Lee subsequently helped to draft the constitution of the new society. Mrs. E.D. Smith of Winona became the first president of the "Mother Institute." The Women's Institutes movement has since become a world-wide organization.

A second plaque, erected in 1967 by the Historic Sites Board, reflected the fact that Mr. Lee had been elevated to the status of a co-founder. — Ontario Heritage Foundation "a wife and mother should have some leisure and time to study improvements in her homemaking," she was concerned about how her activities outside the home might affect her own family. Mrs. Smith was a very busy woman. Involved with her husband's enterprises in the nursery and fruit business, she supervised her own household and provided "careful supervision of the purse strings [to] promote the growth of a business." In addition, she had two young children at that time, and she was concerned that they not be neglected because of her involvements. She settled that dilemma by weighing her hesitations against the contribution that she could make on behalf of other women, and she consented to serve.[14] Mrs. Smith and the other members of the new organization quickly went to work. According to the early official record, the new organization existed for very specific purposes. "The object of women's institutes shall be the dissemination of knowledge relating to domestic economy, including household architecture, with special attention to home sanitation; a better understanding of the economic and hygienic value of foods, clothing and fuels, and a more scientific care and training of children with a view to raising the general standard of the health and morals of our people."[15] Viola Powell, in her important history of the Institutes, observed that "very soon after organization, these pioneer members began to realize the value of their society to themselves and to their families, and wishing to spread the gospel of the Women's Institutes they began to write papers and articles for four different agricultural publications."[16]

The papers and articles written by the women of Saltfleet Township were not intended simply to promote groups meeting for their own sake. Their agenda was not primarily a social one. The meetings were clearly devised to be classes in home economics. Within the first year of their formation, the women at Stoney Creek decided "to undertake the Chautauqua study course in Domestic Science." This American curriculum was an early form of distance education. The women decided to obtain the necessary books and materials, and met once a month "for the purpose of taking up this course of reading."[17] These early meetings, which concentrated on education for improved homemaking and attention to the social problems of health and child-rearing, contained the seeds of many of the themes that would feature prominently throughout the coming century. Reading through reports of the early meetings, one researcher concluded that "these topics and discussions show that the women were blazing the trail along health and child welfare lines which later extended beyond the home into the school and the community at large."[18] While the women worked at the grass-roots level to produce papers, study together and encourage one another to adopt higher standards of homemaking, they also worked to create more new branches. Through the rural press, these women were able to publicize the news that women could finally have a group of their own. The popular Farmers' Institutes now had a parallel forum for women.

With the first group established at Stoney Creek, it became easier for groups of women in other places to follow suit. Two examples are particularly noteworthy: the Women's Institute of Whitby and the Women's Institute of Kemble. These branches, the second and third WIs established in the world, also grew out of the structure provided by the Farmers' Institutes and the enthusiasm generated by female lecturers addressing the local women. For each new group, it seems, there was a pattern that combined groups of interested local women, sponsorship by existing agricultural organizations, and inspiration from animated lecturers.

The lecturer responsible for organizing the second new group, the Whitby Women's Institute, was Miss Laura Rose. Miss Rose was a professional lecturer who taught dairying at the Ontario Agricultural College.

Laura Rose, an instructor of dairying at the Ontario Agricultural College, worked as a lecturer for the Women's Institutes in the early years. She played key roles in organizing new branches, creating the WI pin, and selecting the motto and official colours. — UG, OAC Collection

Firmly committed to the idea of separate spheres of work for men and women, Rose was in full agreement with Adelaide Hoodless's commitment to domestic science roles for women. She was eager to promote increased standards of hygiene among rural women, and she was convinced that women were particularly suited for their roles as wives, mothers and nurturers. For Miss Rose, later Mrs. Laura Rose Stephen, this translated into a lifelong commitment to the Women's Institutes, and she is credited with organizing many Institutes throughout the province of Ontario. She lent her highly respected name and her boundless energy to help with the organization of the Whitby group. Under the leadership of Mrs. Smith, a local woman who was eager to create a group like the one at Stoney Creek for her own community, the second Women's Institute was formed in the summer of 1897.[19]

The next Institute also followed the same pattern, with the same three essential ingredients. "At the Farmers' Institute at Kemble in that same year, viz. 1897, Mr. Creelman [later to become] Superintendent of F.I., gave . . . Mrs. James Gardner a place on the programme, at a joint meeting of the men and women. Mrs. Gardner took as her topic 'Man works from sun to sun, but woman's work is never done.'"[20] Mrs. Gardner's lecture, which was later reprinted in the Annual Report of the Department of Agriculture, shows that she was not resigned to a life of drudgery for women. Instead, she urged the women of Grey County to find more efficient ways of working so that they could take time for rest and for learning. She encouraged her listeners to prove themselves exceptions to the old adage, and to get their work done. She was not suggesting that they should work harder or faster, but more efficiently. She was convinced that by forming a Women's Institute, women could learn to concentrate on the essentials and avoid setting unrealistic goals for themselves. She was particularly critical of women who devoted themselves to "fancy work" and felt too pressured by it to take any leisure time for themselves. Not only did she provide fine speeches, but she also took it upon herself to play the promotional role that Janet and Erland Lee had played in Stoney Creek, travelling "from farm to farm in her buggy to tell the Kemble women of the two branches already formed, and of the possibilities for a similar effort in Kemble."[21] With Mrs. Gardner's perseverance and some assistance from Mrs. Smith of the Whitby WI, the Kemble Women's Institute was established that same year.

The early advocates were not without opposition. Not everyone was happy that these new Women's Institutes existed. In fact, male attitudes to women's organizations were among the biggest obstacles facing the young movement. Husbands apparently were concerned about the cash outlay required to establish such a group. Forseeing that criticism, Janet Lee had proposed a membership fee of only twenty-five cents per year to ensure that the costs were affordable for everyone. "Another sneer was 'Let them try it — all women fight

These early WI members belonged to the Kemble Women's Institute, the third branch founded in 1897. Through the efforts of Mrs. James Gardner, women in Grey County were encouraged to escape the drudgery of endless household tasks. — Kemble Women's Institute Tweedsmuir History and it will break up.'" Janet Lee was prepared with an answer to that jibe as well. "'We'll start with the Lord's prayer,' she suggested, 'That should put us in a good frame of mind.'"[22] According to a report by the Lees' daughter, "No man was in favour of women organizing. The most charitable said, 'Oh, well, let them start, it won't last long without a man to run it.'" But obviously, at least one man, Janet Lee's husband Erland, was supportive. He had taken a risk in suggesting Adelaide Hoodless as a speaker for the Saltfleet Farmers' Institute against the wishes of the male membership, and his invitation resulted in the formation of the first Women's Institute.

It is overstating the case to claim that "no man was in favour of women organizing," since Erland was not just supportive, but instrumental in organizing the Women's Institutes. Moreover, he was not alone in lending male support. There was, for example, E.D. Smith, Christina Smith's husband, who was a prosperous local orchard grower like Lee. Mr. Smith, the founder of the food company that bears his name, was a man with important political connections. He served as a federal member of Parliament and was later appointed to the Senate. His public experience showed him the importance of the rural constituencies and the power of lobby groups. His support behind the new women's organization helped to elevate its status in the minds of politicians and civil servants, and he also helped ensure that the constitution of the new group would provide a flexible and workable set of guidelines. The same is true of Mr. F.M. Carpenter, a member of the provincial legislature, who was married to one of the active charter members of the WI at Stoney Creek. Mrs. Carpenter was elected, along with Janet Lee, to serve as a "director" of the branch, and to assist the executive officers. These early charter members had their husbands' support and political acumen behind them. When the Women's Institute sought official political recognition, twenty years before women in Ontario could even vote provincially, they needed all the male sympathy they could muster. Erland Lee is credited with obtaining official government support for the WI. Undoubtedly the political expertise and knowledge of recent legislation, which he shared with Smith and Carpenter, were crucial to that success.

According to the *Ontario Women's Institute Story*, "Mr. Lee assisted in the drafting of the first constitution and by-laws. He also made the necessary contacts with the officials in the Department of Agriculture to explore affiliation for the women's group with the existing Farmers' Institutes."[23] Lee's strategy in seeking this affiliation was aided by his considerable knowledge of recent provincial statutes. Rural organizations in Ontario were governed by the regulations set out in *The Agriculture and Arts Act, 1895*. That Act was amended in 1896 to allow for the creation of new types of agricultural groups.[24] The new document set out the terms and conditions for agricultural organizations in Ontario that existed "for the purpose of education and improvement of rural life." It provided a way for new groups, not currently under the Department of Agriculture's jurisdiction, to petition for inclusion under the Act by becoming affiliated with existing groups. This would entitle these newly created organizations to the financial support of the government, as long as they were formed for the purpose of "education and improvement of rural life." It is no coincidence then that the objects of the WI were officially recorded as "the dissemination of knowledge" with "a view to raising the general standards of the health and morals of our people."[25] Erland Lee knew that if the Women's Institutes could prove that they existed for the right reasons, they would be entitled to official recognition under the Act. This new clause, amended in 1896, was the one that Erland Lee bore in mind when he proposed the creation of a separate women's chapter of the Farmers' Institute.

The Farmers' Institutes fell under the jurisdiction of the Department of Agriculture and the superintendent of the male groups became, by default, superintendent of the new Women's Institutes. In the early years, from 1897 up to 1904, two different men filled that post. Mr. F.W. Hodson, formerly of the staff of the *Farmers' Advocate*, served in the post from 1897 to 1899. His successor, serving from 1899 to 1904, was Dr. G.C. Creelman, later president of the Ontario Agricultural College. While neither of these men had any idea about the ultimate potential of the newly formed WI groups, their roles are central to the early story. In addition to managing the day-to-day affairs of the groups in the early years, they each contributed in a significant way to the WI's development. Hodson acted upon his very progressive notions about women's public roles, while Creelman brought important structure to the movement through his keen administrative expertise.

Even before Erland and Janet Lee organized the 1897 Stoney Creek meetings, certain people had already been thinking about women's inclusion in rural organizations. One such person was F.W. Hodson. As superintendent of the Farmers' Institutes from 1894 to 1899, Hodson had demonstrated his determination to include women even before Lee requested affiliation.

For the first ten years of Farmers' Institute meetings, from 1884 to 1894, lecturers were typically either professional educators, prominent government spokesmen or prosperous farmers. And they were always male. It was the practice to hold an evening session as part of these special meetings, which became popular among rural people not only for the information but also for the entertainment that they usually included.

The first Superintendent of the Women's Institutes, F.W. Hodson acquired that responsibility by default because he was already the Superintendent of Farmers' Institutes. Hodson hired female lecturers to address the Farmers' Institutes well before the idea was popular, and in so doing, paved the way for Adelaide Hoodless to accept the invitation to come to Stoney Creek in 1897. — UG, FWIO Collection

Ten years before the WI was launched, women already had begun to have a presence in the Farmers' Institute meetings. The North Lanark Farmers' Institute report in 1887 was typical: "Evening Session which began at 7:30, in the shape of a musical and literary entertainment, the principal attraction again being Professor Mills's address on the absorbing question of our High and Public Schools. The hall was literally packed, a pleasing feature being the large number of ladies in attendance." The women who were part of the audience that night had accompanied their husbands and fathers to the meeting. But sometimes women were more than just observers; they provided part of the evening's entertainment. The North Lanark report continued, "It seemed as if the beauty of our quiet little neighboring village turned out en masse to lend a graceful effect to the appearance of the audience, and to assist by music and song, which many of them did willingly and with cheerful hearts, in making the meeting one of the most pleasant and successful yet to be held by the Institute."[26] The East York Farmers' Institute held a similar event with Dr. Mills, and reported that the "Hall was well filled, with Ladies and Gentlemen from all parts of the riding."

Over the next ten years women began to expect more from the meetings than just entertainment. In recognition of the important contributions that women made to work on the family farm, some of the sessions at Farmers' Institute meetings were specifically geared to topics of interest to women. At the South Renfrew Farmers' Institute meeting in Lindsay in 1888, for example, one of the men who spoke recommended that "the Government already should send out dairy instructors more especially among the women of this section as it falls to their share of labour to look after the butter business."[27] By 1896, a paper published as part of the Annual Report of the Farmers' Institutes to the Minister of Agriculture entitled, "Poultry on the Farm," encouraged women to keep careful accounts of their egg and chicken operations and to track their profit margins. Farmers' Institute organizers had begun to recognize women's agricultural production on the farm and to treat it as a serious profit-making enterprise. It is very significant that the topics chosen by the Farmers' Institutes at this time were beginning to incorporate women's interests.

As the new superintendent of the Farmers' Institutes, Hodson was clearly responsible for that change in emphasis. His main function was to coordinate and schedule the speakers who travelled from one county to the next addressing the local Farmers' Institutes.[28] He consciously created a receptive climate for women, thus setting the stage for the Women's Institutes to emerge. The work he did prior to 1897 paved the way for Erland Lee to invite Adelaide Hoodless to address the local Farmers' Institute at that historic meeting. Without Hodson there might never have been a successful proposal for the formation of a separate "women's" Institute. During his term in office, not only did women come to hear the Farmers' Institute lectures, but in some cases, they gave the lectures. Thanks to Hodson's efforts, some of the most engaging speakers who addressed Farmers' Institute groups were women.

Early in his term, Hodson encouraged one Farmers' Institute that was struggling financially to book a female to speak to the group. "How would you like one of the lady speakers sent to the [Farmers'] institute meetings?" he asked. Enthusiastic about female lecturers, Hodson described them as "very capable" and explained that "where they have been sent [they] have drawn large crowds. Their subjects are suitable for evening meetings where ladies are present."[29] Women who lectured to those evening meetings drew crowds because rural women were eager for information and instruction that would assist them in their dairy and poultry production on the farm, teach them more efficient ways of running their homes, and enlighten them on the important social questions of the day.

It was very progressive, even risky, for Hodson to hire and promote the work of these "lady speakers," as he called them. His enlightened thinking is explained in part by the model he and his wife followed in their own marriage. Annie Hodson shared a joint bank account with her husband, and she was the one who handled the business transactions for their farming operation when he was preoccupied with other work. This was not a very common arrangement in rural Ontario in the 1890s. There is further evidence that Annie Hodson herself was a public speaker who was prepared to read papers on women's topics to farm audiences. When Mr. Hodson was making arrangements with George H. Greig, of the *Farmers' Advocate*, for his own trip to Winnipeg in 1895 to address the Central Farmers' Institute of Manitoba, he offered Annie's services as well. "It is possible Mrs. Hodson may come with me," he wrote, and, "if so she will probably come prepared to read one or two papers on Domestic Economy if that is thought necessary." Recognizing that this was a novel suggestion, he asked Greig to explore the idea. "I do not know what the Manitoba farmers think of ladies engaging in this sort of work but the plan is taking quite well in Ontario and also in Wisconsin and other of the West and South Western States. Look carefully into this matter and write me at your earliest convenience."[30]

To promote the work of female lecturers in Ontario, Hodson quietly corresponded throughout the summer of 1895 with two women who taught at the Ottawa School of Cooking. It was Professor J.W. Robertson of the Ottawa Experimental Farm who first suggested the names of Bessie Livingston and Mary

Miller to him. Writing to thank Robertson for suggesting these two women, he indicated that "for some time I have thought of endeavouring to obtain the services of suitable ladies."[31] He was well aware that this might be too radical a move for some of his farm constituencies, and he determined to proceed carefully. Writing to another supporter of the idea, he explained, "I will have to move cautiously during the coming season. . . . Lady speakers at [Farmers'] Institute meetings will at first be looked upon as innovation. You know farmers are very conservative, but if I can use the thin edge of the wedge this season, I hope to make better progress in years to come."[32] The progress that would occur over the next ten years was something of which Hodson undoubtedly never dreamed.

Opposition by members of the Farmers' Institute to the idea of women speakers and separate women's groups helps to explain the relatively slow development of the WIs in these early years. However, Hodson's patient work paid off. His strategy was to introduce women gradually into the Institute program, so that people could get used to the idea. Negotiating in 1895 with Miss Livingston and Miss Miller, both of whom were anxious to begin lecturing immediately under the auspices of the Farmers' Institutes, he explained his plan. "I am not yet in a position to say just what part lady speakers will take in the coming Institute work," he wrote that summer. "I will have to handle it in a very careful manner or it will arouse a good deal of opposition among Institute officers. I think it probable that for the first year or so, we will employ lady speakers only at four or five, or probably a dozen prominent places throughout the province, and be [sic] degrees develop this department of the work."[33] Before launching fully into the program with female lecturers, he wanted to poll the local Farmers' Institutes on the issue. By the end of August 1895, he had heard from only thirty percent of them, and he was anxious to have a broader base of support for the idea.

Later that fall, Hodson decided to go ahead and introduce women to the lecture circuit, and so he asked both Livingston and Miller to provide him with lists of topics on which they could speak. Still, he was determined to proceed carefully. Concerned with how the conservative farm community would perceive him, Hodson explained to Livingston, "I am a new man at the helm and am said to be very radical."[34] He was convinced that this controversial idea of hiring women would ultimately prove quite popular.

Hodson was correct. Women lecturers were very popular indeed. Erland Lee's invitation to Adelaide Hoodless in 1897 is a case in point. Although there was hesitation among the men in the South Wentworth Farmers' Institute about inviting her, the women were eager to attend. After her first visit to Stoney Creek, with only one week to promote the next meeting, the Lees were able to attract a hundred women to hear her speak. F.W. Hodson's work in promoting women speakers was undoubtedly partly responsible for creating the favourable climate in which Erland and Janet Lee could promote and host Adelaide Hoodless's talk. When Erland Lee wrote to the Superintendent to request official status for the first Women's Institute, he was probably writing to the most sympathetic man in all of Ontario.

While Hodson spent his term working to change attitudes and mould public opinion to accept female speakers and to consider separate women's groups, the next superintendent continued that trend and, moving ahead, concentrated on putting systematic procedures in place to encourage more WIs to start. Dr. G.C. Creelman served a term as Superintendent of Institutes, during which he encouraged growth, hired effective lecturers, and saw through new legislation to firmly establish the beginning Women's Institutes. His term was characterized by important developments in the structure of the organization.

Growth up to that point had certainly been slow. The Annual Report of the Farmers' Institutes for 1900 reported only three branches in existence: Grey North (Kemble), Ontario South (Whitby) and Wentworth South (Stoney Creek).[35] Optimistic about the potential of Women's Institutes, George Creelman hoped to see that number grow significantly in his first year as superintendent. A fourfold increase would be very impressive, he thought, and so he set a goal to see twelve new Institutes organized in the coming year. One year later, Creelman confessed in amazement, "We were hardly prepared, however, to see the ladies take the matter up so enthusiastically, and we are pleased to report that thirty-one Institutes are now organized, and holding meetings once a month."[36]

During Creelman's term from 1899 to 1904, "inquiries were pouring in from all over the Province," about how to establish a WI group such as the one in Stoney Creek. In answer to these anxious potential members, Creelman decided to issue the first formal set of instructions on how to organize a Women's Institute. Dated June 1900, this letter outlined the rationale behind the movement, declaring "What Farmers' Institutes have done for the farmers and the farms, Women's Institutes can do for the homes through the instrumentality of wives and daughters." Promising a grant of $10 per year to help with holding meetings, the letter went on to advise:

> The rules and regulations are very simple. The following are the most important:
>
> "The organization meeting may be called by the Superintendent of the Farmers' Institutes, by the head of a municipality, by the President and Secretary of the local Farmers' Institute, or by five ladies of the district."
>
> "Each Women's Institute shall be in affiliation with the Farmers' Institute in that district."
>
> "The object of the Women's Institutes shall be the dissemination of knowledge relating to domestic economy, including household architecture, with special attention to home sanitation; a better understanding of the economic and hygienic value of foods, clothing and fuel, and a more scientific care and training of children with a view to raising the general standing of the health and morals of our people."
>
> "Each Women's Institute shall receive a grant of $10 annually from the Department, on condition that an equal sum be granted by the county council or municipality in which the institute is organized, or from the local farmers' institute, and on such further conditions as are imposed by the 'Act and rules governing Farmers' Institutes.'"
>
> After your institute has been organized and has elected officers, a date will be set for the next meeting. . . .
>
> An organization that will enable each lady in the neighbourhood to get all such information in a practical and systematic form cannot fail to assist in the general upbuilding and improving of women's work on the farm. Some districts have already organized, and twelve others have signified their intention of doing so during the coming season.
>
> We now have a number of estimable lady delegates on our staff, and their services may be secured at any time to assist any proposed institute in organizing or in carrying out any practical schemes of organization.
>
> Trusting you will give this matter your personal attention, I am,
>
> Yours very truly, G.C. Creelman, Superintendent of Farmers' Institutes.[37]

The circular letter proved to be a very effective means of communicating. Its content closely resembles the information that would eventually be compiled into a handbook for members. In fact, the first handbook was published in 1902 as an expanded attempt by Creelman to communicate with the branches.

By 1902, under Creelman's leadership, there were forty-four Women's Institutes in place. His plan for growth had taken root across Ontario. He did not reach his goals singlehandedly, however; eighteen of those new branches were organized by a young woman named Alice Hollingworth. Alice was a student of Laura Rose at the OAC School of Dairying, and like her famous teacher, Miss Hollingworth also worked part-time as an itinerant lecturer for the Farmers' Institutes. In 1899, Dr. Creelman had recruited the young student (whose family lived near Beatrice, in the Muskoka region) as a lecturer for the Institutes. She spoke on Buttermaking, Using Native Trees and Plants to Beautify the Home, Weeds, Healthy Homes, What Women Have Done, Flowers, and Good Housekeeping.[38] Alice wrote her dairying exams at the OAC in March 1900, but in the months leading up to them, she was on a busy schedule of lecturing. "In January and February of 1900 she toured parts of south-western Ontario visiting places such as Ailsa Craig, Beachville, Scotland, Jarvis, Lynedock, and Waterford. In November and December 1900, her travels took her to eastern Ontario: Trenton, Napanee, Sydenham, and Spencerville, among others. After a brief vacation at home for Christmas, she was off again to eastern Ontario. This time her meanderings took her to Peterborough, Havelock, and smaller centres such as Hoards, Wooler, and Baltimore. Such a heavy schedule was followed by a year's respite. She then began another tour at Owen Sound on February 4, 1902, and travelled in a southeasterly direction towards Toronto, speaking at Walter's Falls, Creemore, and Queensville, and numerous places in between."[39] Alice's career as an itinerant lecturer ended when she married Francis Ernest Webster, a Creemore farmer, in December 1902. However, she remained active in WI work in her local branch for the rest of her life.

George Creelman served as the second Superintendent of Women's Institutes. During his five-year term, the Ontario WIs acquired a solid organizational structure, preparing them for rapid expansion in the years that followed. — UG

Women's Institutes were originally thought to be simply a women's version of the pre-existing Farmers' Institutes for men. The earliest WI branches were closely linked to the local men's groups and they sometimes held joint events, such as this 1904 annual meeting of the South Bruce Farmers' and Women's Institutes. — Annual Report of the Farmers' Institutes, 1904

Alice Hollingworth's experiences on the lecture circuit reveal that the male opposition that Erland Lee had encountered when he proposed to invite Hoodless to Stoney Creek in 1897 continued into the new century. In fact, that opposition slowed the progress and spread of the Women's Institutes in the early years. Miss Hollingworth often faced angry objections from men when she toured the province attempting to establish new branches. Years later, she recounted two of those charged exchanges: "At one organizational meeting I received a Full Blast from a professional man whose theme was that when women start going to meetings day after day, and week after week, and month after month, the homes would be wrecked. One farmer said, 'Don't bring the Women's Institute here or we won't be able to get a woman to milk a cow.' His wife was doing duty as housekeeper and hired man, but the Institute came and his wife became a member. I recall these difficulties as proof that we actually did work out a substantial project in clearing away snags for those who have followed us."[40]

Some of the "snags" that slowed the Institutes' development were cleared away by the efforts of feisty women such as Alice Hollingworth. Others required legislative change. In March 1902, an important new act of the Ontario government received royal assent. *The Agriculture and Arts Amendment Act, 1902*, gave the Women's Institutes formal legal stature in the province for the first time. Whereas before, a WI group had to affiliate with an existing Farmers' Institute for recognition, this amendment allowed Women's Institutes to stand alone. Specifically, the new amendment stated: "The formation of Women's Institutes for the purpose of improving rural home life, and of imparting information in regard to women's work upon the farm, shall be permitted under this Act."[41] Local women who wished to organize were no longer subject to the goodwill of the local men's group. With or without the support of the Farmers' Institutes, Women's Institutes now had legal recognition in the statute books. This was a crucial step in building the foundation of the organization.

With clear information on how to organize provided by Creelman's circular letter, great enthusiasm generated by lecturers such as Laura Rose and Alice Hollingworth, and legal stature guaranteed by new legislative amendments, the Women's Institutes received a real boost during Creelman's time as superintendent.

The Women's Institutes of Ontario also developed some of their most enduring symbols during the early years after the turn of the century. Their official motto, badge and colours were all selected by 1904. These important symbols have come to represent the shared experiences of thousands of women and the fondness that members across Ontario have for their organization. The history of these emblems can be traced to the earliest WI conventions. According to the *Ontario Women's Institute Story*, conventions originated "in December 1901, [when] the Executive Committee of the Experimental Union of the Ontario Agricultural College arranged a special session for the ladies at the time of its annual meeting of men in Guelph. This was so much appreciated that in preparing the program for 1902, the Experimental Union decided to devote a whole day of sessions to the women. . . . This was the first Convention and it proved so successful the delegates voted unanimously to continue these meetings annually."[42] The convention of 1903 was held at the newly built Macdonald Institute in Guelph, and it was the occasion for announcing the group's new motto and unveiling the design of the official WI pin.

Recognizing the importance of tangible symbols, delegates to the 1902 convention had appointed a committee to come up with a motto for the Women's Institutes. A saying that was frequently quoted among Institute organizers provided the inspiration. "A nation cannot rise higher than the level of its homes," reformers declared. It logically followed in the minds of

With a pragmatism characteristic of the early WI organizers, Alice Hollingworth wrote, as part of one of her lectures, "If we [women] cannot be both dainty and useful, let us first, last and always be useful." Alice, who worked for the Department of Agriculture as a travelling lecturer, organized eighteen new branches of the WI from 1899 to 1902. — Helen Blackburn, Nottawa, Ontario.

The Agriculture and Arts Amendment Act, 1902

Item 7. Section 46 of
The Agriculture and Arts Act
is amended by adding thereto
the following:

(a) The formation of Women's Institutes for the purpose of improving rural home life, and of imparting information in regard to women's work upon the farm,

This piece of legislation was the first formal legislative recognition of the Women's Institutes of Ontario. The Act, amended in 1902, placed WI groups on the same footing as other agricultural organizations. — Statutes of Ontario, 1902

The official badge of the Women's Institutes, designed by Laura Rose in 1903, declares the organization's official motto: For Home and Country. — *Stoney Creek Tweedsmuir History*

domestic science advocates, therefore, that "we must study and work together to devise ways and means of raising our homes to the highest possible level." Combining the sentiments behind homemaking and nation-building, Laura Rose submitted the winning phrase when she suggested the new motto, "For Home and Country."[43] Miss Rose is also credited with designing the blue-and-gold emblematic pin, a design that has since become the widely used logo of the WI. According to the official record, the badge "was designed from a signet ring [Laura Rose] wore at the time of organization, and was in the form of a small oval in blue and gold. 'If we could have the initials of our Institute, OWI, in the centre it would be fine,' she stated. A small maple leaf was placed on each end and the words of the motto engraved on the oval banding. A clear cornflower blue was chosen along with the gold, and this remains the chosen emblem."[44] There was still one more important suggestion Laura Rose would make for the group. In 1904, again meeting in Guelph for the convention, she proposed blue and gold as the official colours of the WI. They were royal colours, she reasoned, and the city of Guelph, named for Queen Victoria's family, was once again the site of the WI convention.

The annual conventions quickly grew in popularity. The attendance at the 1902 meeting of 53 women doubled to 116 in 1903.[45] Growth in coming years would be exponential. The conventions provided members with a chance to come together to celebrate their successes and plan their programs.

Since those first meetings in 1897, the Institutes had become well established, with their own symbols and structures firmly in place. It is clear that there was much more to the beginning of the Ontario Women's Institutes than the story of one grieving mother. Set in the context of nineteenth-century social reform and scientific agriculture, the beginning of the Women's Institute story involved a whole cast of players. In addition to Adelaide Hoodless, the grief-stricken mother who became known as "the Domestic Crusader," there were Erland and Janet Lee, a farming couple who understood the value of rural organizations for both men and women. Then too, there was an eager group of women from Stoney Creek, women such as Christina Smith, who decided to proceed with organizing despite demanding household duties and the scoffing of men who ridiculed their efforts. There were public-minded women in Whitby and Kemble, eager to bring a good thing to their neighbourhood friends and relatives. There was

190

Member's Ticket

25 Cents

M

Sold by

MRS. J. B. MITCHELL, Secretary.

(BACK)

Each Member is entitled to such Reports and Bulletins interesting to women, as are issued annually by the Ontario Department of Agriculture. If one or more such reports are not received during the year, kindly communicate with

G. C. CREELMAN,
Superintendent of Farmers' Institutes,
Parliament Buildings,
TORONTO, ONT.

A sample membership card used by the South Ontario Women's Institute. In the 1903 Handbook, Superintendent George Creelman suggested that this card was a good model for other branches to use when they canvassed their neighbourhoods for new members.
— Ontario Department of Agriculture, *1903 Handbook for Women's Institutes*

THE INSTITUTE STORY

Farmers from Wentworth County
Gathered at O.A.C.
Erland Lee was there among them
When he heard a woman's plea
To revise our education.
"This system just won't do.
We must teach the art of cooking
And domestic science too."

Much impressed with Mrs. Hoodless,
The public-spirited Lee
Invited her to Saltfleet.
What an opportunity
Adelaide Hoodless came to Saltfleet
And her message roused them all.
They agreed that night among them
To return to Squire's Hall.

On the nineteenth of February,
With the mercury dipping low,
One hundred and one women
Faced the bitter cold and snow.
With a scarf around their bonnets
For the winter wind was bleak,
They hitched Dobbin to the cutter
And set out for Stoney Creek.

What a memorable occasion
An acorn seed took root.
That group of pioneer women
Formed the Mother Institute.
They prompted other branches
(So my story does unfold).
For Guelph and Queen Victoria
They chose the Blue and Gold.

Home and Country was their motto
Adelaide Hoodless did advise.
A little oak kept growing
Till it grew to quite a size.
Branches spread across the province
On and on — from sea to sea;
And they formed two Federations
F.W.I.O. and F.W.I.C.

To the States the torch was carried
Then to countries overseas;
England, Scotland, Wales, and Holland,
Belgium, France, and Germany.
On and on through other nations
Rural women joined the throng
Of the A.C.W.W.
To which you and I belong.

— Stella Muir, "The Institute Story," a poem written for the eightieth anniversary by an Institute member, *Stoney Creek Tweedsmuir History*

F.W. Hodson, an energetic new employee of the Department of Agriculture, who was so convinced of the importance of women's work that he gambled on promoting "lady speakers." There was George Creelman, who brought administrative structure and legislative support to ensure the organization's stability. There were itinerant speakers such as Laura Rose and Alice Hollingworth who lectured on everything from Buttermaking and Housekeeping to Literature and Leisure, urging women to improve their circumstances. And there were scores and scores of women in dozens of Ontario communities who flooded the Department of Agriculture with letters asking how they too could introduce this new organization to their own communities. There was, in fact, a whole company of actors who shared the spotlight and helped to set the stage for Women's Institutes. That is the fuller story of how the Women's Institutes of Ontario began. But it was only the beginning.

One of the first large events to be held in the newly opened Macdonald Institute was the annual convention of the Ontario Women's Institutes in 1903. Financed by the Montreal tobacco magnate, William Macdonald, the school was the brainchild of Adelaide Hoodless and the site of WI annual conventions from 1903 to 1910.

— UG, Macdonald Institute Collection

CHAPTER TWO

Branching Out: Years of Growth, 1904–1914

On the occasion of the Ontario Women's Institutes' third annual convention in December 1904 at the Macdonald Institute in Guelph, Mr. George Putnam was introduced to the delegates as the new superintendent of the Institutes Branch of the Department of Agriculture. It was a historic occasion, because Putnam would remain in that office for the next thirty years, and over that time the WI would grow and develop significantly. In addition, Putnam himself would be forced to reconsider his ideas about the WI. The first ten years of his term saw the most dramatic changes. In his first address to the delegates, the new superintendent revealed his limited vision for the WI, confessing that he was surprised that the WI still existed. "Men are coming to realize," he said, "what the Women's Institutes mean; and to be frank with you, I must admit that when I first took charge of the work, I was inclined to put credence in the statements of some [who said] that I would not have to guide the Women's Institutes for long, as they were sure to disband in a short time. . . . I am glad that I have been agreeably surprised in this matter. The work has been steadily going forward instead of backward."[1] So the WI had already exceeded Putnam's expectations by 1904, merely because it had survived. But he had not seen anything yet. The next ten years would put to rest any doubts about the WI's future. The movement was about to branch out, both in terms of increased numbers and new program directions, for its most explosive period of growth ever.

When George Putnam took on his new job, he saw his role in a very narrow way, simply as a co-ordinator of travelling lecturers. "My work, as you know," he told the audience at the Macdonald Institute that December, "must consist in getting good speakers from whatever source I can, to instruct and assist the ladies throughout the Province; not to address many of the meetings myself, but to send the very best help I can procure. . . . I shall aim to get the very best speakers, and to provide them with facilities for getting information from the very best source, before sending them to you."[2] Evidently, he was underestimating the potential of the Women's Institutes, because he was thinking of them as a mere carbon copy of the more familiar male Farmers' Institutes, where so-called experts travelled to locations across Ontario to lecture to farmers about more scientific methods of farming. He thought that the WI was just going to be a women's version of that same thing, a group that would concentrate solely on formal instruction

Sceptical at first about the future of the Women's Institutes, Mr. George Putnam was the third person to act as superintendent of the Institutes, serving from 1904 to 1934. All doubt about the WI's future was laid aside in the first ten years of his term, as the movement spread throughout Ontario. — UG, FWIO Collection

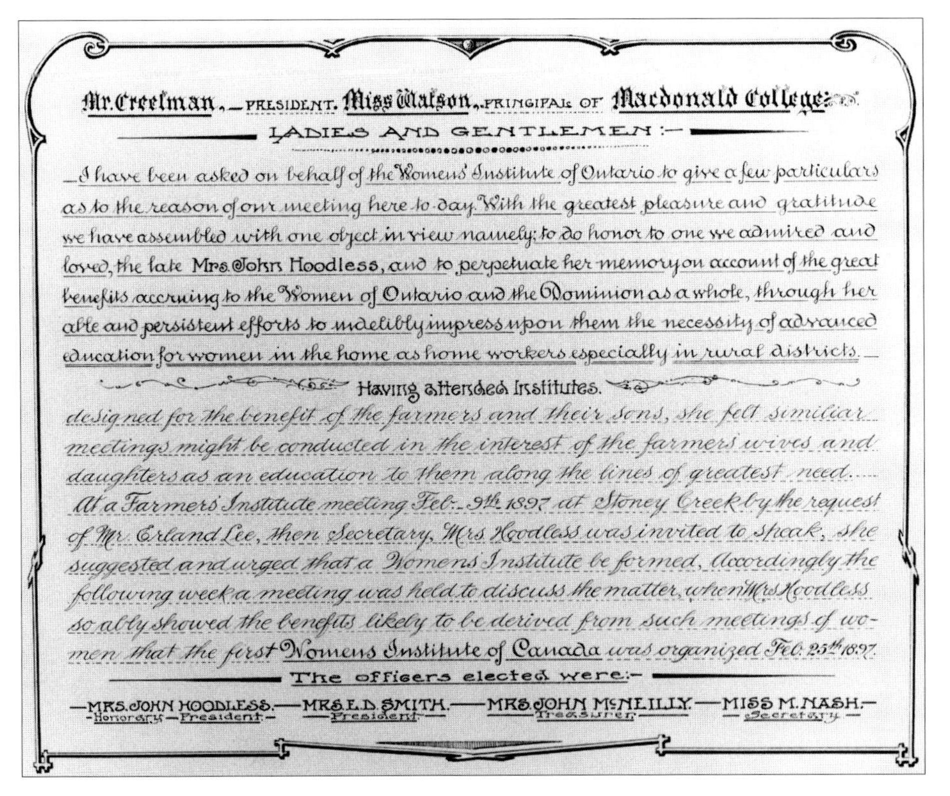

Mr. Creelman, — President. Miss Watson, — Principal of Macdonald College:

LADIES AND GENTLEMEN :—

— I have been asked on behalf of the Womens' Institute of Ontario to give a few particulars as to the reason of our meeting here to-day. With the greatest pleasure and gratitude we have assembled with one object in view namely; to do honor to one we admired and loved, the late Mrs. John Hoodless, and to perpetuate her memory on account of the great benefits accruing to the Women of Ontario and the Dominion as a whole, through her able and persistent efforts to indelibly impress upon them the necessity of advanced education for women in the home as home workers especially in rural districts. —

Having attended Institutes.

designed for the benefit of the farmers and their sons, she felt similiar meetings might be conducted in the interest of the farmers wives and daughters as an education to them along the lines of greatest need. At a Farmers' Institute meeting Feb.-9th 1897 at Stoney Creek by the request of Mr. Erland Lee, then Secretary, Mrs Hoodless was invited to speak, she suggested and urged that a Womens' Institute be formed, Accordingly the following week a meeting was held to discuss the matter, when Mrs Hoodless so ably showed the benefits likely to be derived from such meetings of women that the first Womens Institute of Canada was organized Feb. 25th 1897.

The officers elected were:—

— MRS. JOHN HOODLESS. — Honorary — President — MRS. E. D. SMITH. — President — MRS. JOHN McNEILLY. — Treasurer — MISS M. NASH. — Secretary —

The founder of the Women's Institutes lived to see only the first thirteen years of WI history. When Adelaide Hoodless died suddenly in 1910, the members of the Women's Institutes of Ontario honoured her and credited her with founding their movement. This page from Hoodless's funeral book cites the date of February 25, 1897, as the first meeting of the Stoney Creek branch. In fact, that was the first regular branch meeting after the organizational meeting on February 19.

— UG, Adelaide Hoodless Collection

in more efficient homemaking — women's work but done along more scientific lines. Putnam's vision was very short-sighted.

But the women of the province had a bigger vision. Adelaide Hoodless herself realized that the WI groups had tremendous possibilities, and when she addressed the meeting where Putnam made his debut, she encouraged the delegates with the story of her struggle to establish the Macdonald Institute. "This [school] is the result of about ten years' effort, so imagine . . . what you may do in ten years. You have in this organization a tremendous power for good, and that it may be used to its fullest extent is my most earnest wish for you."[3] Hoodless's real dream was for the spread of domestic science education, and she expended considerable energy in spreading the "gospel of homemaking."[4] Part of the good news of this gospel message was that homemaking could in fact become interesting instead of monotonous. By applying scientific principles to the running of a household, "these Women's Institutes are engaged in applying science and theory to the ordinary practices of the home and farm. Everything becomes increasingly interesting when we know the reason for it. It is possible to do things by a routine that does tend to a deadening monotony, but, when we know the reasons for things, then even commonplace acts take on a new complexion. When we know the reason why we should ventilate our houses and prepare food in proper ways; when we know the reason why we should wage war on flies; when we know the reason why we should choose the best grade of seed, and a hundred other things that relate to the country, all these things become increasingly interesting and the monotony of life will be broken."[5]

But Adelaide Hoodless would not live to see the fruit of the next ten years of WI growth. The 1904 meeting was the last time she addressed the annual convention of the WI. She died six years later. "On the eve of her fifty-second birthday she was scheduled to speak at the Federation of Women's Clubs in Massey Hall, Toronto. . . . She was halfway through a brilliant speech when she stopped, smiled, took a sip of water. Then the glass crashed to the floor. Adelaide Hoodless was dead — February 26, 1910."[6] In a memorial to her, a speaker in 1910 voiced the realization that the WI had long since outgrown that original, narrow concentration on domestic science. "The founders of the Institute undoubtedly had a vision, but that from their small group of homemakers should come forth a powerful world wide organization of rural women, was of a surety far beyond their vision."[7] Indeed, what happened between 1904 and 1914 was beyond the expectations of even the most visionary people. The growth of the organization was phenomenal. Mrs. William Bacon, from Orillia, addressing the ninth annual convention in 1910, remarked, "When, fifteen years ago, a few women met in a sitting-room to talk over household matters, they did not dream that their little gathering was the nucleus of an institution comprising many thousands. Neither did they expect that the watchword which was soon after adopted would be interpreted in its broadest sense. Yet these things have come to pass."[8]

In fact, the numeric growth between 1904 and 1914 was the most rapid in the history of the organization. From just over 5,000 members and 149 branches in June 1904, the Ontario Women's Institutes mushroomed into a force of nearly 25,000 members in 843 branches by May 1914. That growth is phenomenal and the numbers are staggering. "To think of the small membership there was ten years ago to what there is now!" mused one of the delegates at the 1910 convention. This member, Mrs. McTavish from Port Elgin, continued, "It reminds me of the proverbial grain of mustard seed, the smallest of all the seeds, that was cast into the ground and grew and became so tall that the fowl of the air lodged in its branches. Now our Institutes have grown at such a rate that we are just like that."[9] As the graph at right illustrates, the mustard-seed metaphor was no exaggeration.

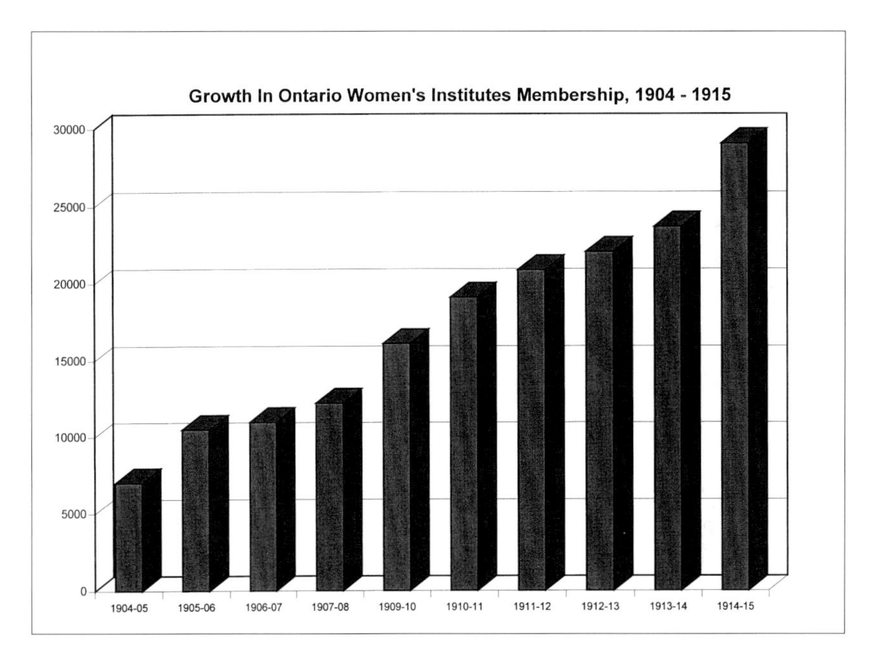

The growth of the Women's Institutes in the years leading up to the First World War was phenomenal. In terms of membership and new branches, it was the largest rate of growth in the 100-year history of the WI.

—Compiled by author from annual reports of the Department of Agriculture

One of the largest centres of Institute growth was Prince Edward County, where the membership by 1909 was "close upon four hundred." That growth was taken as a good omen for the future. "Today we are told there are four hundred members of the Women's Institute in Prince Edward County. The Institutes have grown so rapidly, and are still growing so rapidly, that the question has been asked of me, 'Where is all this going to lead, and where is it going to end? What is to be the outcome? . . .' And I have simply to answer, 'We do not know.'"[10]

One outcome of the growth was a change in the annual convention. For years the group had met at the Macdonald Institute, but by 1910, the convention had grown so large that it was relocated to larger quarters. It moved to the University of Toronto's Convocation Hall, both for the convenience of out-of-town travellers making train connections and also for the larger meeting space. But C.C. James, the Deputy Minister of Agriculture for Ontario, attached a more symbolic importance to the Toronto location when he said, "Some of us can remember when it took but a small room to accommodate the delegates from the Women's Institutes of Ontario. We saw them move into a larger room and find that too small, and so they decided this year that they would come to the City of Toronto, and they have come right into the heart of the University of Toronto. There is some significance in that, I think. I would not have you understand that the ladies intended to take possession of the University, but they have a cause which they believe is worth working out and proclaiming even from the centre of the great Provincial University."[11] James went on to discuss the important roles that women had played in Canadian history, and to remind the delegates that with their numeric strength and their collective determination to effect change, they were indeed at the heart of the nation's future as well.

"Right here in the Province of Ontario, in the centre of the Dominion of Canada, history is being made, and you women especially have it in your power largely to determine what that history shall be."[12] By 1914, another significant restructuring of the convention saw three locations, not just one, as regional locations were established in Ottawa, London and Toronto.

But the expanding conventions were only a symptom. The real growth was happening on a more local level. Across Ontario new branches were springing up — in towns, villages and hundreds of country cross-roads communities. The story of one branch's founding, Manilla Women's Institute in Victoria County which began in 1910, deserves retelling because it is typical of this period.

> Manilla, the place I represent, is a small village with a population of two hundred. It has a splendid outlying country, branching in every direction. The people are above the ordinary — plain, unassuming and hospitable.
>
> Apart from church work, there is nothing of a social nature to bring the homemakers together. This I have long felt was much needed. An invitation came to me in June to visit an Institute southeast of us. I attended for the first time a Women's Institute and heard addresses by Misses Campbell and Walsh. The subjects taken up by these ladies were of such vital importance to every woman in our fair Dominion that I immediately thought, "Now, this is what Manilla needs." I made inquiries from the Government delegates as to constitution, obligations, etc., required by such an organization and decided there and then that I would leave no stone unturned until we were organized. . . . The next morning I called up by 'phone seven or eight ladies, who, I felt confident, would be interested in such work and be willing to use their influence in their different neighbourhoods. I found them favorable to the suggestion, so asked them to visit ladies living near them, and find out how many would like to have such a society formed. In the meantime I was to write to Mr. Putnam, the Superintendent, and find out fully how to go about organizing. We arranged a night to meet and report our success. This we did, and after canvassing found a sufficient number ready to take it up, so proceeded to set a date and corresponded with Mr. Putnam again, asking if it would be possible to have a delegate address us. We found Mr. Putnam most kind, he did everything possible to help us have a successful organization.
>
> We arranged to have our gathering in the form of a garden party, the programme to be held in the house. We made a personal canvass of the entire neighbourhood, more general than at first, distributing literature and explaining to the best of our ability the object of the

New branches were created because of the determination of local women who gathered together with their neighbours to take advantage of the programs and services offered by the Department of Agriculture. The groups appealed to large numbers of women, both young and old.
— Listowel West WI Tweedsmuir History

Women's Institute. You can imagine my pleasure when I received word from Miss Campbell that she was the delegate appointed to come to Manilla. The day arrived and was all that could be desired, the sun shone brightly and the temperature was perfect for our outdoor gathering. The ladies began to arrive until I began to wonder if our home would be large enough to hold them. In counting, we found we had eighty present. This far surpassed our most sanguine hopes. We felt fully repaid for the time spent, for such a hearty response to the invitation meant that the ladies were ready for the Institute. We invited the district officers and three came. When the delegate asked how many wanted a Women's Institute, forty ladies responded by handing in their names. We had Mr. Glendinning, a highly esteemed resident of Manilla, and well-known to [Farmers'] Institute workers. In a few words he expressed his pleasure with the organizing of an Institute in our vicinity and promised to help us whenever he could. After the business of organizing was over, the ladies were asked to each take a chair and go to the lawn, where they would be expected to chat with each other, whether acquainted or not. . . . One and all pronounced it one of the most pleasant afternoons they had ever spent. We were anxious to have our first gathering a success, for we felt confident that if the ladies spent one pleasant and profitable afternoon, they would want to come again, and their speaking well of it would bring others. After holding four meetings, we can report sixty members and we certainly have every reason to feel encouraged.[13]

Members enjoyed the social side of meetings, as this photograph of the Staffa WI, founded in 1903, attests. One member is knitting, a foreshadowing of the new roles that WI groups across the province would take up during wartime.
— Staffa WI Tweedsmuir History

This story illustrates how new branches were most often formed, through the hard work and determination of one or two individuals in a community. Links with other branches in the district during this period provided district personnel and officers to preside over the formation. As well, the links with existing Farmers' Institutes are unmistakable. Influential citizens in the community would lend their support by opening their homes (homes large enough to accommodate sixty or more people) and by encouraging others to join. The support of the provincial office was also indispensible for new branch formation because organizers could obtain information, advice and encouragement in their efforts. Virtually every new Institute in this period has a similar story of its origin. One eager founder, after being exposed to some nearby Institute branch, came home determined to see a local group started in her own neighbourhood. And so the branches spread.

Putnam remarked in 1910 that this was "an organization which is not only extending to new territories from year to year, but is growing in numbers, popularity, and effectiveness of work in those sections where the work was first undertaken."[14] How can one account for this

Women's Institute Meeting

On Monday afternoon, Jan. 22nd, about 40 ladies met in the office of the Department of Agriculture for the purpose of organizing a Women's Institute.

The meeting was called to order by Mrs. W. W. Farley, of Smithfield, who gave a very interesting discussion on the objects of organization and why we should belong to the Women's Institute. It was decided that the "Stirling Branch" of the Women's Institute be formed, and the following officers were elected:

President—Mrs. R. P. Coulter.
Vice-President—Mrs. J. M. McGee.
Secretary-Treasurer—Miss B. Ward.
Directors—Mrs. G. G. Thrasher, Mrs. Thos. Montgomery, and Miss M. Cosbey.
Auditors—Mrs. G. W. Faulkner, and Mrs. W. S. Martin.

There is already a membership of 18.

It was moved, seconded, and carried that the meeting be held on the first Wednesday of each month at 2.30, p.m., in the office of the Department of Agriculture. The subject for the next meeting, which will be held on Feb. 7th, is "Poultry, and Different methods of Cooking Eggs."

Mrs. Farley then very ably answered a number of questions that were handed in, and also gave some hints re easy methods of doing house work, and a number of useful recipes.

After a hearty vote of thanks was tendered to Mrs. Farley for her able assistance, the meeting closed by singing the National Anthem.

The Stirling Women's Institute traces its origin to this meeting in 1912, during the height of WI growth. As more and more branches continued to spring up, doubts about the popularity and the viability of the movement diminished.

— Stirling WI Tweedsmuir History

increase of 20,000 new members and almost 700 new branches in the space of just ten years? According to one member, "we cannot claim it all as Institute workers. We must remember who it was that cast the seed into the ground — our superintendents — and they have not only started it, but they have watched over it and cultivated this Women's Institute, until it has attained the proportions that it has at the present time."[15] It is true that the Department of Agriculture had carefully supervised the growth. Putnam corresponded with and encouraged Mrs. McPhail in her efforts to establish a new branch at Manilla, as he did for hundreds of other local women. Acknowledging the efforts of local people, Putnam remarked that "the greatest responsibility does not rest with the Department." In his mind, it was the local organizers. "You have the greater responsibility and you have the burden to bear. I am sure that you will accept the responsibility and we shall see the Ontario Women's Institutes accomplishing more in the years to come than we have yet dreamed."[16] But Putnam was being too modest, because in fact, the Department played a central role in the organization of new branches, going beyond encouragement and moral support, to providing financial support.

In 1904, Putnam introduced a grant system that put the branches on a solid financial footing. Each branch would receive an annual grant of $3. This money was available to any branch with at least fifteen members, if they had held a minimum of four meetings that year and submitted financial statements to the Department of Agriculture. Announcement of this grant was first published in the 1905 Annual Report, and more fully explained the following year. According to the Superintendent, "giving a small grant to each branch has had the effect of stimulating the work. This has been an encouragement and inspiration to the officers and has enabled them to do much more effective work."[17] Certainly then, Putnam's administration and the government support for the work were very important factors in the growth of branches. One speaker expressed her appreciation for his work saying, "Our Superintendent, Mr. Putnam, is, I think, one of the most wonderful men. To think that he can guide and control an army of 16,000 women!"[18]

But Putnam's so-called control over the women was not really military in style. Although branches were required to meet certain criteria in order to qualify for the grant, one of the secrets to the WI's success over the years has been that the organization is flexible enough to allow for great variation in the running of local branches. Beyond the minimal requirements of record-keeping, local groups had a great deal of independence from one another in this early period. As one speaker quipped, "I think the management of Branches is like the management of husbands — we all have to learn to manage our own."[19]

The delegates were urged not to be bound by precedents or the practices of other branches. "One says they cannot get a large attendance without having afternoon tea and another would say it is better to meet in a hall than a private home. If it suits your locality to meet in a hall, meet in a hall; if you get along better without afternoon tea, do not have it; if you get along better with afternoon tea, why have it."[20] The issue of whether or not to serve refreshments at the monthly WI meeting was debated in 1910, when it came to the floor of the annual convention in Toronto. During the Question Box, a forum set aside at the convention to answer questions about procedure, the following exchange occurred:

Q. Some person has asked the old question about refreshments at Institute meetings. . . .
A. I think that rests with each branch to decide. We have not found it expedient to have refreshments at each meeting. It seems to take away the effect of the programme, and the hostess is thinking of the kettle boiling, and not listening to the meeting. We have refreshments only twice a year. The hostess provides the tea and sugar and cream and the others bring the rest of the refreshments. I do not think it is well to let our meetings run too much to refreshments, because we can get our meals at home.
A Member: That is not our idea. The social part is after our meeting is over, and we have the sandwiches and cup of tea. That is just how we get our members.
A Member: I come from the town of Preston, where we have a membership of over ninety. We found out that our meetings were not successful when held in a hall, so we now hold meetings from house to house, and we assist the hostess in providing refreshments. Some of the ladies come half an hour earlier than the rest and they have everything ready before the meeting starts. At the close of the meeting we help her clear up. We have some ladies who walk in two and a half miles, and it is very nice for them to have a social cup of tea before they go home. We have found that it is very beneficial to our meetings.
Mr. Putnam: This is a matter which must be left to the good judgment of the individual Institute, but we regret that a few Institutes have allowed the lunch part of it to become the most prominent and apparently most interesting feature. We trust you will not do that.[21]

This photograph appeared in a Toronto newspaper in September 1905. The caption below it read: "Mr. G.A. Putnam, Superintendent, is sitting in the centre of the front row, and Principal Creelman of the Guelph College on the left. The value of the work done by the Women's Institutes in humanizing and improving conditions of life on the farm cannot be over-estimated." — UG, FWIO Collection

Evidently, many branches did emphasize refreshments, as for many women, the WI meeting was the only social outing they would enjoy all month.

Reporting for the Lansdowne WI branch, Mrs. John Darling told the annual convention about how her relatively new branch had incorporated suggestions from members to include singing, socials with the Farmers' Club, and fundraising by catering and renting out a piano they purchased. But recognizing the diversity among the branches, she concluded her report by saying, "I am not going to tell you [other branches] what is good to do, because you are older. You may approve of what we have done, or you may not. I have told you the facts."[22] Each local Institute took the liberty of shaping its activities according to local community needs and members' interests. This flexibility made the organization highly successful in a wide variety of contexts throughout rural Ontario. In fact, this may explain why the Women's Institutes actually outlived the Farmers' Institutes despite predictions to the contrary. The

The staff of the Women's Institute branch of the Department of Agriculture was quite extensive in the years leading up to the First World War, and staff included those who worked in the office of the superintendent, and travelling lecturers, organizers, and teachers. Pictured here are the women who lectured for the Women's Institutes in the Summer of 1912. FRONT ROW (L TO R): *Dr. Jennie Smillie, Mrs. W. Dawson, Miss E. Robson, Miss D.I. Hughes, Miss S. Campbell, Miss G. Gray.* MIDDLE ROW: *Miss B. Gilholm, Mrs. Laura Rose Stephen, Miss M. Hotson, Miss M. McKenzie, Mrs. D. McTavish, Miss M. Allan, Mrs. M.N. Norman, Mrs. W.H. Parsons, Mrs. C.H. Burns, Mr. G.A. Putnam (Supt.).* BACK ROW: *Miss M.P. Powell, Miss B. Millar, Mrs. W.J. Hunter, Mrs. M.L. Woelard, Mrs. E.B. McTurk, Miss E.D. Preston*
— AR 1912

chair of the 1910 annual convention hinted at this, recalling a remark made by the Deputy Minister of Agriculture. "I remember hearing Mr. [C.C.] James say, two or three years ago, that he thought they had started at the wrong place when they started with Farmers' Institutes instead of Women's Institutes. I do not want to be too hard on the men, but I do not think the Farmers' Institute offers the diversity to the men that the Women's Institute offers to the women."[23]

Rapid growth and widespread popularity soon made the WI the largest rural organization in Ontario, and through their collective membership, thousands of women caught the attention of the government of the day. They did so outside the realm of formal politics, since women could not vote provincially until 1918. In fact, some members were careful to disassociate themselves from the women's movement, stressing, "we are not suffragists, claiming votes," but rather, hardworking women with concerns about society's direction. "We have been something like Martha, who was attending to everything," but like Martha in the biblical story, WI members came to realize that higher goals than efficient homemaking were worthy of their time and energy. [W]e must not forget to cultivate [our] minds and try to make ourselves better."[24] In the process of coming together, WI members enjoyed government favour because the government was convinced that WIs could improve the quality of rural life and thus help to stem the tide of depopulation in rural Southern Ontario.

At the same time, the provincial government's attention was turned to the north. Settlement in the northern lumbering, mining and agricultural communities was actively encouraged by the government. So were WIs. As new settlements were created and older ones welcomed more women, the WI grew at tremendous rates in the northern reaches of the province.[25] The Department of Agriculture launched campaigns to organize WI branches in the north during the summers of 1905 and 1906. Five different women were hired to spend five to six weeks in the north, travelling by train, giving public lectures on domestic science, and holding over two hundred meetings for the purpose of organizing new WI branches. In 1905, Miss Lillian D. Gray from Toronto visited the Algoma, Manitoulin and Nipissing Districts, while Miss Agnes Smith from Hamilton went to Muskoka and Parry Sound. The following year, Miss Gray, now Mrs. Lillian D. Gray Price, travelled to Muskoka and Parry Sound during June and July, while Miss B. Maddock, an instructor from Guelph, went to Algoma and Nipissing. That same summer, Miss Laura Rose of the Ontario Agricultural College travelled to the northwest, holding meetings in Rainy River and Thunder Bay before going on to Temiscamingue District.[26] The minute books from these earliest northern branches trace their roots to these special summer meetings.

Reporting on the progress of those northern branches a few years later, Margaret McAlpine from Toronto reported how excited she had been to return to the north, where she had spent her childhood, and to find that the WI was very strong in Northern Ontario. "When I got to Mindemoya [on Manitoulin Island] I found two hundred women and a few men gathered [for the annual convention]. They had driven — for you must remember that there is no railway and very few telephones. It still has the romantic cast of early days, and they drove distances of five to forty-five miles to participate in the convention. When a woman will drive forty-five miles to a convention she is in earnest and intends to make it go, and so they made it go. It was inspiring to listen to the reports of those outlying districts, and to know that Women's Institutes are formed in those sparsely-settled communities."[27] McAlpine continued her travels into Algoma District.

> Now the second convention was held at Sault Ste. Marie, and there were present about fifty from all down the line as far as Thessalon and from St. Joseph Island, and away up by Goulais Bay. I was very much impressed by the report of the delegate from Goulais Bay. She says that is the end of civilization; in other words, the end of the world. When you come to Goulais Bay, there are no more settlements and no more clearings, and that is where they work. The women come out and drive for miles and miles, sometimes ten miles, to come to the Institute meetings. They realize that it is a sort of Women's Club. Now you understand that this is the day of women's clubs and institutes and organizations, and so the women at the end of the world at Goulais Bay have the same feeling and cannot do without their club, therefore they would not miss it for the world, and I believe they are taking up studies almost the same as we do in our centers. I am not sure that it was not Browning they were enjoying.[28]

Many women found themselves behind the steering wheel of a car or holding the reins of a team of horses to transport themselves and their neighbours to monthly gatherings or annual business meetings. A WI member is at the wheel of this vehicle with its 1912 license plates. The group posed for a picture at the Institute picnic in Algoma Centre District. — Algoma Centre District Tweedsmuir History

Although Mrs. McAlpine drew many parallels with WIs in Southern Ontario, there were very important differences in the northern experience. These women were very isolated, and they faced many obstacles in trying to organize WI branches in their remote locations. Yet they were determined to organize. "They did not care anything about obstacles. Obstacles do not count with the New Ontario women. . . . Some of the

A district meeting was quite an event for members of the WI and their families. In some areas of the province, attending rallies and conventions meant travelling great distances, often with other members of the family in tow. Some of the delegates who attended the 1910 Area Convention at Barnhart in Rainy River District are pictured here. — Barnhart Women's Institute *Tweedsmuir History*; AR, 1912 women from the backwoods were delayed by a train being late and they walked six miles to get another train, so as to be on time for the convention. One woman said, 'I would not have missed it for anything if we had to crawl on our hands and knees.'"[29] Reports of that kind of enthusiasm and determination were incredibly rewarding for Institute organizers such as Lillian Gray, who had visited Manitoulin Island and Algoma District in 1905 to organize those very branches about which McAlpine reported.[30]

Education for efficient homemaking involved more than just teaching the science of nutrition or the art of sewing. Women were taught to take better care of themselves, and these illustrations about posture drew attention to the importance of working comfortably to reduce physical strain. — Annual Report of the Farmers' Institutes, 1904

Numbers and new branches tell only part of the story. The WI was growing in other ways. The movement grew in scope in the field of domestic science and other fields of education; it grew beyond education to begin to fill several other roles in the lives of Ontario's rural women. The momentum of statistical growth is best explained by these other growth areas: the WI grew because women found something appealing in it. "When you find women [in 1909] driving thirty and thirty-five miles in order to get something to assist them in making the local society a success, we cannot but conclude that there is an earnestness in this work which must result in universal benefit."[31] Furthermore, if women did not find what they wanted already existing in the WI, then they pushed for change and expanded the roles that the WI would fulfill for them.[32]

Although George Putnam continued to define the WI narrowly as an educational forum for women, he did concede that the range of topics was becoming broader. "The day is fast passing when the Institute is looked upon as a place to discuss food topics only," he admitted.[33] Pointing to the newly revised WI Handbook of 1907 and its list of discussion topics as proof of that growth, Putnam reported that women were now encouraged to discuss all manner of things at their meetings.

But even in the delivery of domestic science education, the Institute movement forced the government to become more creative in its delivery of services and to grow in new directions. Originally, according to the vision of Adelaide Hoodless and the authorities at the new Macdonald Institute in Guelph in 1903–1904, young women from rural Ontario would flock to that school to be educated in scientific homemaking. In fact, that never happened. Mary Urie Watson, Principal of Macdonald, confessed in her private correspondence with the editor of the *Farmers' Advocate* that farmers' daughters were not highly represented among the student body.[34] The admission standards may help to explain this, given the fact that normal school was the usual requirement for the courses, and most rural women did not have access to high school in those days. It is not surprising, then, that on the basis of academic requirements alone, many rural women were disqualified from entering the Macdonald Institute. But there were also economic considerations. Education was expensive (one short course at Guelph cost about $60), and farm families had to consider economic strategies for their

In order to extend its system of education throughout rural Ontario, the Macdonald Institute co-operated with the Women's Institutes to introduce a system of short courses. Pictured here is a group of WI members learning to sew in 1913.
— AR 1913

children. If one were to take on the expense of educating a daughter, then teaching, nursing or clerical training might rank higher on the priority list as leading to paid employment.

For whatever reason, few rural girls took advantage of the new facility at Guelph. The Macdonald Institute and the Department of Agriculture had to change their methods. The educational experience became a little more accessible with the introduction of a short course, though financial strain and farm workload still made it beyond the means of most rural girls. How could the resources of higher learning be made available to the majority of the female rural population? Over the years from 1904 to 1914, two strategies involving the Women's Institute became central: the creation of a loan library to put educational materials in the hands of WI members, and a new format for Watson's short courses where the instructors rather than the students would travel. Thus, distance education for rural Ontario women was conceived in 1913. It is worthwhile to consider both of these developments to trace the ways in which the WI grew, and to begin to explain why it was so popular with rural women.

Speaking to the delegates at the WI convention held on the Guelph campus in 1909, Watson addressed her subject, "What the Macdonald Institute is Prepared to Do for the Institutes." "You will remember two years ago I told you that if any of you had any questions or problems that you thought Macdonald Institute could help you with, we would be glad to do so if we could. . . . Last year I renewed that invitation and told you how we were trying to get our material in accessible form."[35] The accessible form was a library of clippings and articles dealing with domestic science. The invitation was for members to write to Miss Watson and request the loan of these materials for a two-week period. And so the loan library service was born. Miss Watson's help became invaluable. WI members throughout Ontario were eager to make use of this resource person and her collected materials on domestic science. Members of local WI branches were charged with the responsibility of presenting papers to one another at their monthly meetings, a prospect that was absolutely terrifying for some women. With little or no educational background beyond elementary school and even less experience in public speaking, most members were daunted by the idea of preparing and presenting these talks. In 1908, Watson had offered, through an advertisement placed in a national women's magazine, to make loan materials available through the mail to any Institute member upon request. The members were quick to take Watson up on the offer. In fact, in November 1909, she reported that she had received 350 requests for information.[36] The correspondence between the principal and the WI members who used the service in those early years has been carefully preserved, and it speaks volumes about the interests, expectations and fears of WI members in these important years of expansion.[37]

A woman from Bluevale, Ontario, wrote that she would "be greatly obliged if you can help me out as it is my first paper [and] I am very green at this business."[38] Another from Ayton echoed these sentiments, saying, "I have never in my life got up a paper so I thought and heard I could get some good points from you [for] which I would be very, very thankful."[39] For younger women especially, the thought of giving a paper to their older, more experienced neighbours was especially intimidating. "I am just a young member," confessed Mrs. Mills from Wingham, Ontario, and "I feel very nervous having to take this subject, so if you could assist me in getting a paper I would be very grateful."[40] Watson provided clippings from magazines on topics of interest to homemakers, specializing in the science of nutrition and other topics related to homemaking, including cleaning solutions and home nursing. Members who were responsible for preparing talks for their monthly meetings found the loan library services indispensible.

The WI was first conceived as a means for bringing domestic science education to the rural women of Ontario. Mary Urie Watson, the Principal of the Macdonald Institute in Guelph, helped achieve that goal by providing loan library services and travelling courses in home economics. — UG

But the services of the loan library were only one aspect of what the Macdonald Institute was prepared to do for the WI movement. Putnam hinted that a more comprehensive scheme of instruction was in the works when he told the delegates of the annual convention in November 1910, "We hope to see some system introduced which will provide for systematic introduction covering three or four months time among some of our Institutes in one or more sections of the Province during the coming year."[41]

In 1913 an important new joint venture between the Macdonald Institute and the Ontario Women's Institutes was launched. It was domestic science education by extension — an early form of distance education.[42] These new courses were different from the three-month variety offered on the campus. This new proposal was for a course that would travel to the students in their own communities. In one sense, the proposal was an expansion of the custom already popular among Farmers' Institutes, where "experts" would travel to various locations and educate the farmers in their own locality. But this was something more. Because the courses were several weeks in length, they allowed for more in-depth instruction, demonstrations and testing. The lecturers who travelled to give these short courses were for the most part graduates of the Macdonald Institute, and so Watson was accomplishing two things at once: venturing into distance education and expanding the influence of the College, and also finding work for her qualified graduates as they took on the role of travelling instructors.

Recognizing that of all the problems standing in the way of launching a series of these courses, "the financial difficulty is the chief one," Watson argued, "Why should the women not claim some of Ontario's

Social outings have always been an important part of local branch experiences in the Women's Institutes because they helped to build a sense of belonging. In 1912 the Winona WI went on an outing in a boat owned by a local fisherman, and their expedition was captured on film. — Erland Lee (Museum) Home, *Winona WI Scrapbook*

wealth from the government?" She supported her argument by pointing out the disparity in government spending between funds directed to men's and women's programs. Referring to the new scheme whereby county "ag reps" had recently been stationed in fourteen counties around the province to act as advisors to male farmers, she blasted the government, asking her audience, "Do you know what that work in each county costs for salaries and travelling expenses and maintenance? $2,100. Do you know the average amount per county the Women's Institute work costs? An average of $125.00. The disparity is too great when the relative importance of the two branches of work is considered." With the Farmers' Institutes in decline, Watson concluded that surely the Women's Institutes would not "be considered unreasonable if we seek some Government assistance."[43] Continuing her critique of government spending on the men's organizations, Watson cited a remark, made by the Deputy Minister of the Department of Agriculture, that he found it "difficult to get the people to support the proposition of spending money freely in teaching the indifferent farmer to drain his land." Turning his rhetoric back on him, she caustically suggested that "Mr. James and his Department might leave those indifferent farmers to ripen a bit and transfer their attention to harvesting a crop of extension classes amongst the women who are hungry for more instruction about their special work. We can assure them of enthusiastic support."[44]

The very first short courses were offered off campus by the Macdonald Institute in conjunction with the WIs of Haldimand County. The Canfield WI was one of the first to take advantage of these courses.

> In 1912 Mrs. W.M. Thompson was appointed by Mr. Putnam as one of the committee of eight to co-operate with him to formulate a plan that the Institutes might have a systematic method of teaching and study in groups. In 1912 Canfield had the smallest branch in the County but we had a Domestic Science class with Mrs. Burns as teacher. Twenty-five members were required, fee $1.00. The class started with 10 but soon had the necessary 25 and finished with 30 in February. The supplies were furnished by each lady in turn giving them. The hall was free and a lady sent a load of wood for the fire. At that time we had a cook stove to demonstrate on.[45]

In these two important ways then, the WI outgrew Putnam's original ideas. First of all, the role he predicted for himself as a co-ordinator of speakers was not central. The WI members did a lot of the speaking themselves, through papers they prepared with the assistance of the loan library services offered from the Macdonald Institute. This had a tremendous personal impact on the members in terms of their personal development and the confidence and public speaking skills that they acquired through the experience. Second, the creation of travelling short courses made the instruction both more thorough and more accessible than Putnam's original proposal for travelling lectures could ever have done. Domestic science education became more accessible for more women, and more women were directly involved in leading and learning than the original model would have allowed. But the emphasis on domestic science was only one part of the growth of the WI during these years of expansion. In fact, many WI branches outgrew their emphasis on domestic science altogether.

Indicating that domestic science was no longer the chief focus of her local WI group, a northern member reported in 1914, "We have got past the recipe stage." A speaker at the annual convention in 1907 echoed that sentiment, pointing out that with the statistical strength of the WI movement, they had the potential to move beyond tea parties and fancy work. "We are a goodly company — ten thousand women. Let us not devote too much time to ice cream, crisp salads, and eyelet embroidery. There are greater things."[46]

What were the greater things, and how would they be incorporated into the scope of WI activities? That remark was made in the context of a story about isolation; the speaker, Mrs. Richmond from St. Jacob's in Waterloo County, had recently visited a woman living in a very isolated location, "away north of Kingston in the Rideau Lake region." After they had visited for a while, the overworked woman, who was grateful for the companionship, revealed, "'I have not laughed so much since I was a girl.' And when the visitor left, she called after her, 'God Bless You,' and 'Won't You Come Again?'" Her point was that lonely, isolated women needed the social interaction and friendship that the WI could offer.[47] The social benefits of the WI were high on the priority list for many Ontario women who made lasting friendships through the local Institute.

Women also acquired skills from organizing their local groups. Many members overcame their fears of public speaking. The challenge of learning how to hold meetings and prepare papers was a positive one for most members. "Now, in a great many Institutes when they began, they did not know much about managing their meetings, and if you asked a woman to speak it would almost be enough to keep her away for good. Now we have not only gotten her away from that, but we have such speakers as Mrs. Howell, Mrs. Thurston, Mrs. Junior and others. You ask what we have done. These are some of our finished product."[48] Most members never became renowned speakers because of their Institute experiences, but almost all gained new levels of self-confidence. Miss Nie, reporting from Fenelon Falls, told of one branch in Victoria

PLAIN CARD—PRINTED ON ONLY ONE SIDE.

WEST ELGIN

WOMEN'S INSTITUTE

Dutton Branch

PROGRAMME

1907

JAN. 25—"Apples."
Mr. J. Lyons
"The Practical with the Scientific."
Mrs. E. V. Docker

FEB. 22—"The Uses and Food Value of Eggs."
Mrs. J. L. Pearce
"Selection and Care of Hens for Eggs."
Mrs. A. F. Bobier
"Fowls as Food; Cooking and Carving."
Miss Effie Graham

MARCH 28.—"Care of the Teeth."
Dr. Paton
"Sweet Pea Culture."
Miss F. McLean

APRIL 26—"Consumption: Its Prevention and Cure."
Dr. McLachlen
"Hints for the Garden."
Mrs. D. Graham

MAY 31—"Patriotism."
Mrs. R. Bobier
"Labor-Saving Appliances for the Housekeeper."
Each Member

Mrs. D. Graham, *President,* *Dutton.*
Miss M. C. Gow. *Sec.-Treas.,* *Wallacetown.*

The program of Dutton WI in West Elgin District — Hand-book for the Use of Women's Institutes in Ontario, 1907

This picture of the 1909 North Wentworth Women's Institute District Annual Meeting illustrates how viable the movement had become, bringing women together to discuss a variety of issues beyond basic domestic science. This event, hosted at the home of Mrs. J.F. Thompson of Christie's Corners, attracted women of various ages, including mothers of young children.
— *West Flamboro WI Tweedsmuir History*

East District, where "it was a decided failure to try to get any person or persons to prepare a paper on any subject, so it was decided that the subject chosen for the next meeting should be dealt with by a three-minute paper from each member. This proved to be a boon to the branch. Every member present prepared a paper and since then every member has been successful."[49]

Women learned about more than just domestic science topics. Guest speakers informed them about legal and financial affairs, and this proved to be a very popular type of presentation, no doubt because the kind of information available through the WI meeting would be difficult and expensive for an individual woman to access on her own. Branches would often invite bankers and lawyers to address them and help them to learn business matters. Such was the case in Orillia, where, as they reported, "One of our lawyers gave us a paper on bonds, law, banking, and told us, among other things, that we should know about money deposited in the bank. We should have our husbands put the bank account in both names, because very serious complications often arise over small sums of money in the bank, after the decease of the one in whose name the account was. He told us such a lot of things that we were so ignorant about, and some of our ladies have already benefitted as a result of that paper."[50]

But the WI moved beyond individual development. The branches developed a group feeling among the women that was new for most of them. "It seems to me that one of the most gratifying results of the Institute's work is the growth of the fraternal spirit. The spirit that men call brotherhood."[51] "We have always heard and read a great deal about the brotherhood of man, but I think it was left for the organization known as the Women's Institute to bring out the true significance of the sisterhood of woman."[52] Or, as another member from Wellington County expressed it, "[I]n many places, chiefly in the country, there are many who are neighbours as far as residence is concerned, yet have merely a speaking acquaintance, and it was not until the Institute came along that those so-called neighbours came to know each other and exhibit a real neighbourly spirit. The Institute affords an opportunity for all sects and classes to come together upon a common ground, and in this lies its chief strength."[53]

The Institutes were surprisingly successful at including a whole variety of people. "The Institute is for women what the public school is for the nation. All denominations and classes meet together and they are one. Class, social position, wealth, religion are all swept aside, and each one must find her own level and each one must be taken on her own merits. It touches the farm homes all over Ontario, making them, with the town and city homes, the largest body of organized women in Ontario to-day. As every politician knows, the rural population is to be reckoned with, and the women of the rural districts will wield an influence as great as the city women."[54]

Despite all the positive outcomes associated with women meeting together for mutual benefits, the Women's Institutes were not content to be just a social and educational group. As Mrs. Brown from Winterbourne in Waterloo County reported, "A noticeable fact is that during the first year or so of a branch Institute, they are very much interested in the planning and preparing of foods, exchanging recipes, etc. But this is invariably replaced by other subjects, such as character building, or the desire of the Institute as a body to be of some definite use to the community."[55] Community work became central to the Women's Institute local branches throughout rural Ontario. Putnam remarked on the changed emphasis of the reports coming in from across the branches:

> In the early days of the Institutes, the reply to inquiries as to how the work was progressing in any particular society was nearly always in some such manner as this, "We have splendid times, I got a most excellent recipe at the last meeting, and many of the ladies were delighted to get a copy of my method of canning raspberries," or "We had a very nice social time, Mrs. Blank provided a splendid luncheon — cakes, sandwiches, coffee, and fruit." In these times the replies are quite different and indicate that the Institutes are not self-centred, but are reaching out to help others at the same time that they are receiving benefit. Local libraries are being established in increasing numbers and Travelling Libraries are being asked for by many of the Institutes. The beautifying of home surroundings and town or village is receiving a just amount of consideration, street lights are being installed, permanent quarters provided for the Institute meetings and libraries. The members of the Institute are not only doing the work themselves, but are successful in enlisting others in such objects as the beautifying of country cemeteries and church yards, and the improvement of rural schools. One Institute replies that they could not send a delegate to the Convention, but would appropriate the funds necessary for that, in securing a teacher to instruct the school children in sewing. Several societies have furnished individual drinking cups for the school children. Committees have been successful in many instances in inducing the members to make better provision for sanitation about the school premises. There is a decided tendency to make the local school the social centre for the community, and we heartily commend this line of work to the Women's Institutes and Farmers' Clubs.[56]

Community work took women out of the kitchen and into the realm of community organization. Mrs. Brethour from Burford invited the delegates in November 1910 to reminisce about the origins of the WI, saying, "I would like to take the delegates back ten years, when, we might say, we began at the kitchen, because it did seem impossible in those days to get up any kind of a good meeting or any enthusiasm, unless we had a demonstration in cooking, but now-a-days it is very rare that that has to be resorted to, to get out a lot of women. The talk now is all about Public Libraries, Travelling Libraries, the improvement of our schools, the health of the school children, and other matters of general interest dealt with on scientific principles. From the beginning at the kitchen, we have not only gone through the house, out of the front door, but into the streets of the Municipality."[57] Some Institutes quite literally went to the streets — and had sidewalks and street lights installed in their communities. In fact, the WI played important roles in infrastructure projects, either encouraging local authorities to act, or acting themselves where local municipal structures did not yet exist.

With such a long and varied list of projects to support, the WI branches turned their attention to fundraising schemes to finance their service work. One of the earliest stories of WI branches doing catering work on a large scale is that of the Agincourt WI. Reporting for that branch, Mrs. Johnston described how they had arranged this work since 1907:

> In our riding we are fortunate to have a Plowman's Association which meets once every year for the purpose of conducting a plowing match. The plowmen found it very inconvenient to get their meals, and especially so when the field chosen for the match was some distance from the village. So our Institute has been catering for them for the last four years.
>
> We usually leave the building accommodation to be arranged for by the men, but try to have this as near the field as possible. A driving shed makes an excellent dining room and a tent adjoining answers the purpose of a workroom or kitchen.
>
> The menu is arranged by a committee of ladies from our Institute, who always provide a bill of fare in keeping with a plowman's appetite. We also divide the baking, so that it does not fall too heavily on any one. The meat is purchased out of our funds, and a number of ladies help in the cooking. One lady is asked to cook ham, another to roast veal; each one thus has her work. We do the same with the bread, pies, etc. Everything is prepared at home, and on the morning of the plowing match each member of the Institute is supposed to be on the ground and ready for work. . . .
>
> The ladies very often come to the dinner with the men, and become so interested that they soon find their way to the kitchen. They are almost invariably delighted with the way we manage things, the good things we have to eat, and decide to become members of the Institute before the next plowing match. Eight new members joined our Institute this year, simply through coming to the plowing match dinner.
>
> Of course, you understand, undertaking this is no idle speculation; we all have to work and work willingly. We have our Motto hung in the dining-room and when we get a little foot-sore we look at the motto, take fresh life and start again. Very often we go away feeling

> better than when we went, and I think that the men, as well as the women, are beginning to believe that the Women's Institute is one of the best organizations we have. . . .
>
> This year we gave about five hundred meals. That is as near as we could estimate.[58]

The funds raised by schemes such as catering were in most cases turned back into community projects, so that the women used the money to introduce new services and improvement to their communities. Three kinds of projects particularly popular throughout Ontario were libraries, hospitals and schools.

The need for a local public library caught the attention of a number of Institute groups. The Burgessville Women's Institute reported on their 1909 project to launch a library in their village:

> Last year our Institute decided to organize a public library in the village. When we first spoke of doing so we were told by some that we would not succeed, as the matter had been talked of for years and seemingly could not be done. Nearly every person wanted a public library, but no person seemed to care about taking the responsibility of organizing one. We finally called a committee meeting and arranged to have a garden party to raise the money. This meant a lot of work and anxiety, but, what was best of all, it was a great success and we cleared above all expenses $81. We thought we were rich then and we went to work with double energy. We had no trouble in getting our fifty members, which is necessary to send to the Government to organize a library. Next we applied to the County Council and they granted us $50, also the Township Council $25. The Government, I believe, gave us from forty-five to fifty per cent of the amount we spent for books.
>
> We then made arrangements with the Shredded Wheat Company to give us a banquet, which they very kindly consented to do, and we gave a concert in connection with it and realized $40 from that. We rented a suitable room and sent for our books. They arrived about a week ago and cost us about $132. I think they are the finest collection of books I ever saw. They consist of history, fiction, biography, etc.
>
> Now, we have enjoyed the work very much, and I think after organizing and establishing a public library, as we have in our village, that the people of that place will not dare to say, "What good are the Women's Institutes?" We intend to keep on improving and adding to our library as fast as we get funds. We have appointed our librarian and everything is ready. We expect to open the library doors to the public next Saturday at 3 o'clock.
>
> In conclusion I might say, if there are any millionaires here who are bothered to know how to make good use of some of their wealth, we would be only too glad to receive your contribution and, if you feel so disposed, you can arrange with me at the close of this meeting. In doing this, I believe we, as Institute workers of Burgessville, would rise up and call you blessed.[59]

In isolated areas of Ontario, the community counted on travelling libraries to supply reading material for the use of women and their families. Where a group could not afford to establish its own collection, members could take advantage of collections offered through the Department of Education. This service, pictured here in 1958, continued for several decades.
— UG, FWIO Collection

Libraries in many, many villages and rural communities across Ontario owe their establishment to a local branch of the Women's Institute.

Where a full public library could not be established, many Institutes took advantage of the provincial government's program of travelling libraries. Cases of books were shipped to the community for an extended period, and the Institute oversaw the circulation and return of these books. One branch in Northern Ontario that made extensive use of the travelling library in these early years is the Kentvale WI on St. Joseph Island in Algoma District. Residents of this remote location were isolated during the winter season when ferry service to the north shore was not operating. At an August meeting, the branch moved that "we return the public library now on hand and try to have another one sent us before the close of navigation."[60] The members of the WI made good use of the travelling library for the season, then returned the collection and received a new one. Where distance or lack of funds prohibited the establishment of a permanent local collection, the branches made use of this innovative public service instead.

Another favourite target of the WI was in the area of health care. Institutes worked very hard to ensure access to health care either through helping to finance hospital buildings and equipment, or raising funds for the salaries of health personnel. The Halton branch near Hamilton explained that their motive in raising money for the Hamilton Sanitorium was that "many of our members being of the opinion that we were getting too self-centred, and that the time had come when we should try to help some who needed help and cheer."[61] The Institutes in Peel County banded together to raise funds, and as Miss S. Campbell of Brampton reported, they had a great deal of community support.

> The Superintendent has asked me to speak of our hospital work in Peel. I was the one who spoke of it first, I think, and suggested that we should have a cot in some hospital where we would have any member go if she were ill, and where we could go and visit her and be able to look after her. I went to several gentlemen, some of the most prominent in the town, and among them a doctor, who said, "Oh Miss Campbell, don't take that cot out of Peel." I went to our Mayor, who has since passed away, and he said, "Well, you go on with your work and I will call a meeting." After a time I said, "Will you give us your sympathy? We want even more than sympathy, we want money." He said, "I will give you money, too." I went to the

Sheriff, and he said he would give us a donation. I went to several of the Institutes, and our County President went with me, and she talked it up. We will have a great many discouragements, I know, but it is worth some discouragement if we are able to float a flag over a Women's Institute Hospital in Peel some day. We had our bazaar last year and made $830 clear, and today we have, as a Women's Institute, over $1,000 to help the list of donations. We have formed a board of five women, who have taken out a charter. I believe they are the first five women who have ever taken out a charter. Now the next step is to see how much we can get in our town before starting to ask for donations in the county. We are planning a banquet for the purpose of interesting the people in our scheme. Now, we do not intend to go into debt. We intend to do just what we can get the money to do with, but we want something good, and I feel that quite a number of the gentlemen are going to give us a donation. One has promised $1,000. Perhaps some others will not be so agreeable, but I do feel that nothing is gained except by work.[62]

Certainly the work of fundraising and administering a project was very familiar to many WI members during these years of growth when the local branches became central to community projects of all kinds.

However, at least one woman reported that her branch at Orillia in Simcoe County did not engage in fundraising activity because too many other voluntary organizations in her community were already doing that kind of work. "We accept the grants that are given by the Farmers' Institute and the Government, and we use our fees, as far as we can, to keep things moving, but we do not make any money, because our town is simply overburdened with making money for the new hospital and for Y.M.C.A. work, besides a great deal of church work; so we felt that we should make the women feel exempt from making money in the Women's Institute."[63] WI performed fundraising when no other groups did so. But if a community had other groups for that purpose, as Orillia obviously did, then the WI abstained from fundraising to prevent duplication of effort and to give the members a respite from that kind of work.

A third area where the Institutes worked in their communities was schools. This was an area that was close to the hearts of mothers particularly, as they extended the concerns of caring for their families outside their homes and into the schoolyards. "The Women's Institutes have done considerable by visiting the schools and offering suggestions to the trustees to improve the conditions surrounding the rural schools. The sanitation of the school has been much improved and scholars and teachers have co-operated in beautifying the school grounds as a result of suggestions offered by the Women's Institute."[64] Sometimes the local school had a very specific need, and the local WI branch would launch a project to provide for that need. Such was the case in Middlesex County, where the Parkhill branch was celebrated as one of the first to "exert their influence wherever the interests of women and children need[ed] them." In one location, "the public school there [had] no fire escape, and in case of fire the little children upstairs would be in great danger of their lives. A committee of mothers went before the educational board and complained of these things, and last month there was a fire escape put in."[65]

Pragmatism took the Women's Institutes beyond the science and theory of homemaking and out into their communities. Most of the members were interested in learning new ways of improving their

While most WI branches were involved in a variety of community projects that required fundraising on their part, the Orillia WI reported in 1911 that they were careful not to compete with other groups in their community that were raising money. Shown here in 1907, the year their branch was founded, the members are dressed in their finest. — *Orillia WI Tweedsmuir History; Hand-book for the Use of Women's Institutes in Ontario*, 1907 homemaking and taking instruction in domestic science. But they did so with very practical goals in mind. The new science of household management promised women a reduced workload because they would learn to work more efficiently and thus cut down on their time and the difficulty of their work. Anything that could promise a well-managed home and time left over to do other things had great appeal. WI members were pragmatists first and foremost. One very practical thing that interested most women was the potential of labour-saving devices. "Our latest expenditure has been the purchase of a vacuum cleaner," a member from Bloomfield WI reported, "the cost of which was $25. This we rent by day to non-members at the rate of $1 a day, to members at 75 cents. We also rent it for half a day, and hope to rent it especially during the winter months, by the hour, as some might wish to clean just a living room."[66] The vacuum cleaner served a dual purpose: making housework more efficient, and at the same time, making money for the branch. Other Institutes also exercised this practical co-operative approach to sharing the equipment they needed. The Ailsa Craig WI in Middlesex County is a case in point. Referring to that branch, one member reported, "they bought a lawn mower, and gave it out to those who could not have one."

In another part of that district, "the Institute had a flower brigade and trees were planted in the country schools, and in my own home town, Parkhill, the most unsightly spot was taken and made into a beautiful park. I think there have been twenty-five or thirty men working at this park already. Besides this, the women in this district, both in the towns and country places, have interested the children in the schools in flowers, and at one of the flower shows, one of the public schools took the prize for the flower boxes." Although these horticultural undertakings were, on one level, signs of a simple concern for community improvement, the speaker reporting on them actually said that for her they represented deeply held convictions about women's roles and rights. "The women believe that this is for the benefit and welfare of their sons and daughters, and through this influence on their sons they will come to see that suffrage should be extended to the home-makers. (Applause.)"[67] Community landscaping meant more than planting trees and flowers. Some members hoped that by fixing up the public grounds, they were actually planting the seeds of political equality for women.

The Women's Institutes grew and changed in remarkable ways during the first ten years of Putnam's time as superintendent. From an organization whose demise was rumoured at the beginning of the century, the Institutes had become 25,000 members strong. They were fulfilling new roles in the educational, social and community life of rural Ontario, and there was no longer any doubt about it: the Ontario Women's Institutes were here to stay. The "army of women" that George Putnam led was about to face a major challenge with the declaration of war in the summer of 1914. Perhaps the military metaphor was an apt one after all.

As the war continued, food production became an issue, and WI members were encouraged to help by respecting the rationing orders and by contributing through their gardening and farming work. This promotional exhibit at a fair was part of the message to encourage women to participate. UG, FWIO Collection

CHAPTER THREE

Knitting Together: War Work, 1914–1918

There has been no organization and could have been no organization so well fitted to vitalize and organize the efforts in the rural communities as has the Women's Institutes at this time." Such was the high praise that W.B. Roadhouse, Deputy Minister of Agriculture, gave to the Central Ontario Women's Institute Convention in Toronto in the fall of 1915. Acknowledging the organization of effort, the collection of funds, and the production of goods that the Ontario Women's Institutes were performing as war work, Mr. Roadhouse was very impressed. "Think what it means," he continued, "to have an organization so ideally spread out, so closely knit together in its efforts and its aims."[1] Perhaps there was no pun intended, but it was very appropriate that he would refer to the Institutes as "closely knit together," because they certainly did a lot of knitting during the war. Woollen socks for soldiers topped the list of items that WI members produced for the war effort. The grass-roots effort of knitting hundreds of thousands of socks is an important symbol of how the Institute developed during the First World War. Not only did they literally do their knitting when they were together, but also they became an even stronger organization because of their wartime experiences. Indeed, members of the Women's Institutes were "knitting together" in more ways than one.

Virtually every branch of the Institutes did war work, "even in the most isolated or poorest sections of the Province," and by 1916 that meant that nearly 900 branches with a total membership of 30,000 women were busy knitting. One Eastern Ontario branch, the Chesterville WI, described how they organized themselves for the knitting bees. "We invited all the women and girls of the community to meet every Friday evening, to knit. We commence at 7:30, knit until 10, then we have a cup of tea. Each member pays ten cents a night which helps to buy supplies. In order to stimulate the work and accomplish more, we appointed captains and chose up sides, and then started a friendly rivalry to see which side will knit the most socks by the New Year. This knitting circle is a little break in the monotony of the lives of some of the women, and we are looking for splendid results."[2] Another branch, the Morrisburg Women's Institute, also in Eastern Ontario, was typical in its 1915 report: "Red Cross garments made 7,780. Of these are 761 pairs of socks and 366 flannel day shirts. I signalize these two items," Mrs. Ashton pointed out, "as we are particularly proud of our hand-knitted socks. One of our workers alone has knitted 53 pairs, and several others are close to this record."[3] Meanwhile, in Haldimand County, a Sock League was organized, with the goal "to give every soldier of the 114th Haldimand Battalion, now overseas, one pair of socks each month. The women of Haldimand to do the knitting." To meet that goal, they needed to produce 250 pairs of socks per month, and through the efforts of the local Institutes, they did just that.[4]

Although observers attempted to calculate how much the Institutes actually produced during the war, most concluded that "how much patriotic and Red Cross work the Institutes in Canada have done in the last two years I suppose no one person really knows. It must be a grand total and a total of which we as members have reason to be proud."[5] For the year ending in May 1918, approximately $850,000 in cash and goods was donated to the Red Cross, and George Putnam, the Superintendent of the Ontario Women's Institutes, estimated that the grand total for the war years was "at least $1,650,000."[6]

Many women had incredible knitting records. Mrs. James West of Kemble WI in Grey County was celebrated for her knitted contributions to the war effort. A charter member of the branch, she is pictured here in 1957, after she had enjoyed sixty years of WI membership.

— UG, FWIO Collection; *Home and Country*, summer 1957

After just one year, the 1915 fall convention of the WI reported that 13,524 pairs of socks had been knitted. "It seems a lot, but it is only a drop in the ocean; nevertheless, it has been a great help," Mrs. McPhedran, the provincial co-ordinator of knitting, remarked, "Shortly after the war broke out I said to a friend, 'In a country like this, where so many know how to knit, we will have no difficulty in securing help.' And she said 'I have no doubt they will give us the most precious part of the work, their time.' I inserted a letter in the paper asking for help, thinking it would bring in about 300 pairs, but we received at once offers to knit 3,000 pairs. This was before the organization of the Red Cross work. The Red Cross took it over after we felt that we could not carry it on any longer as a private enterprise."[7] The call for help went out, and the WI answered. "S.O.S. stands for 'Send Out Socks,'" one Red Cross worker suggested.[8] The women were ready to answer that S.O.S. and they continued to surprise themselves at their collective accomplishments, as each year's work outdid that of the one before.

Looking back, one has to marvel at the volume of the work that was accomplished. It was all done in a spirit of patriotism; women were urged to knit and to believe that, just as "somebody has said, 'the hand that rocks the cradle rules the world,' . . . [so] the women who knit socks are going to help Britain to win this war."[9] In fact, women were told that they had no right not to be involved, since men were risking their lives for the war effort. Women were expected to exert extraordinary effort too. "There is nothing wonderful in our rallying to the call of the Motherland," one modest member declared. "We would be false to every hereditary instinct we possess had we, her colonies, turned a deaf and unheeding ear to her in her distress."[10] Mrs. R. Condie, reporting for the Beachburg Institute to the Eastern Ontario WI Convention in 1914, told of her branch's work, saying, "The keynote of our last two meetings has been patriotism, and feeling in that direction runs very high among the members. The Institute had the honour of starting the first fund in Beachburg and vicinity to help our Mother Country and our own Canadian boys who are gone to fight our battles."[11]

Loyalty to the Empire and to the nation was couched in the language of personal sacrifice. "Women of the Institutes, our beloved Dominion is calling to us today to sacrifice. If we are to meet the needs as they arise it will mean individual sacrifice. If you are living in the same happy, easy, luxurious style you did in the sunshine of last year's prosperity, let me tell you you have no right to do so. Look at your household and personal expenditure and see whether it is all necessary. Do not for a moment think, because you have made some socks or some shirts, that you have done your duty. You have not done your duty until you have done all you can every day, every week, every month till the war ceases."[12] Women's Institute members were reminded to be sure that their own level of sacrifice was acceptable. "Before the war there were a great many of us who had lived, perhaps not richly, but we had three good meals a day, and all the clothes we wanted. Do you know there is a lot of that we can do without, without really feeling it? We can have a less expensive pudding and have fish instead of meat, and not go to so many entertainments, and have no new dresses, or only one instead of two, and, in that way, not only will we gain quite a little for the Red Cross, but we will gain a splendid education in economy which is going to last us all our lives."[13]

The sacrifice of a new dress or a favourite food was not to be trivialized. Women's efforts were elevated to the same level as men's through the use of military metaphors. "The battle today is not man's battle alone," Institute members were told, "but it is the battle of the home; the battle of the mother; it is a battle for the civilization of the world. . . . You women have to take a part in this, some of you already, with a smile on your face but with breaking hearts, have bidden goodbye to your sons and your loved ones who have gone to the front to fight the Empire's battle. Many more of you will yet have to do the same task before this terrible war is closed, but I know the stock from which you have come, and I know the character of the women of Canada, and they will measure up to the highest ideals of the race, the highest ideals, I believe, that have ever been measured up to by any women that the world has produced."[14] Sympathy for the Empire and for the "ideals of the race" meant that women were expected to do all they could, within their female roles, to participate in the war effort. There was no thought of the women going into active combat themselves, but their hearts were certainly close to the front lines.

History Will Congratulate the WI

Speaking to the annual meeting of the Women's Institutes of Ontario in 1916, C.C. James, Commissioner of Agriculture for Canada, remarked in his chairman's address, "Your children and your children's children and their children, and probably their great-grandchildren will, in the future years of the history of this country, be talking of the events of 1914 and 1915, and of 1916, and it will be a pleasure then to be able to recall the things that were accomplished back in those years. Time will show how fortunate it was that there was available for this work an organization like the Women's Institutes of Ontario."

— AR 1916

In fact, the military imagery about women's activity sounded very much like a recruitment drive for women. Speaking at the annual convention in 1916, Mrs. Wilson urged the delegates to remember, "The idea we must all hold to is the need for more work and more giving. If you have done well up to the present you know you can do better. If you are busy then you are the very woman to give more work to, because it is the busy people who always can do the most, for they usually have more system and spend their time the most wisely. And, as our brave soldiers have to get better of their wounds and return to the front, so we must start again and go right ahead and do more, determined to do our share in this terrible struggle which was none of our making and which must be won by us."[15] Busy Institute members were the very ones who would be most likely to find inspiration in the wartime rhetoric.

"The cry is for socks and more socks," a Wardsville woman explained, "which means that we must knit more and pray harder while knitting."[16] A great deal of prayer went into the making of socks. As one district officer reported in 1916, "All are found knitting — 'Knitting with a prayer in every row, that the ones they hold in their hearts so dear may be guarded as they go.'"[17] In answer to that cry, women knitted everywhere. They knitted while on picnics, at church and during every spare minute. They even knitted as they attended the WI convention in Toronto in 1914. Miss E.J. Guest remarked to her audience, "[M]any of us have boys at the front. I saw tonight many in the audience knitting away while waiting for the meeting to begin. We are doing what women can do to make things easier for the boys of the country who are fighting the battle of

Emily Guest was celebrated for her work in organizing the branches of the English Women's Institutes during the First World War. Originally from Middlesex County, Miss Guest helped to organize the Parkhill and Birr Women's Institutes. — UG, FWIO Collection

This pin was presented to Emily Guest by the Women's Institutes of England in 1918 in appreciation for her work in organizing their war efforts. "The beautiful pin is similar in design to the official pin of Ontario Women's Institutes except that at one end of the oval the English rose is designed, while at the other end is the Canadian Maple leaf." The pin was later given to the Birr W.I. in Middlesex County where Emily and her sisters had given considerable leadership. — The Free Press, London Ontario, The Women's Institute 50th Anniversary Edition, June 16, 1947

ideals for the British Empire. They are the ideals for which Women's Institute stands — 'Home and Country' — and as never before in our history, tonight it is 'Country' and it is not only country, it is our Empire, and we are staking our imperial existence in this struggle for the right for freedom, for honour."[18]

York County Women's Institutes reported that they had given up their preoccupation with "fancy work" and turned instead to knitting, making "socks by the hundreds."[19] On Manitoulin Island, a similar trend was reported. "Our community worked hard to help," a contributor to the *Barrie Island Tweedsmuir History* reminisced. "The WI bought pounds and pounds of yarn which were knit into dozens of pairs of socks, mitts, scarves, helmets, etc. We girls at school organized a girls club. I remember it was at the suggestion of Bertha Latta, a chum of mine. We started to do fancy work but as the war was closer we learned to knit. . . . Later we held our meetings in the evening every two weeks in the homes. The boys not only attended but some did some of the knitting. We had a real live organization and besides knitting made money in social affairs in different ways to help win the war."[20]

With so many women knitting and recruiting others to knit too, it became difficult to control the quality of the knitting and the members were urged to give attention to this important aspect of their work.

> I saw one "patriotic offering" and you could not tell whether some of the socks were intended for the hand or the foot; another pair had a leg out of all proportion to the length of the foot; still another pair had many dropped stitches so badly taken up that the recipient would have little ladders in the heels and toes in no time. Some sent in wristlets that never

Knitting became a social activity for many women during the war. For some groups, the knitting was set up as a competitive effort. For many, such as these members from Elgin County, it was something they did whenever they had a chance, literally in every spare moment. — *Hyde Park WI Tweedsmuir History*

> could be persuaded to go over any man's hand. There is no use mincing matters, some of our gifts were far from perfect. If you never made a sock before, don't practise on the soldiers. Make a pair for your own men at home first. They will not be backward in giving you a frank opinion of what they think of your maiden effort. . . . If our men are worth anything, they are worth the very best we can give them. Florence Nightingale, in her report after the Crimean War, said the well-made, good-fitting shirts and socks added real personal comfort to a soldier on campaign. Then let us see to it that any gift we send does not fall short of the mark. Patterns and every direction needed may be had for the asking from the Red Cross Society, 77 King Street East, Toronto. If you are still in doubt as to your intended gift and its requirements, every letter of enquiry will receive prompt attention and a courteous reply. There is no need for any waste of material, time or money. Do the thing you can do best. Service is only service when it is adequate and efficient.[21]

The concerns over well-knit socks were more serious than just appearances. Mrs. Plumptre, a Red Cross worker, raised the question of quality control in relation to the soldiers' comfort. "Some person has asked whether it is a good thing to send in the socks if the heel is not properly turned. We must remember that in war we are dealing with a very unusual state of affairs. If the heel is not properly made it has a very bad effect upon the man when he is marching, causing blisters and sometimes blood-poisoning."[22] Certainly these were serious health concerns, and the theme was often raised that the quality of the offerings had a direct effect on the morale of the soldiers as well. Dr. Patterson urged the women to realize how important their knitting was, because "it is said in military circles that a man is no stronger than his worst foot, and every sock we knit helps to keep his feet in order."[23]

Problems with the quality of the knitting were only part of what the Red Cross had to deal with. Rumours about abuses in the system began to circulate too. While the women who knit the socks made them with the intention of giving gifts to the soldiers, rumours began to suggest that the socks were being sold for profit by the Red Cross. "You are entirely wrong if you think Red Cross goods are being sold," Mrs. Plumptre told the 1916 Toronto convention.

> So far we have not been able to get the address of a single man who has ever bought a pair of socks, and I would like to ask anybody here if they know of any man who has bought a pair of socks in this way. Don't tell me that you know somebody who knows somebody else who knows somebody else whose sister knows somebody who told her that her son at the front was told by another man that he knew of a man who had bought a pair of socks. Don't write and tell me that a miner in British Columbia bought a pair of socks from the Red Cross without giving me the name and address of the miner. Don't tell me that a lumber man in Ontario bought a pair of socks from the Red Cross unless you give his name and address. We have followed up every clue that has been given to us without finding any facts that would go to show that any of our goods have been sold. The impression I want you to carry away is this: If anybody is selling gift socks, or any other gift article to our men at the front, then it must be some absolutely dishonest person who is doing it for their own personal gain, unknown to the Society sending the goods.[24]

These rumours of abuses in the distribution of socks, and also of Red Cross workers being paid high salaries at the expense of the donors, were widespread. Red Cross workers addressed the issues directly, assuring the WI members that their work was all done on a volunteer basis and pointing out that accusations and insinuations were very damaging to the war effort.

The Red Cross explained that they had reached a conclusion about the subversive nature of the stories. "This story about selling socks came in from all over Canada practically the same week. It seemed curious to us that all the stories should come in the same week," Mrs. Plumptre reasoned, "and we came to the conclusion that it was a bit of German secret service work. We believed German agents were

PLAIN HEAVY SERVICE SOCKS

Original Red Cross Instruction

MATERIALS: 5-6 ozs. SPECIAL HEAVY RED CROSS SERVICE YARN or HEAVY 4 ply SCOTCH FINGERING.

For Average Knitter set of 4 No. 11 Steel Knitting Needles. For Tight Knitter set of 4 No. 10 Steel Knitting Needles. For Loose Knitter set of 4 No. 12 Steel Knitting Needles (points at both ends). Bell gauge.

Colours: Khaki, Navy, Grey, Airforce.

MEASUREMENTS: All sizes from 10-12 required.

Length of leg from top of cuff to under the heel from 14 ins. - 16 ins. To make a 16 in. sock add 2 ins. to the directions for leg, making 13 ins. instead of 11 ins.

Cast on 60 stitches, rib 4 ins., 2 plain, 2 purl. Knit plain 7 ins., 9 ins. for 16 in. sock, (11 ins. in all).

HEEL: Knit plain 28 stitches on to one needle. turn, purl back these 28 stitches, turn, knit plain, Repeat these two rows (always slipping the first stitch) 11 times (12 in all), or 24 rows.

With the inside of the heel toward you, purl 15 stitches, purl 2 together, purl 1. Turn, knit 4 stitches, knit 2 together, knit 1, turn, purl 5 stitches, purl 2 together, purl 1. Turn, knit 6 stitches, knit 2 together, knit 1, turn, purl 7 stitches, purl 2 together, purl 1. Turn, knit 8 stitches, knit 2 together, knit 1, turn, purl 9 stitches, purl 2 together, purl 1. Turn, knit 10 stitches, knit 2 together, knit 1, turn, purl 11 stitches, purl 2 together, purl 1. Turn, knit 12 stitches, knit 2 together, knit 1, turn, purl 13 stitches, purl 2 together, purl 1. Turn, knit 14 stitches, knit 2 together, knit 1. Pick up and knit the 12 stitches down the side of the heel piece and knit 2 stitches off the front needle. Knit 28 stitches off the front needles on to one needle; the last 2 stitches knit on to the 3rd needle, on which pick up and knit the 12 stitches at the other side of the heel piece. Divide the heel stitches on to the 2 side needles and knit right round again to the centre heel. First needle, knit to within 3 stitches of the front end of side needle, knit 2 together, knit 1. Front needle plain. Third needle, knit 1. knit 2 together, knit plain to end of needle.

This reducing to be done every other row until there are 56 stitches on the needles (front needle 28, side needles 14 each). Knit plain until the foot from the back of the heel measures 9 inches.

KITCHENER TOE: Decrease for toe—knit 6 stitches, then knit 2 together, knit 6 stitches, knit 2 together. Repeat this to end of the 3 needles. Then knit 5 rows plain. Then knit 5 stitches, knit 2 together, and repeat to the end of 3 needles. Then knit 4 rows plain. Then knit 4, knit 2 together, repeat to the end of 3 needles. Then 3 plain rows. Then knit 3 stitches, knit 2 together, repeat to end of 3 needles. Then knit 2 plain rows. Then knit 2 stitches, knit 2 together, and repeat to end of 3 needles. Then 1 plain row. Then 1 row decreasing if necessary, so as to leave 10 stitches on front needle and 5 on each of the back needles. Graft toe. For Grafting see inside back cover.

ALTERNATE TOE: Decrease for toe. On front needle knit 2, knit 2 together. Knit to within 4 stitches from end of needle, knit 2 stitches together, knit 2. On first side knit 2, knit 2 together, knit to the end of needle. Knit to within 4 stitches from the end of second side needle, knit 2 together, knit 2. Knit 3 rounds plain. Then 1 round decreasing, then 2 rounds plain. *Then 1 round decreasing. Then 1 round plain. Repeat from * until there are 10 stitches on front needle and 5 on each side needle. Now slip stitches from one side needle to the other, making 10 stitches on 2 needles. Graft toe. For Grafting see inside back cover.

This is the pattern that women used to knit socks for the Red Cross. WI members were told that the Kaiser himself was so afraid of their knitting efforts that a German spy campaign was launched to sabotage the knitting campaign.

— Private collection, The Canadian Red Cross Society, Knitting Instructions for the Armed Forces instructed to spread this news in order to prevent our people from knitting."[25] The thought that a systematic enemy campaign had been set up to discourage the Women's Institutes' knitting effort became an incentive for even greater effort. "People here were instructed through German sympathizers to spread these stories and stop the women of Canada knitting. What do you think of that? Are not you glad that the Kaiser himself was afraid of your knitting needles and things you are doing? I do not know when I felt prouder; it gave me so much encouragement to go right along knitting."[26] If the smear campaign was a German plot, it backfired, because, as a prominent organizer for the Red Cross humorously declared, "It will take more than a few yarns to discourage me at this job."[27]

One year into the war, the call went out for supplies the soldiers would need. Mrs. Somerville, from London, explained to delegates at the Western Ontario WI Convention why socks were so urgently required. "As winter is approaching, the soldiers need very warm comforts that the Government does not supply, and we will need to redouble our energies for knitted goods, and I would just like to read you a list we will need for the men in the trenches: Socks — unlimited quantities. During October we sent 1,200 pairs of socks to the men in the trenches and between 500 and 600 to the wounded men in the hospitals. Scarfs, in unlimited quantities. The percentage would be about ten pairs of socks to one scarf. Balaclava caps, fingerless mittens (we need a great many of these), face cloths, small towels."[28] WI conventions were used as information sessions to demonstrate how to make the articles and to distribute patterns. The members received practical advice from Red Cross personnel.

The undertaking of knitting thousands and thousands of items required incredible organization. Commonly, one member in the branch was charged with securing the wool for the group and making the purchase. Wool was bought by the pound and then divided among the knitting members for their own use. They bought in bulk whenever possible, and Miss Watson of the Macdonald Institute used her influence to try to get the best price for the groups' purchases. Using such large quantities of supplies, the Women's Institutes were powerful buyers during these war years, and they were urged to recognize that power and employ it wisely to support their local manufacturers. "I would say to the Institutes, always buy your materials in your home town if it is suitable, if it answers the requirements for the work that is needed for our soldiers both in the hospitals and in the trenches."[29] But hometown loyalty was never to become a substitute for quality goods. "In connection with wool," Mrs. Somerville urged the knitters, "if it is possible, do not get it too coarse. Our soldiers complain when they must walk so far, the hard sock hurts the foot, and I would ask that the socks be washed before they are sent in; they are so much softer and better for the foot."[30]

Buying good-quality supplies to produce comfortable, well-made socks was an expensive proposition because good wool came at a high price. There was some initial misunderstanding among WI members about how the supplies for knitting would be provided. "So many people write and say that they understand the wool is free," Mrs. McPhedran told the delegates to the Central Ontario Convention in 1916. "There is no such thing as free wool. I have so often wished that I could just go into the garden and gather free wool, but we are all practical, and we know that, if we spend $1,000 in wool, we cannot spend that $1,000 again for more wool, we must have more money. At first we paid 60c a pound for the wool, and now we have to pay $1 for the same quality."[31]

The Chairman of the Executive Committee of the Canadian Red Cross Society, Mr. Noel Marshall, addressed the Central Ontario WI Convention in Toronto in 1914, reporting that 409 packages containing about 500,000 articles had already been received from the Women's Institutes of Ontario. "I don't know where the money's coming from," he said. "A few days ago we received $40 from a little hamlet in the north, that must have meant a sacrifice for some people. Every day some gift comes in that has meant most rigid economy or work, depriving the giver of perhaps even the necessaries of life, and I want to say that these gifts are just as much appreciated as the thousands from some millionaire. We've done a lot but we're just beginning. We are bound to win, but we will win at an awful cost, and I feel that the women of the Institutes will stand by us when the next appeal comes."[32]

If Mr. Marshall did not know where the money was coming from, the women did. In part, it came from the members' thrift and careful use of supplies. One story from Perth is a good example of extreme thriftiness. "We keep a drawer where the people who bring back their knitting put all the little scraps of yarn that were not used. All these little bits of yarn were given to one woman knitter and she brought back three pairs of socks from them. So we want to practise that old Scotch habit of thrift."[33] The Institutes in Western Ontario also contributed $750 in 1917 to local hospitals. According to Mrs. Donald McLean, the president of the Women's Canadian Club in London, and a prominent women's organizer, "This is wonderful evidence of self-sacrifice." Mrs. McLean was well aware of the effort involved. "This money does not grow out of the mud. We all know how hard it is to have extra money during these trying times. That the women in the rural districts are able to do all this work and then contribute so much real money is indeed wonderful."[34]

However, thrift only went so far. The supplies still had to be purchased with real money. The greater part of that money came from Women's Institute fundraising projects, which were very much a community affair. As one branch reported, "Arrangements are being made for a systematic mode of giving and the women are making an effort to visit each home and solicit a weekly donation of five or ten cents each."[35] Members of the WI asked for money from everyone and in some places, they earned themselves a reputation which was not very flattering. "In fact, one of our members, canvassing for the Red Cross Fund was told, 'Oh yes, I have heard of the Women's Institute; they are a bunch of busy-bodies.' Whether it be east or west, the women are busy, busy; we are not satisfied to let well enough alone. That is not in us."[36] Indeed the women were busy in their efforts. In November 1915, George Putnam reported that "the total givings in cash and goods by the Institutes of the Province of Ontario is certainly over $200,000, or about $7.00 per member. In cash alone they have contributed $42,200 to the main office of the Red Cross Society in Toronto, while many of the Institutes, especially in the eastern and western sections of Old Ontario, have contributed considerable amounts to local Red Cross societies."[37] Evidently, the work of the canvassing "busy-bodies" paid off.

The war years were a relatively prosperous time for Ontario farmers. There was more cash in the hands of the rural community during the war because of the increased prices farmers were receiving for their goods. Dr. Robertson from Ottawa urged the women to go after the farmers for funds. "May I say one thing more?" he asked the delegates. "Get the men who are farmers to give money to the Red Cross. I do not say that because I think the farmers ought to give more than the city people. . . .The farmers can afford it better than any other class of people at present. This year the farmers in Canada will get at least twenty-five per cent more for their crops than in all probability they would have got if there had been no war. That is the bald truth —

cheese at 16c. a pound; hay much higher, oats higher, wheat higher. People say, Look at the financial stringency. Think how it would have been in Canada at this time but for the war. If the farmers got twenty-five per cent more because of war prices, and then gave the whole of it, they would just come out even, and that would be an enormous gift. It would meet the needs of the Red Cross work and all other benevolent patriotic work in the most abundant, lavish way."[38]

In addition to generous donations collected through neighbourhood canvassing, WI branches sometimes received support from local municipal councils or other sources of public money. Most branches, however, depended on their own resourcefulness in fundraising as a means of supporting their wartime projects. In some cases, the money itself was the donation that was turned over to the Red Cross, or to the Belgian Relief Fund. Most often though, the money was used to buy supplies, and the knitted articles became the donation. Including these contributions of money and goods in kind, one estimate suggested that the WIs had raised over four million dollars during the four years of the war. That figure was based on a calculation that put a price tag on the women's products and the labour that had gone into making the socks and other articles.

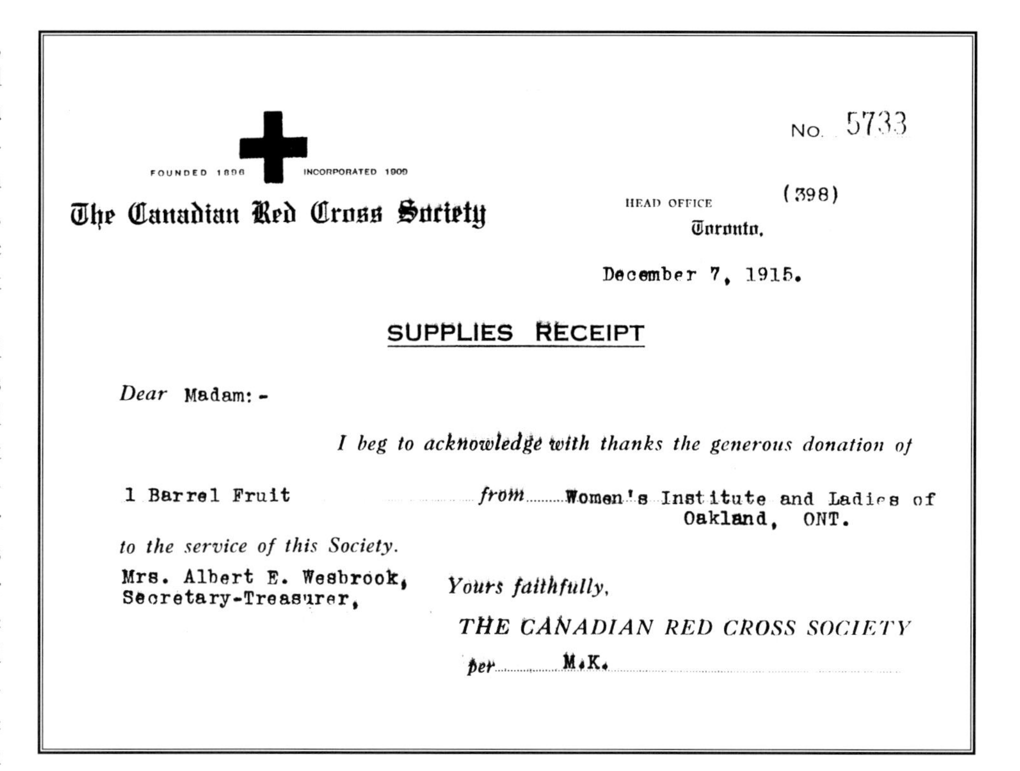

FOUNDED 1896 INCORPORATED 1909

The Canadian Red Cross Society

No. 5733

(398)

HEAD OFFICE Toronto.

December 7, 1915.

SUPPLIES RECEIPT

Dear Madam:-

I beg to acknowledge with thanks the generous donation of

1 Barrel Fruit from Women's Institute and Ladies of Oakland, ONT.

to the service of this Society.

Mrs. Albert E. Wesbrook, Secretary-Treasurer,

Yours faithfully,

THE CANADIAN RED CROSS SOCIETY

per M.K.

Special efforts were mounted to collect money for the Red Cross through subscriptions and community events. Donations of supplies were also very common, as these receipts from Oakland WI illustrate.
— Oakland WI Tweedsmuir History

In their continuing efforts to generate cash, some means of fundraising proved controversial among Institute members. For example, one member posed this question at a convention: "Is it wise for an Institute to sell tickets on a quilt to raise funds? Is not that just a polite way of saying they had a lottery, and are lotteries legal in Canada?" Mrs. Shortt said in reply, "It is illegal without the permission of the Chief Executive of the locality or municipality. If anyone wants to have a raffle or lottery, according to the law of Canada, they must get permission from the Mayor or Chief Executive in that locality, and that has been done in a great many cases since the war."[39] For the most part, branches took whatever steps were necessary to get approval for their fundraising schemes.

Mrs. E.H. Edwards from the Pakenham branch reported to the Eastern Ontario WI Convention in 1914 the ways in which her WI had raised funds for the war effort:

> Since the outbreak of the war sewing has been carried on one afternoon each week, all members contributing an extra twenty-five cents to assist in providing materials for a start. In this work we have received much assistance and generous donations from those outside our branch who have become interested in the good work. A large consignment has already

An example of the parcels that Institutes prepared for overseas shipment. This shipment, containing knitting projects, bandages and supplies, was prepared by the Onondaga Women's Institute, Brant North District, in 1915. — Onondaga WI Tweedsmuir History

> been sent for the Hospital Ship, also mending kits, etc., to our boys before they left Valcartier. A carload of clothing, potatoes, cheese and many other things has also been shipped to aid the brave Belgians in their distress. Now to accomplish all this work during the past sixteen months it was necessary to find some means of raising funds. The first method employed was an afternoon tea held at the home of the President. This brought in over $40, and was repeated again this year, adding $40 more. A sale of "novelties" was held after business was concluded on one of our regular meeting days, $10 more being realized in this manner. In August of this year a patriotic concert was held under the auspices of the Institute, the entire programme being given by local talent. Our net receipts from this were $115, and this amount was at once forwarded to the Patriotic Fund. Scott Bros., general merchants, very kindly offered their store to the women of the Institute for one Saturday in September. This offer was gratefully accepted and the sale most successfully carried out, a cheque for $100 being handed by them to our President as the result of our day's labour. This amount has also been used for Red Cross work.[40]

Despite their impressive record of fundraising, delegates to the 1915 annual convention were urged not to rest on their laurels but to step up their efforts.

> We have learned with pleasure that we have given $35,000 in cash as an organization. It sounds a goodly sum of money. It is, but, before you take all the credit to yourselves of a generous offering, will you recollect that much of the money was made by concerts, socials, tag days, etc.? Do not misunderstand me. I am not condemning the raising of money or criticising the ways and means. You did the work, achieved the object, raised the money, got noble returns, but the fact I want to emphasize is, that it does not mean the personal sacrifice of the members of the Women's Institutes. Look at it in another way. We are an organization of 25,000 women; that sum total up to the present time represents a little more than $1 a head. Is that what your country is worth to you? Do not look at your neighbour and size up your situation from her standpoint. You, and you alone, are responsible for your actions.[41]

Of course, knitting and fundraising were only two of the types of war work that Institute members performed. In fact, most of the women and most of the branches produced a whole variety of goods. When the contributions were collected and their value tabulated at a provincial level, the combined effort looked most impressive. As Mr. Putnam reported in 1916, "During the past year the Institutes have come into prominent and favourable notice through what they have done in response to the various patriotic appeals made necessary on account of the war." He admitted that it was a difficult thing to keep track of all the contributions, because donations in kind were not easily classified. Realizing this, Putnam reported, "A 'bundle' is, of course, very indefinite. The following gives a list of supplies in a representative bundle:

17 pairs bed socks
121 pairs socks
1 Balaclava cap
28 handkerchiefs
4 mufflers
21 pairs wristlets
3 shirts
18 pneumonia jackets
20 abdominal bandages"[42]

50 flannel bandages
gauze, soap, euthymol, anti-serum tablets
old linen
48 gauze pads
4 packages absorbent dressing
3 packaged bandages
12 bandages
24 absorbent bandages

As the contents of the typical "bundle" suggest, a large part of what the Institutes were contributing were health supplies for overseas field hospitals. The bandages, pads and dressings were contributed directly to the Red Cross for their work with wounded personnel. Although the women usually lumped their war efforts into one category of work done "for the soldiers' comfort," the Red Cross made a particular distinction between medical supplies and other generic "comforts" that the women wanted to forward to individual soldiers.

The Red Cross had a very clear understanding of its role in health care, and its representatives urged the WI delegates to get a clear understanding of the differences too. "I might say that the comforts for the 'well' men in the training camps and the comforts for the men at the front are not provided by the Red Cross Society. That is not Red Cross work," Dr. James Robertson instructed the WI members. "It might even be regarded as contravening the International Convention that gives protection to the Red Cross workers by its flag. Red Cross work is volunteer aid for the sick and wounded and prisoners of war only." He was concerned that WI members consider how their volunteer efforts could be put to best use. "But, if the women, out of the wealth of their affection and desire to do good, want to supply some comforts for the soldiers, let them do that," he continued. "There is a Canadian Society in England for that purpose — the Canadian War Contingent Association to which the Red Cross Society sends the boxes we get that are marked 'Field Comforts.'" However, he urged the women to think carefully about where they directed their efforts. "Do not deflect one pair of socks that you can send to the Red Cross into the Field Comforts box. Never before were there put in the field armies so well equipped as the British and Canadian armouries are now, in clothing, in comforts and in everything needed. If you wish to give some extra comforts to the men — and it heartens them to be remembered — let it be out of the abundance of your good will, but do it in addition to the Red Cross work."[43]

Although Dr. Robertson thought that the comfort boxes to well soldiers were less important than the medical supplies his organization so urgently needed, returning soldiers had a different perspective. They placed a very high value on the women's comfort boxes. Veterans encouraged the women not to underestimate the impact of their so-called extra comforts. "The only sunshine a man gets are the letters and gifts from home," one veteran remarked, "and I can assure you the men appreciate more than I can tell you what the women of Canada are doing for them, and they know the women are doing everything in their power to do their bit, and they appreciate it."[44]

According to all accounts, personal "ditty bags" and cheer boxes were particularly welcomed by the men. The reason for shipping these personal items was, in part, an expression of local community support for the armed personnel from their own communities. The delegate from Carleton Place Women's Institute pointed this out after listing the efforts her branch had made on behalf of the larger campaign. Although her branch regularly made large donations to the Ottawa Red Cross Society, she explained that "we as an Institute did not wish to give up our own identity, so we continued to send comforts to our own boys at the front. These parcels consist of day shirts, socks, handkerchiefs, salve, note-paper, envelopes, pencils, insect powder, etc."[45] Institutes often held work bees to pack such boxes earmarked for individuals they knew personally from among their own families, friends and neighbours. The contents of the boxes were often itemized in the branch minute books. They commonly contained soap, gum, tobacco, cigarettes, jams, cheese, Christmas cake and, of course, socks. One puzzling reference mentioned that the women were packing boxes and into each one, they put a "housewife." The term referred to a small sewing kit that the soldier or sailor could use for small sewing repairs.

At least one of the items in these comfort boxes proved to be controversial among the women: cigarettes. Members of the Women's Institutes were divided over the issue of supplying tobacco products to Canadian young people. During the First World War, prohibition groups such as the Women's Christian Temperance Union worked to limit the use of alcohol, but were equally concerned about the use of tobacco products. Membership in the WCTU and the WI sometimes crossed over, and therefore, some WI groups had determined not to include cigarettes in their boxes to the soldiers. However, Major Strethune, from Ottawa, who had just returned from the front, told the WIs to rethink their position on cigarettes and not to be too committed to their prohibition instincts.

> I have often been asked, "Do the men really appreciate all that is being done?" And I always tell them the same thing: "If you could only be out there in France . . . when the quarter-master brings along a couple of cases, you would see a number of men gathering together. They sit down . . . and open up the parcel; sometimes it is a bale of socks or tobacco. . . ." I think the men enjoy the cigarettes more than anything else. And, if there are any members of the W.C.T.U. here I would just like to say — and probably you will think me a very naughty man — I would certainly advise you to let the men have cigarettes. It does not do them half the harm that the nerve strain does under heavy shell fire. They say a lot of young chaps who never smoked before learned to smoke. There may be a few who do that but there they are under a big nerve strain; they have nothing to occupy their minds but to wonder where the next shell is going, and, if a little cigarette will take their minds off that, let them have the cigarette.[46]

The issue surfaced in questions dealing with war work when Mrs. Plumptre answered questions at the Central Ontario WI Convention in November 1915. Supporters of the WCTU position posed the question, "Why do persons send cigarettes to the soldiers when they know they are injurious to them?" Mrs. Plumptre was diplomatic but firm when she answered, "This is a question of principle with many people. For my own part, I would send cigarettes to the soldiers. Some of them receive terrible injuries, and, although I do not say that cigarette smoke is sufficient, I do say that it has an extraordinary soothing effect upon the nerves of the

With Greetings and Prayers
from
THE WOMEN'S INSTITUTES OF ONTARIO
for
The Empire
and
World Peace.
FOR HOME AND COUNTRY

This little tag was included with the comfort boxes that the Institutes prepared for soldiers overseas. Loyalty to the Empire was part of the motivation behind sending such parcels, but so too was the opportunity to support members of their own community who were serving the war effort.
— Sheffield Women's Institute

men; and the doctors, as well as the nurses, allow the men to have the cigarettes even in the hospitals. I remember one nurse who went from here telling me of the frightful injuries one man had received. His body was almost torn in pieces by shrapnel, and she said that when she sees a man like that in dreadful agony asking for a cigarette, she thinks it right to give it to him."[47]

Furthermore, women were told that neither health reasons nor economic reasons should prevent men from smoking. While some members argued that tobacco was a waste of money that could be better spent on more important war supplies, one woman, a physician, argued that women could not criticize on that grounds. "Well, ladies," she retorted, "as long as we see women trotting around the streets with high heels and high-priced shoes, with trinkets of more or less value hanging from the flesh of their ears, with hats on their heads, the price of any one of which would keep a man in tobacco for years, for goodness' sake let us hold our tongues. (Applause). But I can tell you," she continued, "tobacco is not all bad. Anyone who has lived in a house with a nervous man can tell you that. I have known some men who were really very companionable as long as the old briar pipe was around, but as soon as that was gone he was unbearable. Now, men are bound to be doing things, and I think we had better bear this evil that we know than fly to others that we know not of."[48]

Although the women disagreed over the merits of supplying soldiers with tobacco, on most other issues they were firmly united. As the war dragged on, concerns about food production came to the fore, and WI members made concerted efforts to work together on the problem. The harvests of 1914 and 1915 were abundant, but with poor conditions in 1916, concern arose over the Allied countries' food supplies. The causes of the food shortage were many. Dr. James Robertson of Ottawa explained that the problem was cumulative, the result of a variety of factors including reduced harvests, inclement weather, reduced rural work force due to enlistments and wartime factory work, losses due to enemy submarine activity, and the extravagant buying and high living of prosperous munitions workers.[49] As the government encouraged farmers to increase their production, consumers were urged to respect the rationing, and to decrease their consumption of certain foodstuffs, specifically wheat, bacon and beef. The government launched a campaign that involved food pledge cards, which were to be filled out by householders and displayed in the window as a sign of compliance with the government initiatives. This was clearly an arena where homemakers could make a difference.

As one official explained to the Institute members, "The [Food] Controller never asked anybody to go hungry, but he asked you to conserve food, to the extent of eating bacon at five meals a week instead of seven, and so far as possible substitute some other cereal for wheat which is needed for our allies." Members were assured that this "was a necessity, not a fad, not a political propaganda, not a chimera; it was a ghastly reality that the Allies had to have more beef, bacon and wheat, and the only way to get it was for the people on this continent to save one-quarter of what they usually consumed."[50]

In this realm of food management, the educational work of the WI became central again, teaching homemakers about nutrition and helping women to learn how to increase food production through courses on gardening and home canning. In 1917, 100,000 bulletins were distributed throughout Ontario on canning and preserving.[51] The Institutes enthusiastically took up this emphasis in their program, and "as a result 184 meetings were addressed by speakers on 'Back Yard Gardening.' Literature was widely distributed and large numbers took advantage of arrangements made with a reliable seed company to supply a collection of vegetable seeds at a price considerably below retail price for the season. Following this, many requested demonstrations in Canning and War Time Cookery, in addition to the circulars which they received on canning, drying, and war-time cookery."[52]

One important collective effort on the part of WI members concerned about food supplies during the war was in canning food. "The establishment of Canning Centres, under the auspices of the Women's Institutes in co-operation with the Canadian Red Cross Society, resulted in a large output of fruit, jams, jellies, pickles and chicken for the soldiers overseas. The results are as indicated in the following table:

PLACE	**OUTPUT** (in pounds)
Barrie	46,799 lbs
Guelph	22,336
Mapleton	18,840
Niagara-on-the-Lake	21,781
Parkhill	26,238
Stratford	14,000

The value of the goods put up at the six centres was at least $35,000. Institutes in Eastern Ontario were equally generous. As Mrs. A.H. Robertson reported in 1915, "[O]ne barrel of jam in pint sealers was sent to the Red Cross headquarters Montreal, for hospitals at the front" by the Maxville WI.[53]

In addition to this kind of help aimed at alleviating the shortages overseas, some Institutes had the opportunity to be directly involved in providing for the soldiers at home. For example, "at Grimsby Beach a considerable quantity of jams, soup, etc., was put up for the Aviation Camp at Beamsville."[54] Some local Institutes in the Niagara area were called upon to feed soldiers who were en route to training locations or marching drills. There was also an effort to encourage home canning as a means of conserving foodstuffs for home use. Through special wartime lectures prepared for the Women's Institutes, members were taught how to preserve their own produce so that the foodstuffs on the market could be released for export rather than home consumption. In 1916 the report from Mr. Putnam indicated that this new emphasis was very successful. "The Gardening and Canning Campaign, managed and assisted by the Department [of Agriculture], has been well taken up. We are planning to furnish seeds and gardening literature to 2,500 members for the season of 1917, and the interest stimulated in gardening and home canning through this campaign shows encouraging promise."[55]

Farm women were directly affected by these calls for increased production. At Glasgow Station WI, for example, "Women regretted that not as much patriotic work as they had planned for could be carried out, owing to the fact that so many of the women had to work in the harvest field. This, however, is patriotic work in the truest sense of the term. Fifty-nine dollars was sent to the Prisoners of War Fund. Quilts and clothing were sent to the French Relief and to fire sufferers in Northern Ontario."[56] The members from Bonnechere Valley WI in Eastern Ontario reported that the calls for increased production gave a seasonal rhythm to their war efforts. "During the winter months, we do knitting and sewing for soldiers. This is suspended during the summer, as we are a rural Institute and feel we can best serve our country by doing our bit on the farm. We raked and forked hay, donned overalls, and worked in the garden. When summer work is over we resume Red Cross work."[57]

With this seemingly endless rhythm of war work, it is difficult to imagine that women could maintain the exhausting pace through four years of war without losing momentum. Yet each year's contributions were higher than those of the year before. According to one estimate, of all the goods collected by the Red Cross, sixty percent were contributed by the members of Women's Institutes.[58] Patriotic appeals provide only a partial explanation of why women worked so hard for the war effort. Moreover, an accurate picture of women's experiences in the Great War must go beyond simply celebrating the enormous amount of work that they performed. For many women, the war years were nothing to celebrate. "We women must rise to our responsibilities and meet, as best we may, this tide of sorrow and worry that has been thrust upon us," one member mused. "We have been called upon to give our sons as sacrifices and the women of Canada have risen to it in a noble and marvellous way. . . . The response and the generosity of the women for the Red Cross work has run into thousands of dollars. I do not believe in weighing things by dollars but I do love to weigh these Red Cross garments by the love that every woman stitches into them. The quantity supplied has been marvellous and none have contributed more than the Institute women."[59] Not only were women working and knitting together in a literal sense, they were knitting together emotionally both as individuals and as communities. As the Athens WI branch reported, "[T]he great women's heart of our Institute has throbbed very close to the firing line, as so many of our own town boys are in the trenches."[60]

Dr. Annie Backus was a frequent speaker at WI conventions and in the press. She commented on the emotional cost of the war when she addressed the Western Ontario WI Convention in 1914. "It is difficult . . . to concentrate our thoughts upon any question but war . . . and our anxiety is so great as to the final results of these events, that sub-consciously we are waiting and listening for some definite news. This only do we know, the world is filled with bereavement, and for years mothers will still be mourning for their slain and maimed children — many Rachels weeping for their children because they are not."[61] "It was a very anxious time," one Tweedsmuir curator recorded with honesty. "I remember three of the mothers sitting and crying through part of the WI meetings. We had memorial services conducted by Rev. Wiseman three Sundays in succession in the church. . . . I think that was the year we had no Christmas concert. No one had the heart for it."[62] For the same reason, Carleton Place WI, in Eastern Ontario, reported in 1915, "we dispensed with our yearly picnic, and spent all our spare time in work for soldiers."[63]

Grief associated with the casualties of the First World War touched many, many women in Ontario at a very personal level. They were the lovers, mothers and sisters of soldiers who died. By working together during the war, the women felt that they could do something to help one another cope with the war, rather than just sit by and wait. WI members were determined to support the individual soldiers they knew who were serving and dying overseas, but the women were not just meeting together to support their men. Their loyalty was to "first the mothers; mothers of our fallen heroes, mothers of our boys at the front, who woman-like must stay at home and wait and dwell on the details of war rather than the great issue at stake. We must get them away from themselves. Grey knitting is the only pastime and, while the needles clink, someone may read a good book, a bit of poetry or a good essay. Then how easy to have a social hour with plain bread and butter, salad or jelly, plain cake and the cup that cheers. All jealousy will fly away and a true spirit of friendliness will grow up. Sacrifice and sympathy should be the keynote of all our endeavour this winter."[64] They met together to support one another. Patriotism was at work here, but so too was a more personal force. Institute women recognized the comfort they could be to one another. Members turned to the WI group for the support they needed to live through the emotional stress of the war. "The work of our hands is still going on," one woman explained, "even though our hearts are heavy as we think of the husbands, sons, yes, even the daughters we have bidden God-speed to at the call of our country."[65]

During these difficult times, the WI did not abandon the social side of their meetings. "At no time in the ten years that we have been an organized band of women, working for home and country, have we lost sight of the social side of our meetings. Even during this terrible war," one branch spokeswoman reported, "we feel that after the musical and literary part of our programmes is over, we are better fitted and able to carry out the plans made during the business part of our meetings."[66] It seems that the women drew emotional strength from the social escape that the monthly meeting provided.

We have seen how individual women combined their efforts to amass an incredibly high volume of funds and goods, and how women welcomed the personal support they could draw from their meetings. How did this preoccupation with the war affect the organization of the Women's Institutes? Some observers worried that total concentration on war work in the branches would obscure the other purposes of the WI and result in a decreased membership at the war's end. Others were convinced that the opposite was true. War work, they reasoned, would only cause growth. Statistically, it is difficult to resolve the debate. After the sharp growth during the ten years preceding the war, the 1914 report shows that there were 843 WI branches operating in Ontario, with a membership of 25,000. In the first year after the war, 1919, there were 920 branches and 30,000 members. Obviously then, the numbers went up, but not at the same rate as before the war. Perhaps the growth would have been even greater had there been no war. Whether the war enhanced or inhibited the rate of growth is difficult to say.

Record-keeping during the busy war years was not a high priority, and many branches failed to file annual reports, especially during the years 1917 and 1918. This could be interpreted in one of two ways. Perhaps the members were so busy with the all important war work that they did not want to waste their precious time making reports to the Department of Agriculture. However, some people worried that a casual attitude toward report writing might mean that the women were losing interest in the formal aspects of the organization, and that after the war, they might let their memberships lapse altogether. Each explanation seems plausible. Debate raged within WI circles about whether the war would actually be a catalyst to further growth or put a halt to their incredible prewar progress.

Feeding the 5,000

"During the trek of the soldiers from Niagara, the ladies of Clarkson and Lorne Park fed the soldiers pies, cakes and sandwiches for five days, representing the feeding of about 5,000 men."

Reports of the Institutes, Clarkson and Lorne Park Branch, Mrs. P.W. Hodgetts, Clarkson — AR 1916

In the first two years of the war, optimism was high. Putnam predicted growth because of the war in the spring of 1915, saying, "We have, at the present time, more applications than usual for the organization of new branches and confidently look forward to a considerable extension of the work during the coming months."[67] Furthermore, the WI had recently taken the decision to split their annual convention into three locations rather than one, and this was unanimously regarded as a sign of unstoppable growth.

Yet the Institutes gave so much emphasis to the war that some branches gave up regular WI business altogether, in order to fully devote their time and attention to the task of war production. In the Question Box of 1915, the question was put to George Putnam, "Is it to the advantage of branches to omit their regular business to do Red Cross work, or should it be an extra?" In his answer, he gave evidence of the fact that the WI and the Red Cross were working so closely together that their efforts were difficult to measure separately. "I would not hold many regular meetings if they are going to interfere with your Red Cross work," he said. "I believe however, that, with a little extra effort and bringing to your assistance all local resources, both Red Cross work and a limited amount of regular Institute work can be carried on. Why not consider many of your Red Cross meetings as regular Institute meetings?"[68] Some branches took that advice so literally that they considered Red Cross work to be their only work.

Concern arose, however, when the suspension of WI activities for the duration of the war was constantly reported. The issue came up repeatedly at the 1915 conventions. "The Women's Institutes have been able to do the work along Red Cross lines on account of its peculiar organization which has been reached after seventeen years of building up," Mrs. K.B. Coutts of Thamesville remarked. "While we have been doing Red Cross work, we must not forget the distinctive features of the Institute," she urgently reminded her fellow members, because "there seems to be some danger of this. . . . A number of the branches have dropped all their other work. We must not lose our individuality or we will lose the very spring of the usefulness that we have shown, the very spring of the benefits we have been able to confer upon the country during this crisis." Mrs. Coutts was part of a committee selected to compile the Annual Report of the Institutes for 1916, and that group made a conscious decision to edit the branch reports. The committee wanted to remind the membership that there was more to the WI than war work.

The reports that were selected for reprinting that year highlighted the fact that in the midst of war projects, WI groups were very busy with a whole variety of activities, including drama, fall fairs, baking contests, sewing competitions, Grandmothers' Days, renovation of halls, picnics, demonstrations of domestic science techniques, landscaping schoolyards, parks and cemeteries, catering at plowing matches, and donating to hospitals.[69] Institutes were not being asked to make an either/or decision about war work versus regular activity. In fact, it seemed that the branches most active in war work were often those that managed to keep up their regular affairs as well. "When we receive a report which indicates that the individual members have been working night and day for months in order to do patriotic work, we naturally conclude 'Well, they have given up their regular Institute work,' but we find that the aggressive Institute along patriotic lines is the Institute which has been able to carry on regular work to a limited extent at least. We refer to this," the committee rationalized, "for the purpose of suggesting to the Institutes that they should not give up their regular work altogether."[70]

These Riverside WI members in Brant North District pose together on the occasion of a barnraising for which they supplied the food in 1913 or 1914. Hundreds of WI branches could be mobilized to undertake war work because of their experience in working together on practical projects, a national asset that was widely recognized in wartime.
— Riverside WI Tweedsmuir History

The more optimistic among the Institute workers were not worried about the competition of war work. Instead, they hoped that the Women's Institutes' reputation in war work would help to recruit new WI members at the end of the war. Mrs. Amos, from the Exeter WI, explained how her branch was counting on that turn of events. "As soon as the call for Red Cross work was given, our members met, and feeling how very inadequate our numbers were for such work and knowing there was not time to spend in then endeavouring to increase our membership, we immediately called a public meeting of all the women of the town and from that meeting our Patriotic League was formed with a membership of over two hundred, and it is doing splendid work. We are constantly bringing our Institute work to the notice of these workers, feeling confident that, when the urgent work for the Red Cross Society and the need has somewhat abated, we may gather in many new members."[71] Thinking about the young women who had become associated with the WI through war work, the Superintendent urged the membership to think about how to hold their loyalty once the emergency had passed. "As soon as the war is over, it will be necessary to have something of real benefit and interest to offer these girls."[72] The alliance with the Red Cross and Patriotic Leagues did not have to be seen as a threat, then, if the WI was careful about its postwar membership drives.

Women's Institute Convention Toronto, November, 1915

Women of Canada, I pay
My best respects to you to-day.
We're banded here, as women should
In hopes to get and give out good.

Women of Canada, you know
That we gain much by doing so;
So that is why we gather here
And meet in council once a year.

We've got to think and glean and plan
And work as only women can;
For there is lots of work to do
For good of Home and Country too.

There's much has been already done,
But we have only but begun;
For women now must work, not weep,
If they the benefit would reap.

And women now can take their place,
And never think it is disgrace,
To help along the outside show,
For men oft need our help, you know.

Our homes are first, our duty's clear —
We tend and serve our loved ones dear;
But after that, our Country's next,
With various tasks between, betwixt.

Women of Canada, be true,
Do well the work allotted you;
It does not all depend on strength
The pace we go, or what the length.

If we take God to be our guide
And keep Him with us, by our side,
And go forth in His armour dressed,
We safe can leave with Him the rest.

Then if the Germans should prevail,
Or if the Government should fail,
And every other thing to boot,
There still will be "Our Institute."

Mrs. Walter Buchanan, Ravenna WI, Grey County

— AR 1916

In some cases, the war work proved to be a boost not only to the recruitment of new members, but also to the creation of new branches. Several Ontario branches trace their origins to the First World War. Groups of women who had met together to do war work but were not formally affiliated with the WI chose to become affiliated after the experience of war work. Some chapters of the Red Cross converted into WI branches at the end of the war.

The motto "For Home and Country" took on new patriotic meaning during the war, and there was much discussion about how the women were fighting the war by giving up their men, by knitting for victory, and by running their households loyally through careful use of rations and attention to shopping patterns. Mrs. R.V. Fowler from Perth told the Eastern Ontario WI Convention in 1914, in her report on the District of Lanark South, "Since the war we find that the latter part of our motto is not an empty one. All our women have done well, and are still busy sewing and raising money for Red Cross work, the Patriotic League, and Belgian relief work."[73] The war effort made WI members more committed to the groups' aims and objectives. "Just as the term 'Canada' means more to Canadians and the world than it did a decade ago," Mr. Putnam remarked in 1915, "so the term 'Women's Institutes' implies a greater field of activity than it did eleven years ago, when I took charge with some misgivings."[74] The war was partly responsible for broadening the organization's mandate.

Nevertheless, news about the end of the war was obviously a welcome announcement. This is the report of one Women's Institute community on Manitoulin Island,

> There was great rejoicing when the war ended on November 11, 1918. There were no radios then so we depended on telephones and newspapers for news. In fact, Mr. Latta the mail carrier often brought bits of news about the war when he heard it in town. We had only Monday and Friday mails until someone got a petition to ask for mail on Wednesday too. We were so anxious to get the overseas mail. When a batch came over, the good news went around . . .
>
> The morning the war ended and word came, Mr. Wiseman, who with his family of seven lived on the farm to the south of us, was on his way to the barn with a pail. He was on the way to feed his horse . . . I remember going out to our stoop and calling him. He stopped and I yelled 'The war is over.' He threw the pail in the air and came over as fast as he could walk. He was as delighted and excited as any of us.
>
> That evening people from all over the country went to town to celebrate and watch a stuffed effigy of the Kaiser burn in a huge bonfire on the bluff west of town.[75]

When the war was finally and officially over, war memorials were erected in communities all across Ontario, often with the Women's Institutes as key sponsors. As early as 1915 the local WIs began to publicly commemorate the deaths of local victims of the war. "We had a tree-planting day in May," Mrs. Robertson reported of the Maxville WI, "when our lawns were beautified by the planting of evergreens in memory of the boys who have given their lives in defence of our country."[76] Wherever the local community had worked on supporting the war effort, they now turned their attention to celebrating victory. While the dead were commemorated with solemn ceremonies, the living were welcomed home with joyous parties, dances, receptions, honours and community gifts. The WI women were always part of those celebrations, overjoyed to mark the end of the terrible war.

War work among WI branches across the province was very effective in bringing the efforts of women together in a way that no other organization could have done. One speaker congratulated the organization and expressed her satisfaction at the Institutes' accomplishments, "I, of the rural population, say, 'Well done, Women's Institutes.' Little did Mrs. Hoodless know how well she was building when she laid this foundation for our Canadian women to build upon."[77] Others were similarly impressed. "Of all the various women's organizations in Ontario no other could have reached that remote country woman with her home-knitted socks, her pint of jam and glass of jelly, the product of her own hands, and laid them on the altar for the cause of patriotism and the good of all. Woman's best and grandest work has been done for her boys in the trenches, for the sick and wounded ones in the hospitals, and in the mother's heroism in giving up her sons for the glory of her country."[78]

Not only did the Institutes provide an effective forum for wartime production and personal sacrifice by the women, but they proved to be an effective way for women to support one another emotionally during that time. The war was also a catalyst for change within the women's organization itself. Recognizing the combined effect of their wartime effort, women in the Institutes learned unforgettable lessons about strength in numbers. The wartime experience of knitting together, both literally and figuratively, ultimately led to a new pattern of organization when the Federated Women's Institutes of Ontario (FWIO) was established in 1919.

TO WELCOME YOU

Mr. J. S. Thompson

DEAR FRIEND:

We, the members of the St. Augustine Women's Institute, welcome you home with hearts full of joy and thanksgiving to our Heavenly Father who has spared you to return to your loved ones.

It was with a great deal of interest and pride that we saw you leave your home to journey accross the ocean and meet a fiendish enemy on another continent, so that peace and happiness might still hold sway in our dear beloved Canada. After all you have done and borne for us it is with pleasure beyond expression, that we welcome you home.

We wish, in some way, (though inadequately) to express our appreciation of your noble and heroic services on the blood stained fields of Flanders, and ask you to accept this gold headed cane as a token of our gratitude to you. May the kind Father, who has spared you through the conflict of war, guide and prosper you in all your undertakings. May we ever bear in mind the sentiment so beautifully expressed in those words of Kipling:

"The tumult and the shouting dies;
The Captains and the Kings depart;
Still stands Thine Ancient Sacrifice,
An humble and a contrite heart,
Lord God of Hosts, be with us yet,
Lest we forget! Lest we forget!"

Signed on behalf of the Institute by

MISS R. THOMPSON, President.
MISS ELLEN THOMPSON, Secretary.

St. Augustine, August 20th, 1919.

Community celebrations at the end of the war took a variety of forms, but most centred around the contributions that local soldiers had made. This official "welcome home" certificate expressed the sentiments of the St. Augustine WI in Huron West District. — Private collection, St. Augustine WI

Nutrition became a vital concern for Institute members working in rural school reform in the 1920s. WI involvement continued, and in 1955, Mrs. W. Sohm (right) and Mrs. J. Graham, two members from the South River WI in Parry Sound South District, watched as schoolchildren drank milk provided by the local Institute.
— UG, FWIO Collection; *Home and Country*, winter 1955

CHAPTER FOUR

Instituting Changes: Federation and Reform, 1919–1929

They say the women should get on the School Boards. How are we to get there?" This was the question a member from the Ravenna Women's Institute in Grey County asked her audience at the Central Ontario WI Convention in 1915. Then Mrs. Buchanan answered her own question, "I tell you, ladies, somebody has got to go first, and it takes a lot of nerve." She confided to her listeners, "I have never been to a school board meeting yet, but, ladies, I intend to go." She urged others to do the same, saying, "I hope a number of you will go to these school board meetings, because somebody has got to take hold of the work. We have heard a great deal about the work we have done, but we haven't heard about the power behind the work. I think there must be a great many trained women connected with the Institutes, or the work that has been done could not have been accomplished."[1] Convinced that WI work had prepared women very well for taking on other public roles, Mrs. Buchanan challenged her listeners to act on their expertise. "I remember the first Women's Institute meeting in our neighbourhood some fifteen years ago," she recalled. "I asked the neighbour next to me if she would go and she said she would, and when we got to the village we secured one more woman, and that was all that came, but from that day to this you cannot keep the women at home, and it will be the same with the school board." This newly found confidence about women's potential to contribute to public policy making was widely shared among Women's Institute members in the 1920s. Faith in the future was based on three pillars: the new self-perception that WI members had gained from their remarkable record of war work, the new political status women enjoyed as electors, and the newly created provincial level of the Institute organization.

In the midst of the work they were doing during the First World War, it became clear that the Women's Institutes were perceived in new ways because of their accomplishments. The Superintendent of Institutes had come a long way from his more tentative predictions of his early days in office when, in 1916, he declared, "The day of the Institute is just dawning. Keep up the good work and go on to greater things. You will have your reward in a sense of duty well done, and you are certain of more marked public recognition as time goes on."[2] Not only did the Ontario Women's Institutes get marked public recognition after their wartime contributions, they got a whole new identity. In 1919 the branches organized themselves in a new way by forming a provincial body known as the Federated Women's Institutes of Ontario (FWIO). By joining together provincially, the local branches were declaring that their organization was greater than the sum of its parts. The war work was impressive, but the women wanted to create a new organization so that even when the international crisis of war no longer existed, they could still rally together for strength and co-operative efforts. In addition to the new provincial organization, a similar national federation was created in the same year to tie together all the Women's Institutes across Canada under an umbrella organization known as the Federated Women's Institutes of Canada (FWIC).

Creation of the provincial federation meant that, in addition to Mr. Putnam's direction of matters relating to the Department of Agriculture, the organization was now headed by a committee of women who represented all the various regions within Ontario. The need for that organization had been felt for some time, but preoccupation with war work had delayed the process of making such changes. The war, however, provided more than just a delay. It actually became a catalyst for change, bringing a new sense of collective action based on wartime achievements that served to strengthen the Institute members' resolve to make those changes. When women in Ontario were granted the right to vote in 1918, change was even more certain. There was a consensus that the day of women's organizations in general, and of the WI in particular, was at hand.

"It is not so very long ago that a woman's organization, or club, was made the butt of many jokes, and the woman's club rarely had the approval of the municipality or community in which it existed," Margaret Patterson remarked in 1918. "Yet it is a fact that most of the laws re sanitation, hours of rest, work, etc., were first talked of in these clubs. When so much has been accomplished by women's organizations, laboring under such hardships, there is absolutely no limit to what we might expect of an organization like the Women's Institute, an organization with Government approval, practically every part of the Government, Dominion wide, and never had an organization such opportunities to wield its powers of healing and saving and comforting as we have just now; we have done wonderful things, but we are only beginning."[3] In the 1920s, Ontario's Women's Institutes turned their energies to social reform. With new organizational structures in place and new levels of public respect, the WI was determined to bring social changes to rural Ontario.

That determination was based on more than just changed opinions about them from the outside. Women's Institute members had actually changed the way they thought about themselves. During the war, Institute members began to realize the power of their concerted efforts and of their collective influence. Long before the war was over, members began to remark that their organization was doing more than anyone had ever dreamed it would do. "The Women's Institutes have long since passed the experimental stage," Mrs. Stock of Tavistock told her audience in London in November 1916. "For example, when the call came some two years ago for help in the way of Belgian relief, soldiers' comforts, and hospital supplies, the women from the large centres looked to the workers in the Women's Institutes for help, and they did not look in vain. We took out our knitting needles, we took out our sewing machines, and we set to work. The result of the joint work . . . was a great surprise, even to the women themselves." Women's Institute members were beginning to see themselves in a new light, as social reformers. Mrs. Stock went on to predict that these new ways of thinking would continue to have an impact in WI circles even after the war was over. "When the need for this work is ended," she said, "we will not fold our hands, even though we weep for those who are not, but we will equip ourselves the better to train the sons and daughters that are left us, to be good Canadian citizens and to conserve the lives of those yet to be born."[4] This resolve to shape the future was based on a new level of commitment to reforming society. It was also based on a new way of thinking. Speaking about Canadians in general, Archdeacon Cody told a gathering of WI members in Toronto that "this [war experience] is our growing time, both in our production and in our thoughts of ourselves, and that higher thought will certainly lead to higher achievement."[5] Applied to the Women's Institutes, his words were prophetic.

Others were echoing the same sentiments. As the chair of the opening session of the Western Ontario WI Convention remarked, "The Institutes of the Dominion have . . . established a precedent. Woman has come into her own, and I am sure that all doubt will be forever laid at rest as to woman's ability to cope with the issues of the nation." Looking back to the origins of the WI, she remarked that "its formation was as a prophecy in our national life, a forerunner of the time when women would be needed by the nation. In no other way could every woman have been reached, and her time, ability, means and interest centred on her country's glory."[6] It was clear to everyone by the end of the war that the WI had long since outgrown its original mandate. Institute women were claiming their places on the public stage.

"You will all agree with me that this war has been a war of many revelations," Mrs. Lang remarked in 1916. "It has revealed to us many things that we did not know before. One of the things it has revealed, perhaps as never before, has been what organized, consecrated devotion of the women of any country can mean to that country. To some people this has been a bit of a shock; they did not realize that women are as far advanced as they really are. It does not come as a shock to those of us who have been in women's work for many years. It seems centuries to some of us. We have always known that the women of any country might be an enormous asset to that country. I have not the slightest intention of making a suffrage speech, but it is only fair to suffrage women to say that, in the first days of the war, it was to them the Government of the country turned, and it seems to me that was a very natural thing. These women have been organized for a long time to fight for the weaker part of womanhood. Suffragettes have been fighting for political freedom."[7] Although Mrs. Lang was hesitant about making a suffrage speech, many WI members actively supported the idea of women receiving the vote.

The question of the vote became a very controversial one in Institute circles. Many local branches were quite actively supporting the developments toward equal political rights for women by discussing the question, circulating petitions and campaigning for it. Other branches were strictly opposed to the idea and felt that women had no place in these political controversies nor in exercising the franchise. The Department of Agriculture agreed with the second position. The question was raised at the Central Ontario WI Convention in the fall of 1915, as a member posed it through the Question Box. Mr. Putnam was put on the spot to explain his Department's position on the issue. "There is one question which I hesitated to answer," he explained to his audience, and it was, "Why is it that suffrage questions are debarred from our meetings?" Recognizing that his audience was quite divided on this point, he tried to defend his conservative stance. "Now I am in trouble," he began.

> I think it was at London [at the Western Ontario WI Convention] that we had a similar question and I said to the ladies there, as I say to you, that the Institute is an organization which is supposed to appeal to all classes in the community and to be of service to all. There are so many questions which are of interest and value to every woman in the community that we think it unwise at this particular stage in our progress to take up what may be considered questions of controversy or anything that is likely to be a political issue. I think we can class the suffrage question in this first class. I have had a great many women come to me during this Convention and say, "If you introduce the question of suffrage as a plank in your platform you are going to antagonize a lot of people." Women have come to me who I know are quite in favor of the suffrage movement and they have said to me, "Don't take

> up the question of suffrage in connection with the Institute." I think they are right, and I think we will do well to avoid the suffrage question at the present time. It is not that these people are opposed to Women's suffrage, but they are opposed to introducing it in the Institute, because they know it will antagonize a great many people. I would not say to an Institute, "You must not debate the suffrage question in your meetings." If you want to discuss the question in your branch the Department would not offer any objection. This is a free country. The Women's Institutes have been a great success in the past and will continue to be, especially if we adhere to those lines of work which cannot be objected to upon good grounds.[8]

Mr. Putnam was giving mixed messages about whether or not he approved of suffrage debates within the Institutes. On issues of meeting structure, there was a great deal of flexibility, and to a certain extent, also on the content of the meetings, but Putnam did draw the line when it came to the question of suffrage. On another occasion he advised the members, "You may discuss whatever subjects you think well, but we strongly advise, and we are very serious in our advice, that you avoid all controversial or political questions. There is such a large field of work without taking up these questions. The Institute is yours." In the same breath, however, he continued by reminding the women that they were dependent on the Department of Agriculture for funding and services, and they needed to obey his mandate about staying out of politics. "We send our speakers, we give you a grant and all the assistance and encouragement we can." He concluded by remarking, "[W]e do not say to you: 'You must do this or that' at your own meetings."[9] But in fact, he did tell them what not to do. He ordered them to avoid politics. He suggested that if they wanted to work on the suffrage issue, then they should join another organization devoted to that purpose.

However, local Institutes were not always obedient to Putnam's directives. At branch level, some of the women were convinced that the WI should promote suffrage. They argued that wartime projects had given them the credibility to be listened to when they asked for the vote. Members had no intention of stopping their discussions of suffrage. Some WI branches went further than merely discussing the issue and campaigned for it. The Kentvale Women's Institute on St. Joseph Island in Algoma District was one such branch. At their September 28, 1916, meeting a motion was presented, "that we undertake the work of canvassing for names of those in favor of women of Ontario receiving the franchise." The motion carried, and at the next monthly meeting they followed through by ordering "one dozen blank forms to canvass for names." Presumably they were working in co-operation with some formal suffrage organization from which they ordered their supplies. By December of that year, the women resolved to have each member "take a petition form and get the granting of the Franchise to Women."[10] A member from the Lee Valley Women's Institute, just outside Massey in Northern Ontario, defied the head office when she reported to their 1917 annual meeting in Toronto that she and her fellow northern members had no intention of complying with Putnam's directives. "There was a strenuous effort to keep suffrage out of the Institute. However, it was of no avail. We have got the suffrage microbe in our District, and we are hopelessly infected. Headquarters may give all the orders they like, but when women get interested in anything, it is going to come out in the Institute, and indirectly our Institute, although officially opposed to suffrage, has been the best medium we have had to spread the suffrage doctrine."[11] Although Putnam was convinced that infection from the suffrage bug was bad news for the Institutes, other people obviously had other opinions.

There was no consensus, even among the male authorities associated with the WI. Some men, such as Dr. G.C. Creelman, President of the OAC, came to the conclusion that extending the vote to women would be a good idea. He revealed that he had been influenced by Nellie McClung to be more sympathetic to the suffrage cause. "I have been watching the trend of women's work all over the world, and as a climax I was chairman of a meeting last week when Mrs. Nellie McClung addressed a large audience of men and women, and after listening to that excellent address, that most splendid series of facts, good-naturedly delivered, of woman's sphere in the concrete, and the necessity of organization for women all over the country, I came to the conclusion that she had convinced that entire audience of men and women that there were things women can do if they were allowed to do them, and there were things women are doing now, and that converted me wholly to the side of the woman question."[12]

But Mr. Putnam was not a convert. He and several of the WI's own membership held firmly to their conservative position. They did not want to see women involved in politics, but wished for a quieter, more "dignified" approach than the suffragettes were taking. "I have thought it over carefully and discussed it with many of you," he told the delegates to the 1915 annual convention, "and I have yet to be met with a strong argument why we should take up Woman's [sic] Suffrage in connection with the Institute work." In reply, a delegate from the floor asked him, "Should our Institute members not be prepared to meet the responsibilities the suffrage will bring us?" Putnam's answer was carefully crafted to recognize the members' political influence, while still sidestepping the issue of working toward achieving suffrage. "Allow me to state that the Women's Institutes are doing more," he retorted, "than any other organization to educate the woman [sic] along lines which will place them in a position to intelligently exercise the franchise if they ever get it; and if you continue along the lines which you are following with such credit your appeals will have great weight."[13] Putnam was arguing that women were already exercising political influence, and he was convinced that they could continue to do so very effectively just by maintaining the status quo. Even without the right to vote, he argued, Institute women were well recognized by politicians. "Cabinet ministers, Departmental officials and others in public places are asking to co-operate with the Women's Institutes in important work which they have in view. They look upon the Women's Institutes as the one medium through which they can best reach the women in the towns, villages and rural districts. And they can depend upon the Institutes for sound advice, liberal support and united action in solving many of the problems that must be dealt with."[14]

Although George Putnam remained rigidly opposed to the discussion of suffrage in WI circles, he could not stop women from voting after 1918, nor could he deny that the Institutes were evolving. In his 1918 report, he suggested that the activities of the Institutes were now threefold: home, community and nation. "When the Institutes started, we thought the home alone was sufficient to take the whole attention of the women," he observed, "but it was unnatural for the motherly . . . thoughtful, progressive women, to confine their thought and action to the feeding and clothing and housing of the family, and the production and conservation of food, without sooner or later extending their activities to community interests. In community interests one of the first to claim their attention is the school . . . Then in regard to national matters I am confident that the women of the Institutes, especially since they will have the co-operation of many other

After achieving the vote, members of the WI continued to be greatly involved in a variety of public activities, and very often that included owning property and constructing an Institute hall for community use. The Colpoy's Bay WI in Bruce County erected this substantial hall in 1927.

— Colpoy's Bay Women's Institute

Emphasizing social reform as an extension of their domestic responsibilities, the local WI group brought together homemakers of various ages to work for improvements to their community. In 1928, at the Colpoy's Bay WI and other branches across the province, this meant that children often accompanied their mothers to the monthly meetings.

— Colpoy's Bay Women's Institute

women's organizations, will see to it that, with the added power which they now have through the franchise, the laws of the land, especially those affecting women and children, are amended to meet present-day conditions."[15] Putnam was echoing the sentiments of so-called maternal feminists when he reasoned that women's expertise in nurturing their families would logically be translated into concern over public matters. According to that view, a woman with "a motherly heart" would soon turn her attention to issues outside her own home. The extension of her home interests was the basis for WI activity in the arena of social reform. It was seen as a logical progression for women to move "from exchanging recipes to a discussion of food values; from suggesting games in the home to providing public amusements for the young people of the community and establishing rest rooms; from household sanitation to cleaning up the village and making it beautiful with public parks; from having a few books in the home to establishing libraries."[16]

Certain issues were deemed to be particularly suitable for Women's Institute members to take up. Specifically, Dr. C.C. James, in speaking to a WI audience, echoed the idea that women, as mothers and WI members, should serve on rural school boards.

> The thought I would like to impress upon you is that you will find awaiting you in the rural parts of this country a problem to solve which has never yet been solved by anybody else in this province. For one question, and as far as the rural parts are concerned, they have — I was going to say utterly failed — perhaps not as badly as that — but the men of this country have not yet solved that problem, and it looks very much as if they would not solve it very soon. It means more to you than it does to the men. The education your boys and girls are to get means more to you than it does to your husbands, brothers and your fathers. I should like to see the women of this country take up that question. Study it in all its bearing and then take hold of it and solve it. Perhaps, you say, we shall have to get on the school boards to do it. Then get on the school boards. Why not, if we men cannot solve these problems by ourselves, I think it is only right and fair that we should welcome upon the school boards of this country, at least upon the rural school boards, the women who represent the farm homes — and then probably something will be done. This idea is not thrown out in a haphazard way. It is something that has been pursuing me in my educational work for some years, and, the longer I live and the more I see of educational problems, the more I am convinced that it is up to you women to help solve this great problem of rural education.[17]

The problems associated with rural schools were enthusiastically taken up by local WI branches. Their reform efforts were advanced on several fronts, including attention to nutrition for schoolchildren, improvements to school buildings, concern over the curriculum, and campaigns for medical inspections. Some women followed the advice of Dr. James and of Mrs. Buchanan and positioned themselves to serve on school boards to formulate and implement policy changes. Others worked with a more hands-on approach, one that was more directly related to their homemaking skills and that brought more immediate results. The hot lunch program is an example of this second approach. In the spring of 1919, the offer was extended by the Department of Agriculture to supply each WI branch with two free packages of vegetable seeds.[18] The

Typically, Women's Institutes acted out their concern for the rural school reform in very practical ways. One common project that continued for many years was the provision of hot lunches for students. The members of the Skead Road WI are pictured here in 1951 serving soup to local schoolchildren.

— Skead Road WI, *Sudbury Star*, Jan. 14, 1951

plan was that women would plant the seeds and use the food that they harvested to make soup for the local schoolchildren. This was an idea that was enthusiastically adopted by many branches around the province. On Manitoulin Island, Institute members took it even further. One of the Institutes there reported in 1923 that it had supplied three of the schools in its district with all the equipment they would need to make hot lunches. Other WI groups kept schools supplied with cocoa, sugar, milk, vegetables and other groceries that would be used to make hot lunches.[19] In some places the WI simply gave the food; in others, the members came to the school to prepare and to serve the food to the children. In 1925, one community-minded WI branch decided to share the responsibility for the hot lunch with the trustees and the parents. As the Annual Report for that year revealed, "A committee from the Institute attended the school meeting and explained the matter to the trustees, who agreed to bear any necessary expense. In order to help them and to get the work started immediately, one Institute member loaned her coal oil stove, others provided cooking utensils and a dishpan, and the children brought their own serving dishes from home. The parents took turns in providing materials to be cooked, while the School Board supplied the necessary cupboards and table. With the Government grant received this year the school lunch will be thoroughly established."[20] Almost thirty years later, some WI branches were still making lunches, buying groceries, and supplying the dishes and equipment needed for the serving.[21] In 1947, the Hoyle WI in Cochrane District voted to purchase forty-five sets of bowls, cups and spoons plus a large soup kettle for this purpose.

The lunch programs were just one example of practical assistance that the local Institute women gave to the schools. According to the 1923 Annual Report, "A number of branches have installed sanitary drinking fountains, one branch . . . where the water supply for schools or homes is a real problem, paid fifty dollars to have a well dug at the school and are proud of having struck flowing water. Others have had the school cleaned and redecorated, supplied wash basins and paper towels, and in general improved the sanitary condition of the school and surroundings. Proper seats to suit the needs of growing children, better heating and lighting systems have been put into several schools through the influence of the Institutes, and sometimes through their financial assistance, while it is a common feature of Institute work to present the school with such things as library books, first aid kits, playground equipment, historical pictures or prints of classic paintings, gramaphones, pianos, weighing scales, [and] screens to keep out flies."[22] The local Institute was supplying basic needs and improving the experience of the local schoolchildren, fulfilling a role that would later be assumed by Parent and Teacher Associations or Home and School Organizations.

The members' input extended beyond the provision of physical improvements to the schools and into the realm of the curriculum. Because high schools were not accessible to rural communities, students often had to travel to other locations to attend the higher grades. "One Institute, finding that a number of their children going to a strange town to write their entrance examination suffered from nervousness, approached the inspector and had arrangements made to have the entrance examination put on nearer home."[23] A few years later, concern arose in Kenora District over the high cost of textbooks, which parents had to provide for their children. A resolution was put forward by the Kenora WI in 1935, "Whereas owing to the frequent change of text books, many schools find difficulty in providing used Books for these children who are unable to purchase their own. Be it resolved that those responsible for the change of text books, be requested to restrict as far as possible any change which is not absolutely necessary."[24] At the same meeting, it was proposed that a system should be set up for sharing used books and soliciting donations of books for school libraries. The suggestion was that "in country places where books are required for a school library, applications for such be sent to the District Secretary or one of the larger Branches so that donations of secondhand books suitable for [a] school library can be solicited. Each application should be accompanied by a list of books required by the teacher."

For children in Ontario's rural schools, instruction was often limited to a very basic set of course offerings; under the auspices of the WI, the range of subjects was extended. In Halton County, the Institutes provided musical instruction and began to sponsor an annual music festival starting in 1926.[25] The New Hamburg WI in Waterloo County was so committed to introducing music into the curriculum at their local school in the 1920s that "for three years the salary of a music instructor for the public school was raised by presenting concerts, plays and teas." Later on, the local school board took over that responsibility, but the WI had initiated it.[26] Another enterprising Institute agreed to "financing a music teacher to come to the school once a week to teach the children singing. They are undertaking this for a period of six months. At the end of this time they will hold a concert, inviting the parents and trustees, with the hope that the school section will continue the lessons and take on the responsibility of paying for them."[27]

To some people the introduction of music was seen as an extra that schools could do without, but the Institutes called for more practical subjects as well. One of their main concerns was to make sure that rural education was relevant and accessible to rural children. To that end, they worked to see that "manual training" and household science were introduced. In some cases this meant providing the equipment for the courses, and in others it meant finding the extra money to pay an additional salary. In 1927, "groups of Institutes assisted in organizing classes in manual training and providing work benches, while the local School Board gave assistance and the Department of Education paid 75 per cent of the salary of a special instructor who spent his whole time among the five centres organized."[28] In 1923 the Superintendent reported that he knew of one Institute "where a number of children in a farming section were ready for high school but would never have an opportunity for further education unless the public school opened a continuation class, and the school had no funds available . . . The trustees appealed to the Women's Institute, and they responded with a few hundred dollars to make up the additional teacher's salary."[29]

Relationships between the school officials and the Institutes were not so congenial in every instance. While some school trustees no doubt welcomed the support the WI could provide in extra funding for special projects, others felt threatened by the intrusion of women into their jurisdiction. Viola Powell discussed the roles that women played in local schools, and after citing a long list of achievements, she added, "This all took time, for at first the trustees were not altogether favourable to this move on the part of women, and it required no little tact and good management to bring about these needed changes."[30] Working toward improving the schools meant that the women took on projects and made provisions, but before long they tried to convince the school board officials to take over these roles. As Putnam explained, "[S]upplies [are often] furnished to the schools by the Institutes, but the tendency is to induce the trustees to provide these things to which the children are entitled."[31] Venturing out to public meetings to argue with elected male officials about what the children needed was a new and daunting task. Perhaps those women who first dared to go to the meetings of the School Board and make demands had good reason to be apprehensive. As Mrs. Buchanan had told them, "it takes a lot of nerve."

Their courage paid off. One of the most important aspects of WI reform in the schools was in the area of health. Institute members argued for medical inspection in the schools so that children who needed medical and dental attention would receive it. Under the direction of the local WI branch, doctors visited in the schools, "to medically inspect the schools and operate on the children who needed it."[32] Removal of tonsils and adenoids was a standard procedure performed on children whose families could otherwise not afford the surgery. According to the Annual Report of 1919, over four hundred children were operated on at one clinic sponsored by the Women's Institute. As the children were all being treated at the same time, members believed that not only were they assisting families financially, but they were helping the children experience less fear than they would if they went to a doctor alone. Dental clinics were also standard, with "all the children in the school [having] their teeth attended to and temporary and permanent fillings were put in wherever necessary." That same year, the Superintendent announced the results of a province-wide survey of Ontario's schoolchildren. "During the year 1918, 7,192 were inspected in various parts of the province. Approximately 70 per cent of the children were found to have defective teeth; 33 per cent have enlarged or diseased tonsils and adenoids, 19 per cent have impaired vision, and 10 per cent have defective hearing . . . If we can judge by what was done in a few districts, we are safe in saying one-third of the children needed attention."[33]

This increased activity in the area of health inspection had grown out of activity prior to the First World War. In Parkhill WI, local women did a survey to determine whether medical inspection of the schools was necessary on a larger scale. Working in five schools, 351 students were examined, and 134 homes were visited by a nurse. A few months later, over 800 students were examined, and then several hundred more. Those initial visits revealed that there were serious health concerns among students in rural schools, and action needed to be taken. At the convention of 1913, a resolution was passed requesting the Department of Education "to take steps for the early establishment of a provincial system of medical and dental inspection of school children."[34] By 1919, the Superintendent declared that the Women's Institutes had now fulfilled their goal in

One part of the public health campaign was the information bulletins published by the Ontario Department of Agriculture in cooperation with the Ontario Agricultural College. These circulars, distributed through local Institutes, instructed women on how to improve standards of domestic hygiene. — UG, FWIO Collection

Ontario Department of Agriculture

ONTARIO AGRICULTURAL COLLEGE

CIRCULAR NO. 29

Disinfectants and Their Use

on the Farm and in the Home

D. H. Jones, Professor of Bacteriology, Ontario Agricultural College, Guelph.

The main purpose of disinfection is to destroy disease germs and thus help to prevent the spread of infectious diseases which are caused by these germs. Tuberculosis, anthrax, black leg, contagious abortion, hog cholera and foot-and-mouth disease are some of the infectious diseases which are liable to affect stock and cause heavy financial losses through sickness and death of the affected animals. Some of these diseases, as anthrax, foot-and-mouth disease and hog cholera, are highly infectious and often rapidly fatal, and call for strict quarantine of the herds where they occur until the disease is wiped out. Others, as tuberculosis and contagious abortion are of a more chronic type, and whilst it is necessary to isolate the affected animals if the spread of the disease is to be stopped, yet the government regulations do not require quarantine of the premises where these diseases occur. In the control and eradication of any of these infectious diseases, however, it is always essential that effective disinfectants be used on the floors, walls, fittings, etc., of the stables in which the animals are or have been housed, because the discharges from the animals will contain large numbers of the germs or bacteria that cause these diseases. Hence the stables get contaminated and healthy stock are liable to contract the disease from the contaminated buildings and their contents.

As we frequently get requests for directions for disinfection of farm buildings, it has been decided to prepare a short bulletin dealing with the subject.

Preparation of the Buildings for Disinfection.

Before applying any disinfectant to a building, the walls, floors, and fittings should be well scraped, and swept, and the refuse gathered up undertaking medical inspections in the schools; namely, they had changed public opinion. The women had managed to convince authorities in the Department of Education that province-wide inspection was necessary, that medical personnel should be employed at provincial expense to do follow-up work, and that health officers and school nurses should be employed on a permanent basis. The Women's Institutes had begun to lobby for change, and had successfully pressured the province to set up one of the earliest forms of publicly funded health care in Ontario by insisting on health reforms in the schools.

By 1926, Ontario's Women's Institutes had taken up the suggestion about reforming rural schools, and much more. They certainly could boast an impressive array of various contributions, extending beyond the home and even beyond the school. The WI Handbook that year included a section entitled,"What the Institutes Have Secured and Introduced," and it was indeed an impressive variety.

> Among the advantages being enjoyed by rural Ontario, as a result of the introduction of Women's Institutes, may be mentioned the following: Rural school medical inspection; systematic instruction through classes organized by the Women's Institutes; additional equipment for community activities — community halls, parks, skating rinks, libraries, etc.; the leadership of women in community work; the establishment of classes for grown-ups, as the regular monthly meetings of Women's Institutes have well been named; an increased volume, a wider distribution and better utilization of literature of interest to women and bearing chiefly upon health matters, food problems, clothing, housing, lighter forms of agriculture; discovery, utilization, and development of local talent; the creation of a more general desire on the part of teenage girls for information bearing upon the responsibilities of womanhood.[35]

In that summary list, Putnam modestly described the work of the WI as "organized philanthropic service seasoned with neighbourliness." But that description was an understatement of the real effects, because there was far more going on than simple community service. "The greatest work, I think, the Institute has accomplished," one district officer declared in her report to the Superintendent, "has been in raising the level of self-confidence amongst our members (and here something really remarkable has been done), and the stimulation of interest in public affairs and the cultural and philanthropic activities of the world. It has been the greatest factor I know of — far greater than church work — in developing in our women fuller, nobler, more beneficient mental powers. It is upon this point particularly that I tend to grow enthusiastic in speaking of Institute work."[36]

Women were developing leadership skills and political acumen, two side effects that should not be underestimated. As Mrs. Dawson from Parkhill WI explained, this was not an official goal of the WI, but nevertheless it was an undeniable result. "Leadership was not the first thought of the organization. The members met in the beginning for different reasons, to talk, for a cup of tea, to exchange recipes and discuss housekeeping, hygiene, or food questions; perhaps sometimes they came through curiosity. What has this accomplished? The development came by steps and the women did not realize that they were becoming leaders because they were going through a process."

Programme 1921-22

MANOTICK BRANCH

County Carleton

Women's Institute

Meeting—Every 2nd Wednesday, 2.30 p.m.

August

Meeting at the home of Mrs. Calvin Blair—"Better wear out than rust out."
Roll Call—Answered by a proverb.
Paper—"The Legal Status of Canadian Women," Miss Beatrice Dunlop.

September

Meeting at the home of Mrs. Harvey Hicks—"The proof of the pudding is in the eating."
Roll Call—Answered by a conundrum.
Recipes for pickles by members, followed by discussion.

October

Meeting at the home of Mrs. A. M. Rowat—"The only way to have a friend is to be one."
Talk on making tea, coffee and cocoa and the effects of each on the system, by Mrs. J. A. Wilson.
Paper—"Opening our Eyes to the Wonders of Nature," by Miss Fair.

November

Meeting at the home of Mrs. J. Patterson.
Roll Call—Answered by remedy for burn or poison.
Method of making bread and rolls, by Mrs. A. A. Chambers.
Yeast making, by members.
Paper—"Citizenship." by Mrs. Calvin Blair.

December

Meeting at the home of Mrs. F. C. Gray.
Suggestions for cheap Christmas gifts and baskets for the needy.

January

Meeting at the home of Mrs. J. A. Pritchard—"A cheerful grin will let you in."
Debate—"Resolved, that a cranky good provider is preferable to a shiftless good-natured one." Captains, Mrs. Gray and Mrs. Calvin Blair.

February

Meeting at the home of Mrs. Walters—"Punctuality is the politeness of kings."
Roll Call—A book I have recently enjoyed.
Demonstration on buttonhole making, by Miss Brownlee.

March

Meeting at the home of Mrs. Wm. Eadie.
Roll Call—Exhibit of something of my grandmother's.
Recitation—Miss Elise Dunlop.
Paper—Miss Dunlop.

April

Meeting at the home of Mrs. Leach.—"Make hay while the sun shines."
Address—by Rev. C. H. Brown.

May

Meeting at home of Mrs. R. H. Lindsay.
Annual, Election of Officers, etc.

MRS. R. H. LINDSAY, Sec.-Treas. **MRS. GEORGE CLARKE,** President.

She did not preach a sermon, nor quote a Bible phrase
She did not reprimand us for all our evil ways.
She did not look at us askance and plead why not be good
She only gently smiled and prayed our weakness understood.
She lived the Ten Commandments instead of shouting them
Faith, hope and charity to her were each a gem.
She knew that by example she'd help us find a way
And at His feet we'd worship with her another day.
And if we ever reach the height it will be because she knew
To teach another godliness one must be godly too.

This poem was written in tribute to Mrs. Thomas Daley of Fort William, District Secretary from 1922 to 1934. More than just a touching portrait of one woman's leadership, it describes the Social Gospel ideals that motivated so much of the Institutes' reform efforts.
— *Thunder Bay District Tweedsmuir History,* Paipoonge Museum Collection

That process led to two kinds of results — practical ones and political ones. As Mrs. Dawson put it, "[W]e have accomplished some things. We have bought rinks and playgrounds; we have laid miles of cement sidewalks; we have put pianos in halls for public amusement; we have had lecture courses, sometimes on subjects of health, sometimes on university extension work; we have educated the people of Ontario to think medical inspection of schools is necessary; and now we have begun to lay our hands on Provincial laws and Federal laws." In order to get their hands on those laws more effectively, WI members recognized that they needed a whole new structure for their organization. Although the Department of Agriculture had been more than generous in its support of the organization, that support had certain limitations.

Putnam's hesitation over the issue of suffrage was only one example of the limits that Department of Agriculture sponsorship entailed. When the WI became active and vocal on a wide range of public issues, pushing for things like school reform and rural health inspections, it became clear that they were moving into areas that were outside the jurisdiction of the Department of Agriculture. The women were asking for changes that Putnam's department could not make, nor even influence. After repeated reminders that it was not appropriate for one department of government to lobby another, the women took steps to organize themselves into an official body which could act outside the auspices of the Department of Agriculture. By declaring independence from Putnam's department, they would have better success in their attempts at lobbying.

Several factors led to the creation of the Federated Women's Institutes of Ontario (FWIO). First, it was in part a political move designed to provide a forum for the Institutes' increased activities in the realm of social reform. It should not be interpreted, though, as an act of defiance or a complete breaking away from the sponsorship of the Department of Agriculture, since a special relationship would remain firmly in place for several decades to come. Putnam's branch of the Department would continue to provide the Institutes with educational opportunities, published materials and financial support. Creating the FWIO was not an act of revolution, but rather an evolution in the WI's development. Education had always been an important component of the program, and with continued government assistance and departmental leadership, it has continued to be central throughout the century. However, by the end of the First World War, social reform was an increasingly important aim of the group, and the new provincial level of the Institutes would oversee that part of the work, giving the women a stronger voice with which they could make their demands and protests known to a variety of government departments.

Second, the new FWIO would feature women prominently as leaders. According to Mrs. William Todd from Orillia, who became the first provincial president of the FWIO, women had gained credibility because of the war work — and there was no turning back. As she saw it, that work was at once an extension of previous work and a good omen for the WI's future work. "The silent, unobtrusive work of the fifteen

The 1919 Convention of the Women's Institutes of Eastern Ontario, held in Ottawa, provided an opportunity for women in that area of the province to gather and learn about the direction that the WI movement was taking. — UG, FWIO Collection peaceful years that went before the war is really what made possible all the work of the last twenty-four months, and I think, while we emphasize the war work and must continue to do it, we must not forget that the Women's Institute is an organization for all time. There is no circumstance in which it cannot serve, and its vigorous growth and the life that is in it, mean a future for it." The WI had very strong endurance and "come back," according to Mrs. Todd. In an intriguing comment about the power of women's achievements in the Institutes, she remarked, "You cannot put them down; the harder you put them down the more they bob up."[37] One is left to wonder what specific events Mrs. Todd was referring to when she mentioned being "put down" and "bobbing up" again. While there is room for speculation about that, there is no doubt that her rise to leadership as head of the new FWIO was a celebrated moment for Women's Institute members throughout Ontario.

Among these delegates, a dapper George Putnam is conspicuous as the only male. In this photo, taken in the 1920s, he is on the edge of the group, instead of occupying the centre as in previous group shots. This is symbolic of the real shift in leadership, since women assumed greater responsibility and direction after federation.
— UG, FWIO Collection

Although Mr. Putnam was fondly regarded by most WI members, the lack of a female head for Ontario's Women's Institutes was conspicuous. Dr. C.C. James, the Dominion Commissioner of Agriculture, pointed this out in 1915 when he drew attention to Institute organization in the other provinces. "Go to Quebec, and [WI] work is carried out by a lady on the staff of Macdonald College. Go to Fredericton, and you meet the lady superintendent; go to Prince Edward Island and you meet the lady superintendent; go to Nova Scotia and you meet the lady superintendent; go to Manitoba, Alberta or Saskatchewan or British Columbia and it is the same thing. You ask, where is the man? You have to come back to Ontario to find the man. This is the only Province where the Women's Institute work is wholly directed by a man."[38] It was time for Ontario to catch up to the other provinces by appointing females to positions of leadership, and the creation of the FWIO was one way to do that. The Superintendent of the Institutes had consulted with prominent women from time to time, as Mr. James observed. "Mr. Putnam has called to his help and assistance and direction you women, and he was wise enough to know he could not do it of his own accord." With the creation of the FWIO, Putnam retained his authority over some aspects of the organization, but women's leadership of the Institutes was finally formalized and brought into line with the practices of the other provinces.

Developments in other provinces stimulated the federation process in another sense as well. Because each one of the other eight provinces had established Institute work by this period, some formal means of communication was required to maintain contact between the regions. Ontario, as the province with the longest experience in WI work and the largest membership, needed an efficient and formal organization both as a model and as a means of maintaining its leading edge in Canadian WI work. It is no coincidence, therefore, that in the same year as the FWIO was created, a national group, the Federated Women's Institutes of Canada (FWIC), was also established. The creation of these umbrella organizations was no sudden turn of events, since the possibility of federation had been discussed for some time before 1919.

Even before the war, there had been some discussion about new levels of organization. "Mr. Putnam expressed regret that the Institutes were not nationally organized." In November 1915 he told the Western Ontario WI Convention that plans had been underway, but postponed because of the war. "Three years ago I attended a meeting at which there were representatives from all the provinces except one, where Women's Institutes and similar organizations have been established, and we formed a Dominion organization. They appointed me as president and Mrs. Watt of British Columbia, secretary, but little has been done. A year ago this fall I took up the matter of a Dominion-wide organization with the Dominion Commissioner of Agriculture, Dr. C.C. James, and plans were about completed for calling together representatives from all the provinces at Ottawa last January, but the war intervened. I have no doubt that the Dominion officials will take steps in due course, after the war has ceased, to organize the Institutes nationally."[39]

Organization at the provincial level made way for new kinds of co-operative efforts. Not only did the WI lobby the government for change and reform, they implemented new measures and delivered these new services very efficiently. Typically, the WI would identify a problem, suggest change, and then help to implement new measures to solve the situation. Explaining the two-way relationship that was typical of this era, the Annual Report for 1925 noted, "The Institutes have built up a form of organization and method of carrying on which is a great national asset. Efficiency, with a minimum of red tape and expense, appears to have been their motto . . . The Institutes are cooperating more and more with various departments of the Government in making their efforts of the greatest benefit to the community. The Departments of Education, Health, Amusement, Provincial Secretary, and Agriculture, value the Institutes as a cooperator in making administration, education, and service more effective at a minimum of cost."[40] Government departments were eager to welcome the participation of the Institutes because the women's work in implementing reforms was a very cost-effective means for them to deliver government services at the local level. There was the other side to the relationship too. Because the WI was effective at the local level, and the departments came to depend upon them, the WI earned their respect. When Institutes made suggestions and requests, government listened.

Part of the WI's efficiency stemmed from the networks of local effort that were established during the First World War. It can also be traced to new initiatives in the 1920s, specifically, the creation of a series of eight "standing committees." These committees, first mentioned in the Annual Report of 1926, included Education and Better Schools, Health, Agriculture, Home Economics, Immigration, Community Activities, Legislation, and Historical Research and Current Events. These committees existed as part of the provincial board of the FWIO, but each local branch was encouraged to select one member to be the representative of these various topics as well. Thus, while the provincial board worked at that level to promote these concerns,

This 1923 Baby Welfare Day organized by the Institute in Dundas came about because of WI public health concerns for the local community. These events were pioneering efforts in public health promotion. — AR 1923

each branch was encouraged to mimic that structure in order to effectively bring the issues to the attention of the local community. What is clear from the description of these various committees is that rural women were active on several fronts, studying social questions and equipping themselves to act for change. The range of their interests is impressive in its own right, as the descriptions of the committees suggest.

The provincial standing committee on Education and Better Schools grew out of the Institutes' efforts to improve the local schools, both in terms of physical facilities and trained personnel. The provision of better sanitation, offering of hot lunches and hiring of more qualified teachers were centred in this committee. With the force of their provincial organization behind them, the Women's Institutes were determined to make an impact on public education policy. When discussions about restructuring the local school boards were initiated, the Institutes planned to play an integral role. The women were keenly interested in seeing their own local initiatives translated into permanent changes to the system of rural education. By the mid-1920s, it seems, many women had taken to heart Mrs. Buchanan's advice about attending school board meetings, and not only did they intend to have a local presence, they intended to inform themselves about the larger trends so that they could participate in talks aimed at restructuring the provincial system.

Health concerns were a major motivation for the Institutes to be involved in the schools, but health of schoolchildren was only part of it. Under the standing committee on Health, WI members determined to educate themselves, specifically, "taking a keen interest in health education, physical training, and preventive measures, while they [were] acquiring through literature and the demonstration lecture courses in 'Home Nursing and First Aid' greater efficiency in acquiring and conserving health and caring for the sick and defective." The women were determined to improve the general standard of health, and in order to achieve that goal, they started with educating themselves. The courses they took under government auspices were widely popular. In 1926, 1,486 women and girls registered for two-week courses on health concerns offered in fifty-four locations across Ontario. From the knowledge they gained in their studies, Institutes made practical applications, "holding a number of sick and well baby clinics, and [using] their influence in securing public health nurses and . . . [giving] financial assistance." Evidently, in this period prior to the establishment of a full-fledged social welfare network, urging governments to act did not preclude the lobbyists from taking action themselves. The Women's Institutes took it upon themselves to become informed, to urge government action, and to help organize and fund initiatives to provide greater access to health care and information.

A third standing committee was one created on Agriculture. While not all of the rural women involved with the Institutes were farm women, those who were found important access to information about services

While reform work dominated the Institutes' agenda throughout the province, local branches also continued to enjoy more traditional female pursuits as seen in this Fort Frances craft exhibit. — Fort Frances Museum, *Fort Frances Tweedsmuir History*

and activities of both the Provincial and Dominion Departments of Agriculture through this committee. At the local level, this same committee was the one that encouraged women to be actively involved in fall fairs, particularly regarding the participation of schoolchildren. But this was not just an extension of the WI connection with the schools; it was very much a forum for economic self-improvement. According to the Annual Report of 1926, "women and girls on the farm are following some special feature as a means of adding to the farm income, poultry raising, bee-keeping and the growing of small fruits being the chief activities." For women who wanted to learn, there was the opportunity to consult with the local agricultural representatives, and the Superintendent of Women's Institutes noted that WI members were showing "special interest" in "quality production and better marketing methods." Women's economic contribution to the farm income was an important concern for large numbers of Institute members. It must be remembered that for many of the members, their efforts in voluntary associations and efforts at social reform were only part of their work. The Institute women were not primarily "club women." Many were farmers. Through this committee, they were able to acquire information about agricultural production that they could apply to their own farming operations.

A display of current fashion underscores the Women's Institute's continued emphasis on home economics. Practical and up-to-date instruction in clothing design and care kept the educational mandate at the forefront of the organization.
— UG, FWIO Collection

While farm women were participating in production on the local farm, they were also chiefly responsible for the home. The fourth standing committee, which dealt with Home Economics, was thus of interest to all the members, whether they actively farmed or not. Making a study of "housing, clothing and feeding," Institute members could avail themselves of information from the Department of Agriculture through a series of "bulletins" published in order to bring instruction to individual homemakers. Nutrition, home canning, food values and meal planning were part of the standard fare offered through these pamphlets. However, the committee was concerned with more than just a standard home economics curriculum. This committee was striving to provide a forum for discussion on a wide range of problems. Among them was the issue of housing itself. "How to remodel and make more convenient the old house is one of the leading problems, since building is very expensive."[41] Another main theme of this committee was the "study of labour-saving devices, equipment and methods . . . making for greater efficiency in rural homes." It is no coincidence that the topics of improved rural housing and greater conveniences should arise in the 1920s, since there was a widespread concern in this period about the trends toward rural depopulation. Part of the reason why so many people were choosing to leave the countryside, they thought, was that women were dissatisfied with their quality of life, and if life could be made more comfortable, perhaps the women would opt to stay. This standing committee had a widespread appeal then, both for women who had no intention of leaving the local farm and for those who did. The promises of convenience, comfort and practical instruction were welcomed by a wide variety of WI members.

Another committee dealt with Immigration. Under this scheme, the Institutes served as an extension of the government: "[T]he local [WI] branches are notified [by the Immigration Department] when a new settler is to arrive, with the request that they make the newcomers welcome and invite the womenfolk to join the Institute and take their place in community activities." This was another example of the kinds of roles the Institutes could serve by virtue of the fact that they were so widespread across the province. Under this same committee, local branches might agree to sponsor orphans and dependent children, either through donations to local children's shelters or direct contributions on behalf of individuals. The consensus in the 1920s was that "the Institutes will, no doubt, be an important factor in welcoming and absorbing a large number of newcomers who will be brought to Canada."[42]

There were other activities that the Institutes provided for the community as well. A standing committee struck for Community Activities listed a wide variety of responsibilities highlighting the provision of equipment, facilities and community activities. Recognizing that the local Institutes had provided "libraries, community halls, parks, skating rinks, games, amateur theatricals, debates, etc.," the provincial organization struck this sixth standing committee to deal with such contributions.

The seventh standing committee focussed on Legislation. With the provincial federation in place, WI members had the mechanisms for making resolutions to various government departments, and so attention was turned to studying existing legislation. In introducing this committee, the Annual Report of 1926 explained, "Many of the Institutes have made a study of Provincial and Dominion legislation and methods of administration, especially as they affect women and children and property rights. The laws bearing upon the nationality of married women, legalized gambling, education, property rights, the franchise, etc., are receiving more and more consideration." To complement this newly organized committee, many local branches continued to inform themselves of their rights and their status by inviting local lawyers and bankers to address their meetings, to teach them how to take control of their personal finances and legal affairs.

The last committee, a new interest for Institute members in the mid-1920s, dealt with Historical Research and Current Events. Under this committee, local members were encouraged to begin to compile historical scrapbooks that would provide a chronicle of the history of their local community. This was the forerunner of the Tweedsmuir history books, which would be launched in the 1940s. It is interesting to note that the Institutes' involvement in compiling local history predated the official start of the Tweedsmuir projects by twenty years.

After 1925, the Superintendent of the Institutes structured his annual report around these standing committees. Putnam was always careful, however, to emphasize that the chief objectives of the Institutes were still firmly in place. Concluding his report of the various activities of the standing committees, he remarked, "It will be seen from the above that a wide field of activity is included in the programme of the community organization known as Women's Institutes. We must not, however, forget that the chief object of the Institutes is to make for efficiency in the home, and it is gratifying to be able to report that the original aim and object of the organization has always been kept to the fore."[43] Whether more efficient homemaking was really the main concern for all WI members is debatable. What is clear, however, is that Putnam was attempting to reiterate to the government officials that the WI was still true to its stated objectives of disseminating knowledge about domestic science and improved rural living. The annual report was his opportunity not only to report new initiatives, but also to illustrate and prove that the Institutes were true to their original mandate, and thus still eligible for the funding and support they received from government sponsorship.

Providing meals to local Plowman's Associations was one of the earliest means of raising money for the WI. The menu offered by the Ilderton Women's Institute in 1928 is posted on the blackboard: "Plowman's Dinner 50 cents Menu: Roast Beef or Roast Pork, Potatoes and Carrots, Cabbage Salad, Raisin Pie, Coffee." BACK ROW (LEFT TO RIGHT): *Mrs. Roy Bloomfield, unknown, Mrs. Bev. Needham, Miss Demary (Waddell), Mrs. Tom Martin, Mrs. J. Ardiel, Mrs. J.W. Freeborn, Miss Ethel Robson, Mrs. Elmer Roberts, Mrs. Batie McNair (holding Bev. Robb), Mrs. Leslie Scott, Mrs. Jack Needham, Mrs. Ernie Robson, Mrs. W.R. Scott;* FRONT ROW: *Mrs. Dick Scott, Mrs. John Douglas, Mrs. Wm. Whilliams, Mrs. Walker Reeve, Mrs. Geo. Charlton, Mrs. James McNair, Mrs. Geo. Lipsitt* CHILDREN: *Marjorie Freeborn, Mary Carmichael*
— Ilderton Women's Institute Tweedsmuir History

Indeed, that reminder was a necessary one, because after thirty years of activity, the Women's Institutes had developed a large variety of activities and interests. Here was a place where a woman could come to find information on a number of topics: her legal rights and status, increased efficiency for her agricultural production, new initiatives in school board structures and public health initiatives, immigration policy, historical research techniques, and the impact of her purchasing choices on consumer trends and national productivity. The WI was clearly much more than a simple class in home economics. It is difficult to generalize about the experiences of members in this period, because with such a wide range of potential topics available, members obviously might have had very different experiences. For some WI members, the Institute still meant that they would get out socially once a month to exchange recipes with the neighbours over a friendly cup of tea. For others, the Institute was the opportunity to educate themselves on issues ranging from nutrition, health, and legislation, to sewing and history. For still others, involvement in the Institute meant the heady experience of taking their concerns to politicians, knowing that their opinions would be taken seriously.

In 1927 the Women's Institutes of Ontario were thirty years old and could boast 1,070 branches, with a membership of 38,000 women. According to the 1927 Annual Report, 59 new branches had been established in the previous twelve months. The practice of holding annual conventions was still firmly in place, and in fact was expanded in 1927 to include conventions at twelve locations. The conventions were well attended, ranging in size from a gathering of 75 delegates at Bruce Mines in Northern Ontario to 550 delegates at Toronto. In total, 3,700 members, approximately one member out of every ten, attended a convention that year.

Celebrating the first thirty years of the Women's Institutes in Ontario, George Putnam observed that "the undertakings of the present day in hundreds of [Women's Institute] groups would have been looked upon as impossible by the leaders of twenty-five years ago." In his summary comments of his 1927 Annual Report, he wrote, "May I be allowed to repeat that the most valuable development in the Women's Institutes is a realization on the part of the women of rural Ontario that they have within themselves the power to acquire information of practical, everyday value, and to render most valuable service to the community." On the eve of the Great Depression, the people of Ontario were about to enter a devastating economic crisis, and there would be ample opportunity for the Women's Institutes to demonstrate exactly what they could do for their communities.

The friendships forged through local branches were a very important means of coping for women facing severe economic hardship during the Depression. This group of neighbourhood women from North Russell WI posed together for an informal picture in 1930. — North Russell WI Tweedsmuir History

CHAPTER FIVE

Supporting Roles: Welfare and Education, 1930–1939

The Cookstown Women's Institute summed up its activities for 1932–1933 with a report that was typical of many branches. "In lieu of a meeting in July and August, we held a picnic for the women of the community and the Junior Institute. Having heard of the need of a mother and infant just home from the hospital, we supplied them with clothing and groceries. Since so many men were out of employment this year, we assisted four families with the staple articles of food by paying for a weekly amount at the local stores . . . We prepared and served a banquet to the Masons, thus increasing our finances. In December we appealed for donations of fruit, candy, groceries, clothing etc. These greatly aided us in making up ten Christmas boxes which we distributed to families in the community."[1] In the Great Depression, community activity took on heightened importance. The social aspects of mutual support helped women to cope with grim circumstances. The monthly WI meeting with the neighbourhood women became, once again, a welcome respite to the drudgery of difficult times.

The importance of those social affairs should not be underestimated. One report of an Institute's so-called hen party in Elgin County was more than it seemed. "Following a fire in July, which destroyed the entire flock of poultry belonging to an ex-member," the report for 1931–1932 recounted, "the members held a 'hen' shower at her home, taking refreshments with them, and spending a pleasant evening socially." The well-wishers brought more than just sympathy, sandwiches and good cheer. They made their support very concrete. At the end of the evening, the fire victim was encouraged both emotionally and financially. Each of her guests from the Institute contributed, and together they supplied her with "about twenty hens [which] formed the nucleus for a new flock."[2] Those expressions of neighbourly support and mutual aid were repeated on countless occasions as women from the WI banded together to give one another various kinds of help.

The economic crisis was yet another context in which the Institutes could rally around a cause. One might predict that during such severe economic conditions the organization would have adjusted to more modest goals and acquiesced to a certain defeatist attitude. On the contrary, the 1930s saw new organizational initiatives among the Women's Institutes, at the local level, within the provincial administration and, indeed, around the world. The international arm of the organization, the Associated Country Women of the World (ACWW), traces its origin to this same decade. Just as the crisis of the First World War had been a catalyst for the development of the WI, so too was the economic crisis of the Depression.

Over the course of the ten years from 1929 to 1938, the provincial membership increased slightly, from just over 40,000 members to 42,100. Fifty-four new Institutes were created in 1929, bringing the total number in Ontario to 1,115 branches. By the end of the 1930s, that number had climbed to 1,366. However, that growth trend should not be misunderstood; it was not a steady increase without setbacks. For example, in 1933 forty new branches were organized, a fact that the Annual Report was happy to celebrate. What went unreported, however, was the fact that twenty-five other branches found it necessary to disband that same year. For each local Institute, the dilemma about whether or not to continue was very real. Recognizing that the previous record of growth, fundraising and reform could not be sustained in the Depression, local branches considered their options. The Superintendent addressed the problem in 1933 in a special column of the new Institute publication, *Home and Country*.

> Some branches take the attitude that since they are not able to raise funds as readily as some few years ago, the value of the Institute has decreased. Not necessarily so. . . . The worth of the Institute consists in its educational value, the assistance which it can give to the needy, support of community undertakings, and the opportunities which it can provide along social lines; so do not be discouraged because of a decrease in financial resources. The trying times through which we have been passing have been the means of strengthening the bonds of friendship and cooperation; so the advice of the Department and your Provincial Board is not to disband a branch or slacken your efforts at a time when the need is so great, both so far as the individual, the family and the community are concerned.[3]

In the same issue of *Home and Country*, Mr. Putnam advised the branch officers not to embarrass their members by asking them for money they could not afford to give.

> We find that a few of the branch Institutes continue to take up collections at their regular meetings (monthly). This practice is likely to result in some women, who are hard-pressed financially, not attending the meetings and thus depriving themselves of the educational advantages and social opportunities afforded. It has always been advised by the Department, and I think approved by the Federation, that funds in excess of the 25c membership fee, be raised in some other manner than to require each member to contribute at each meeting she attends . . . [U]pon payment of Twenty-five Cents (.25c) per year . . . no individual is *required* to contribute anything beyond this amount.[4]

The expenses of supporting the FWIO and financing community projects were over and above that regular twenty-five-cent fee, and many women found that even that basic amount was beyond their means in the difficult years of the Depression. Putnam encouraged the branches not to exclude people who could not pay the annual fee. Rather, they were told to "let it be known that members of the previous year who do not feel able to pay the fee may continue to attend the meetings and take advantage of the educational and social features." [5] Indeed, the President and the Board of the FWIO agreed with the idea that collections at meetings should be discouraged.[6]

The Superintendent encouraged the members not to worry about collecting money, nor about maintaining their previous reputation as effective fundraisers. The achievements of the war years, or indeed, even of the social reform years in the 1920s simply could not be duplicated in the economic stress of the

Depression. Branches were advised to stop pressuring their members for those extra contributions, or at least, to be more subtle about their collection techniques. "If it is decided to ask for contributions at the monthly meetings, it would be preferable to follow the plan adopted by some branches, — have a box placed near the entrance and let it be known that those members who wish to contribute may put their donations in the box, either upon entering or leaving the hall." If they decided to receive money, it should be strictly on a voluntary basis and strictly confidential.[7]

Putnam admitted to the Board in April 1934 that the "membership had dropped off somewhat in recent years, but was about the same this year as last year," yet he predicted that "during the coming year, there would be a substantial increase in membership." That hopeful forecast was matched by reports from some of the districts. The President of the Kenora District WI told the delegates to the 1932 annual meeting that "the Depression has not held down the Institutes [in Northwestern Ontario], but rather they are working harder than ever all branches carrying on well." Instead of reporting a decreased activity level or lower morale because of the severe economic conditions, Women's Institute leaders believed that rural women were rising to the challenges of the day. In keeping with that optimistic outlook, the Kenora reporter urged her members to keep up the good work, stressing the fact that coping with the economic hardship was just another form

The annual conventions provided opportunities for delegates to exchange reports and information on Institute programs. The setting for this banquet of the 1934 Central Ontario Convention at the Royal York Hotel in Toronto seems extravagant, especially since some of the members in local branches found it impossible to continue to pay their annual membership fee of twenty-five cents a year.
—UG, FWIO Collection

The relief committee made the following purchase:

90 1/2 lbs. rolled oats	*$2.90*
98 lbs. flour	*$2.50*
12 cans Bordens Milk	*$1.38*
20 lbs. sugar	*$1.16*
21 lbs. beans	*$ .70*
5 lbs. butter	*$1.25*
TOTAL	*$9.89*

In many communities, the WI served as a welfare agency, distributing groceries among the needy. The relief committee of the Dane WI in Temiskaming Centre District purchased these supplies in 1932.
— Englehart and Area Museum, *Dane WI Minute Book*

of "women's work for which we are well trained."[8] With the idea that women were already accustomed to being frugal, running their homes carefully, and surviving setbacks with cheerful mutual encouragement, that report from Northwestern Ontario is representative of the spirit of determination that kept Women's Institutes across Ontario strong, even flourishing, despite the economic hard times of the 1930s. The hard times, in fact, gave local WI branches a very concrete purpose in their communities.

In many cases, the WI became the recognized social welfare agency, providing financial and practical aid to needy families specifically, and community organization and recreation for their neighbourhoods in general. To be ready for the emergency needs of its neighbourhood, the Maple Grove Women's Institute in Waterloo County reported in 1930 that they had made arrangements with a local retailer in Breslau to purchase unsold inventory and distribute it among needy families. Thus, layettes and other dry goods were held on hand until the moment of need arose.[9] At the Fulton–Grassie WI in Lincoln County, the members "bought a fleece of wool, washed and picked it, and used it for comforters. Six were made during the winter. Tops were pieced from remnants, bought at five pounds for a dollar." Many branches kept quilts such as these on hand so they could respond quickly to help families who had house fires. Another branch came to the aid of a family whose barn had burned. The Keward WI in Grey County did "a large share of the baking for the meals for some 75 men who worked on the barn raising."[10]

The Stanley Women's Institute in Thunder Bay District held grocery showers for newlyweds, and assumed the responsibility to pay the house rent for another family in need.[11] At the Iroquois WI in Dundas County, they "outfitted three fatherless Indian boys for school, bought glasses for children, and sponsored an oratorical contest."[12] At Kentvale WI on St. Joseph Island, they undertook in 1934 "to purchase proper food for a local diabetic case, and have continued this for some months. When funds became low the neighbours contributed cream, eggs, vegetables and other foods."[13] This kind of help made the issue of relief a very touchy one, since independent survival was a matter of pride for many people, and branches strove to be sensitive to that by "providing aid without publicity."[14] The WI was celebrated for its effective distribution of services to those in need. Deemed superior to the urban welfare efforts, because of the "personal touch and neighbourly spirit" of their work, the Institutes tried to be sensitive to issues of pride.[15] The Institutes were described as working under "the neighbourly cloak of relief activities,"[16] because their activities in providing relief were not widely publicized. But neither was their service anonymous nor unrecorded. Families in need were often named in the local minute books, and the provisions that branches made for them are clearly spelled out. For example, in East Rainy River the district minute book for 1931 names a widow with five children whose husband had recently died. The Institute decided to give the woman $35, instead of using the money to send a delegate to the Institute convention. This kind of help is why Institutes across Ontario were said to be the mobilization of "responsibility and resourcefulness."[17] In these years before the welfare state was in place, while battles raged about which level of government should assume responsibility for poor relief, the WI pragmatically went ahead with their efforts and provided assistance wherever they could. As new government programs were introduced, the WI continued to give support in neighbourly ways, but they also acted to support measures such as the system of Mothers' Allowance introduced in the 1920s, a program that could offer women like the widow in Rainy River a more regular means of support.[18]

Relief was not restricted to families outside the Institutes' own membership lists. Often the recipients were members themselves, as the case of the Dane Women's Institute in Northern Ontario illustrates. In that community, Institute members established a system of distributing groceries. They established a committee to administer the distribution of these foodstuffs among their neighbours' and fellow members' families. Some of the names on the distribution list are the same as those in the membership list, showing that the members themselves were among those who were helped by this system. The Institutes' programs for relief were not simply a case of the fortunate members of the community helping the poor in a system of charity. In some cases, the Institute was a way for members to help themselves, as well as their neighbours, in a system of mutual aid.

The case of the Dane Women's Institute program is interesting for another reason. Not all of the money they spent was from a local source. The minutes reveal that "Groceries and Merchandise . . . was [sic] purchased by money received sent by the Wexford WI which came in handy at the time." The more prosperous branch from York County (present-day Scarborough) had sent $30 for these purposes.[19] This was a common pattern, as Institute branches in the south (or "Old Ontario" as it was sometimes called) helped to support their fellow members in the north. Examples of this arrangement abound. The Sheffield Women's Institute in Wentworth County passed a motion in January 1923 to send quilts and a donation of $25 to the New Liskeard WI, "to be used as they find necessary to help the fire sufferers of that district."[20] The Thornhill WI, just north of Toronto, was also active in this type of work, sending children's clothing to the settlers in Cochrane District. That WI set up a committee of five women who met at a central location to pack and ship the parcels to the north.[21] The Wexford WI continued to send supplies and gifts to the women of Dane WI for many years.

The experiences of Northern Ontario settlers had first pushed the WI toward a systematic, province-wide relief effort as the Institutes in Southern Ontario came to the aid of fire victims throughout the 1920s.[22] During the early years of settlement in New Ontario, when risk from forest fires was constant, generous help came from southern WI branches who sent clothing and other kinds of aid in response. This became a rallying point for organizing assistance from other parts of the province, and that assistance for was formalized in the 1930s through the establishment of a special fund designed specifically to help relieve the hardships experienced in the north. In 1935, when parts of Southern Ontario already were recovering from the worst of the Depression, it was noted that "hardship and want were still ever present in the north, and 970 pounds of bales were sent."[23] In 1938, twenty-five bales of clothing were shipped to the north, in all 1,268 pounds of goods, valued at $83.75. The cost of shipping the goods was covered from a special fund established for that purpose. The Putnam Fund (named for the provincial Superintendent) remained in place for twenty years, until the FWIO voted in 1955 to close it as the Institutes in the north felt it was no longer needed.[24]

The Women's Institute

(Written by Gladys Luck Hall, a member of the Inman Road W.I., 1934)

There's a band of willing workers
Scattered throughout the land,
Who stand prompt and ever ready,
To lend a helping hand.
To the weak and heavy laden,
Who stumble along life's way—
Their labour of love and protection
Continues from day to day.

Wherever the call of suffering,
No matter the class or creed—
Their ears are always open,
To the cry of the ones in need.
This band of christian women,
To no call of distress is mute,
And the home of these tireless workers
Is the Women's Institute.

God bless the noble toilers,
Who, with earnest hearts and true,
Among their fellow creatures,
Their deeds of mercy strew
And He will, in His infinite goodness,
When their crown of life is won,
In the last great day receive them
With the blessed words "Well Done".

— Gladys Luck Hall, Inman Road WI, 1934. Printed in *The Women's Institute in Haldimand County, Cayuga*: Advocate Print, 1938.

During the Depression years, Institutes sometimes held their own picnics, a chance for the women to relax and enjoy one another's company. Evidence that this tradition continued long after the 1930s, this 1949 picture captures the members of the South Tarentorus WI savouring a much-needed break from routine.
— *Algoma Centre District Tweedsmuir History*

Community picnics were an important way for Institutes to provide entertainment for all on a limited budget. Institutes were largely responsible for fostering rich community life during difficult economic times, and picnics and socials were a tradition that would continue for years. This 1950s sack race of the Prince of Wales WI is reminiscent of the community spirit of Depression-era Institute activity. — *Prince of Wales Women's Institute Tweedsmuir History*, Algoma Centre

As the Depression decade drew to a close, the Annual Report of 1938 confessed that local relief work had been an important feature "in practically every Institute's activities,"[25] but that in reality, sharing financial resources and providing physical relief were only part of what the Women's Institutes did in response to the Depression. Not all of their energy was spent in social welfare work, because in addition to the practical relief, WI branches provided a kind of emotional relief to their neighbourhoods by organizing community leisure and recreation activity. In a 1938 address to the leaders of Institutes across Canada, Lady Tweedsmuir, the Honourary President of the FWIC, emphasized the importance of the social aspects of the monthly WI meetings themselves. She gaily suggested that meetings "should be good parties, occasions where members shed cares and troubles, and should not be nests of envy and jealousy." She said they should be "delightful, inspiring, interesting and pleasant." Urging the Institutes to pay attention to their own needs and to spare no expense in booking the very best lecturers and planning their programs, she reminded the members, "You are not relief or welfare agencies. Do not be used by every institution that wants money. Keep your money for your own work — let it come first."[26]

Institutes were not prepared to make that either/or decision about welfare versus socials. Most of the local branches were already paying attention to their social agenda. While they were generous in their support of relief projects, they did not neglect their own mental health, nor their communities' needs for entertainment. Monthly meetings were a bright spot on the members' calendars; as many of the elderly members recall of these Depression years, "We made our own fun." Even the brief respite of a social hour at the monthly WI meeting was a welcome change of attitude for many members who claimed that the little break restored their "vigour and brightness."[27] The Minnitaki branch reported that "the best results of Institute work in this branch have been getting the women out to meet other women who rarely left their homes before."[28] One of the branches reported in 1938 that "a very enjoyable picnic was held for the members and their familys [sic] . . . Races were held for all, candy, nuts and ice cream was also enjoyed by all it was a lovely day."[29] When luxuries were unavailable, little extras like ice cream and prizes at the picnic made a great deal of difference, and fond memories survive about the 1930s and the rich community life made possible across rural Ontario because of Women's Institute events.

The benefits of socializing were not limited to the membership itself. At the Gore Bay Women's Institute, for example, the group was committed to the idea that "our first duty is to our community."[30] This sentiment was never stronger than during the Depression, when many branches turned their attention to the viability of their community social life. Social occasions sponsored by the Women's Institutes were said to be a "strong stabilizing factor" for the life of countless communities throughout the province.[31] "The best meetings are Christmas parties and community fun nights when husbands, children and friends are invited," one branch declared. "We do not have to look beyond our community for skilled singers, instrumentalists, actors and play writers."[32] Dances, parties, dramas and concerts provided an outlet for the stress of economic hard times, and by depending largely on local talent, the Institutes were once again giving evidence of their pragmatism, a quality some called "resourceful self-reliance."[33] In 1937 a full listing of typical community work was reported. "Local enterprises sponsored by branch Institutes are many and varied and are governed by the special needs of the community concerned. In many cases the work entailed has been spread over several years and has provided a structure of lasting value. Rest rooms and libraries have been established and are being supervised. Hospital wards have been furnished, grounds for parks and athletic fields purchased and cemeteries beautified. Motion picture machines for community use have been purchased and sports and other forms of wholesome recreation encouraged. Local institutions for the unfortunate are given assistance and in recent years local relief has played an important role in practically every branch's activities."[34]

The attempt to entertain the whole community sometimes caused problems, as well as solving them. For example, while the WI prided itself on representing all classes and creeds, there could be fundamental disagreement over the kind of leisure activity that was acceptable. One Institute discovered, when they proposed holding a dance in the schoolhouse, that the school board disagreed with their chosen form of entertainment. Trustees refused their request, stating that the school was only to be used for educational purposes, not for dances. The same issue divided the Sundridge Institute in Muskoka District. They had recently acquired a hall that had formerly been a church. Some of the members would not support dancing in a former house of worship, and the issue threatened to deeply divide the branch.[35] However, in many other communities consensus was reached on what was acceptable for entertainment, and dances and card parties

Throughout rural Ontario, the WI hall was the centre for community activity in the 1930s. This hall in Middlemarch, typical of many others across the province, was given to that Institute in 1937 by the trustees of the local Grange movement.

— Middlemarch WI Tweedsmuir History

proved to be very popular pastimes.

For Institutes fortunate enough to have their own meeting space, a Women's Institute hall was undeniably the centre of community life, and that public space was usually the result of tremendous co-operation and effort on the part of community members and Institutes working hand in hand. The legislation governing halls dated from the 1920s when the provincial government created regulations for their establishment. The 1936 Handbook advised members that the legislation concerning halls had been revised, and they were instructed on the steps they should take if they intended to hold property.

For some branches, the hall was a memorial tribute to the fallen soldiers of the First World War, and memorial cairns or honour rolls of local soldiers who served are a common sight on the grounds of these community centres. For others, the creation of a Women's Institute hall was not a tribute to the men of the community, but to the women themselves. One branch claimed that "in the minds of the older generation the Hall is a fitting monument to the women of the past who made their dreams come true by hard work and devotion to their community."[36]

In Eastern Ontario, the Finch WI began a project in 1928 to build and finance a hall, but they ran into financial difficulty. When the contractor threatened legal action to collect the outstanding payments, the women appealed to the local council for help. In 1932, the Town of Finch assumed the debt and became the owner of the hall. Under an agreement struck at that time between the municipality and the WI, the Institute was granted free use of the facility for their functions for as long as they remained active in the WI movement.[37]

Other WI branches throughout Ontario arrived at similar arrangements, where the women retained free use of the community hall space for their own purposes, and often they maintained a public kitchen facility, for which others had to ask their permission to use. Braemar WI installed hydro into their community hall in 1930 and continued to pay for the service after that. The Roseland WI in Essex County owned their hall, but they shared it with the community. In 1936, they were "assist[ing] Girl Guides and Brownies, Boy Scouts and Cubs, by allowing them the use of the Institute Hall free of charge." To help with expenses, the members of those groups were "responsible for fuel and any breakage which might occur."[38]

In one northern community, Stratton, the WI hall was used as a temporary shelter for families evacuated from their homes during the forest fires. "In 1938 forest fires raged in the northern unorganized sections of the District. The people living in Sifton Township were in great danger. Several men from the Forestry Department brought out sixty-eight women and children in trucks to the village of Stratton for safety. The men and older boys were left to fight the fires from their buildings, and try to save their livestock. The fire had come so quickly that the pitch off the evergreens burned into the backs and necks of those who crouched in their gardens. They put soda on their backs to put out the fire. When the trucks came they had no time to collect anything. They were housed in the Women's Institute Hall and in another large house. The Forestry dept [sic] supplied them with blankets and food, and [the] WI [was] in the kitchen."[39]

The ideal location for WI short courses was the Institute hall. The Institute would provide equipment available locally and the Department of Agriculture would provide paid instructors. Under the watchful eye of King George, these women received hands-on instruction in patient care. True to the slogan "For Home and Country," patriotic decor was typical of Institute halls.
— UG, FWIO Collection

Throughout the years, Women's Institute halls have served multiple purposes. Institutes have also been responsible for a variety of community properties besides halls. In Northumberland County, the Hastings WI created a park space and beautified their community at the same time. In 1935 they reported that they had "bought a piece of property in the village, have filled in old cellars, cut the weeds, removed stumps, and levelled the ground, and established a creditable community park."[40] The Mt. Healey WI in Haldimand County was proud to report the following year that they had "performed a dual service" by hiring an unemployed man to clean the local cemetery.[41]

The Wiarton branch went even further in its effort to make creative use of public space. They went into business by developing a park and tourist facility at Colpoy's Bay. The fall 1937 issue of *Home and Country* gave a full report of their business plan:

> The Wiarton branch in its development of the Blue Water Beach on Colpoy's Bay has demonstrated that a local Women's Institute may initiate and manage a successful community project. Until 1921 the present site known as Blue Water Beach at Wiarton was merely an old sawmill yard and considered a strip of waste land along the shore. During the hot summer of that year, the local Women's Institute built bath-houses to accommodate bathers who frequented Colpoy's Bay. At the same time the officers of the Institute, headed by Mrs. Hough, the president, saw the possibility of a tourist camp. They negotiated to get control of the old sawmill property and in 1923 the town council granted the Women's Institute a long lease.

The beach was cleaned and landscaped and, for the first few years, fire-places were provided for the use of tourists and picnic parties. In 1927 the Institute purchased an old boathouse and converted it into a kitchen. This was followed in 1928 by the making of a good playground and providing tables, benches and swings. A diamond was levelled for soft ball. A demand started for accommodation for tourists. Two sleeping cabins were partitioned off the girl's bath-house. As the demand grew, another building was added with better toilet facilities. The Park Commission donated a band stand. For the last few years, the Wiarton Band gives a concert every Sunday evening during July and August.

In the last year or two, a refreshment booth, which caters to the needs of campers, and new cabins have been added. A protected swimming place with spring boards and slides for little children has been provided. This fall holes have been dug for the planting of more trees next spring.

The first year the camp was self-sustaining was in 1936. All money taken in was used to pay the expenses of the splendid caretaker, laundry, equipment and improvements for the camp. The Institute manages this good-sized enterprise by having a park committee to take care of all the business.[42]

Short courses were an important part of Depression activities. In 1932, these Buriss Institute women had just completed a course in home nursing, as their numerous bandages and dressings attest.
— Dorothy Redford, Fort Frances

The scope and variety of these community activities would be impressive at any time, but even more so in the context of the 1930s and their great economic hardships. Yet branches worked hard to pool their resources and raise money to support their projects. One creative project from the East Rainy River District in 1937 was the idea of patched aprons. At the district annual in 1937, "Mrs. Armstrong told of a money-making scheme in which each branch would make an apron, pass it about among members and friends, who would slip a coin under a patch which they put upon the apron. The various branches undertook to have an apron patched to swell the funds of the District in 1938." When the aprons were opened at the district annual the following year, they found that $8.85 had been raised.[43] The Omemee WI in Victoria County reported that they "augmented the treasury by filling quilting orders. During the year 1936, 30 quilts were quilted at a charge of $1.00 each."[44]

Thirty dollars was a real boost to the branch treasury, especially at a time when government grants were reduced because of the Depression. As the Superintendent explained to the members in 1933, government cutbacks were widespread. "The funds available [to the Women's Institutes] through Government sources have been somewhat reduced during the past two years, in keeping with the general policy of retrenchment found necessary on the part of the Government, and the Institutes have willingly accepted the reduction. With some readjustments in our methods of providing service through Conventions, district meetings, short courses and various group meetings . . . we have been able to maintain a level of services which compares favourably with that of former years — in fact, in one respect the results have been most gratifying, for it has created in the minds of the members generally a keener sense of their responsibilities."[45]

Branches were encouraged to give up the government grant voluntarily, if they did not need it. This money was then applied to other purposes, such as WI publications. Some of the more remote branches and districts argued that they really did need the money, but in truth, government money only represented a small and relatively insignificant proportion of the total budget of the branches. The East Rainy River District financial records for 1937 provide an interesting example. The district was composed of five branches and therefore qualified for a $15 grant, but the total receipts that year were $1,086.25. In other words, the grant represented only 1.3 percent of the total budget, enough to cover the telephone bills. Of the five branches in that district, Atikokan Women's Institute (undoubtedly one of the most remote in the province, let alone the district) actually managed to raise the most money through its local community moneymaking projects. From dances and card parties alone, Atikokan raised $146.50 and $159. This very isolated branch evidently sponsored some very well-attended community functions. Perhaps the isolated location actually meant that the WI experienced less competition for community resources than in communities with more activities and organizations to support. It seems the people of Atikokan were quite single-minded in their support of the WI.

The combination of local effort and government support is one of the fascinating things about the Ontario WI. While there is no doubt about the community resourcefulness displayed by these Institute members, it is also important to recognize that in addition to the cash grant, they did receive several different types of support from the province through the Department of Agriculture. As they were reminded in 1933, "The Department [of Agriculture] undertakes to give service to the Institutes [through the Institutes Branch] by way of lectures, short courses, literature and general service, and advice through correspondence to all who wish to take advantage of the same."[46]

The 1934 Staff Conference was one of the last gatherings of these remarkable leaders. Within two years, George Putnam and Emily Guest had both passed away, and the leadership direction had changed considerably. BACK ROW (LEFT TO RIGHT): *Miss E.A. Slicter, Mrs. Clarence Hayes, Miss Alleta Smith, Miss M.E. McDiarmid, Miss Ethel Robson, Mrs. Hugh Bertram, Miss Harriet Graydon* SECOND ROW: *Miss Elizabeth Warner, Mrs. William G. Towriss, Miss Gertrude Gray, Mrs. Fred H. Graham, Miss L. Petty, Mrs. Joan Hamilton Shearer, Miss E. Appelbe, Miss E.M. Collins, Mrs. J.M. Percival* FRONT ROW: *Miss Emily J. Guest, Mrs. Jas. Patterson, Mrs. Laura Rose Stephen, Mr. G.A. Putnam, Mrs. J. W. Stone, Miss M. V. Powell, Miss F.P. Eadie* — UG, FWIO Collection

The historical emphasis on education continued. However, the courses were offered in a new variety of forms, including versions that lasted for three months, two weeks, or shorter courses of only two or three days. The shorter courses were proposed in order to allow busy farm women to have access to the material.[47] These were very often courses on nutrition. In 1935, there is a reference to the WI as "the rural university," with students from ages sixteen to eighty. Courses were popular because the Depression meant that families had less money to spend, and there was a definite interest in learning skills to help homemakers to run their households more cost-effectively.[48] The Department offered the courses to the branches at very little expense. As Putnam explained in 1933, "Briefly we may state that the locality concerned is required to provide a suitable hall, or in some cases a private home, free of cost to the Department. The only charge to the members of a Two Week Class is Twenty Five Cents for Institute members and Fifty Cents for non-members; while for the Three Day Courses, it is left with the instructor and the members of the class to make such collection as is found necessary to cover the local expenses."[49]

Some very important changes occurred in the provincial office of the Institutes Branch in this decade, and it all began in 1934 with a change in leadership. After thirty years in office as superintendent of Ontario's Women's Institutes, George Putnam retired. The decision to leave was not his own. Mrs. R.B. Colloton, the FWIO president at the time, revealed that "Mr. Putnam has been asked to retire from active leadership."[50] As the Annual Report put it, he "was superannuated." Putnam revealed his reaction to the decision in an open letter to the members, saying, "It is with mixed feelings that I am severing the official relationship which has existed between us for the past thirty years; but the decision which has been reached by those in authority cannot sever that bond of friendships which has been established while working together in the interests of the women and girls of rural Ontario."

The full details surrounding the decision to release Mr. Putnam are not clear, but his feelings about the decision are unmistakably bitter. Putnam used his farewell letter to say that he felt grateful to have served the WI over the years; but he also took the opportunity to openly criticize the government, saying that in his mind, no government during his time in office had ever given the kind of financial support to the WI program that the women really deserved. He assured the members that he intended to continue to support the WI in his retirement years. "While we must part officially, my interest in the welfare of the Institutes will continue," he asserted, "and now that I am relieved of the detail work, I hope to give much of my time to the interests of the Institutes, and I shall, as opportunity affords, pass on what, I hope, will prove helpful information and suggestions to the leaders in the Institutes. Possibly as a private citizen, I may impress more forcefully both the members of the Institutes and those responsible for service to the Institutes with the importance of the work."

Putnam was not in good health when he left his post. Apparently, he had been sick for some time, though he claimed that "I am fully recovered from my recent illness and am feeling better than for several years past."[51] However, his recovery was short-lived. George Alfred Putnam died two years later, on November 4, 1936, in his sixty-seventh year.[52] The obituary published in *Home and Country* magazine was an endearing tribute to the man who had been so very important to the work of the Ontario Women's Institutes. As a memorial to him, the Women's Institutes renamed the fund that provided money for relief efforts among the Institutes of Northern Ontario. Putnam had established that fund a few years earlier, and to commemorate his commitment to the northern region, the fund became known as the Putnam Memorial Fund.

EMILY J. GUEST

Ontario Institute members have learned with very deep regret of the death of their friend Miss Emily J. Guest. During the many years of her connection with the Women's Institute Branch of the Ontario Department of Agriculture, she visited practically every Institute District in the province. Through her courage, wit and common sense she left each community more competent to carry good plans to completion.

Miss Guest was born on a farm in Middlesex Co. and was a graduate of Toronto University. She studied also at Columbia and Oxford Universities. She was one of the chief organizers of the Institutes of Great Britain during the time of their inception. In both Canada and England she will be held in grateful and happy remembrance.

Among Miss Guest's books, her sister, Mrs. Earl Grose, found a notebook which Miss Guest had used shortly before her death. In it was a message to the Women's Institutes.

"Good-bye to the Women's Institutes who have done so much for a beautiful Canada. It was a privilege to be one of those grand women and girls; especially to live and see the second generation under our new Superintendent carry on so well.

"I leave them, myself joyous and confident, and shall hope to see them come with the same feeling."

— *Home and Country*, July 1936

After thirty years of continuous involvement, Putnam's departure marked a very critical shift in Institute history. The next years were transitional both in terms of leadership and direction. Mr. Putnam was not the only well-known leader that the Institutes lost in these years. In September 1933, *Home and Country* reported the death of Mrs. William Todd, the first provincial president of the FWIO, and later president of FWIC. Her passing was a solemn occasion for the FWIO. As well, just months before Putnam's own death, Miss Emily Guest, a prominent leader of the Ontario WI who had helped to organize the Institutes overseas, also died.[53] Losing Todd, Guest and Putnam in the space of three short years meant significant change for Ontario's Institutes. Shortly before her death, Guest revealed that she had a sense of the changing of the guard; as she remarked, the leadership of the Institutes now rested with a second generation. When she was welcoming Putnam's replacement to the office of superintendent, Miss Guest had commented that she was convinced that the organization would "carry on well." It would certainly carry on differently.

Upon Putnam's retirement, the Ontario Women's Institutes were finally placed into the hands of female leadership, something that had already been true in all the other Canadian provinces for more than twenty years. As Ontario's first female superintendent of the Institutes, Miss Bessie Cameron McDermand served the organization for only four years, but during that time she oversaw some important changes in the relationship between the Department of Agriculture and the Institutes. According to the September 1934 issue of *Home and Country*, McDermand was "a Canadian by birth with experience in Women's Institute work in both Ontario and Alberta, and extension service in New York State." With that experience profile, the FWIO executive reported that "we feel that we are extremely fortunate in the happy choice which the Minister of Agriculture has made. We extend hearty greetings and best wishes to Miss McDermand together with the hope that the relationship between us will prove not only profitable but very happy for all concerned."

When she took up her new post as superintendent, McDermand directed her full attention to the educational roles of the Institutes, and she concentrated on developing a wider variety of educational schemes for the Department staff to offer to the women of Ontario. In her first annual report, she reminded the branches that they should keep their priorities straight. McDermand insisted that although their activism in community projects was commendable, the Institutes were, first and foremost, "an educational, not [a] charitable or money-raising organization." Evidently, McDermand intended to refocus the energies of the Institutes away from community service, and bring the emphasis squarely back to domestic science education.

The new superintendent announced her resignation in the fall of 1938. Miss Bess McDermand, Superintendent of Women's Institutes and Director of Extension Work in Home Economics, was leaving her post, the members were informed, to become Mrs. Guy Skinner, homemaker. "I assure you," she told the readers of *Home and Country*, "I shall always remember the Women's Institutes of Ontario. At the fireside of our New England home, my Canadian husband and I will often discuss your fine ideals, activities and accomplishments." McDermand's replacement, Miss Mary A. Clarke, was hired in November 1938. Miss Clarke, a former lecturer at the Macdonald Institute, intended to continue in her predecessor's footsteps by concentrating upon the Women's Institutes' education mandate. However, Clarke's term as superintendent, which extended through the war years up to 1945, was not what she or anyone else had expected. Wartime concerns meant that the Institute members could not afford to continue to pursue educational opportunities with the same single-minded attention they had enjoyed during peacetime.

When McDermand set out to renew the emphasis on education, she had very significant resources at her disposal to help accomplish that goal. During this period, the provincial office of the Ontario Women's Institutes had a very large staff, a luxury it could only afford because of its status as an arm of the Department of Agriculture. In 1935, there were ten staff members at the head office in Toronto, along with ninety-six field workers who performed duties as travelling instructors. Attention was paid to the professional training of these workers, with an emphasis on hiring only those with qualifications in sociology, home economics and education.[54]

Contact with local branches kept the office staff very busy. In 1936, for example, eighty-two circular letters were distributed among the membership with a circulation of 23,000 copies each. The work of preparing that material for typesetting and printing was very labour intensive. A further 15,000 individual letters were answered during the 1935–1936 year. With the popularity and growth of the local branches, there was plenty of office work to keep the staff of ten clerical workers very busy.

McDermand used some new approaches to organize her staff, especially those who worked as instructors of courses for the Women's Institutes. "In November [1936] the annual conference of the entire staff was held at Macdonald Institute when the instructors in the senior and junior programme in extension education in Home Economics and in the one-month and three-month short courses in Home Economics met for four days. The staff of Macdonald Institute brought to the conference information concerning recent research in Home Economics. This gathering, characterised by group discussions, helped to strengthen the workers in their own fields. In addition they learned what instructors in related programmes were doing and became better informed concerning all the services offered by the Women's Institute Branch."[55] Indeed, there was much to learn, because under McDermand's leadership the Ontario Women's Institutes' programs were quite varied and wide ranging.

In her first year, the new superintendent created what she called the Cooperative Programme in Home Economics. As the branches understood it, "the Cooperative Programme [was] the name given by Miss McDermand to the work of the Federation with the Branches."[56] McDermand travelled around Ontario explaining that it was simply an all-inclusive term for the educational courses that the provincial office could provide to the membership. She was convinced that her staff could deliver the kinds of information and instruction that were greatly in demand by the women of rural Ontario.

The wide variety was a necessity because, as McDermand recognized, any one format could never meet all the needs of all the members. One of her first recommendations was to provide short courses that respected the homemakers' busy schedules. As she explained in the Annual Report, the existing format of two-week courses had been problematic. "Because of the difficulty homemakers have experienced in finding time to attend a two-week course regularly, the time was shortened to provide for five-day and three-day courses, the length of the course governed by the type and amount of subject matter covered."[57] Adjusting the content of the courses and the techniques of teaching them in various formats were among the issues which the staff discussed at their annual conferences.

McDermand's goal was to get instruction to as many women as possible, in spite of the obstacles. That was the real aim of her new program. As she explained, it "was planned to meet the most urgent needs of the majority of homemakers in the Province. It had to recognize the possibilities and difficulties of establishing sound educational procedures by taking into account limited funds; the diversity of social and economic conditions in the Province; the varying mental and physical abilities of homemakers; the widely differing demands and limitations set up by ideals and beliefs; varying climatic conditions and occupations; and the tradition of previous programmes . . . An endeavour was made to make the programme flexible and elastic and at the same time to give it a simple fundamental organization."[58]

Part of that new flexibility included listening to the branches to determine what kinds of courses the women really wanted. Rather than simply announcing what was available, McDermand decided that her staff should consult with local members. Accordingly, she "tried to encourage the Institute branches to analyze their own needs and be conscious of their interests." She was convinced that this was necessary in order to run a successful program. By 1937, she was encouraged to report that members had begun to "understand that they must help to plan the activities they wish to carry out successfully."[59]

This onus on local initiative was an important part of McDermand's concern, as she was determined to reach the greatest possible number of women. The previous educational model, which concentrated on sending trained "experts" to speak to groups of Institute members, was the one that had been in place since before Putnam assumed the office of superintendent in 1904. The old model, based on the practices of the Farmers' Institutes of Ontario, was one that McDermand wanted to update. While the so-called speaker service would still be available to Institutes who requested it, McDermand was proposing something new. Her alternative, introduced in 1935, was called "training schools for local leaders." This was a scheme whereby the instructors on staff would work with local women in a new way. Individual members of Institutes would from now on be "trained to conduct schools in phases of home economics, in their home Institutes, thus reaching an infinitely larger number of women." Women who took the courses went home to teach that same course to their friends and neighbours. There is no doubt that the new arrangement was designed in part to save money. However, it achieved much more than that.

Within just one year, the statistics proved that the scheme was indeed very successful. In Eastern Ontario, thirty-one local leaders from four different districts took advantage of one of those training schools, and just how many women they reached after that is hard to know. We do know however, that "eight [of those] local leaders in south Renfrew held two meetings each with a total attendance of 265."[60] At that rate, the thirty-one leaders probably reached one thousand women altogether. Throughout Ontario, the program trained 350 local leaders from 48 counties. The potential of this new model was exponential. Indeed, it was an idea that proved so effective it would remain in place for decades to come, as it was adopted heartily by women eager to learn so they could teach their peers.

There was a wide choice of possible topics that these local leaders could learn to teach. Records show that courses were offered in everything from meal planning (as in The Use of Whole Meat, a course that the Manitoulin, Algoma and Thunder Bay Districts took up in 1937) to individual health and diet, to home nursing techniques. That same year, some Institutes took up the topics Gaining Weight, and Relieving Constipation. Such instruction was enthusiastically received, and members wrote to the Superintendent to thank her for the program, with reports such as "no more headaches," "feel better in every way," and "have gained six pounds." That type of feedback encouraged Miss McDermand and her staff to press on with the plans to emphasize the educational work of the Institutes.

Members also enjoyed courses in sewing, cooking and home renovations. Courses in crafts also proved popular, and for women in rural districts such as Rainy River where sheep raising was common, a new course introduced in 1935, Home Utilization of Wool, proved to be in high demand. The course included "a survey of the wool industry from the raw material to the finished products — quilts and quilting, knitting and the making of leather gloves."[61]

Consumer education was also part of the curriculum. During 1936–1937, over three hundred women attended leader training schools in Buymanship. This study was so popular that those local leaders went beyond teaching it to their Institute branches; several of them "accepted invitations to address other organizations and [to give] assistance to school teachers in special study groups."[62] A consumer course was originally proposed in 1932 to emphasize the importance of buying Canadian-made goods, of buying locally whenever possible, and of learning about world markets for Ontario's surplus goods.[63] The goal of McDermand's new course was different. It was designed so that "as a result more women will 'buy' their household furnishings rather than be 'sold' them." The emphasis was on women becoming active buyers rather than passive consumers. Enabling WI members to make active choices based on good information, these courses were a source of real empowerment for many women.

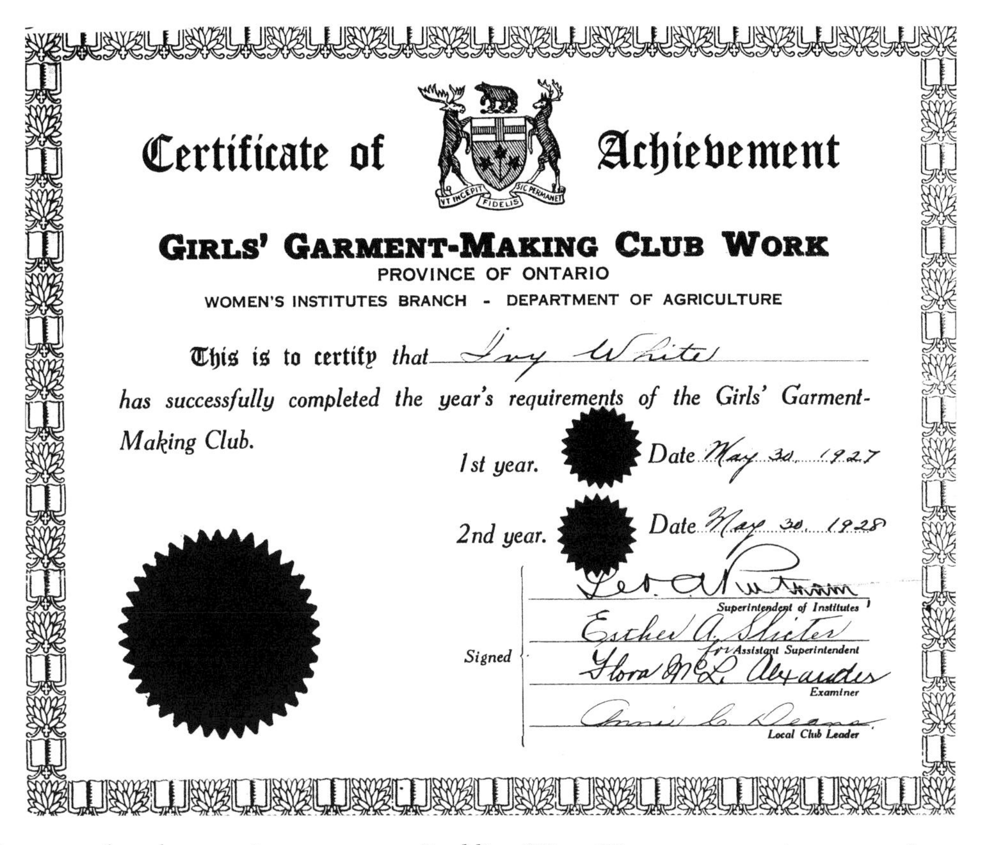
Certificate of Achievement

UT INCEPIT FIDELIS SIC PERMANET

GIRLS' GARMENT-MAKING CLUB WORK
PROVINCE OF ONTARIO
WOMEN'S INSTITUTES BRANCH - DEPARTMENT OF AGRICULTURE

This is to certify that Ivy White
has successfully completed the year's requirements of the Girls' Garment-Making Club.

1st year. Date May 30 1927

2nd year. Date May 30 1928

Signed
Superintendent of Institutes
for Assistant Superintendent
Examiner
Local Club Leader

WI courses were an important early form of extension education and something to take pride in completing. Ivy White (now Iva Irwin) kept her WI Certificate of Achievement in Garment-Making, which she earned as a teenager in the 1920s. These courses were often the only opportunity for formal educational training available to rural women.
— Iva Irwin, North Bay

Other courses took the students outside the realm of home economics altogether, focussing instead on current legislation that affected women and their families, or teaching them parliamentary procedure so that they could be confident of their ability to lead meetings effectively. The Crosby WI in Leeds County was convinced that the branch was instrumental in the personal development of its members. "Our meetings have broadened our views, solved many problems of the homemaker, educated us in many ways, given us more self confidence in conversing and discussing topics that are of interest to the rural women making us less afraid of the sound of our own voices, brought out hidden talent that was previously unknown to exist."[64]

Clearly, the educational programs were more than just classes in cooking and sewing. Although those topics were available, and very popular among the women, they were only part of what was offered. Training in public health, legal matters and consumer education was equally popular. The Komoka WI in Middlesex County reported in 1935 that they had had a debate, "Resolved that the woman exerts a greater influence as homemaker than as lawmaker," and, surprisingly, "the supporters of the law were the winners." In 1935 the

Superintendent of Women's Institutes Resigns

Bessie Cameron McDermand

Miss McDermand completes four years of service in the Department of Agriculture.

Dear Women's Institute Members:

The last four years have been both busy and happy ones for me, and I am glad I have had the opportunity of spending them in Ontario working in the Women's Institute Branch. Your friendliness and kindly co-operation have been important factors in whatever progress may have been made.

I assure you I shall always remember the Women's Institutes of Ontario. At the fireside of our New England home, my Canadian husband and I will often discuss your fine ideals, activities and accomplishments.

With best of good wishes I am,

Very sincerely yours,

BESS McDERMAND,

(Mrs. Guy Skinner).

— *Home and Country*, fall 1938

Superintendent looked back over thirty-seven years of Institute programming, and remarked that, though "the Women's Institutes have evolved into a rural university," the goal was not to impose a standard academic curriculum on the members, but rather "to offer valuable training in self-development."[65] In fact, the goal was articulated by a twofold aim. "We strive," the Superintendent revealed in 1937, "to make women better homemakers and to make homemakers better women."

In part, the process of "making better women" meant starting earlier, with younger members. Consequently, considerable emphasis was placed on junior programs. Junior Women's Institutes had already existed since 1915 when the first junior chapter was founded on Manitoulin Island. During the 1930s, though, McDermand focussed very directly on developing specific education programs for junior members, and again, significant changes were introduced.

In the spring of 1935, "definite changes were made in the Junior Programme. In its new form it aim[ed] to foster in young women a sense of satisfaction in achievement, rather than too keen a desire for competition." Florence P. Eadie headed up the program for juniors in this period, and she defended this new model vigorously.[66] In keeping with this new initiative, young women were presented with certificates of achievement and silver teaspoons for the courses which they completed. Records were kept of their studies, leading them through the levels of the program, up to the attainment of a special "County Honours" award for completing six units, and eventually "Provincial Honours" for twelve.[67] This girls' work was the forerunner of the familiar 4-H Homemaking clubs program that existed until the early 1980s. Although the name "4-H" was not yet used to describe the program, references to the "four Hs" (head, heart, hands, and health) were already in place in the 1930s.[68]

In 1938, the Annual Report proudly declared that the junior work was strong. That strength was based in part on variety. Educational opportunities for young women took many forms beyond the Homemaking clubs. Up until then, girls' courses had adopted the male model of competition in their training. They were taught to judge food and clothing at fairs, using the same model that was in place for boys judging crops and livestock. The most successful young women were rewarded for their competitive spirit and their accomplishments with coveted awards. The most valuable prize was a trip to the Royal Winter Fair for the lucky entrant from each district who managed to outdo all her competitors. She would travel to Toronto with all expenses paid, attend the fair, and be an honoured guest at special luncheons and concerts sponsored by Eaton's at their College Street store.

The popularity of the annual Girls' Conference at Guelph is evident in this photograph of the young women who attended in 1938.
— UG, FWIO Collection

A statistical report of the participation in the winter of 1936–1937 indicated that 35 one-month schools in Home Economics had been held with 1,038 girls enrolled. Although the ages of attendees ranged from 10 to 70, the average age was 20 years. Of the participants, 41 percent had not attended high school and 28 percent had attended 2 years or less. Only 9 percent had the advantage of special training in nursing, commercial and normal school and university. Over 69 percent were farm girls, 24 percent were village girls and 3 percent were town girls. Only 15 percent of them had previously been members of a Homemaking club.[69] This was obviously proving to be a very popular and effective way of providing educational opportunities to young women who otherwise would not have studied beyond elementary school.

The seven-month schools in Home Economics reported similar success. There were 244 enrolled, ages ranging from 12 to 26; the average age was 19 years. Thirty-two percent had not attended high school, 20 percent had attended two years or less. Only 7 percent reported having had the advantage of special training in nursing, commercial and normal schools and university. Some 72 percent were farm girls, 16 percent village girls and 12 percent town girls. Only 28 percent had at any time been members of a Homemaking club.[70]

In 1938, plans were discussed to establish courses in child behaviour and family life, meant to equip junior members with the skills they would need to parent more effectively. Clearly, there was an emphasis on very traditional roles for women, both in homemaking and in mothering. One story from 1937 reported that a junior member who learned the advantages of using cod liver oil communicated those benefits to her mother, who then introduced that supplement to the entire family. This was the kind of story that the Department of Agriculture proudly recounted to demonstrate the effectiveness of their junior work, not just as an investment in the future of rural homemaking and mothering, but more immediately in the lives of the members' own families.

In girls' work competitions at local fairs, young women were given an opportunity to display their homemaking skills. Four of the officials who acted as judges of girls' work take a moment to pose for the camera at a fair in Peterborough. They are Lillian Howell, Flora Durnin, Greta Pollard and Florence P. Eadie. — UG, FWIO Collection

But again for the girls, as for their mothers, the training was not exclusively limited to homemaking. In that same year, 1937, four courses were offered with the goal of leading young women into part-time employment in one of four areas: Catering for Tourists, Marketing Home Baked Goods, Rugmaking, and Simple Dressmaking and Remodelling. These were offered in conjunction with the Dominion-Provincial Youth Training Programme, a government program intended to provide an antidote to the chronic youth unemployment problem of the 1930s. The Institutes used the program to fund and develop courses for young women who wished to generate income through part-time business ventures in hospitality, food services or dressmaking — an extension of their homemaking skills. Statistics about participation in this program for 1938 indicate that 622 women were enrolled, and their average age was 20 years. Of these women, 34 percent never attended high school, 41 percent attended two years or less, 14 percent had specialized training of some kind. Also, 45 percent of them had been previously employed. The enrolment by urban/rural difference was as follows: 60 percent from farms, 23 percent from villages and 11 percent from towns. At the end of the courses, several had plans for setting up their own businesses. Thus young women were introduced to business opportunities through the programs offered by the Women's Institute Branch of the Department of Agriculture. They also could take courses in public speaking and parliamentary procedure. Although the emphasis on home economics was important, junior members of the Institute were exposed to a wide variety of opportunities. For many of rural Ontario's young women, these courses in the late 1930s made a lasting impact on their lives.

Beyond the various educational programs and the all-important community roles that Institutes played, two other developments during the 1930s are particularly noteworthy, and both of them occurred in 1933. That was the year in which Ontario Women's Institutes launched their very own publication, *Home and Country* magazine, and the international level of the organization, Associated Country Women of the World (ACWW), began.

HOME and COUNTRY

Published through the co-operation of the Federated Women's Institutes of the Province and the Women's Institutes Branch of the Ontario Department of Agriculture.

Published by
The Ontario Women's Institutes at Toronto, Ont.

EDITORIAL COMMITTEE:
Mrs. R. B. Colloton   Mrs. I. Graves
Miss M. V. Powell   Mr. Geo. A. Putnam

Note:—Copies are being sent free to each branch and district president and secretary, the officers of the provincial board, convention area chairmen and secretaries, chairmen of standing committees for the various conventions, and the leaders in rural women's organizations in other countries. Correspondence to be addressed to Institutes Branch, Parliament Buildings, Toronto.

Volume 1   MAY, 1933   Number 1

Masthead of the first issue of Home and Country, *Volume 1, Number 1.*
— *Home and Country*, May 1933

Home and Country was designed to be an effective communication link between the Institute membership at large and the two leadership bodies, the FWIO and the Institutes Branch of the Department of Agriculture. In 1933 the province was still in the grips of the Depression, provincial spending was being cut back, and the editors deliberately attempted to encourage local Institutes to carry on despite those hardships. The provincial president, Mrs. Colloton from Lorne Park WI, opened her front-page remarks with a poem:

It is easy enough to be pleasant
When life goes along like a song:
But the man worthwhile
Is the man who can smile,
When everything goes dead wrong.[71]

Colloton further remarked, "It has taken a lot of courage on the part of most of us these trying times to summon up that smile and keep it on the job." In part though, *Home and Country* was designed to help put that smile back on the faces of the Institute members, and that determination back in their actions.

Communications from the provincial office to the members already had a long history when *Home and Country* made its debut in 1933. The Department of Agriculture devoted a great deal of money each year to publishing and circulating its annual report, putting out informative bulletins on new homemaking techniques, and producing circular letters to the membership. But the idea of printing its own magazine was new. In the earlier years, the Ontario WI had used the pages of the *Canadian Home Journal* as their official news organ. A few pages of each issue were dedicated to WI purposes as early as 1907. These columns contained some news from the branches, and very often an essay by an Institute leader or promoter. Special subscription rates were offered to Institute members, and many members took advantage of that offer. Women were also invited to sell subscriptions, and a reward program was established as an incentive. For example, a member from Sheffield WI worked to sell subscriptions to her fellow members during 1914–1917, and in so doing, she could have a free subscription for herself. By selling even more subscriptions she could earn pieces of Limoges china or a silver tea service.

Although the pages in the *Canadian Home Journal* were a good start, they did not compare to having a whole publication produced by one's own organization and dedicated solely to its purposes. The first issue of *Home and Country,* produced in May 1933, was an important event in the provincial history. More than sixty years later, the magazine continues to be published (though it has undergone a variety of changes and different formats) and to serve as a source of information and inspiration to the membership. However, those first issues were very different from today's publication.

For the first eighteen years, from 1933 to 1950, the format was a four-page (or sometimes up to eight-page) newspaper in tabloid size. The publication was well received and economical to produce. In 1934 the announcement came that *Home and Country* was to replace the annual reports that the Department had published since the early 1900s.

The editors made a real attempt to reach members with information in these first special issues, and to establish a legitimate role for the publication. They took the opportunity to explain aspects of the organization's structure, such as the difference between the WI Office at the Department of Agriculture made up of its paid staff of superintendent, assistants, office workers and educators, and the FWIO Board, made up entirely of volunteers elected from the various parts of the province. The only paid person on the Board was the secretary-treasurer. In another issue clearly marked "Keep This Copy for Reference," the programs of the various standing committees were outlined and explained. Each one of the provincial convenors contributed a column about her committee's concerns and accomplishments. The standing committees that had served the FWIO so effectively during the 1920s era of social reform were still in place and still functioning as an efficient way to organize the work around Health and Child Welfare, Home Economics, Legislation, Relief, Community Activities, Education, Agriculture, Immigration, Historical Research and Canadian Industries.[72]

But beyond that kind of organizational information, these issues were designed to communicate directly to the individual member and give her some very practical help as she faced her task of homemaking in the Depression years. To that end, the issues in 1934 contained recipes and household tips, and even fitness instruction. Dr. Annie Ross of the Macdonald Institute wrote a piece for the August 1934 issue, entitled "Health Exercises for Every Day," giving instructions on stretching and toning exercises. Recognizing that women might feel self-conscious about exercising, since daily fitness regimes were not widely practised, she counselled her readers, "you may think that you are only wasting time in foolishness, but what you are doing is inviting good temper, cool judgement, and good circulation and the joy of life to come and dwell with you." To reduce stress, Dr. Ross recommended the following relaxation exercise:

> Relax when you are worried to death by stress and strain. Lean lazily back in your chair, with your head supported, and completely let go. Loosen for a moment every kink and knot in the nerves and muscles and brain. Let go. Just for one minute let everything go. He who made you what you are, let Him say to you:
>
> I know the anguish and the helplessness.
> I know the fears that toss you to and fro,
> The hosts of little cares that pull
> About your heart and tear it so. I know.[73]

Advice about how to exercise in order to reduce stress and find peace of mind during the height of the Depression's economic strain may indeed have struck some readers as foolishness, but others no doubt welcomed the opportunity to take that little escape, however brief.

And so the earliest issues of *Home and Country* were not all official business and administrative structure. The August 1934 issue, an expanded eight-page edition, reveals that there was an attempt to communicate with women on an individual level and provide them with tidbits of practical advice, hints for personal well-being, and suggestions for leisure activities. Despite its news-tabloid format, the publication was really attempting to go beyond an organizational newsletter and become a women's magazine. The editorial committee seemed convinced that *Home and Country* could give WI members a cheerful boost each month. Readers were reminded in September 1934 that such a treat came with a price tag. That special August issue cost the FWIO over $300 for its share of the contribution toward printing costs. Although it was a pleasant idea to publish a breezy, conversational journal for women, economic realism overtook the editorial policy.

In January 1935, *Home and Country* returned to its original four-page, news-based format and a circulation of only 18,000 copies. The total membership at this time was over 40,000, but rather than attempt to place one copy into the hands of every member, the editors urged the branch secretaries to share the issues among the membership. If a woman wanted to ensure that she received her own personal copy, then she could pay a ten-cent subscription fee to the branch secretary; the prepaid copies were not for individual use. The experiment to become a personal magazine for women had proved too costly. The renewed mandate to publish news of the organization was reflected in the January 1935 edition. A new feature, "News Flashes from the Branches," offered a page of snippets about local activities that served not only to report activity, but also to offer new program ideas for local branches. After twelve issues were published sporadically between May 1933 and October 1935, a new system of production was introduced in January 1936, and from that date on, *Home and Country* became a quarterly publication, on a regular production schedule of January, March, June and September. Within two years, the policy of printing one copy for each member was back in place, and branch secretaries were charged with the responsibility of promptly distributing the new issue to every member, at the earliest opportunity.[74] To finance the increased circulation, the Department began to redirect the funds that had been distributed previously as grants to branches. Branches were urged to voluntarily give up their grant in order to get a better magazine. This appeal was reiterated at the district annual meetings in 1937.

The purpose of *Home and Country* in 1937 was "keeping branches alert and well informed." To that end, *Home and Country* began to run a regular column that featured a fictitious character, "Mary," who had discussions with her nephew whenever he visited her on his returns from the Ontario Agricultural College. Mary talked to him about a whole range of organizational problems, including how to write minutes, the importance of parliamentary procedure, the proper way to make a motion and amend it — issues that

To Members of The Most Progressive Women's Club in the World

We give members of Women's Institutes of Canada a special half price of 50c. for yearly subscriptions to the Canadian Home Journal.

This special rate is made possible only through the efforts of some member of every branch, usually the Secretary, to secure large club orders for us. In many branches every family has subscribed.

A woman's magazine has a very great influence for progress and refinement. Every copy has suggestions for making the home life better and more attractive. Household suggestions, recipes, home and table decorations are of practical assistance.

Every mother owes this self improvement to her children if she wants them to start life with the greatest advantages, because they learn so much from her and their home surroundings. **The young wife will be better fitted for her duties** if she has studied a magazine devoted to her needs.

At a cost of four cents a month, there is not a member who cannot afford the Journal. No matter what other magazines are taken, **the Institute department, editorials, and special Canadian news are worth double the price to every reader.** Every one of those who are not giving their support to the Journal would feel it a great loss to Canadian women if it were to be discontinued.

We are confident that you, like many other Institute officers, will count the Journal a most valuable auxiliary to the Institutes in creating a desire for better knowledge of women's interests, and we hope to have your active assistance.

Very cordially,

William G. Rook,
President.

Canadian Home Journal
Toronto.

Before the launch of Home and Country, Women's Institutes were offered special subscription rates to the Canadian Home Journal which devoted several pages each issue to WI news. — Sheffield Women's Institute

When the ACWW met in Washington in 1936, several of the delegates and dignitaries took the opportunity to travel to Ontario. Mrs. Alfred Watt, the ACWW President, visited in Stoney Creek with several charter members of the "Mother Institute." — Home and Country, July 1936

This historical plaque marks the birthplace in Collingwood, Ontario, of Mrs. Alfred Watt, the first president of the Associated Countrywomen of the World. She held that position from 1933 to 1947. LEFT TO RIGHT: *Mrs. Gordon McPhater, Past President of the FWIO; Mrs. J.R. Futcher, representing the Historic Sites Board; Mrs. Arnold Elliot, niece of Mrs. Watt; Hon. Rev. A.W. Downer, MPP; Mayor A.C. Carmichael of Collingwood; Mrs. T.C. Kells, President of Georgian W.I.; Rev. W.L. Young, Collingwood First Presbyterian Church*

— UG, FWIO Collection

surfaced all the time in WI meetings. The true identity of the author of the column was never revealed, but it probably was the FWIO president, Mrs. Colloton. The issue that reported Mrs. Colloton's obituary had no column about Mary, and three more columns did appear after that, but they ended in the fall of 1938. Mrs. Colloton apparently was noted for her sense of humour and her attention to organizational details. Mary's columns began to appear during the period when Colloton was travelling from branch to branch, and was experiencing frustration at the ignorance of the members about standard operating procedures. The remaining columns that appeared after her death may have been written prior to her death, or they may have been written by another person. The final column about Mary appeared in the fall 1938 issue, when Mary told her nephew Donald, "I may take a long holiday this winter. Our plans are uncertain, but sometime in the future I hope we shall have more discussions."[75]

While Mary taught the members how to run their meetings and have orderly discussions, *Home and Country* was sometimes used to tell members what they should not discuss. Certain subjects were removed from the roster of WI topics, and the same argument that had been used to discourage women from discussing the issue of women and voting rights was invoked again. Some topics were apparently just too divisive. "As most WI members are now aware," a special notice in *Home and Country* announced in 1934, "the subjects of Sterilization and Birth Control, by reason of their sectarian ramifications, have been ruled out of WI discussion. However, those who desire to inform themselves on both sides of this question will be interested to know that an impartial summary of the most up-to-date medical and lay findings on these subjects have [sic] been gathered and presented in book form by Dr. Helen MacMurchy. Publishers: Macmillan Co of Canada Ltd., 70 Bond St. Toronto. Regular Price $1.50; special to WI members, $1.25, postpaid."[76] That prohibition was a rare announcement in a publication that was overwhelmingly positive in tone.

One of the most celebrated themes in *Home and Country* was the launch and continued activities of the international organization, Associated Country Women of the World (ACWW), which began the same year as the new publication. Creation of yet another level of the Institute organization was taken as evidence of the WI's maturity and widespread influence. Readers were encouraged to celebrate the new international organization and particularly to recognize that Ontario's Women's Institutes were a fundamental part of that story. Institutes had been emerging around the globe since the 1910s, and the First World War was an important boost for the Institutes of Great Britain in particular. Women from Ontario such as Emily Guest and Madge Watt were directly responsible for leading the Institutes in Wales, Scotland and England. Their involvement was a reminder that it was Ontario's own Adelaide Hoodless who had first started the movement thirty-six years before, in Stoney Creek. This new international level was one more reminder that Ontario's role in Institute history was highly esteemed because of the earliest branches here. Members were encouraged to feel proud of that heritage, and to offer their support and good wishes to the new worldwide organization composed of members from twenty-two different countries.

For most WI members, contacts with the ACWW were vicarious, by way of reports from the few who were privileged enough to travel internationally and participate in the planning meetings for the ACWW and the founding conference in Stockholm in 1933. The Canadian and Ontario Institute representative at that founding meeting was Mrs. W.R. Lang from Toronto, and her experience was featured on the front page of *Home and Country* in the September 1933 issue.

This memorial cairn was erected in 1937 at the junction of Highways 5 and 24 near the birthplace of Adelaide Hunter Hoodless. The inscription reads "To commemorate the birthplace of Adelaide Hunter Hoodless 1858–1910, who founded the Women's Institutes on February 19, 1897. Erected by the Women's Institutes of Brant County."
— UG, FWIO Collection

The second ACWW conference, held in Washington, D.C., three years later, was much closer to home for the Ontario membership. The FWIO appointed official delegates to attend, but many districts throughout the province also sent representatives. This was a wonderful opportunity for Institute members to be part of a meeting of 7,000 women from countries around the world, including England, South Africa, New Zealand, Australia, Germany, Sweden, Norway, the United States of America, Finland, Holland, Czechoslovakia, Bulgaria, India, Estonia, Kenya, and Palestine.[77] After the Washington meetings, several of the international delegates took the opportunity to visit points of interest throughout Southern Ontario, including the Guelph campus of the Ontario Agricultural College and the Macdonald Institute, where some were billeted, and of course, Stoney Creek, where they viewed the first minute books of the mother branch.

After the exciting events and exchanges of 1936, many Ontario WI members felt they had a more personal involvement in the ACWW. Contacts were established, and sixty-three branches began to correspond with rural women in England, Australia and other places. This new interest in international themes and continued contact through the "Pen Friends" project brought the ACWW much closer to the hearts and minds of Institute members throughout Ontario. When announcements were made for the third ACWW conference, this time to be held in London, England, in May 1939, interest ran very high. The royal family's visit to Canada that same year only served to heighten the excitement, since Her Majesty Queen Elizabeth herself had a very close association with the Women's Institutes of Great Britain.[78] In the end, nine WI members from Ontario attended the London conference, and their adventures were fully recounted in the pages of *Home and Country* in the fall of 1939, with an issue almost entirely devoted to their reports.

The heady days at the end of the decade seemed a far cry from the pessimism that dominated throughout the Depression years. But the excitement of transatlantic travel was still the experience of only the most privileged. The great majority of Ontario's WI members would only read about those exciting global exchanges. For most, their own adventures consisted of more humble but nevertheless rewarding experiences — the experiences of providing community service, establishing lasting relationships with fellow members locally, and taking advantage of educational opportunities offered by the Department of Agriculture. Above all, Women's Institute members in Ontario were learning — learning to support one another, learning to improve their lives and learning to be leaders.

Self-sufficiency and mutual support were the hallmarks of Institute activities in the 1930s. Camaraderie among women of all ages is evident in this picture of the Derry West Institute, Peel County, 1939.
— Derry West Women's Institute, Peel South

Leadership was one lesson that Ontario's WI members learned very well during the 1930s. With the combination of practical community projects, educational courses and local leader training schools, and a new means of keeping up-to-date through the pages of *Home and Country*, women had the information and the forum they needed to put their skills to the test. Now that they also had an international level to their organization in the ACWW, Ontario's WIs were ready to take on the world. Celebrating their achievements during the Depression years, the Annual Report had boasted, "In brief, during a period of considerable unrest, the Institutes were a steadying force, progressive, yet sane in outlook."[79] Another period of considerable unrest was just around the corner, and in the fall of 1939, the WI would once more be called upon to put their steadying influence to work in a nation once again at war.

Jam-making was an important part of the WI effort during the Second World War. Members of the Oakland WI are pictured here with the cases of peach jam that they were sending overseas through the Canadian Red Cross Society. The branch produced 1,000 pounds of homemade jam for overseas.

— Oakland Women's Institute Tweedsmuir History

CHAPTER SIX

Serving the Country: At War Again, 1939–1947

Just twenty years after the close of the Great War, the winter 1939–1940 issue of *Home and Country* declared the war efforts that the Institutes were once again launching. "The keynote of every convention was the earnest desire of each member present that the Institutes should serve their country in the best possible way during the war. The Institutes pledged themselves to continue to accept their responsibilities for home and community life, and at the same time, to carry on special war efforts." To be specific, the commitment to war work meant that the provincial president, Mrs. T.J. McDowell, offered the services of the Women's Institutes of Ontario to the Premier of Ontario, "in whatever capacity the Government may wish to use them."[1] Once again, the members would take up their knitting projects, and throw themselves fully into the war effort. To many members it must have seemed as if history were repeating itself. However, the story is not that simple. Although the knitting patterns had not changed, the Institutes themselves had been through some important changes since the first war, and those developments were reflected in the Institutes' war work.

Miss Mary A. Clarke served as the Superintendent of the Women's Institutes throughout the war years, from 1939 to 1945.
— UG, FWIO Collection

One of the most significant changes centred around the ways in which the women thought about their work. Mary Clarke, the provincial Superintendent of the WIs who had succeeded Bess McDermand in 1939, urged the members to be very conscious of their mind-set as they undertook their war projects. In her addresses to the conventions in the fall of 1941 she challenged the members with a simple adage, "Make your thinking as valuable as your knitting." Women were asked to turn their attention to peace proposals and postwar plans. Clarke's advice was taken very seriously by one of the former board members from Pembroke, Mrs. David Porter, who decided to promote it to the women of Canada. She created cards with Clarke's motto printed on them, and with the approval of the provincial Board, worked out a distribution scheme whereby women would purchase the cards at a price of two for five cents. The spring issue of *Home and Country* promoted this simple idea, and the distribution began. Mrs. Porter and Miss Clarke were eager to ensure that the WI membership would be intellectually engaged with the war effort, not just preoccupied with the busy work of mass-producing the necessary articles.

The goal was to keep the women informed and, specifically, to help them focus on problem-solving efforts that would ensure world peace in a lasting way at the war's conclusion. Throughout the 1930s, the standing committee on Peace and International Relationships had been one of the most active subcommittees of the FWIO Board. When war was declared in 1939, the women who had been working so hard for world peace "felt their task a difficult one," but they conceded their pacifist ideals and resolved to enter into the war effort, emphasizing "that women should still hold the ideal of peace before their eyes, planning for peace so that they shall know what they wish to do when it comes." Through these efforts, members of the Institutes kept up their own morale by focussing on what life would be like when the war was finally over.

Some new branches were created during the Second World War as groups came together to contribute to the war work organized under the auspices of the FWIO. This is the organizational meeting of the Dewars WI, Renfrew South District, May 20, 1941. BACK ROW, LEFT TO RIGHT: *Mrs. E. McLean, Mrs. R. MacMillan, Mrs. A.S. Dewar, Mrs. John Jahn, Mrs. W.J. Stevenson, Mrs. Donald Dewar, Mrs. W.A. Bromley, Mrs. Crawford Dewar, Mrs. J.H. Findlay.* FRONT ROW: *Mrs. Duncan Stevenson & Ruth, Mrs. Dorothy Gain and Robin, Mrs. Angus Carswell, Zelma Cameron, Mrs. Stewart Carmichael and Carrie, Mrs. George McLeon, Mrs. Susan Dewar and K. Carmichael*

— *Dewars WI Tweedsmuir History*

Mrs. Emma M. Duke, the provincial President in 1941–1942, wrote to encourage the members to keep up the knitting and the postwar planning: "I know a good many of you, like myself, have knitting at different places in your homes where it can be picked up in the spare minutes. One by the radio, perhaps, where you may sit for your favorite programme or newscast; another handy to the table to pick up while you indulge in a second cup of tea; and another in the knitting bag ready to take out. What unseen thoughts, plans and prayers are woven into these articles we are making? We are thinking of the day when this world will be at peace. I do not mean cessation of war alone, but permanent peace. How can we insure this peace for those who follow where we leave off? This all needs serious thought."[2]

The most outstanding feature of Institute thinking during the war was the focus on internationalism. With the experience of the First World War still current in the minds of many people, the added confidence of women's reform efforts throughout the interwar years, and the emphasis on overseas links through the ACWW, Institute members were thinking on a larger scale than they had during the previous war. In particular, contacts with England were being cultivated through the celebrated visit of the royal family in 1939, the ACWW conference in London that same year, and programs such as "Pen Friends." Since the creation of the international level of the Institute organization six years before, women had established links with pen pals in other parts of the British Empire. In the 1941 Annual Report, the Superintendent reported that "there has been a steadily increasing interest on the part of Ontario Institute members in establishing and maintaining closer bonds of friendship with overseas members." The provincial office co-operated with leaders from overseas in "linking up" almost two hundred writing partners that year, so that Ontario women were corresponding with women in England, South Africa, Australia, New Zealand, Scotland, Wales and Lithuania. Such personal connections made world war very real to Women's Institute members throughout Ontario. Sally Jones, Secretary of the Kidwelly WI, in Wales, wrote, "As you hold this letter, I felt that across space and expanse I shall be clasping your hand in friendship, loyal and true, members of the British Commonwealth of Nations. Will you clasp it tightly on behalf of our little branch of the Women's Institute and the Federated Women's Institutes of Ontario?"

Women appreciated those bonds of friendship and the opportunity to learn about each other's experiences. On both sides of the ocean, homemakers were learning to adjust their household routines in light of the war restrictions. They wrote about changing their menus to include more vegetables and less meat, and stepping up their home-canning efforts while still respecting sugar rations. "We are not really short of anything," one overseas correspondent from Wykes Regis WI wrote, "(except butter — only 2 oz. of that a week per person) [and] the meat ration is not large. We all eat far more vegetables than formerly and the health of the nation is grand. We have a very large garden here . . . and grow all we can to supply some of the sailors on the ships which come into the harbour."[3] Another WI member from Britain described in some detail how food rationing had affected her, and then added, "I hope I haven't bored you with all this." Her account was certainly not boring, as Institute members throughout Ontario were eager to compare notes on these experiences, and to hear about life overseas. The member from Britain closed her letter by saying "If any of your members would care to write to me, I would be delighted."[4] Throughout the province, Institute members did keep up regular correspondence with their pen friends overseas, but the women sent more than just cheerful letters.

Make your Thinking as valuable as your Knitting.

Mary A. Clarke

Mrs. David Porter of Pembroke thought Miss Mary A. Clarke's adage so important that she organized a mass printing of these cards. WI members purchased them as they once again took up their knitting for the war effort. — AO

Throughout the war, Women's Institutes across Ontario expressed their support for fellow members in Britain by shipping several thousand pounds of vegetable seeds. The program, "Seeds for English Gardens," grew from a suggestion made by Lady Tweedsmuir. It was a practical attempt to help offset the food shortages in England, and when a formal request for seeds came from the National Federation of Women's Institutes in England, the members of the Central Fund Committee (the FWIO committee responsible for wartime fund-raising) were unanimous in favour of the idea. They took it up eagerly, hoping "to serve English Institute members, feeling that this was an opportunity for service close to the heart of every rural woman." Under this scheme, donations of money were used to ship planting supplies to the Women's Institutes throughout the United Kingdom. As *Home and Country* reported in its spring issue in 1941, "Because of the early English season, it was urgent that seeds be sent at once."[5]

Later that year, *Home and Country* proudly reported that two tons of garden seeds, valued at $1,926.76, had been shipped. The cost of packing, transportation and insurance was $206.62. To make donations such as this possible, the FWIO worked with several horticultural societies in Eastern Ontario and gratefully acknowledged their support: "The name of each organization is printed on the labels of seeds purchased with its donation. Horticultural Societies — Almonte, $10.00; Arnprior, $25.00; Manotick, $26.50; Ottawa, $25.00; Pakenham, $5.00; Renfrew, $14.50; Welland, $40; Smiths Falls, $54.81."[6] Each ton of seeds was thus described: "One thousand assortments of seeds (approximately 2,000 pounds) have been purchased and shipped, each assortment consisting of: 1/2 lb. peas; 1/2 lb. beans, climbing; 1/2 lb. beans, dwarf; 1/2 oz. carrots; and 1/2 oz. onions. Varieties chosen are suitable for English growing conditions. Small packages were chosen to facilitate distribution in England." [7]

MAY 7 1945

Norda Brows.
Burgh-by-Sands.
Carlisle.
15th April 1945

Miss Mary Clarke
Department of Agriculture,
Toronto.
Ontario,
Canada.

Dear Madam.

I am writing to thank you for the very generous gift of Canadian grown vegetable seeds I have received from you through our Women's Institute County Secretary Miss Beckton,

I will watch their growth with great interest and hope to have good results at our Vegetable Show in the Autumn,

again many thanks.

Yours faithfully

Phyllis A Graham.

In keeping with their international outlook, WI members throughout Ontario rallied together to lend practical support to their sisters in Britain. This thank-you letter reveals the personal impact of the FWIO's "Seeds for English Gardens" program. — AO

Letters of thanks from English Institutes poured in, revealing the strategies that had been used for distributing the seeds. "We have nearly 150 Institutes in our County, so that we decided that we should ballot for them," one grateful member revealed.[8] One of the fortunate winners, Mrs. E. Qualdling of Suffolk, England, wrote to express her delight at receiving the seeds. "In July [1941] our WI secretary brought along some Ontario seeds to our meeting. We drew for them and I was lucky enough to get the carrots. After taking up some early peas, I put in the carrot seed and have just had two delicious boilings of young 'spring carrots.' Many thanks! They were delicious and there are heaps more for later on."[9]

"I have waited to say thank you until I can now say that every seed must have germinated," a member from Wokingham, Berkshire, wrote. "They are growing splendidly and every visitor to this house has to walk down the garden to look at the onions from Ontario." Other letters echoed the same sentiments of gratitude, and explained the creative means by which the seeds had been distributed. The Copdock and Washbrook WI in Suffolk reported, "We divided the seed into 16 packets suitable to the size of our gardens. At our meeting these were drawn for and the 16 members who received them were quite delighted. They, and all our members, send many thanks and we appreciate this splendid token of the unity of the Empire and this instance of the Women's Institute spirit." Letters of gratitude flooded into the provincial office of the FWIO, and the English members made reference to the international links that were being established. "We hope these will prove [to be] 'seeds of friendship' which will still be thriving when this struggle is ended," one woman said. Another revealed her thoughts about peace saying "Once again, may we thank you not only for the gift but also for the kind thought which prompted it. We hope that when the war is over we shall be able to entertain some of your members over here and show them by more than mere words how grateful we are. It is our earnest hope that the united influence of all WI members throughout the world may help to play a large part in making future wars impossible."[10]

"We are very, very grateful to you all and thank you from the bottom of our hearts for all your thoughts for and kindness to us," the West Kent Federation of Women's Institutes of England wrote in November 1941. "At the meeting of the Half Yearly Council of the Federation, a most hearty vote of thanks was carried with acclamation to our very kind friends in the FWIO for all the beautiful packets of vegetable seeds which have been sent to us. Several speakers expressed hope that we would some day be able to repay Canada and America, and that an even greater bond of friendship will unite our countries. In spite of a very bad year for some crops, the Canadian seeds did remarkably well."[11]

The seed program continued throughout the war, and in the fall of 1942, *Home and Country* reported that the target for contributions that year was raised to $3,000. "We have received lists of seeds which they prefer, and which do best in their soil and climate, and hence we feel the requisite seeds are reaching them. Orders have been placed for 4,550 assortments each including the following seeds in quantities suitable for a home garden: — bean, carrot, onion, leek, cauliflower, tomato, beet, spinach or lettuce, turnip, cabbage. The seeds will be packed in cartons of 50 assortments so that they will not have to be repacked for distribution in England."[12]

Wartime conditions meant that the seeds were sincerely appreciated because food shortages and rationing in Britain were forcing people to adopt some new lifestyles. "Wartime diet necessitates that some of our meals shall be mostly vegetarian so here again we shall think with deep appreciation of your generous gift, and with admiration of the efforts of our sailors in bringing them to us."[13] As well, the exigencies of wartime transportation meant that the parcels' safe arrival could never be guaranteed. In the summer of 1944, there was some concern about whether the shipments of Ontario seeds had actually arrived at their intended destination. "After some anxiety about whether the last shipment of seeds had escaped the submarines, we were happy to hear that all arrived safely."[14] Providing the seeds was a tangible expression of support that gave the Ontario WI a vicarious presence overseas, as "letter after letter tell us that our Canadian seeds are growing everywhere in England." It was a clever scheme that gave support both emotionally and practically because the harvests were "enjoyed in English homes, exhibited at vegetable shows and fairs, canned for winter, sold to raise money for war work or saved for seed."[15]

Seeds were not the only commodity that the Ontario WIs shipped overseas. There were large transatlantic shipments also organized under provincial auspices; many of them centred on Ontario sharing her agricultural products. The FWIO used the pages of *Home and Country* to call for participation, reporting that "recently a request has come from the Navy League for maple sugar for the men on the high seas whose need for energy is so great. This request has been forwarded to every Institute in Lanark, Leeds, Grenville, Frontenac, and Parry Sound districts and to a few other Institutes in other counties where the maple sugar industry is commercially important. If Institutes in other parts of the Province are in a position to secure maple sugar locally they should write the Women's Institute Branch, Department of Agriculture, Parliament Buildings, Toronto, for further particulars. The maple sugar should not be sent to the Department. Maple sugar would also make an excellent gift for members of the Scottish Rural Women's Institutes, who visited us two years ago. Should you desire to send maple sugar to Scotland, please write the Women's Institute Branch for particulars and addresses."[16] Institute branches eagerly took up this project and by the summer of 1941, an estimated 1,875 pounds of maple sugar had been shipped to the Navy, in "cakes of about four ounces each. . . . May I tell you of one letter received from a sailor who said he was so pleased to receive his cake of maple sugar, and such treats were so scarce in England, that he was preserving his cake for his wife and little family at home."[17] WI members were pleased to hear these stories of gratitude and personal appreciation. Such tales spurred the members on to even greater things.

In addition to the maple sugar and the seeds, jam production became a third key project, and one of the earliest forms of work that the FWIO took on. In the fall of 1941, this enterprise was already in its third year. It began in Norfolk County in 1939, when Women's Institute members decided to "put into practice the idea of utilizing home grown fruits for jam for evacuated British children and adults, or for Canadian troops in hospitals overseas. Ten thousand pounds were shipped that fall. In 1940, the jam-making enterprise, carried on co-operatively by the Women's Institutes of Ontario and the Ontario Division, Canadian Red Cross Society, was so successful that approximately one hundred and ten thousand pounds were shipped to the Canadian

Red Cross Warehouse in England and to Lady Reading's Committee for Civilians. It all arrived safely."

Again the women were assured that their donations were having a significant impact thousands of miles away. "I thought perhaps that you might like to know how we were using the jam which you were kind enough to send to us," one letter began. "In Exeter, we have a Hostel for aged refugees from a blitzed city — the baby of the party is sixty-eight and the eldest ninety-five, I think — and our canteen workers go in every day to help them get to bed and to listen to all their troubles and lend a hand generally. They found that the old people were suffering from shock in many cases and thought that an extra sugar ration might help in restoring their vitality. So they applied to us and we gave them a case of your raspberry jam. Unless you have seen them, I don't think you would ever realize how much pleasure this gave them. It was not only the actual jam, but the psychological effect of knowing that you in Canada were taking a personal interest in them, and showing your interest in such a very kind and practical way. Will you please accept our very grateful thanks."[18]

The goal for 1941–1942 for all of the Institutes across Canada was 300,000 pounds of jam, and 150,000 to 200,000 pounds of it were to come from Ontario. This kind of work was particularly suited to areas of fruit production such as Ontario's Niagara region, where the co-operation of commercial producers made the task easier and most efficient. WI members appealed to the owners of canning factories who "have given their time, labour and supervision" to jam production for England. Commercial producers were not the only ones who lent support to the jam project. The Canadian Red Cross helped with the packaging, supplying "the four-pound cans, labels, packing cases and free transportation of the cans to a central Red Cross branch, as well as transportation of the filled cans to the Canadian Red Cross Warehouse overseas."[19]

A second strategy was the use of "home or community kitchens by groups of women under local supervision using pure jam recipes. Strawberry, raspberry, currant, gooseberry, grape, peach, pear, plum and apricot jams and apple jelly all have been made." Community kitchens meant that women improvised to make the best use of existing facilities. For example, one WI branch found that "the Institute was already in possession of a kitchen, a coal stove and a coal-oil stove, all at the rink, where hot dogs and coffee are dispensed to hungry skaters in winter. It did not look very convenient at first but proved amazingly so."[20] The notion of making do with existing facilities and using up surplus fruits was closely linked to the Institutes' educational agenda. The so-called pure jam recipes ensured that women at home were well-informed about the latest technical and nutritional considerations in making jam. Using up surplus fruits and meeting together to make the jam were logical extensions of WI war work and practical ways for Ontario women to demonstrate concern for their overseas sisters.

Participation was obviously highest in the fruit-producing regions of the province, but WI members in other parts of the province were not excluded from contributing. As the account in *Home and Country* revealed, "where fruit is not plentiful, cans have been filled with honey." Still other districts contributed by purchasing sugar to be used in jam production. With the rationing that was imposed for the duration of the war, sugar was both scarce and expensive. At the FWIO executive meeting in 1941, "It was recommended that a sugar and fruit fund be established to which Institutes in localities where fruit is not in abundance may contribute." Encouraged to send their cash, the branches eagerly complied. "Contributions to date [to the sugar fund] amount to $1,058.80 of which $624.40 has already gone to Institutes making jam."[21]

Although British WI members were grateful for Ontario's gifts, they were eager to participate in jam production schemes of their own. Mrs. E. Qualdling of Suffolk, England, wrote to the FWIO in October 1941 with a full report of the British efforts. "They also made me secy.-treas. [sic] of the fruit preservation scheme and what a time we've had collecting jars, sterilizing them, buying fruit, rounding up workers and making jam! We had just used about 6 cwt. of sugar and made 1,078 lbs. of jam, as well as 257 lbs. of pickles and some bottled fruit. We have a W.I. Hut with a rather antiquated valor stove. We had to borrow the preserving pans from the members. The water has all to be pumped up at the Village Pump and carted half a mile — the village has neither a water supply nor artificial light. Then, owing to the weather, there was dearth of fruit. Nature relented when the blackberries came along and we had a special day holiday to pick, and how many do you thing [sic] we got? 2 cwt. 1 1/s lbs.! The very sad part of this jam making scheme is that we can't even buy one pound of the jam for ourselves. After making over 1,000 lbs., each person can have only her ration through her grocer."[22]

WI donations were not only devoted to shipping Ontario jam overseas; they also were used to purchase canning equipment for the use of the British WI branches. Kent County District Women's Institutes in Southwestern Ontario sent the first equipment, and later this picture of an exhibit of British canning appeared in Home and Country *in the fall of 1942.*

— *Home and Country*, fall 1942

Direct support for that move toward independent British production came from the Ontario Women's Institutes when they helped to supply canning equipment to the British Institutes. In the summer of 1942, the FWIO decided to use money from the Central Charities Fund to send eleven tin-can sealing machines to England. This was a move that followed the example of the WIs of Kent County in Southwestern Ontario, who sent equipment the year before. The canning machines would be put to good use by people such as Mrs. Qualding and her team of jam-makers as they geared up for production after they were "asked by the Government to be responsible for the preservation of fruit."[23] Providing food for overseas was an extension of the work that women were learning to do for their own homes here. Enabling women in Britain to provide for themselves by supplying them with canning equipment was an ideal way for Ontario's Institute members to act out their commitment to supporting their overseas sisters.

Of course it was not only the women who were helped through the wartime efforts of the Ontario WI. Service personnel were not forgotten. The production of comfort boxes for soldiers was again a big part of the war effort, either for local enlistees, or those who were adopted through more formal arrangements. At the Wabis Valley WI in Temiskaming, the minute book records that in 1940 the members each brought one article to make up a box for their adopted soldier, Private E. Beck. Two women were appointed to pack and ship the box.

To standardize the production of handmade goods, the Red Cross distributed these pattern books.
— Mlle Florence LeClerc

Another branch sent knitted socks to the soldiers they were sponsoring at Camp Borden, but as they prepared their parcels for shipping, they took the opportunity to play Santa Claus. "Each stocking was filled with handkerchiefs, nuts, candy, gum, cigarets, and all nicely wrapped." The contents of the parcels were carefully monitored, as one Institute learned much to their chagrin. The Milberta WI recorded in their minute book of November 1942, "A special meeting of the M.W.I. was held at the home of Mrs. McDonald to pack Christmas boxes, going to the boys now Overseas. 8 boxes were packed, among the articles enclosed were waxed oranges, therefore the boxes were stopped at the local Post Office, and Mrs. E. Jibb and Mrs. McDonald had the dubious pleasure of opening them all & extracting the offending forbidden fruit." The boxes eventually arrived at their destination, and at the January meeting, "thanks were read and other messages were delivered by the Mothers present from grateful boys who received our gifts of remembrances at Christmas time."

That kind of goodwill was particularly appreciated. A thank-you letter from Private Martin F. (Chub), who was stationed in England at Christmastime in 1940, is preserved in the *Oakland WI Tweedsmuir History* book. "I received your most welcome Xmas box today and wish to thank you for all your fine Xmas spirit," he wrote. "I am going to wait until Xmas day to open my box as it will help make it a little more cheerful. I noticed the label [of contents] on the box and everything is just what a soldier appreciates. It is nice to know that friends back home haven't forgotten me and especially at this time of year. I wish your Institute every success in the coming year." The Stanley Park Women's Institute in Thunder Bay District received a similar letter early in 1941 from Private Roy Coppin, who was stationed at Camp Borden. "Received your parcel on New Year's and was very pleased to get it. May I take this opportunity to thank your Institute for the gifts. It helps a lot to feel the ones at home are thinking of us. May your Institute enjoy 1941 and again thanking one and all."[24]

Members of the Junior Women's Institutes throughout the province also got in on the act, sewing clothes for children in Britain. One-month clothing classes were held, and Homemaking clubs and Junior Institutes were encouraged to put their new skills to good use. "Bolts of rose, green and brown spun-rayon material have been cut into skirts and bloomers for six, eight and ten-year old girls by clothing classes and senior homemaking clubs," one report pointed out. And some of the junior chapters decided to begin a fund to purchase wool for sweaters. "The Brooklin Juniors in Ontario County could not think of all these club skirts without sweaters, so started this fund and offered to knit some sweaters. With other junior institutes making similar offers, it is evident that there will be Junior Institute sweaters for the Homemaking Club skirts. Applications to date indicate that over 100 bloomers, skirts and sweaters will be completed during April through the co-operative efforts of these willing juniors. The garments will be handed over to the Red Cross for shipment to Britain."[25]

Youthful enthusiasm was put to good use in a variety of ways. One woman recalled her role in assisting her mother's friends with their wartime quilting. "In the war years, my parents owned a store in a small village, so it was a good source for information and public relations for the Women's Institute. My mother seemed to always have a quilt in the frame, and many times it was a W.I. war quilt, hence women off the street dropped in while at the store and sat and quilted while time allowed. Plus the quilting bees! and the chatter! and as young girls we were asked to keep the needles threaded and helping with the rolling."[26]

Institute branches devoted a great deal of their time to war work, and their meetings were often conducted knitting needles in hand, or sitting around the quilting frame. These five women stitch on a pieced quilt, an item that might either be donated to the Red Cross or raffled to raise funds. — UG, FWIO Collection

Branch records reveal that the rate of quilting justified the creation of a corps of girls just for threading the needles. Working at an astonishing rate, it was not unusual for a WI branch to complete at least one quilt every time they met, and sometimes they managed to complete up to three quilts at a time. Although some of these may have been simple tied quilts and smaller crib quilts, others were obviously much more elaborate. Pieced quilts were most common, and the Wabis Valley branch sent each member home from the January 1941 meeting with very specific instructions. "It was decided to make a quilt, each member to make 3 squares composed of 25 blocks each 3 [inches] square before sewing. These to be sent to Mrs. Poupore as soon as possible for assembling. The next meeting will be a quilting bee on February 12th at Mrs. Bradley's home."[27] Sometimes the quilts were donated directly to the Red Cross, but they were often sold as fundraisers.

The Second World War was clearly a time when the Institutes were preoccupied with making money. There were two main ways in which the Institutes contributed funds to the war effort. The first was through the Central War Charities Fund, an account administered by the FWIO that was used to sponsor projects such as the seed program and the jam production. The second was through local efforts and individual branch contributions to other wartime agencies.

The creation of the FWIO's Central War Charities Fund was a major departure from the practices of the First World War, when branches simply contributed to other groups' coffers. The fiscal responsibility and administrative independence of the provincial

The members of No. 9 Mosa WI display their handiwork in this pieced quilt that they completed in 1941. — *No. 9 Mosa Women's Institute Tweedsmuir History*

WI organization in the 1940s is evident in the detailed records they kept. Whereas in the First World War the WIs' efforts were all channelled through the Red Cross, and only estimates of production and donations could be made, this time there was much more careful account-keeping. *Home and Country* published these records and urged the branches that had not yet reported to be part of the grand total. The efforts were very impressive indeed.

The Central War Charities Fund began in January 1940 with an appeal from the provincial office for each WI member in Ontario to contribute five cents toward the cause. That initial appeal was accompanied with an explanation of the three uses to which the money might be put: (1) to assist Institutes in outlying districts, or those unable to raise funds locally, by supplying them with wool or other material for war work; (2) to contribute gifts of money or equipment to meet bona fide appeals; and (3) to provide a reserve fund that would be quickly available in the event of emergency or disaster. At the time of the appeal, the province boasted a membership of approximately 40,000 women, and at five cents each, this campaign should have netted at least $2,000. In fact the results were more modest than that, with just over half of the members participating. In the first three months of 1940 they raised $1,147.38 by this means. It was a good start for the new fund, and future contributions would average close to $9,000 per year until the fund was officially closed in the spring of 1946. In all, more than $50,000 was collected in the Central War Charities Fund.

CENTRAL WAR CHARITIES FUND

Jan. 1940–Mar. 31, 1940	$1,147.38
Apr. 1940–Mar. 31, 1941	8,581.09
Apr. 1941–Dec. 31, 1941	7,445.90
Jan. 1942–Dec. 31, 1942	11,122.89
Jan. 1943–Dec. 31, 1943	8,952.33
Jan. 1944–Dec. 31, 1944	6,079.83
Jan. 1945–Dec. 31, 1945	8,607.77
TOTAL	$51,937.77

LOCAL LEVEL CONTRIBUTIONS

	Total Money Raised
up to Mar. 31, 1941	>$40,000.00
Apr. 1941– Mar 1942	124,069.49
Apr. 1942– Mar. 1943	123,294.57
Jan. 1943– Dec. 1943	176,935.58
Jan. 1944– Dec. 1944	156,400.38
up to Oct. 1945	40,653.94
TOTAL	$661,353.96

— Compiled by the author from Annual Reports

While the fundraising for the Central Fund was impressive, it was only a small portion of the total monies that the Women's Institutes of Ontario actually raised. The annual reports called for careful records to be kept of the work done at the local level, and the results are astonishing.

Amounting to more than $650,000, the money raised at the local level was well over twelve times that collected by the FWIO's Central War Charities Fund! The local branches were obviously very effective at raising money, and they were determined to maintain control over how that money was used. Rather than donate the total amount to the central fund administered from Toronto, members decided that the funds could be put to good use in a variety of ways at the local branch level. Most of the branches contributed at least some of their money directly to other organizations, chiefly the Red Cross.

Significant local funds were also spent in purchasing the supplies for the boxes they packed for enlisted personnel. Over $150,000 was spent in that way during the period from 1942 to 1945. Another $160,000 was donated to war charities other than the FWIO Central Fund or the Red Cross. More than $25,000 was invested in war bonds and certificates, which the groups purchased as acts of patriotism and also as good financial management.

In addition, members used the money to buy the supplies needed to make knitted and sewn garments that they then donated to the war effort. A careful record of Institute members' handiwork was maintained.

The Middlesex District Women's Institutes combined their resources in 1943 and purchased a mobile canteen which was donated to the Department of Civil Defence for Canada. This local initiative prompted the FWIO to purchase a second mobile canteen with monies from the Central War Charities Fund. In this picture, Miss Jean McLachlan presents the key to Mr. Donald Murie of the Department of Civil Defence. — UG, FWIO Collection; *Home and Country*, fall 1943

Two main types of articles were recorded: knitted items including socks, balaclavas and sweaters; and sewn articles including shirts, pyjamas and bandages. The charts at right record the quantity of the articles, although their monetary value is difficult to calculate.

Institute members in Ontario created almost one million (917,369) handcrafted articles over the course of the war. Although a concerted effort was made to track the contributions of the branches at the local level, these statistics do not represent a full report. Compilers of the FWIO annual reports continually urged local branches to co-operate by submitting full reports to make the statistics more complete, but despite those efforts, there was never a 100 percent rate of return. The statistics in the 1944 Annual Report, for example, represent only about 80 percent of the total number of branches in the province. The actual accomplishments may well have been up to 20 percent higher than these statistics reveal. It is no wonder then that government officials were thrilled to receive the FWIO President's offer of assistance for the war effort.

HANDMADE GOODS

	Knitted	*Sewed*
up to Mar. 1941	76,577	61,910
Apr. 1941–Mar. 1942	126,807	104,300
Apr. 1942–Mar. 1943	102,639	101,759
Jan. 1943–Dec. 1943	73,851	134,238
Jan. 1944–Dec. 1944	57,244	42,754
Jan. 1945–Oct. 1945	15,022	20,268
TOTALS	452,140	465,229

— Compiled by the author from Annual Reports

Not every aspect of the Institutes' wartime story was positive, however. In organizational terms, the Institutes were at a very low ebb in 1945. Membership had fallen by 10,000 members since 1939, approximately a 25 percent drop. The number of branches had also decreased by almost 150, falling from 1,391 branches in 1940 to 1,248 five years later. Also, in 1945 the contributions to the Central Charities Fund reached their lowest levels for the entire war. The provincial superintendent, Miss Clarke, resigned at the spring board meeting in April 1945, forcing the organization to seek a new person to fill the role of liaison between the FWIO and the Department of Agriculture.

DECLINING MEMBERSHIP

	Members	Branches
March 1939	42,100	1,374
March 1940	40,300	1,391
March 1941	40,200	1,367
March 1942	38,000	1,333
March 1943	36,700	1,294
March 1944	34,000	1,257
March 1945	32,000	1,248

— Compiled by the author from Annual Reports

There are several explanations for this discouraging outlook, and it is important to understand that the statistical realities of 1945 were not a sudden turn of events, but rather a result of a five-year trend. The number of members who did not renew their memberships and the number of branches that were disbanding had been increasing steadily from 1940 to 1945.

In her annual report for 1942, the provincial Superintendent was pressed to try to explain why so many branches had disbanded during the previous year. Between 1940 and 1941, the total number of branches dropped from 1,391 to 1,367, but that final total was bolstered by the creation of a few new branches. In fact, forty-two branches had disbanded in just twelve months. It was the first time in the history of the Ontario WI that a negative growth trend was noted, and Miss Clarke offered a twofold explanation. "Of the Institutes disbanded," she explained, "50 per cent were Junior Institutes which found it impossible to continue because of the number of young women leaving the communities." Evidently, the need for women to work in war production was taking its toll on the membership of the Junior Women's Institutes as patriotism and good wages drew these women away from their rural communities and into urban factory work. The fact that so many senior Women's Institutes also disbanded was explained by the fact that women were anxious "to devote all their energies to war work." For some of them, that meant that the formalities of submitting reports to the FWIO and the effort they normally gave to their organizational commitments took a lower priority than making an all-out attempt at supporting the war effort.

Institutes that did continue to function often set aside their regular business in order to deal with the more urgent need of war production. As the minute book of the Milberta WI in Northern Ontario reported, at the August meeting in 1940, "the program for the day was given over to Red Cross work and all other business suspended. A quilt was quilted also a crib quilt completed." The following year, the same branch continued to concentrate on its war work, and regular WI business was only a secondary concern. "As the members arrived [at the March 26, 1941 meeting], work was immediately commenced on the Red Cross quilt, and during the quilting several items of business were discussed."

Many Institute members throughout Ontario were actively engaged in agricultural production, and during the war, their participation in farming operations was more direct. The leisure time they might otherwise have spent in Institute work no longer existed as their time was taken up with farm work. The contributions that women were making to Ontario's farms during the war was acknowledged, though it was hard to measure. As the FWIO prided itself on the statistical record of the contribution its members were

The popularity of Girls' Conferences in Guelph led to similar events in other areas of the province. Young women from Eastern Ontario gathered at the Kemptville Agricultural College in 1940. They were taught from the curriculum "The Club Girl Stands On Guard," a wartime unit specifically designed for Junior Institute members.

— UG, FWIO Collection

making in fundraising, food preservation, knitting, sewing and special war projects, there was a regret that no system existed for recording the contribution of WI women to the agricultural production of the province. In 1942 a special campaign was launched to "recognize the splendid contribution of labour made by those girls working on their home farms by registering them with the Ontario Farm Service Force." The following year, the Annual Report of the Institutes proudly declared that approximately 1,000 girls had received special "Certificates of Merit" to acknowledge their agricultural work, and in 1944, 825 others were similarly recognized. The FWIO president, Mrs. Ernest Duke, also acknowledged these farm women's contributions, and in her travels to the district annual meetings she congratulated Institute members who were farmers on "helping to raise food which was essential in helping to win the war." She treated this contribution as parallel to those of "women in towns and cities [who] did sewing and knitting for the Red Cross work."[28]

There were therefore at least three different explanations for why the membership was falling and why branches were unable to carry on with their regular affiliation as Institutes. Each explanation had to do with some kind of war work — young women were moving out of the rural areas to work in factories; regular members were taking up work on volunteer projects to the exclusion of regular Institute business; and farm women's work in agricultural production left them with little time for organizational life. These trends meant that WI members across Ontario were preoccupied with war work, and as a result their formal participation in Institute work dropped.

Even if members had not been otherwise occupied during the war, the Institutes' Co-operative Education Program was offering far less to hold their interest. The ever-popular short courses, which had always been an important means of attracting new members and holding the interest and loyalty of existing members, were curtailed during the war years. The educational programs that were offered were directly related to war projects. The 1941 Annual Report, for example, revealed that "22 one-half day courses in Emergency Knitting were held," in which "406 young women received instruction." The unit for juniors, entitled "The Club Girl Stands on Guard," was introduced in 1940–1941. However, the variety and scope of programming that Miss McDermand had introduced during the years before the war could not be sustained. When she took office in 1938, Mary Clarke was simply not able to match the offerings of her predecessor, and if she took the job thinking she would continue in McDermand's steps, the exigencies of war proved her wrong. It would be unfair to fault Clarke personally for the limited curriculum; she was severely limited by the context of the war.

Educational opportunities were not the only casualty of the war. The Institutes were also ordered to cancel their annual area conventions because of restrictions on travel and gas rationing. In 1945, Clarke explained that "because of Wartime Prices and Trade Board Rulings it was necessary to cancel area conventions, with the exception of one convention which had an attendance of 137. Eleven convention committee meetings were held with an attendance of 271." This was a severe blow to the organization, since the annual roster of area conventions was a highlight of Institute activity. Attendances of 137 and 271 were a far cry from the numbers recorded in the fall of 1944, when thirteen conventions were held with an attendance of more than ten times that number.[29] The restrictions of the Wartime Prices and Trade Board were both a symptom and a cause of the declining membership. Without annual events such as the conventions, it was difficult to sustain existing membership levels, boost membership morale or attract new members.

At the end of the war, people throughout Canada welcomed the end of those restrictions, but for members of the Women's Institutes, there was even more to celebrate. With the end of the war, the Women's Institutes of Ontario could concentrate their energy on concerns that were more central to their own organization. The loss of membership, curtailment of curriculum, and cancellation of annual functions were all behind them as they entered the prosperous postwar years. On the brink of that postwar promise, however, it was time for the organization to look back. An important anniversary celebration of the founding of their organization was close at hand. Reaching the fiftieth anniversary of their founding, the Institutes were reminded in the years just before 1947 that they had a long legacy to celebrate. Many special events and initiatives marked that momentous occasion, but two are particularly noteworthy: the official launch of the Tweedsmuir history books, and the anniversary celebrations at Guelph.

The Tweedsmuir history books are familiar to most people who have even a fleeting knowledge of the WI movement because of the important role these books play as chronicles of local history. The books, which vary in form from a simple scrapbook to a more elaborate series of volumes bound in leather, wood or the formal blue-and-gold cover, contain a wealth of information about the local communities they represent. Sometimes they take a whole township as their scope. Others focus more closely on a village or particular settlement area. What is not widely known, however, is that the Tweedsmuir books were actually launched as an anniversary project to mark the occasion of the fiftieth birthday of the movement.

Lady Tweedsmuir, who had recently been widowed, was delighted to approve the idea that the local history books should be named for her late husband, the former governor general of Canada. She had suggested that Ontario's Women's Institutes should keep local history books as the WIs in England did. The idea of documenting local history was a fitting project to mark the fiftieth anniversary celebrations, and so in 1945 a campaign was launched to encourage every WI branch in Ontario to prepare a volume of history about their community before the celebrations of 1947 took place.[30] The books would include a history of the local WI branch, but they would not be limited to that. In addition, they were to include a history of the earliest settlers in the area, the agricultural practices and industries that formed the basis of the local economy, the social institutions such as churches, schools and community centres, and local personalities including the local war veterans. With that outline, and the suggestion that each volume should acknowledge the roots of the WI movement traced to Adelaide Hoodless, the idea of local history writing was promoted. It proved to be a very popular project, and within ten years, a report to the provincial Board pointed out that 989 branches were compiling Tweedsmuir history books.

The name of the books, "Tweedsmuir Histories," was new, but the idea of WI members writing history was not. The Women's Institutes had actually been part of the process of writing local history for at least twenty years already. In 1925 a special standing committee of the FWIO was formed, to be known as the Committee for Historical Research and Current Events. The Annual Report of 1927 described the work of the committee: "[I]n some some counties, they have already undertaken to compile a history of the whole county and in many Institutes a beginning has been made on local history, including individual farms, industries, public buildings, etc. A record is being made of the first farms, industries, public buildings, etc. A record is being made of the first settlers, their methods of living and their accomplishments, the history of the first schools and the first church in the district is being recorded. The committee suggests that a little more time be given to the study of local history, and thus gain a greater insight into the lives and thoughts of our ancestors in this country. They are proceeding on the belief that every community has a history which should be preserved."[31]

The history books were only a prelude to the celebration of the anniversary itself. The official celebration party was held on the grounds of the Ontario Agricultural College at Guelph, on June 18, 1947. By all accounts, it was a grand occasion. Anticipating an attendance of 6,000 women, the organizers were hard pressed to accommodate the 12,000 who actually showed up on that day. Thousands of women thronged the grounds, and accommodating all of them proved to be a remarkable feat in and of itself. One in every three members was present on that occasion. It was a day when history was made, not just celebrated.

The visitors were treated to a historical pageant entitled "Let There Be Light," which depicted the history of the Institute movement in several acts. The play, filmed for the National Film Board of Canada, depicted a highly romanticized version of the history of the movement, in which Adelaide Hoodless figured prominently as an "angel of light," and the Institutes themselves were the salvation of countless numbers of rural women

The fiftieth anniversary celebrations were an unprecedented success. Organizers expected approximately 6,000 members to attend, but close to 12,000 women crowded the campus of the Ontario Agricultural College at Guelph. "Hundreds of parties settled down on the campus to eat lunch in picnic style," stretching the resources of the campus food services. The commissariat "worked wonders, because after preparing tea-hour bags of sandwiches and urns of coffee for some 5,000 people, they had to go into action and raise the count to 9,500." The highlight of the celebration was the performance of "Let There Be Light," a pageant especially commissioned for the day. This piece chronicled the movement's history, impressing the legacy of Adelaide Hoodless upon the hearts of the audience.

— UG, FWIO collection; *Home and Country*, summer 1947

who, like Hoodless herself, were delivered from their grief, ignorance and isolation through the vehicle of the groups. This account immortalized the grieving Hoodless, celebrated the throngs of women who had since taken up the cause, and firmly fixed Stoney Creek as a site worthy of pilgrimage. The pageant included a huge cast of actors who dressed as historical figures, heavenly visitors and exotic international characters to depict the origins, importance and scope of the movement over the previous fifty years. It was intended to paint a grandiose picture, and the effect was certainly achieved. The romantic picture of the movement's origins and resultant influence were indelibly impressed upon the audience that day. It was a version of the history that painted the characters at the helm of the WI as larger than life, and it was a version of the history that still dominates the perception of the thousands who attended and enjoyed the day.

In a very real sense, the anniversary celebrations were part of the rising crescendo of attention and celebration that surrounded the Institutes in the early postwar period. Although they did not know it, that building mood was appropriate, because the postwar years did represent the height of the Institutes' greatness, at least from a statistical point of view. Within the next five years, all traces of the slump of wartime fatigue were gone, and the Institutes enjoyed their "glory days" with their highest-ever membership figures and number of branches. The postwar years were very good times for Ontario at large and for the Women's Institutes in particular.

River Road WI members and their families sit down to enjoy their anniversary meal in 1947. Such special events were highlights in the lives of countless communities throughout Ontario. — *River Road WI Tweedsmuir History*

CHAPTER SEVEN

Belonging and Community: Postwar Branch Activity 1947–1966

Belong to the W.I.? Well I guess so! I first attended in my baby basket. My friends and I were always welcome to go to the W.I. meeting and perform whether it be a piano solo, or a singing duet or a chorus from the school. The lunch was always good too, as I remember!"[1] Helen Redman, who is now a member of Scugog Island WI in Ontario County, continued the story of her involvement by explaining her long Institute pedigree. Her grandmother had been a charter member of a WI branch, and her mother joined a branch in Hastings County as soon as she was married. When Helen married a farmer and moved to Scugog Island, it only seemed natural that she would join the new WI branch when it was formed. "So that is how I became a member, mainly I guess because there was WI always in my background." Countless other women recall that they were drawn into the local WI branch by their mothers, mothers-in-law, sisters or enthusiastic neighbours.[2] During the postwar years, women flocked in droves to local Institute meetings throughout Ontario. Membership had never been so popular. In 1950, a report to the provincial board boasted proudly that "in less than three years our membership shows a gain of 10,000 members."[3]

After the war, women were eager to settle into new routines of family life and community activity, and for women in more than 1,500 locations across the province, those new routines included the monthly Institute meeting. With the baby boom in full swing, Helen Redman's experience of attending her first meeting in a baby basket was no exception. The Institute provided a forum for women of all ages to meet and to mingle. In the process, long-standing women's networks were created and the WI became the main community organization where the local women could come together for support and social exchange. "As most of our members were young we held a number of baby showers," Dorothy Walton recalled of her branch in Temiskaming Centre District. "It was the custom to have a shower at the meeting the month after the baby's arrival. Sometimes there was two showers at once and twice we had showers for twins. If a community member didn't belong to the WI we still held a baby shower for her." Postwar marriages were celebrated and new brides were showered with gifts. Walton continued, recollecting, "I received a table cloth in 1953 which cost $2.00 (from the records) a pair of towels for another bride cost $2.25 in 1955. During and after the 1960s we gave wedding showers for all brides in the community which included the boys' brides." That kind of support continued for decades. When the children of that baby boom grew up and got married, they received the same treatment that their mothers had. "In the 1970s and 1980s we gave bridal showers for the babies we had showers for in the 1950s and 1960s."[4]

Institute activity and influence spread beyond the women themselves to include all the members of the family. Sometimes the monthly meeting spontaneously became the nucleus of a bigger social event. In 1953, for example, the Milberta WI minutes reveal that "the meeting was carried on while the men played cards and

Named for one of the early Institute organizers, the Laura Rose WI in Waterloo County was honoured to host Mrs. Laura Rose Stephen at a meeting in 1949. The guest of honour is seated in the centre of the couch. — *Laura Rose WI Tweedsmuir History*

After the intensity of the war work, Institute members welcomed the chance to concentrate on their own needs and branch activities. Social events such as this evening of music with the Goshen WI fostered warm relationships between women of all ages. — UG, FWIO Collection, *Home and Country*, fall 1957, *Ottawa Evening Journal* photo the children played among themselves."[5] Most often though, community socials were the result of long planning sessions and hard work. The Hunta WI in Northern Ontario made plans to mark Labour Day in 1954 by hosting a community picnic. Instructions were laid out in the minute book: "Everyone to bring a basket lunch, and Mrs. Shier to see to getting chocolate bars, freshie and sugar for same. Events to be held in the School Grounds and lunch in Hall. Two o'clock to be starting time."[6] That kind of casual potluck event was still relatively easy to plan. Formal community banquets involved more elaborate plans, with tables crowded into the community hall or the local school. Institute events were an occasion for visiting with the neighbours and marking important occasions. Whether it was the commemoration of an Institute anniversary or the celebration of another significant event in the life of the community, the Institute women were invariably there behind the scenes. The Kenora District minute book referred to the WI as "the spark plug" of the community because they were such a source of energetic leadership.[7]

Catering continued to be an important source of income for local Institutes, but often more was going on in the kitchen than just food preparation. Relationships were forged and memories were made. Preparing to serve a noon meal in the I.O.O.F. hall in the winter of 1947, Ilderton WI members Violet Hall, Hope Hughes, Gladys Coverhill, and Florence McNair were in for a surprise. The women were hard at work when the hall caught on fire. Undaunted, they quickly moved to the Ilderton United Church and served the meal while the hall burned to the ground.

— Ilderton WI Tweedsmuir History

By catering to community banquets, branches provided a service to the community and usually made a good profit. Renowned for their culinary skill and unparalleled in their organizational life, Institutes throughout Ontario became the caterers of choice for wedding receptions, card parties, dances, and the meetings of other service clubs. In St. George, Ontario, the tradition of catering to the Lions Club continues, as it does in many villages and communities throughout Ontario, where the WI prepares the monthly meal. Yet for many WI members, women who have carved more turkeys and served more pies than they can even remember, there is more to catering than preparing food or making money. In the winter of 1947, while they were preparing to serve a noon meal in the I.O.O.F. hall, Ilderton WI members had an experience they have never forgotten. The women were hard at work when the hall caught on fire. Undaunted, they quickly moved to the Ilderton United Church and served the meal while the hall burned to the ground.[8]

The experience of several Waterloo County Institutes at the 1954 International Plowing Match was another particularly memorable one. The match that year was held near Breslau, and the WI realized a profit of about $600. What the members have never forgotten, however, is "how grateful they were to arrive home safely after Hurricane Hazel struck." Dinner was served in Kitchener Memorial Auditorium at the conclusion of the match and gifts of blankets were distributed to hurricane victims.[9] Working together on co-operative projects sometimes meant coping with extremely unusual conditions, but usually things proceeded uneventfully under more ordinary circumstances. For the women at Ilderton and Breslau, and thousands of other Institute members like them, catering meant that relationships were forged and memories were made because of their branch activities.

What is the Women's Institute?

This is an organization of rural women from farms, villages and towns. It is non-sectarian, non-partisan and non-racial.

What is its aim?

Our aim is to develop a more abundant life for the rural people of Ontario by

(1) developing better homemakers

(2) developing happier and more useful citizens

(3) stimulating and training leaders

(4) encouraging appreciation of the things near at hand.

How do you become a member?

By attending the nearest branch Institute paying the annual fee and taking an interest in Institute activities.

How does the Women's Institute function?

All Women's Institutes in Ontario are federated to form the Federated Women's Institutes of Ontario (F.W.I.O.).

The diagram on pages 3 and 4 illustrates the relationship between the branch Institute, the district, the convention area and the Federated Women's Institutes of Ontario.

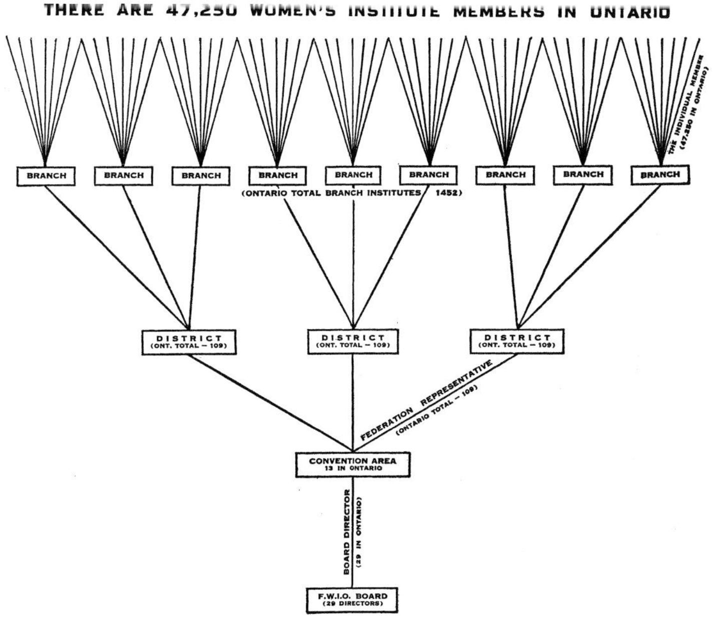

Committed to the idea that the local branch was the most important element of the WI structure, Anna Lewis created a promotional brochure containing this diagram. Note that the power flowed from the local branches down to the provincial Board; a reversal of classic organizational structure. The text of the brochure emphasized the grass-roots nature of the movement.

— FWIO Federated Women's Institutes of Ontario brochure, submitted by Rockley WI

Anna Lewis, the Superintendent of the Women's Institutes from 1945 to 1955, recognized how important the branch experiences were. Miss Lewis was well-qualified for her role as superintendent because not only was she a trained home economist, she was also the daughter of an Institute member. Coming from an Institute family herself, Anna understood that the local level of the organization was really the heart of the WI movement, and during her term as director, she capitalized on that strength.

Miss Lewis was not just an idealist with homespun ideas about the organization's structure. As a pragmatist, she was also very conscious of membership revenues and statistics. In 1949, she made a bold move to increase the membership fees. When the first WI branch was formed at Stoney Creek in 1897, every effort was made to keep the membership affordable, and a fee of twenty-five cents was introduced. The fees had remained unchanged at that same amount for over fifty years. The fact that the WI was able to provide so many services, short courses and publications is evidence of the critical monetary support that was provided by the Department of Agriculture. However, after more than fifty years of being subsidized, an increase in membership fees was long overdue. The new rate was announced in the Annual Report of the Minister of Agriculture, which explained that "to take care of the rising costs of administration the annual [WI] membership fee was raised from 25 to 50 cents."

Lewis also urged members to pay attention to their recruitment of new members and ensure that the local branch did not become exclusive. At the annual Board meeting in November 1949, she brought it to the attention of the delegates that an American organization, the Home Bureau, had conducted a survey among its members in an organization that parallelled the WI in Ontario. The survey asked questions about people's hesitation to join the organization, and Lewis was convinced that its findings might be instructive to the Ontario WIs as well. "Non members in the community where the survey was made were asked to tell why they were not members of the Bureau. Some of the replies were: We were never asked; We do not feel welcome; We know very little about [it]; We have no one to look after our young children and we have not been encouraged to take them to meetings; Local units are not run well. Cliques make it very difficult for newcomers to be taken in until they have been in the community for a long time." [10]

Alarmed by the downward trend in membership statistics that had occurred during the war years, Lewis and the FWIO were determined to see that trend reversed. Beginning with the anniversary celebrations of 1947, the tides turned. The 1948 Annual Report was full of optimism, reporting, "Our horizons have broadened and our responsibilities have increased. In meeting the challenge of the day our women are ready for constructive action. Membership in the Federated Women's Institutes of Ontario is higher than ever before recorded and members in Junior Institutes and Homemaking Clubs are correspondingly high." The optimism was well-founded, as numbers continued to rise for the next five years. In terms of individual memberships, the all-time high was reached in 1950 when 47,250 belonged to the organization in 1,449 branches across Ontario. Measured by the number of branches, 1953 was the high point when 1,503 branches were active.[11]

MEMBERSHIP AND BRANCHES
1947–1953[12]

	Branches	Members
1947	1,267	35,000
1948	1,310	37,500
1949	1,401	44,150
1950	1,449	47,250
1951	1,468	46,100
1952	1,481	45,767
1953	1,503	45,457

How can one explain this surge in numbers and account for the increased popularity of the Institutes in the postwar years? At the 1950 board meeting, this explanation was offered: "The reason [for the growth is] that our organization has proved to rural women that it is a vital, alive, Christian movement." Beyond that superficial explanation there are more concrete reasons that explain the positive growth trend. Anna Lewis's influence can certainly not be overlooked, but her enthusiasm and capable leadership only provide a partial explanation.

For many new members, there was a very practical reason to belong to the Women's Institutes: health insurance. More than twenty years before the introduction of universal health care coverage in Canada, WI branches across Ontario sought out private group health insurance plans. In Elgin East District, the Central Yarmouth branch was created in 1948, and health insurance was one of the top priorities. As Marguerite Young, a charter member, explained, "Blue Cross had just come into existence, you see, and everybody wanted it."[13] At that one branch, the membership quickly rose to more than fifty women, proving that the insurance coverage was a very popular measure indeed. Once again, the Women's Institutes were taking the initiative to address real concerns for many women. In many branches, memberships soared almost overnight when health insurance was made available to members' families. As one woman recalled, the plans were certainly very popular, though the members who joined just to get the coverage were "maybe not the most committed members." Minute books throughout the province recorded that "Blue Cross was discussed and an effort will be made to form a group."[14] There is no doubt that the insurance schemes were a boost to membership numbers.

At the urging of local branches, the Board of the FWIO took up the cause of the local branches in their efforts to get affordable health insurance. In 1950 the Board forwarded a resolution to Blue Cross asking for preferential rates for the WI membership, so that their premiums would be at the same price as payroll deduction groups. Blue Cross denied the request, explaining that a women's group such as the WI actually made heavy demands on the plan, "both as to number of persons entering hospital and the length of stay of such persons."[15] One of the criteria that may have made WI members very

"The Branch Institute is the first and most important part of the whole Women's Institute organization. From it has grown every part of the organization and to serve it all else exists.

By voicing her opinion and carrying a vote in the branch Women's Institute, the individual member in the organization is shaping the policy of the Women's Institute organization as a whole.

The Women's Institute organization is democracy at work."

"Our organization of rural women is vital and alive — interested in home, community and world betterment and worthy of your interest and support. Will you share in this satisfying work?"

— FWIO Federated Women's Institute of Ontario brochure, submitted by Rockley WI

"This picture was likely taken in 1951 at the Women's Institute Area Convention in Emo. Before the road was built which joined Fort William and Fort Frances, the only way to attend the Area Convention at Fort Frances, Emo or Rainy River was by train or by car the long drive by way of Kenora. For a few years during this time, the CNR rented the Thunder Bay Women's Institute a pullman car, which they pulled to the meeting place, switched it to a side line, equipped it with water and lights, and picked it up in the middle of the night to return it to Thunder Bay.

This car was the old type pullman with upper and lower berths separated by curtains the full length of the car and one single room at the end of the car. With one wash room equipped with three basins and one toilet, you can imagine the confusion as thirty women or so prepared for the morning session. After a long day of meetings Thunder Bay delegates and visitors gathered in the pullman for the night; Margaret Sideen with her mouth organ kept them singing while Mrs. Bonnet and Mrs. Paul organized crazy costumes and tricks. The noisy Pyjama party kept the coloured porter in suspense.

The spirit of camaraderie which developed will always be remembered by those who attended the Area Conventions during those years.

— Rainy River District Women's Institute Museum, *Northwestern Ontario Area Tweedsmuir History*, Mrs. Edith Purcell

expensive to insure was the fact that more and more rural women were using hospitals for birthing. Despite the cost, many branches opted to continue the plan because it provided health insurance for rural families that was otherwise unavailable. At the same time, WI membership skyrocketed. Although some people undoubtedly joined just to get the insurance, many of them remained on as committed members, and came to appreciate the organization for its full range of activities.

Through activities at the various levels beyond the local branch, rural women such as Mrs. O'Hare, a member of Providence WI, broadened their horizons. Reporting on her experiences in 1949, she recounted, "This was my first convention. To say I was thrilled and inspired is putting it mildly. I think no woman can really understand the vastness, the scope of this work and the fellowship of working together For Home and Country until she has, herself, attended a convention." Mrs. O'Hare commented particularly on the scope of the organization. "To see 700 ladies in one area meeting, to hear we are nearing [the] 50,000 [member] mark in Ontario, to learn about Institute activities throughout the world, to realize that our very own women take an active part at the world meeting and to know and understand that we are each a part of that whole," she said, that is when "we begin to realize that here is something big and worthwhile."[16]

With a membership of almost 50,000 women, Ontario Institutes were a force to be reckoned with, and they turned their collective strength into political pressure. At area conventions such as the one Mrs. O'Hare attended, decisions were made about how to lobby for change on particular issues and a great deal of energy was spent turning the collective concerns of Institute members into formal resolutions. By far the greatest emphasis in the 1950s was on issues connected with homemaking, and the Women's Institutes became an important voice in consumer lobbying. By some estimates, women were responsible for spending up to 80 percent of the income of Ontario households, and so it is not surprising that WI members should turn their attention to the quality of consumer products. In particular, faced with the task of purchasing and maintaining the clothing for their families, WI members were concerned about the quality of clothing available to them through the retail market.

For instance, the problem of pockets in men's workpants became a women's issue. At the FWIO Board meeting in November 1955 at the Royal York Hotel, a resolution came forward from delegates representing the Kingston Area: "Be it resolved that pockets in men's trousers be made of a more durable material, that a more generous seam allowance be made and that bindings be more firmly secured." It was unanimously approved that the resolution be sent on to the Consumer Association of Canada so that pressure could be applied to the Canadian Manufacturers Association to improve the standards. Exactly the same concern had been voiced two years earlier at the November 1953 meeting by delegates from the Guelph area, showing that concerns about mending pockets were widely shared. With strength in numbers, Ontario Institute members were learning that they did not have to settle for inferior goods.

In 1955 the Kingston Area Women's Institutes launched a campaign to improve the quality of men's work pants. The steps in formulating a resolution to address this consumer complaint are shown on the placards. Mrs. Essie Kennedy of Verona demonstrates the problem while Mrs. Arthur Hamilton of Godfrey looks at the improved product. — UG, FWIO Collection; *Home and Country*, winter 1959

A number of similar issues were raised at Board meetings throughout the early postwar years. In 1950, a resolution was put forward from the Ottawa area complaining about the improper construction of shirts. With sleeves sewn in wrong, the shirts were not only uncomfortable to wear, they wore out before they should have. From the Guelph area, the same meeting of the FWIO Board heard the following resolution: "That sales people who fit shoes be required to take a course in shoe fitting, the manufacturer of shoes to be responsible for providing such a course, and further, that manufacturers of shoes be requested to clearly mark width and size of shoes."[17] Other concerns centred on the quality of belts of ladies ready-to-wear dresses, the standard of material and workmanship in children's shoes, and the problem of inadequate labelling about flammability on sleepwear. In November of 1951 the Board turned its attention to the packaging of bacon, which was wrapped in striped cellophane, giving the impression of more lean meat than was really the case. Most of these problems were directed to the Consumer Association of Canada, and in some cases, to the appropriate department of government.

Not all of the resolutions were concerned with consumer issues; some were overtly directed at improving the status of women. A 1951 resolution on pay equity was directed to the federal government, calling for "equal pay for equal work or hours of labour for men and women in factories, skilled labour, business offices and executive work throughout Canada."[18] In 1953, the FWIO Board endorsed the following resolution: "Moved that we consider the resolution of the Canadian Federation of University Women re: changes in Dominion Succession Act making women partners in business, half of the estate passing from deceased husband to his widow be declared rightfully hers." Support for the resolution carried on this issue of inheritance, one that undoubtedly represented the concerns of many rural women across the province.[19]

Members actually got carried away with the making of resolutions when, for example, at the November 1953 annual meeting at the Royal York Hotel in Toronto, seventy-seven different issues were considered. In these marathon Board meetings, which sometimes lasted until almost midnight, it became evident that many of the ideas were too local in nature to be pursued, others were too vague, and still others were directed to the wrong level of government. Some resolutions were lost because they were proposed on religious grounds, and this was not the focus of the FWIO. For example, at the November 1953 meeting, the following resolution was lost: "That our honourable Prime Minister, Mr. Louis St. Laurent, and his cabinet call a Day of National Prayer for rededication, giving thanks for our many National Blessings and asking for wisdom to carry out His Will in National and International Affairs."[20] True to their organizing principles, the Board turned down that resolution. It was an important reminder that the Women's Institutes did not exist to promote religion. Instead, their membership was to be inclusive of all women, regardless of religion. On those grounds, they could not entertain a resolution calling the prime minister to prayer. However, this did not preclude more practical expressions of political activism.

Women's Institute members were encouraged to become involved in politics at every level. At the New Liskeard Area Convention in 1950, one speaker "urged that all women seize or make opportunities to take part in any public office — above all to be interested and active in municipal affairs."[21] Members definitely rose to the challenge. At the Southampton WI in Bruce County that same year, "the president of the Women's Institute achieved the distinction of being the first woman to be elected as a Member of the Southampton Town Council, and two other Institute members were elected to serve on the Southampton Public School Board." There was a definite link between their political activism and their WI involvement, because for all of these individuals, "the interest aroused by the study of Citizenship and Education led to [their] election."[22] "An Institute background must be an excellent preparation for public life, for I was practically raised in the Women's Institute," Marjorie Hamilton declared in 1952, while she was serving as the mayor of Barrie.[23]

Even for women who did not serve as elected officials, municipal projects were important. WI members played important supporting roles in a series of postwar "Well Baby Clinics," reminiscent of the public health efforts of earlier years, and held throughout the counties of Ontario. Emphasizing the importance of preventative measures, good nutrition and regular checkups, mothers were encouraged to attend the clinics so that children could be measured and weighed, and mothers themselves could be advised and educated. Across the province, these clinics held under the auspices of the local Public Health Unit took on different forms, sometimes held in public halls, and even in private homes. Institute members promoted the clinics by their own attendance, and also helped to staff them as volunteers.

The activism of Institute members was not limited to issues of municipal politics or local public health; it stretched around the world. In the postwar years, the pen friend tradition continued as individual members

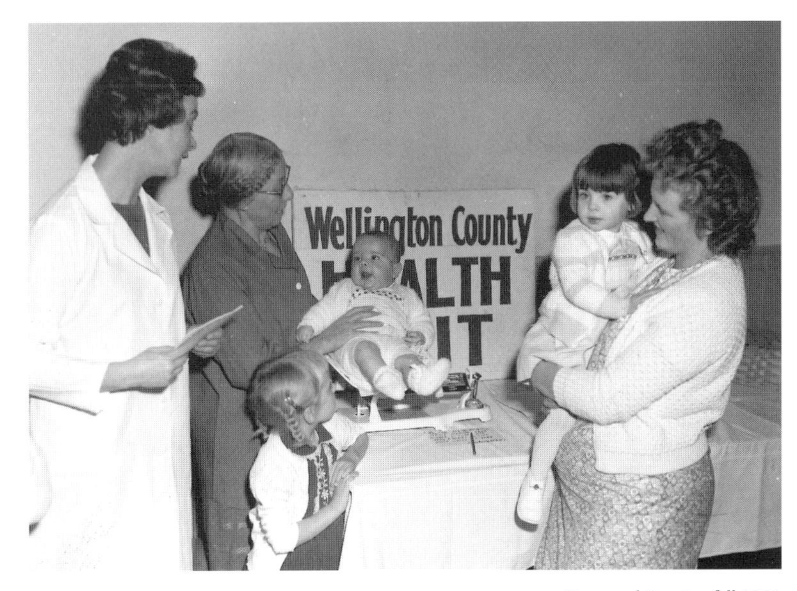

Home and Country, fall 1964

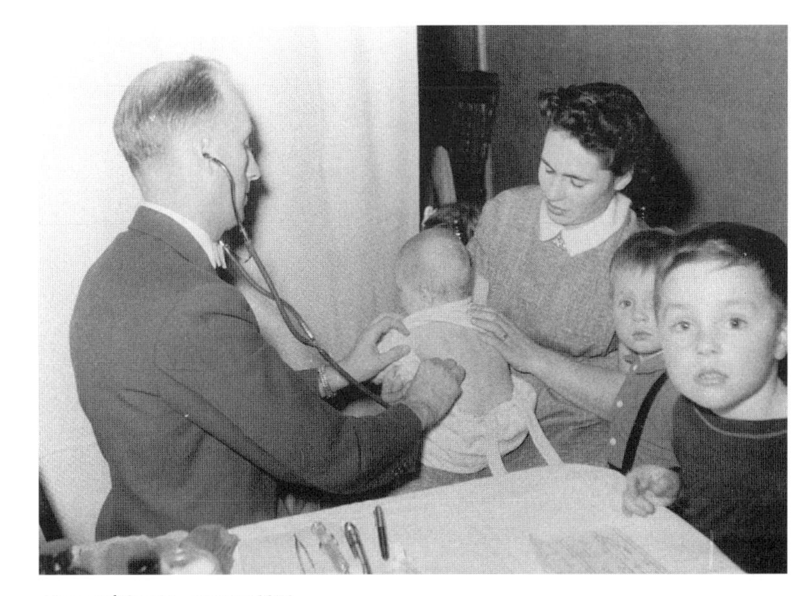

Home and Country, summer 1956

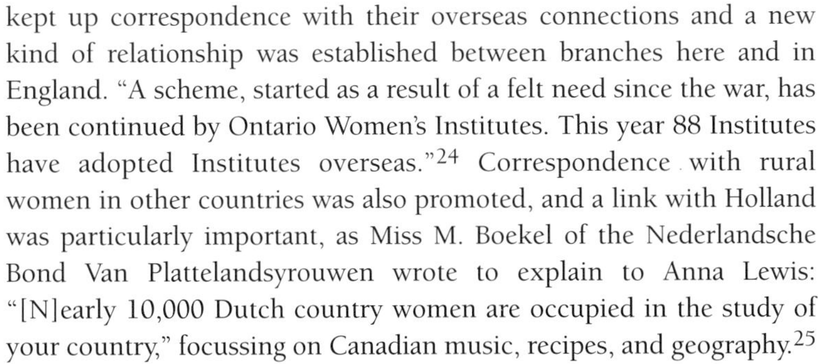

kept up correspondence with their overseas connections and a new kind of relationship was established between branches here and in England. "A scheme, started as a result of a felt need since the war, has been continued by Ontario Women's Institutes. This year 88 Institutes have adopted Institutes overseas."[24] Correspondence with rural women in other countries was also promoted, and a link with Holland was particularly important, as Miss M. Boekel of the Nederlandsche Bond Van Plattelandsyrouwen wrote to explain to Anna Lewis: "[N]early 10,000 Dutch country women are occupied in the study of your country," focussing on Canadian music, recipes, and geography.[25]

But these exchanges were not undertaken in a light-hearted manner. WI members were reminded that this was, after all, the Cold War. Concern over communism and so-called enemy agents was heightened. A resolution on the FWIO's Cold War position was passed at the November 1954 FWIO Board meeting, reiterating that "Canada should continue its active support of and participation in the activities of NATO in order to play its part in the joint effort of the free Nations of the West to resist Communist aggression," and further, that "persons professing Communism, or in sympathy therewith, are not fit to hold

Home and Country, winter 1959

Working in conjunction with local Health Units, the WI sponsored Well Baby Clinics in the 1950s. (1) At this clinic in Wellington County, a note on the table from the public health nurse was a reminder for WI helpers: "To the volunteers: Please remind each mother to guard her baby against falling while being weighed." (2) Eden Mills and Eden Crest Women's Institutes also sponsored a Child Health Clinic. (3) Other temporary clinics such as these in Rosemont and Rockwood were set up in private homes and involved visits by health professionals. — UG, FWIO Collection

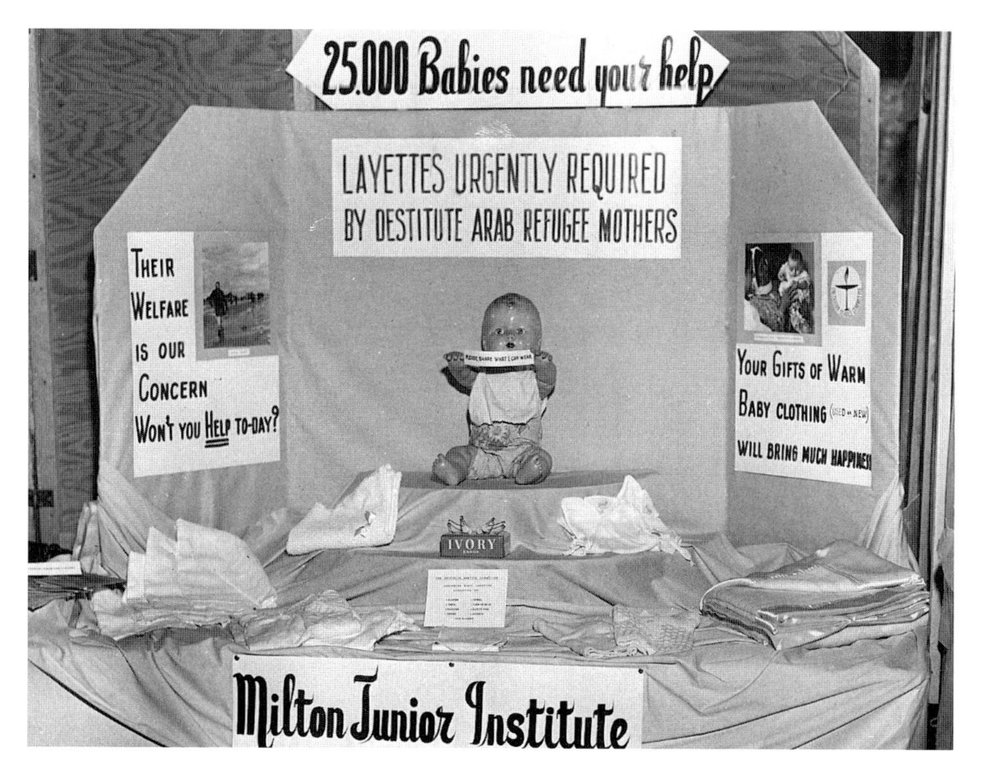
25.000 Babies need your help
LAYETTES URGENTLY REQUIRED
BY DESTITUTE ARAB REFUGEE MOTHERS
THEIR
WELFARE
IS OUR
CONCERN
WON'T YOU HELP TO-DAY?
YOUR GIFTS OF WARM
BABY CLOTHING
WILL BRING MUCH HAPPINES
IVORY
Milton Junior Institute

This display at the 1958 Milton Fair attests to the international scope of WI relief work. The Halton County Junior Institutes presented complete layettes to the Unitarian Service Committee's director, Dr. Lotta Hitschmanova, during her cross-Canada tour.
— UG, FWIO Collection; *Home and Country*, winter 1959

elective or appointed office, nor teaching posts, nor positions in its Labour Unions."[26] Individual members were reminded that they had a role to play in warding off communist advances. *Home and Country* admonished its readers, "When writing to Pen Pals in other lands, the FWIO wish to advise you not to divulge any information which might prove of value to enemy agents, e.g. location of industrial plants, etc."[27]

Heightened attention to conditions in other countries was brought home to many of the Institutes very directly because new Canadians were finding their way into WI membership in several Ontario communities. In Middlesex County, for example, the Prospect Hill WI reported in 1949 that one of the recent immigrants to their community described "her native Hungary and the present conditions in that land. She made a plea to send warm clothing to the needy in Europe."[28] Several new Canadians used the Institutes as an opportunity to improve their language skills, and they accepted positions on the branch executive, most often as secretary, to have opportunity to practise their writing. At the area convention in Stratford in 1950, the suggestion was made to "use the mail order catalogues as an aid in teaching English to new Canadians."[29] Sometimes these new arrivals were in need of other kinds of support, and the WI extended a helping hand to them, as one Dutch war bride found out in York County. This woman, the mother of two small children, was grateful to receive the help of the local WI when her husband was killed in a railway accident. "An hour after I returned from my husband's funeral the Nobleton Women's Institute gave me a cheque to carry me through the week," she said.[30]

Extending help to new Canadians was a local and personal extension of the Women's Institutes of Ontario program of international relief projects. One of the projects they donated toward was an effort of the Unitarian Service Committee's relief work in Greece. "In 1950 most of our material went to Greece, where guerilla warfare did not end until November 1949," explained Dr. Lotta Hitschmanova, the Director for Canada of the USC, in a letter acknowledging the contributions of the Ontario Women's Institutes. "If only you could have seen their happiness when they took off the tattered rags and newspapers and wrapped their half-naked babies, and clothed them — 'like baby princes' they said — in your beautiful layettes! Many of you are mothers yourselves," she continued, "and responded again with motherly generosity when I launched our 'March of Dimes' for Greek babies last Autumn. . . . a great number of your Ontario Institutes have also sent urgently-needed soap, or money for soap. Many of you have held community-wide clothing collections, to gather warm clothing for adults and children to wear."[31] The FWIO reported in 1951 on "The Tractor and

In 1952, Mrs. Purcell, FWIO President, presented a representative of Cockshutt Company with a cheque to purchase this tractor for Greece, a country devastated by civil war. Mrs. Emberley, a local vice president, looked on.
— UG, FWIO Collection; *Home and Country*, summer 1952

Flour Fund for Greece," a fund they had established. "A total of more than $9,000 was raised. From this a tractor with plough and disc harrow was sent to Greece through the Unitarian Service Committee of Canada and a cheque for $1,200.00 was sent to pay for fuel and supplies. The remainder of the fund, over $1,000 was used to purchase Canadian flour for Greece."[32]

Other branches took on the role of "foster parents" for international children through the Save the Children Fund. Maynard WI in Grenville South, for example, adopted ten-year-old Yamilla Abdallah in 1946. Four years later they reported that they had "sent an average of eight parcels each year containing food, clothing, shoes and school supplies. They supplied the clothes for her first communion as well as clothing for other members of the family. Each Christmas they sent toys and sweets." A member of their local community visited the family during an overseas excursion, and "he found them truly in need and most grateful for help received."[33]

To further orchestrate international aid, Ontario WI members participated enthusiastically in the fundraising campaigns of the Associated Country Women of the World. The ACWW raised funds through a program known as Pennies for Friendship, based on the idea that every little bit would help. This simple fundraising idea, which was promoted throughout the world and continues to the present day, encouraged individual women to save their coins and donate them to help finance the operating costs of the ACWW, a group renowned for its relief projects. It was another means for women to feel a closer connection with the international level of their organization, an affiliation that was particularly popular in the years after the Second World War. For a few privileged members, this connection meant international travel. In 1950, Anna Lewis led a delegation of WI members from across Canada to visit with "sister members" throughout Britain and Europe. "At the request of the Federated Women's Institutes of Canada, Miss Anna Lewis, Director of the Branch, acted as organizer and business manager for the tour. Countries visited were England, Ireland, Scotland, Wales, Norway,

Funds for the international organization, ACWW, were collected through a scheme known as "Pennies for Friendship." In 1962 branch representatives from the Institutes of Ontario North District prepare to count their coins. From that event, 3,165 pennies were sent to ACWW. — UG, FWIO Collection; *Home and Country*, winter 1962

Young flag-bearers assemble on the grounds of the University of Toronto in preparation for the August 14, 1953, opening ceremony of the ACWW Conference. — UG, FWIO Collection

Sweden, Denmark, Holland, Belgium and France. This tour included the fifth Triennial Conference of the Associated Country Women of the World."[34] It was an important occasion for these lucky women, not just because of the rare opportunity for international travel, but also because it meant that they felt personally connected to the ACWW and its projects.

While overseas travel was not a possibility for most members, direct contact with international sisters did become a reality for hundreds of Ontario WI members when Canada hosted the ACWW conference in Toronto in 1953. The feeling of belonging to something that was much bigger than the local branch was greatly enhanced that year. The conference site and date were chosen early: the Royal York Hotel in Toronto, from August 12 to 23, 1953. Announced first at the November 1951 Board meeting, plans were underway two years in advance when six women were named to a committee "to consider ways and means of raising money for hospitality re: ACWW Conference."

One of those ideas resulted in the distribution of maple leaf pins with the words "1953 ACWW Canadian Hostess" on them. At the November 1952 Board meeting, the convenor of the registration committee for the ACWW conference asked that "anybody who has a car who can come into the city for the time of the ACWW Conference, and at her own expense, [to] put car and self at disposal of ACWW to act as 'Joe boy' [should] let Mrs. Purcell [FWIO President] know."[35] Indeed, there was much work to be done and many errands to be run as "some 1,000 delegates were entertained." Suggestions about how to entertain the visitors flooded in to the FWIO executive. The Oliphant WI in Bruce County had suggested that the delegates should be divided into groups and taken into the various districts so that the privilege of entertaining the delegates could be shared among members from various areas.[36] That idea was rejected. Instead, the international visitors spent their time based in Southern Ontario (Toronto and Guelph) with excursions to visit points of interest.

Of course, one of the most popular destinations was Stoney Creek itself, so that the ACWW members could retrace the steps of Adelaide Hoodless and the other Institute founders. Much preparation preceded the visitors' tours. In 1951, a plaque marking the location where the first WI had been organized was placed on the buildings at the site of Squire's Hall. As well, plans were reported to fix up the second-floor room of this building as a museum containing furniture connected with the organization of the first Women's Institute. The display was to be opened to the public at the time of the ACWW conference in August 1953.[37] The creation of a temporary showcase of Institute history was an important precursor to the preservation projects that the WI would soon undertake on a much larger scale. Within the next two decades, the FWIC and the FWIO would each create a more permanent site with the restoration of both the Hunter Hoodless Homestead near St. George and the Erland Lee (Museum) Home near Stoney Creek.

The exercise of hosting international delegates was a heady experience for the Ontario Institutes and one they welcomed with great enthusiasm. The ACWW conference was one indicator of the scope of the organization. There were many other occasions for ceremonial celebrations, and two of particular note occurred later that same decade. In 1957 the Federated Women's Institutes of Canada held its first national convention, and once again, Ontario was the chosen site, this time in Ottawa. Addressed by an impressive list of notable officials, including the Right Honourable John Diefenbaker, the Institutes were clearly enjoying a season of prominence throughout the province. When Her Majesty Queen Elizabeth II visited Canada in 1957, the Women's Institutes of Ontario sent official greetings. As an Institute member herself, the Queen was treated to a visit to Stoney Creek so that she too could explore the site of the movement's founding meeting.

The pomp and circumstance of these official functions of the Ontario Women's Institutes can be interpreted in at least two different ways. On the one hand, these official visits reflect the importance that was attributed to the WI as a group that included 50,000 women in its membership. This was clearly a group to be reckoned with, and with such a large membership base and a high-profile lobbying effort, it was only natural that the Institutes would occupy a prominent public position. On the other hand, such high-profile events served to attract even more members because the Institutes were seen as a very influential body. For most of the members, though, these memorable public occasions were noteworthy because they were exceptions to normal WI activity. To host international delegates, hear an address from the prime minister, or accompany the Queen on a

In 1957, Prime Minister John Diefenbaker addressed the opening session of the Federated Women's Institutes of Canada convention in Ottawa. This gathering to celebrate the sixtieth anniversary of the Institute movement was also the first national convention.

— UG, FWIO Collection; *Home and Country*, winter 1958

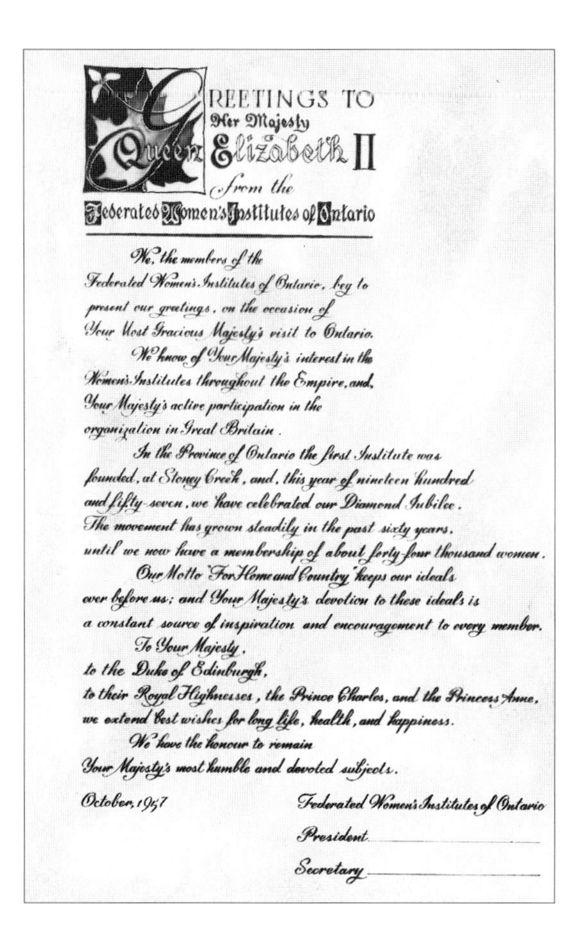

GREETINGS TO
Her Majesty
Queen Elizabeth II
from the
Federated Women's Institutes of Ontario

We, the members of the
Federated Women's Institutes of Ontario, beg to
present our greetings, on the occasion of
Your Most Gracious Majesty's visit to Ontario.

We know of Your Majesty's interest in the
Women's Institutes throughout the Empire, and,
Your Majesty's active participation in the
organization in Great Britain.

In the Province of Ontario the first Institute was
founded, at Stoney Creek, and, this year of nineteen hundred
and fifty-seven, we have celebrated our Diamond Jubilee.
The movement has grown steadily in the past sixty years,
until we now have a membership of about forty-four thousand women.

Our Motto "For Home and Country" keeps our ideals
ever before us; and Your Majesty's devotion to these ideals is
a constant source of inspiration and encouragement to every member.

To Your Majesty,
to the Duke of Edinburgh,
to their Royal Highnesses, the Prince Charles, and the Princess Anne,
we extend best wishes for long life, health, and happiness.

We have the honour to remain
Your Majesty's most humble and devoted subjects.

October, 1957

Federated Women's Institutes of Ontario
President ____________
Secretary ____________

The year 1957 was also the occasion of the Queen's visit to Ontario. The Federated Women's Institute of Ontario sent her formal greetings.

— UG, FWIO Collection; *Home and Country*, winter 1958

tour of Stoney Creek was truly a "once in a lifetime opportunity," and hardly a typical WI experience.

In an effort to maintain good relations between the provincial executive and the local levels of the organization, Mrs. R.G. Purcell (FWIO President from 1950 to 1953), travelled extensively throughout the province during these years. "Realizing the need for a closer relationship between the FWIO and the WI member," she attended the 1952 district annuals of Kenora and Rainy River Districts in Northwestern Ontario, and that fall, "attended the 13 Area Conventions which kept her from home almost continuously from the middle of September to mid-November."[38] This was an important gesture on the part of the FWIO President, because her visits helped to bridge the gap between the privileged few who represented the Institutes at those official state functions, and the bulk of the membership, who rarely ventured outside their own districts.

Meanwhile, back at the branch level, the postwar years were filled with opportunities close to home. While the provincial leadership concerned itself with those public occasions of national and international importance, individual members in rural communities concentrated on domestic interests. Because of the renewed attention to the home and to homemaking skills, home economics instruction was at the top of the agenda for local Institutes.

With a provincial staff of instructors numbering over fifty, the Institutes Branch of the Department of Agriculture was determined to fulfil its mandate "to provide the women of Ontario with the type of Homemaking education which they most desire and which will be most helpful to them." Keeping a watchful eye over those programs, the FWIO Board was concerned not only that the instructors hired by the Department of Agriculture were well qualified to teach the courses, but also that they were paid fairly. Accordingly, the Board was happy to hear in the 1954 report that "the staff salaries of the Home Economists in the WI Branch had recently been adjusted and are now more in line with the salaries paid to Secondary School Teachers." Driven by the popularity of the courses and the high value that the membership placed on the short course instruction, the Board directed their secretary "to write to the Minister of Agriculture commending his Department on their action of increasing salaries of the [Home Economists of the Women's Institute Branch and Home Economics Service], and [to] recommend that this policy be continued so that the salaries may remain in line with those of the Secondary School Teachers."[39]

The funding of those courses was no small expense, yet the cost to each member was minimal because the Department of Agriculture was underwriting the service. Mindful of this arrangement and the fact that the instructors needed to make a decent living, the FWIO tried to act with fiscal responsibility. In the same year that they congratulated the Department for raising the instructors' salaries, the FWIO Board voted to end the fifty-year-old granting system. The minutes of the Board meeting tell the story: "Emanating from Miss Lewis' Report was the question, 'Should the grant of $3.00 per branch be continued?' Many branches do not ask for the grant and so more money is available for other worthwhile Institute work. Discussion followed. MOTION moved "That the Provincial Board recommends that the Legislative Grant of $3.00 to each Women's Institute Branch — which is now available to the branches when certain conditions are met — be discontinued. CARRIED."[40]

To support the burgeoning education programs of the Women's Institute Branch and Home Economics Service, the Department of Agriculture employed close to fifty staff. Superintendent Anna Lewis is seated in the second row, fourth from the right. — UG, FWIO Collection; *Home and Country*, winter 1953

For a variety of reasons, most of the members agreed that the cash grant seemed redundant. First, the WI branches had proved themselves to be more than capable of raising funds both in wartime and peacetime and the three-dollar grant was not a significant portion of the local budget. Moreover, since the Department was paying for the educational programs and subsidizing publications such as *Home and Country*, it seemed a bit much to also expect direct cash grants. Finally, many members sensibly concluded that the grant money (which amounted to approximately $4,500) might be put to better use as a lump sum in the hands of the Department, rather than being handed out in three-dollar allotments.

In 1948, under Lewis's leadership, the Co-operative Programme in Home Economics had been changed, with the intent to place "special emphasis . . . on the needs of the young matron and courses were re-vamped to help our women cope with new postwar responsibilities."[41] The course content was evidently very popular, as the 1952 Annual Report could boast that 551 short courses had been offered that year, with a total enrollment of 14,498 women representing 1,194 of the branches.[42]

For many rural homemakers one of the new realities that had a profound impact on their lives was hydro. A report in the Tweedsmuir history of Barnhart WI, in the Fort Frances Museum Collection, describes the coming of electricity in 1950. "The average farmer of Barnhart never dreamed of having electric lights. These, he thought, were for the city folk and the Eastern Farmers. Yet, on April 18, 1950 most of us had the power on, our electric lights in use and at least a few electrical appliances to try out. About 1947 the hydro fever

This photo of a cooking class attended by members of the Arkell Women's Institute is a reminder of the postwar emphasis on domestic skills. — UG, FWIO Collection

In Northern Ontario, where rural French-speaking communities are common, the Women's Institutes of Nipissing District exist side by side with parallel groups for Francophone women, known as "Cercles de Fermières." — UG, FWIO Collection; *Home and Country*, winter 1956

swept the Rainy River District, of course we all signed up for it. 'It won't help any of us because we are so far from town' . . . was the usual comment. Even in October 1949, when the poles were being put in along the road, we still doubted we'd see it by spring. It was with mixed feelings that the people of Kingsford heard the news . . . the lights came on this morning at 11 o'clock. Now with electric fridges, vacuum cleaners, irons, toasters, hot plates, kettles and washing machines in use; we wonder how we ever managed with the ice box, broom, dustpan, sad irons, wash board, tub and the old kettle singing on a stove heated with wood."[43]

Hydro-electricity had a particularly profound impact on another part of the province — the communities in Stormont County that were flooded because of the construction of the St. Lawrence Seaway Hydro Dam project. Under that scheme, three "lost villages" disappeared as they were literally flooded after the dam was built. Ontario Hydro built a new subdivision in Ingleside, Ontario. Residents of Farran's Point, Aultsville and Wales were relocated to new homes in that carefully planned new community. For the WI, it meant that three branches were also amalgamated, and a new branch, the Ingleside WI, was created. The logistics of bringing three different branches together and combining three membership lists and three different executives were not easy.[44]

Though other communities were not so directly affected as those that formed Ingleside, they still felt the impact of provincial electrification projects very deeply. At the Belleville Area Convention, attention was centred on "How the Economics of Agriculture Affects Farm Women," and respondents turned to the introduction of hydro as a case in point. "The hydro offered conveniences with deep freezers, electric stoves, washers, ironers [sic] and other equipment. More leisure time can now be devoted to children, home life and the community. Some people defined the modern farm home as one where switches control everything but the children."[45] As a result of the changes sweeping through Ontario with the universal presence of hydro service, the WI curriculum began to reflect this new reality. "Courses in Home Management to include economics of the household, conservation in the home, the purchase and use of electrical equipment" were offered.

Women seemed to have an insatiable hunger for more short courses in home decorating, new cooking techniques, and child

Home and Country, summer, 1958

psychology. Interests deferred during the war years were taken up with new enthusiasm. Enjoying the calm afforded by peacetime, and the accompanying levels of unprecedented prosperity, attention to home economics flourished. Some women, particularly new brides, took up these interests for the first time and appreciated the WI as a forum in which they could learn much-needed domestic skills. For others, the postwar period was clearly a time to enjoy the educational opportunities and take the short courses as a form of leisure. Whether out of necessity to learn how to run a household, to figure out how to save money, or just for fun, WI members enthusiastically enjoyed every single course the Department of Agriculture had to offer. "I have never been at an Institute meeting that I didn't come home with new ideas and I have learned something really worthwhile," Claire White from Enniskillen Branch in Lambton County declared. "It was my mother-in-law, God bless her, that introduced me to it and . . . I can say just one thing. I've taken lots and lots of short courses, and led a lot of the short courses and Institute has been a big influence on my life."[46]

Home and Country, winter 1955

Home and Country, winter 1953

Instruction in home economics enjoyed wide popularity throughout the province as women turned their attention to home life. (1) In Caledon, women admire the finished products of their course, "New Lamps for Old." Local leader training schools were an effective means of equipping more instructors. (2) A millinery course is given in Guelph by Miss Nora Creyke (standing back to the window). (3) Chisholm Institute members, Parry Sound District, stand by their newly reupholstered chairs — UG, FWIO Collection

Close to fifty Native delegates representing eight different reserves registered for the third annual Homemakers' Club Convention at the Whitefish Lake Reserve Indian School in 1958. A close parallel to the Women's Institutes, the Homemakers' clubs were sponsored by the federal government in order to provide domestic science instruction to First Nations Women. LEFT TO RIGHT: *Mrs. A. Meawasige of Serpent River near Cutler; Mrs. J. Petahtagoose of Whitefish Lake (seated); Mrs. Mary Napose, Mrs. A. Naponse and Mrs. Flora Solomon, all of Whitefish.* — UG, FWIO Collection

"At the Central Ontario Women's Institute Convention two young married club members, following their part in the programme introduced their children. The husband of one of the girls came to help with the children and incidentally show his approval of homemaking club work. LEFT TO RIGHT: *Mrs. Leslie Thompson with her two children, Mr. Douglas Earle and Mrs. Earle with their family."*
— UG, FWIO Collection; *Home and Country*, winter 1957

"I'm a Toronto girl and there was no Institute anywhere near where I was that I am aware of," Ruth Burkholder of the Bethesda WI in York East District explained. "But of course I married into an Institute family. One of the first things I remember about the Institute was going to a short course for making hats. [That was] in the 1960s and I remember that, and that was basically my first introduction."[47] The hatmaking courses were particularly popular since hats were considered a fashion necessity for women in the postwar years. Explaining the rationale behind offering these courses, Helen McKercher (the Director of the Branch who succeeded Anna Lewis), told the Board meeting in 1959, "It's more than just making a hat. We want to develop people." There was more to the program than one might realize. "Millinery courses continue to be very popular. These, with the course on Hospitality Foods, are frills. This is the criticism that we get, but . . . if they can make their own hats or cook a good meal, then we are giving them a sense of security." The social side of learning together was a very important component of this experience. "We could [simply] supply literature for her to take home, but how is she going to get the supplies there? And where is the comradeship with other women that is so important?"[48]

The one constant theme that emerges from this profile of postwar activity among the branches is that women found in the WI something for the individual herself. For some, the WI meeting meant an antidote to isolation in an era when women were once again relegated to their homes. The short course or the monthly evening meeting was "Mom's night out" for countless women. Women devised a variety of strategies for getting themselves to those meetings, often bringing the children along. Helen Anderson from Haldimand West District recalled that afternoon meetings were difficult for her as a young mother with three children. When she mentioned this to a neighbour, she learned about

Home and Country, fall 1960

Home and Country, fall 1952

Home and Country, summer 1952

A favourite program begun in 1949, the Women's Institute Holiday Week was designed for personal growth and relaxation. A variety of activities made up the week on the campus of the Ontario Agricultural College. Women could enjoy cultural activities, domestic science workshops, and recreation.
— UG, FWIO Collection

the Clanbrassil WI, which met in the evenings. "I said, 'Boy that would suit me fine. My husband can put the kids to bed.' So in 1960 I joined and I've been there ever since." Asked how her husband felt about this arrangement, Helen replied, "That's the only things we went to, Institute and Church. That was the only thing at the time you were involved with . . . and Institute was only once a month. But he didn't mind at all putting them to bed. It worked out well."[49]

One delightful example of a program designed solely for the member's own benefit was the Women's Institute Holiday Week. This was an opportunity for women to go to the campus of the Agricultural College at Guelph, live in the residence for one week, have all her meals provided, and enjoy a whole range of activities. Guests of the college might take art lessons, learn flower arranging, go swimming, or enjoy Shakespearean theatre on an excursion to the Stratford Festival. The first holiday was offered during the summer of 1949, and at the Board meeting that fall delegates heard all about it. "The Women's Institute Holiday at Guelph was reported a success with 49 rural women spending the full week and over 900 attendance in part time. . . . Due to the success of the venture, the second week of July has been set aside for an Institute holiday."

As the news of the Holiday Week spread, Institutes chartered buses to bring participants to the day program. A formal request from the Ottawa Area Convention area in 1951 called for the establishment of a parallel event to be held in Eastern Ontario. Note the contrast between the delegates arriving at Guelph by bus and those touring the Kemptville Agricultural College on wagon rides.
— UG, FWIO collection; *Home and Country*, winter 1953

Who are we? We are the best
We are the girls from Aylmer West
Cakes, pies, meats and slaw
Aylmer Institute rah, rah, rah.

— *Home and Country*, winter 1949–1950

Two years later, the holiday week at Guelph had attracted more than one hundred overnight guests to the residence for all or part of the week, with attendance during the day exceeding 1,000 as thirty-two bus loads of women came for the shorter day program version of the holiday. A letter was received at the November 1951 Board meeting asking for a WI Holiday Week to be established at the Kemptville Agricultural College so that women from Eastern Ontario could enjoy the same kind of experience without travelling all the way to Guelph. The following year that request became a reality as about fifty women attended the newly created Women's Institute Holiday Week at Kemptville. Meanwhile the Guelph experience continued to be very popular: sixty women stayed as overnight guests in 1952, and over 1,600 participated altogether, including those who came in daily by bus.[50] The formal programs were appreciated, but so too were the opportunities for informal relaxation. According to a report in *Home and Country* "numerous 'after hours' parties added zest and hilarity to this happy occasion."[51]

The second holiday site was established partly through local pressure and partly through the work of Miss Lewis and Mrs. J.R. Futcher, FWIO President from 1947 to 1950. The two of them had been appointed by the FWIO Board to investigate the possibilities of several holiday centres being set up throughout the province. Despite the hopes of establishing holiday centres in even more areas, Kemptville and Guelph were the only two places where women could take part in the luxury of a week away from home responsibilities. There were some notable differences between the two programs, because the event at Guelph, which attracted delegates from a much larger geographic area, had consistently higher attendance than the one in Eastern Ontario. As well, with its central location, Guelph afforded a wide range of cultural activities, including close proximity to the Stratford Festival. Hundreds of women took advantage of the opportunity to be part of the holiday, flocking to the campus by bus, especially for the popular day programs.

Although the cost of overnight accommodation on the campus was only $2 per day,[52] the freedom to be away for a whole week was not something that all WI members could afford. Predictably, the women who were able to take advantage of a week in residence at the agricultural campuses were those who lived in villages or towns, or if they were from rural areas, they were not involved directly in the chores of farm production. Furthermore, they were not tied down with children or with paid work off the farm. Even so, the logistics of getting away for a week were complicated for any homemaker, and the women who managed to do so looked upon the experience as a well-deserved break from their domestic routines. Some women appreciated the structured programs that were provided, while others used the week to pursue other activities, and the organizers of the event wondered how to solve the problem of delegates who preferred to "go shopping rather than attend the sessions."[53] By 1962, Miss McKercher, the Director of Home Economics and a key organizer of the event, was working on plans to replace the holiday with an alternate event that would focus on educating the members about their responsibilities as branch officers.[54]

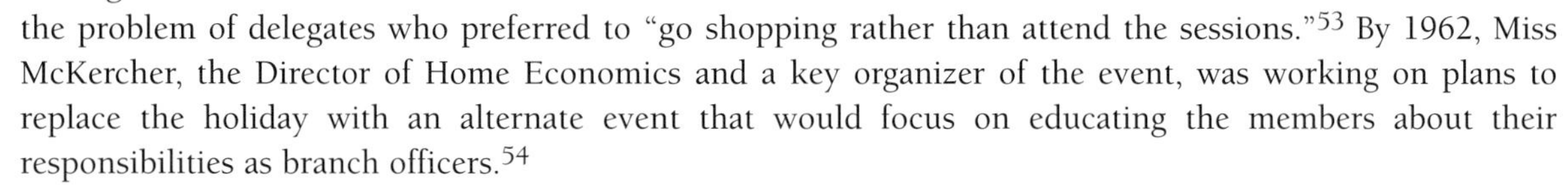

As the enthusiastic chroniclers of local history, Tweedsmuir curators expressed their creativity in the design and presentation of their books. At this Grey County workshop on leathercraft, instructor Mrs. Charles Agnew demonstrates different binding techniques to an unidentified woman (left) and Muriel Johnson.

— UG, FWIO Collection; *Home and Country*, summer 1965

One of the most popular responsibilities of the local Institutes during the postwar years was the continued attention they devoted to compiling the Tweedsmuir history books. After the attention the books received in 1947 at the time of their official naming, and the celebration of the fiftieth anniversary, even more attention was devoted to them throughout the 1950s and 1960s. Women explain that they value the books because of the contribution they make to posterity. "Would you like to know why it's important to me?" one Tweedsmuir curator asked. "Because my grandson came in to find out when his great-grandfathers and so on came over . . . When you start talking and start telling them, the look of amazement [on your grandchildren's faces] about what happened makes you think more, and gather up more things."[55] Institutes have used their books over the years to teach family history, but they are also consulted by curious schoolchildren, Heritage Day organizers, and genealogists hoping to learn more about the community.

In 1949 the Institutes across Canada were honoured with an Award of Merit from the American Association for State and Local History. Presented to the FWIC, the award served to raise the profile of the history books and create even more public interest in their compilation and preservation. One of the biggest

Expertise in keeping local history books meant that WI members often got involved in other local heritage preservation projects. Some of the women who lent their support to the Elgin County Museum were Mrs. J.R. Futcher (standing left) and Mrs. J. McCormick; and kneeling, Mrs. H.C. Duff and Miss Edna Scott.
— UG, FWIO Collection; *Home and Country*, summer 1957; *St. Thomas Times-Journal* photo

boosts to the history project was the appointment in 1957 of Mrs. R.C. Walker, of St. George, as the FWIO's first provincial Tweedsmuir history curator. Mrs. Walker took her new role very seriously, and set out to raise the standards of WI history work to an even higher standard. One of the first steps was to get an accurate picture of the number of Tweedsmuir history books that existed throughout Ontario. This was no easy task.

For the next three years Mrs. Walker pleaded with the Board members to encourage the local branch curators to report on their historical activities by sending her information about the books they were compiling. She was convinced that a great deal of local work was going unreported. By 1964 she was able to report that all levels of the organization had begun to take the Tweedsmuir history books seriously. "All Areas have Tweedsmuir Curators, and 109 Districts have District Curators. There are 1,209 Branch Curators, and Branch Histories recorded are well over 1,100."

Encouraged by that scale of activity, Mrs. Walker decided to pursue the job of bringing uniformity to the history books. Prizes for the best Tweedsmuir history book had existed since 1947 when Lady Tweedsmuir provided a silver cup to be awarded annually. Academic historians and bodies such as the Ontario Historical Society lent their services to act as judges in the competitions. The provincial curator was delighted with these competitions and the fact that some standard measures were being applied to the local works. In keeping with that emphasis, she introduced workshops known as Tweedsmuir workshops to teach the fundamentals of making history books to the volunteer curators scattered across the province.

To supplement the workshops and emphasize conformity to the model, Mrs. Walker released the first Tweedsmuir Handbook in 1962. Designed to serve as a guide for local curators who were charged with keeping and displaying the Tweedsmuir books, the manual outlined how to go about compiling a local history book. It was a set of practical guidelines, providing everything from the official first pages to the table of contents, to details on the type of paper, adhesives and covers to use. In her 1964 report, the provincial curator assured the Board members that "there is no regulation book," and yet she had certainly created some stringent reporting procedures. "A list of the table of contents of every Tweedsmuir History is to be submitted to the Provincial Curator; also any change of Curator is to be submitted to the Curator at the next level and also to the Provincial Curator."[56]

Mrs. Walker's work and that of the hundreds of local curators did not go unnoticed. The Tweedsmuir history books continued to stand as a record not only of the Institutes' community activities, but also of the changing face of rural Ontario. At its annual meeting in 1962, the Canadian Historical Association honoured the Women's Institutes with a Certificate of Merit for their outstanding contribution to local history in Canada. Honoured to receive these distinctions, some local curators were troubled by the kind of attention their work was attracting. "Judges [should] realize that these Books are not being compiled by Historians, history teachers, etc., but by women of ordinary calibre and by family members of the communities concerned, with the object of preserving the history of said community, and with human interest stories. . . . therefore [they should] be judged in that light. The content of the books should not be compared to texts of history books."[57] The complaint behind this concern was that the keeping of Tweedsmuir history books was becoming too regimented and local curators were losing control over their own projects.

Nevertheless, over the next several years, as Canada's centennial celebrations approached and rural Ontario underwent unprecedented sociological change, the roles of the Tweedsmuir history books and of the WI as the keepers of local history were even further enhanced. Mrs. Walker offered a challenge to the keepers of the local history books: "For 1967 — could we make definite decisions re the preservation and protection of these valuable histories, and plan special events to emphasize them?"[58] As rural communities throughout Ontario celebrated the centennial of the country and the province, Women's Institute historians would play very prominent roles, and their work in compiling the local history books would indeed be emphasized.

Kent Centre WI members put the finishing touches on their quilt celebrating both the branch's twentieth anniversary and Canada's centennial. The quilt was later auctioned at a euchre party where it was purchased for $111 — UG, FWIO Collection

CHAPTER EIGHT

Changing Society: Rural Transitions, 1967–1981

"Attics are being ransacked for the articles that grandmother tossed out as junk and that are now considered precious and known to be irreplaceable. Clothes are being taken out of old trunks. Stories are being recalled and there is a growing appreciation of the deeds and hardships of the pioneers," readers of *Home and Country* were told in the summer of 1967. It was Canada's centennial year, and the opportunity to look back and celebrate the past was taken very seriously by members of the Women's Institutes throughout Ontario. The report "Centennial and the Women's Institutes" continued by pointing out that "the Women's Institutes for many years have been conscious of the importance of preserving the history of their communities. This year they are the leaders, in many cases, in planning Centennial programs."[1]

The Institutes' expertise in collecting local history was central to the celebrations in most rural communities. Tweedsmuir history curators became consultants to whom most local organizers turned. Mrs. R.C. Walker, the provincial Tweedsmuir curator, emphasized that work in her annual report to the FWIO Board. "Curators have spent a busy year on centennial commissions, assisting people with publications, arranging displays of histories and in other ways acquainting people with their precious volumes. [Tweedsmuir] Books have been widely scanned for informative background of our local communities."[2] The Women's Institutes were the undisputed authorities in matters of local history, and in 1967 there was a real appetite for all the history they could serve up.

Under the careful direction of Mrs. R.C. Walker, provincial curator from 1957 to 1977 and historical research convenor for three years before that, the importance of keeping Tweedsmuir Histories was emphasized and guidelines for compiling the books were circulated. Here Mrs. Walker (second from the right) shows the Provincial Tweedsmuir book to Mrs. Norman Coulthard, Miss Lily Dempsey and Mrs. Wilker. — *Home and Country*, summer 1973

Virtually every single Institute across Ontario did something special to celebrate the nation's anniversary, and with 1,363 local branches, that was a lot of activity. Tweedsmuir history books are replete with photographs of centennial floats, commemorative quilts, historical costumes and other reports of special projects conducted during that year. Each member was encouraged to undertake some special individual project to mark the anniversary. "Be a participant rather than an on-looker," Ethel Demaine urged in a featured article in *Home and Country*. "Attempt a novel work of art; invent a useful gadget; design a new creation, or a new design; refurbish an old relic; trace your family tree, or history, and so on — but you take it from

As the country celebrated its centennial, WI members were called upon for their expertise in local history. Here Whitby WI members Mrs. Russel Sanders and Mrs. Earl Ward examine their Tweedsmuir History at the branch's seventieth birthday party.

— UG, FWIO Collection; *Home and Country*, fall 1967

here, keeping in mind that your personal centennial project should have a distinctly Canadian flavour."[3] So many festivities and projects were taken on that the office of *Home and Country* was flooded with reports. The editors promised to publish as much of it as they could throughout the year, and though approximately six pages per issue were devoted to the centennial festivities at branch level, this was only a small sample of what was going on. *Home and Country* attempted to summarize the flurry of activity. It was a long and impressive list of accomplishments.

> Community centres were built, restored, furnished and landscaped. Parks were improved, cemeteries restored, beaches and playgrounds cleared and improved. Libraries were opened, books donated to them, and in several instances, encyclopedia and geographics presented to schools. Little red school houses, abandoned in the progress of education, were bought and preserved for meeting places. Countless school bells have been set up on cairns of all descriptions. Signs showing homes of Women's Institute members as well as entrance signs to settlements were erected. Centennial art shows, old-fashioned garden parties, balls, maple syrup festivals, "Portraits of the Past" and other fashion shows of old hats and clothes, etc. created real interest. Centennial queens were sponsored, flags bought and floats entered in community parades which always featured some of the vast number of centennial gowns fashioned for the year. Cook books were edited containing old and new recipes, antique displays of quilts, rugs, etc. revived crafts of years gone by. Histories were written, cabinets made in which to display them and Canada's history reviewed in the Centennial Train and Caravan.[4]

The centennial celebrations provided welcome opportunities to glorify the past and momentarily forget the rapid changes that were transforming rural women's lives. "They are having a wonderful time," said Ethel Chapman, the editor of *Home and Country*, speaking of the Women's Institute members. "And they are teaching the younger generations Canada's history in a painless and delightful way."[5] The chance to teach history in such a positive way was a diversion from some of the rather painful and distressing trends that Institute members observed occurring around them. In 1967 rural Ontario was a society in transition. Major sociological changes were occurring, and these developments were such that most rural communities would never again be the same.

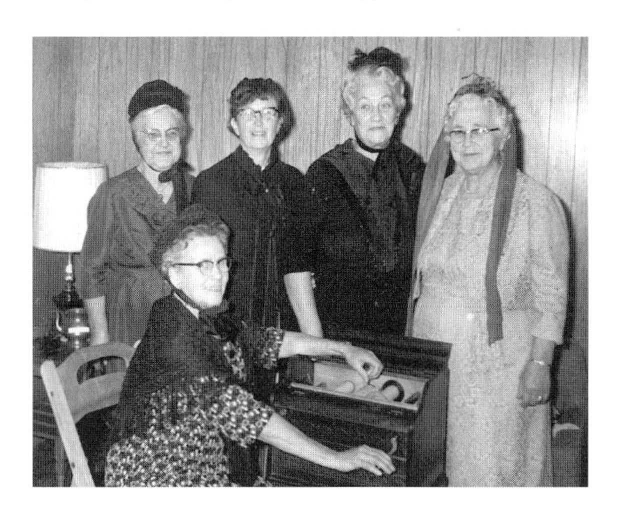

Many WI members enjoyed dressing in costume for Canada's centennial celebrations, wearing gowns that they made to represent the fashions of 1867. Members of the Haysville WI are shown here with a "grind organ," one of the antiques they displayed at their Pre-Centennial Tea.

— *Haysville WI Tweedsmuir History; Home and Country*, winter 1967

For women caught up with portraying and glorifying the pioneer era, there were many troubling forces to be faced when the excitement of the centennial had passed. Over the next fifteen years, three particular challenges faced the Institutes. First, rural communities were changing beyond recognition as school consolidations throughout Ontario were finalized. Second, there was a sense of alarm about the future of the family as a spirit of so-called permissiveness drew attention to non-traditional family structures. Third, the women's movement was gathering strength, and the WI was being forced to consider its position with reference to "women's lib." To add to all of this, by the early 1980s, the Institutes would be challenged to justify their very existence as the provincial government restructured its various ministries and the services they provided.

This was a time of dramatic change for rural Ontario. Recognizing those realities, organizers of the Officers' Conference in Waterloo in 1974 invited Dr. C.T.M. Hadwen, a sociologist from the University of Guelph, to speak on "Stress in Rural Areas." Dr. Hawden posed the rhetorical question, "Are people in rural Ontario under any more stress than the urban dweller?" and then pointed out that the rural communities had experienced tremendous change that added to their stress. "Some of the changes that affect rural life: many of the local churches are closing, the loss of local institutions, regional schools have taken over, these are a few changes that have changed the life style of the rural resident. Rural folk now live in a wider circle, bigger environment, deal with strangers and personal involvement appears to be less, which leads to a loss in personal quality of life. . . . Pressures on the farmer are great: Marketing Boards and government regulations have undermined his traditional independence; part time jobs sometimes create problems; the fact so few young people remain on the farm." In the report of Professor Hawden's talk, *Home and Country* optimistically reported that in the process of change, "the WIs can play a role. They traditionally have worked with rural people, have a strong feeling of local life and could improve the quality of life by bringing all together on a common ground to talk things out — relieve stress."[6]

WI branches may have played that proposed role to a certain extent, but the fact was that many branches themselves were experiencing the same stress caused by the same factors. Young people were leaving the community, women were taking on part-time work outside the home, community institutions were collapsing, and the new consolidated

The Stroud WI members combined their loves of history and homemaking to the amusement of onlookers, with their float in the parade that celebrated the centennial of Simcoe County. — UG, FWIO Collection; *Home and Country*, winter 1954

The Alvinston WI decided to commemorate the centennial year by erecting street signs in their community. This activity harkens back to WI community improvement campaigns early in the century. LEFT TO RIGHT: *Mrs. John Walker, Mrs. Robert Tait, Mrs. Art Yost, Mrs. Leland Pavey.*
— UG, FWIO Collection; *Home and Country*, summer 1967

Community life across rural Ontario changed dramatically with the consolidation of rural school boards. Where once Institutes had played vital roles in school reform, now they presided over historic commemoration of those schools. In a 1964 presentation, members of the Mount Elgin WI stood by a cairn they built to preserve the bell of their local public school. — UG, FWIO Collection

schools were competing for families' attention beyond the small rural neighbourhoods. The unravelling of rural community life was proceeding at an alarming pace, and despite the optimism, no amount of "talking it out" would reverse that trend or its inevitable consequences for the WI.

The Institutes' statistical record was not at all encouraging. By 1971, WI membership had fallen to just over 30,000 women, a drop of 17,000 from the postwar high twenty years earlier. Membership totals had not been so low since the 1920s. Branches were rapidly disbanding too. There were only 1,300 branches in 1971, a number that almost matched the wartime lows of the 1940s. The postwar boom for the Institutes was definitely over.

Nevertheless, Margaret Zoeller was undaunted. As past president of the FWIO and Provincial Convenor of Resolutions in 1971–1972, she urged the members to resolve to increase the membership through more effective recruitment. Her annual report ended with a challenge, aptly phrased as a formal resolution, and she suggested that every member should act upon it: "WHEREAS there are many young married women in (name Community); and WHEREAS few of them belong to the Women's Institute; and WHEREAS they may join if they are approached to do so; THEREFORE BE IT RESOLVED that every member will do all in her power to see that these people are invited to attend a meeting with a view to becoming a member."[7]

Mrs. Zoeller's suggestion got results. The membership drive resulted in an increased membership in more than 140 branches; each of those WIs recorded more than a 20 percent increase in membership over a twelve-month period during 1972–1973. The same year, 77 other branches were very close to reaching that goal. Again in 1973–1974, some 144 branches could report the same 20 percent growth rate in membership.[8] It was growth, but not enough to reverse the trends.

Beyond the recruitment of new members for the branches, Institutes responded to the changes in rural society by turning their attention to youth work, concentrating specifically on 4-H Homemaking clubs. In the late 1960s, the Institutes were already

The 4-H Homemaking club program depended heavily on the Institutes to provide local leaders for the clubs. Shirley van Den Dries from Iona Station demonstrates what she has learned in her program, Embroidery Yesterday and Today.
— UG, FWIO Collection; *Home and Country*, fall 1970

heavily committed to these Department of Agriculture clubs for girls ages twelve to twenty. In 1968, for example, 2,459 4-H Homemaking clubs were active in Ontario, and according to estimates, a full 95 percent of those groups were sponsored by Women's Institute branches.[9] Although it included financial support, sponsorship took a variety of forms. Most important was the direct involvement of local women (usually WI members) who agreed to act as leaders in the 4-H club work. Leaders attended training sessions to master the course content in the various home economics courses focussing on nutrition, crafts, sewing and personal development. These women generally opened their homes to the young women of the neighbourhood once a week to share their kitchens or their sewing machines as they demonstrated the new skills. Course units typically lasted for up to ten weeks and culminated in an Achievement Day, when the members displayed their workbooks and projects, and received a silver teaspoon to mark their accomplishment.

Some WI members claimed that as 4-H leaders, they learned just as much as the girls. "I became a 4-H leader, I worked in 4-H for a number of years. I had my daughters in it at the time. . . . My eldest daughter had eighteen projects . . . and after she was married she said she learned more through 4-H than anything she could ever have done through school. She said it helped her so much in homemaking and I think for myself the same thing. You learn so much through 4-H clubs."[10]

There was much more going on in these 4-H clubs than the simple transmission of homemaking skills or an attempt to offset rural migration to the cities. This was not an attempt to curb the trends that were drawing young women toward the larger urban centres. Rather, it was a means of equipping them with life skills — skills they would use wherever they ended up living. The courses were designed above all, to concentrate on the girls' personal development, and leaders fondly speak about young girls who gained confidence through the club work and learned to articulate themselves through the public presentations they made. The clubs were very much like an apprenticeship into Institute work, as girls learned to conduct meetings, perfect their home economics skills, and make public presentations.

The clubs were equally effective in recruiting adult members for the local Institutes because many of the mothers of 4-H members found themselves involved in the Institute for the first time, or involved in new ways because of their daughters' club work. "I was a city girl and when I got married I went to the country," Margaret Penning, from Woodstock North WI, explained. "It was our girls, our two oldest girls who were at the age where they could go to 4-H and one of the 4-H clubs suggested that perhaps I could get Woodstock North

Home and Country, fall 1970

Home and Country, fall 1972

Supporting young women who went on to higher education was an important part of Institute activity, and many districts set aside funds to create awards. TOP: *Linda Smith of Wyoming received the Lambton North WI Scholarship from Mrs. Earle Gibb in 1970.* BOTTOM: *Anne Shifflett (left) and Carol Thomson were the winners of the the Wellington South WI Scholarships presented by Mrs. L.A. Jefferson in 1972.* — UG, FWIO Collection

Sponsoring 4-H clubs throughout rural Ontario, the WI often provided leadership and financial help to this important youth organization. Pictured here at the 1974 Eastern Ontario Area Convention, some WI officers admire an information display showing that more than 1,500 young people in Eastern Ontario were involved in a variety of 4-H programs emphasizing food, sewing and personal development. LEFT TO RIGHT: *Mrs. Graham Spry, Deputy President ACWW; Mrs. McLean, President Eastern Ontario; Mrs. Noblitt, FWIO President; Miss Helen McKercher, Director; Mrs. Lucien Lamoureaux; Mrs. Hugh McMillan.*

— UG, FWIO Collection, *Home and Country*, winter 1974

WI to sponsor a club again. They had sponsored one before. Anyway so that was the thing. I approached them and at that time was invited to join and that was the beginning, I guess you could say."[11] For Margaret, like so many other women, there was a close connection between 4-H and the Institute. In this case, the 4-H club got the local WI to be their sponsor, and the WI got a 4-H mother as their newest Institute member.

Some 4-H club members were invited to participate in Girls' Conferences at the OAC campus in Guelph. Institute leaders used those occasions to challenge the highest achievers among the 4-H membership to feel a sense of anticipation about their future roles. At the same time, the conferences were designed to instill traditional values into members' lives as an antidote to the perceived threat of the so-called permissiveness that was dominating the 1970s. This theme surfaced several times in the early 1970s. Citing the views of her friend and colleague, Ethel Chapman reiterated that "there was an ethical standard in anything Maryn Pardy wrote that must have been a joy to women troubled by the much publicized permissiveness of the times." Specifically, Pardy had argued in one of her 1972 editorials in *Home and Country* that "a society is headed for trouble unless it is prepared to indoctrinate its children with certain values; honesty, truthfulness, work well done, kindness and compassion, respect for law and democratic rights."[12]

Reinforcing traditional values was a common theme for Ethel Chapman herself to stress, and in her leadership role at the Guelph Girls' Conferences she spoke about the theme several times. This was not, however, a stern morality divorced from modern realities. In one of her addresses, Miss Chapman urged the young delegates to think about preparing themselves for a career, not as an alternative to marriage altogether, but as an alternative to early marriage. "If a girl delays marriage for a career, her horizons may broaden and her choice of life partner may be quite different than it would have been if she had married earlier." Chapman reminded the delegates to this conference, who ranged in age from sixteen to their early twenties, that "when choosing a mate, far more important than looks or brilliance is what he thinks about God, money or a crying baby."

Attention was still being given to marriage as a model and to the place of moral values, but times were definitely changing, and the conference speakers were recognizing that fact and trying to keep pace with it. Mrs. Woof, who introduced a panel discussion on careers, pointed out to the 4-H delegates the new realities and range of choices open to young rural women like themselves. "Looking at you, I find the potential awesome. . . . What future mayor, parliamentarian, mother, nurse or surgeon sits beside you?" She continued

Dr. Ethel Chapman sits with delegate Brenda Vanpatter, St. Thomas, looking at Chapman's book, From a Roadside Window, *at the 1973 Girls' Conference. Young women from rural Ontario looked up to Chapman for her advice and her experience.*
— UG, FWIO Collection, *Home and Country,* fall 1973

Building on the wealth of experiences she had received as a 4-H member and leader and a WI member, Pat Salter entered municipal politics and served for twelve years, including three years as Reeve of the Township of Peel. Pat is just one example of rural women who trace their early leadership training to their experiences in 4-H and Women's Institute. — Pat Salter

to urge the teenagers to think creatively about their futures. "The stereotyped picture of a woman marrying, raising a family and working at home which was not long ago is not so valid now. Statistics indicate that 8 out of 10 women work outside the home at some time in their lives and more than one third of all married women are working. Consider what job prospects you will have after you finish your education. It is easier to get that education now than it will be after you are married and have children. Many women return to a profession after having children. So now take advantage of opportunities to find out about various careers. The door is wide open to you."[13]

The choice of domestic science education was undoubtedly promoted as one option, but 4-H club members were strongly encouraged to pursue a range of academic training. To make such postsecondary education possible, the Women's Institutes created several scholarships, which were presented annually to daughters of WI members with promising academic potential. Several new universities and community colleges were created throughout the province in the 1960s to cater to the young people who were the product of the baby boom. Those young women would go on to higher education in far greater numbers than their

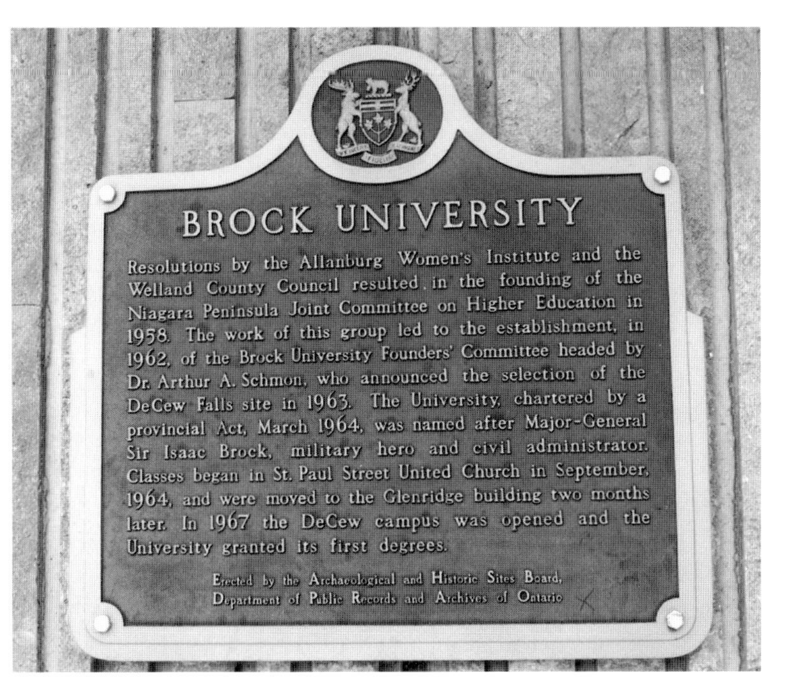

BROCK UNIVERSITY
Resolutions by the Allanburg Women's Institute and the Welland County Council resulted in the founding of the Niagara Peninsula Joint Committee on Higher Education in 1958. The work of this group led to the establishment, in 1962, of the Brock University Founders' Committee headed by Dr. Arthur A. Schmon, who announced the selection of the DeCew Falls site in 1963. The University, chartered by a provincial Act, March 1964, was named after Major-General Sir Isaac Brock, military hero and civil administrator. Classes began in St. Paul Street United Church in September, 1964, and were moved to the Glenridge building two months later. In 1967 the DeCew campus was opened and the University granted its first degrees.
Erected by the Archaeological and Historic Sites Board, Department of Public Records and Archives of Ontario

Commitment to higher education sometimes went beyond financial support for individual students. Several new universities had opened in Ontario by the early 1960s, among them, Brock University in St. Catharines. A historic plaque erected by the Archaeological and Historic Sites Board points out that the Allanburg Women's Institute was instrumental in helping to found the new university.

— Jean Egerter, *Allanburg WI Tweedsmuir History*

mothers had done. In the 1940s, less than four percent of the population attended university, and with limited access to high schools, most of Ontario's rural youth did not proceed beyond eighth grade. Things were very different by the 1960s and 1970s. New academic realities meant that the young women of Ontario would not be following in their mothers' footsteps. They needed to prepare for different experiences.

The message of the new realities of the future was one that the Institutes were also trying to process for themselves. Two events of the 1970s that were evidence that the women's movement was in full force were the publication of the *Report of the Royal Commission on the Status of Women in Canada* and the celebration of International Women's Year. It was time for the Women's Institutes of Ontario to look to the future, declare their position, and take up the issues of the feminist movement. These were not themes that most WI members were eager to address. While contemporary developments demanded attention, the 1970s were also the decade of important historical celebrations for the WI, including the seventy-fifth anniversary of the movement and the acquisition of important historic sites. Members and leaders were torn between embracing an uncertain future and celebrating a nostalgic history.

For many WI members, concentrating on the past was much more comfortable than contemplating the future. Two events helped the Institutes to focus on their own history: the acquisition of the Erland Lee Home as a historic site and the celebration of the Women's Institutes' seventy-fifth anniversary.

According to *Home and Country* in the fall of 1973, "Women's Institute history was made on August 9th when over 400 Women's Institute members from across the Province and interested friends from all over gathered at the Erland Lee Home, Ridge Road, Stoney Creek, for the official opening of the 'Home.' Eight bus loads came from as far away as 350 miles to be present for the memorable event. The occasion was to celebrate the acquisition of the property by the Federated Women's Institutes of Ontario in June 1972, and to honour Erland and his wife Janet."[14] Acquiring that property was an important milestone for the organization and the timing of it, falling as it did during the year of the WI's seventy-fifth anniversary, was no coincidence.

Negotiations with the Lee family had been ongoing for a number of years. In July 1969, Katherine Lee (wife of Frank Lee, and daughter-in-law of Erland and Janet) granted to the FWIO an option to purchase the property, and after her death in November 1971, the Institutes exercised that option. The purchase price was $40,000, and according to the legal documents outlining the conditions of the deal struck between the FWIO and Mrs. Lee's estate, the Institutes agreed that "the above described lands and premises shall be used by it in accordance with the aims and objectives of the Federated Women's Institutes of Ontario, and further that in the event that the said lands are no longer required by the grantee for its purposes, the grantee will transfer the said lands to a recognized Society or authority for the sole purpose of the preservation of the property as an historical site."[15]

When the FWIO acquired the historic property of the Lee family near Stoney Creek, a new emphasis was placed on the role of Erland Lee as co-founder of the WI. One of the most famous objects in the Erland Lee (Museum) Home is the dining-room table where the original constitution of the Women's Institutes was first drafted. — UG, FWIO Collection

Acquiring the property and highlighting the involvement of Janet and Erland Lee meant that the interpretation of WI history had to be adjusted to accommodate a more central role for this Stoney Creek couple. The story of the founding meeting had been retold countless times whenever Institute history was highlighted, but now careful attention was paid not only to the vision of Adelaide Hoodless, but also to the couple who organized the meeting at which she spoke. A new historical plaque was placed on the property in 1967, and the FWIO's Lee Homestead Committee formally declared that Mr. Lee should share the accolades with Mrs. Hoodless, and from that time forward, the WI had two recognized founders, not one. Janet Lee was not elevated to the same level, and so, ironically, while Canadian women carved out more recognition for themselves during the 1960s and 1970s, the leaders of the Women's Institutes voted to reinterpret their history, bringing forward a male co-founder to share centre stage with Mrs. Hoodless.

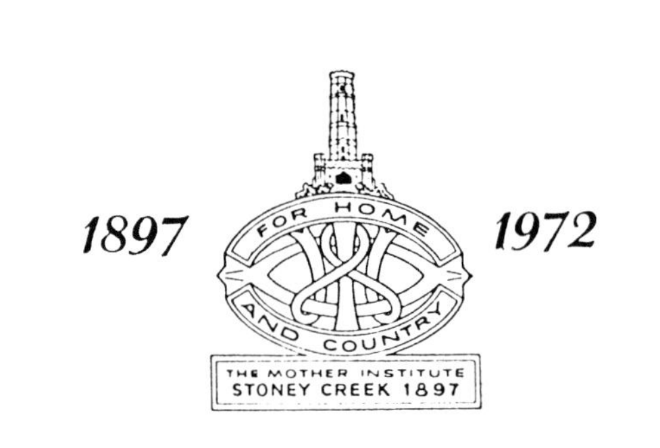

The STONEY CREEK
WOMEN'S INSTITUTE
(The First in the World)

Celebrates its
75th BIRTHDAY

Sidonia Hall

FEBRUARY 19th, 1972

1897 1972

75th Anniversary
of the
Mother Institute, Stoney Creek
on Saturday, February 19th, 1972
Sidonia Hall
232 Barton St. E., Stoney Creek
Entertainment
Tickets $5.00 *Dinner 6.30 p.m.*

— *Stoney Creek WI Tweedsmuir History*

The plan to honour Erland Lee by acquiring his property had been in the works for some time. In 1966 the Winona WI had requested that the Historic Sites Board recognize Mrs. E.D. Smith with a plaque because she had served as the first branch president of the Stoney Creek Institute. Around the same time, a request was initiated to declare the Lee property a historic site. The provincial Historic Sites Board turned the decision back to the Institutes, asking them to settle the matter about where a plaque should be placed, and what and whom it should commemorate. In October 1967 the matter was settled with the unveiling of a plaque at the Lee Homestead, one that acknowledged Erland and Janet's contribution but also recognized Mrs. Smith as first president and the Stoney Creek branch as the first Institute.

As the FWIO approached its seventy-fifth anniversary, the new property became the focus of a great deal of energy, and the Lee Homestead Committee pursued a variety of strategies to try to raise the money they needed to buy the property. Since 1968 that committee had been authorized by the Board "to accept funds from all possible sources, with the definite intent to purchase the home. The funds so received would be administered by the Finance Committee of the FWIO."[16] Recognizing that owning the property would represent an ongoing financial commitment to maintain it, the FWIO Board was determined to raise the necessary funds. At the spring meeting in April 1972, having decided to go ahead with the purchase, Board members held a discussion about the possible uses to which the home could be put — for displays, storage of archival materials, tour groups, or even as a provincial office for the FWIO. After a lengthy discussion, a motion was passed granting freedom to the Erland Lee Homestead Committee and Margaret Zoeller, as Chair of that committee, to "do what they deem necessary with regards to the Home, for the period just after the Home is purchased in June until the Annual Board Meeting in November 1972."[17]

While the purchase of the Lee Home dominated the business of the FWIO in the second half of 1972, the year had begun with another important event — the celebration in February of the seventy-fifth anniversary of the Women's Institutes in Ontario. Plans for the birthday celebration began several months in advance. With a budget of almost $10,000, the special anniversary luncheon was a gala affair. In total, 1,613 people attended the February 12 event at the Royal York Hotel in Toronto. Guests at the head table included several provincial dignitaries, and a special guest of honour, Mrs. Olive Farquharson, the President of the ACWW, who addressed the meeting. The banquet room was suitably decorated with the Institute colours and members were treated to a special birthday cake, a replica of the Erland Lee Home designed by Mrs. Jean Gingerich, of the Haysville WI in Waterloo South District. By all accounts it was a wonderful success, and Bernice Noblitt, the FWIO President from 1971 to 1974, acknowledged the work of the Anniversary Committee with gratitude.

Although the anniversary celebrations were a grand event, many members who wanted to participate could not be present. While provincial leaders strategized over how to raise funds for the Lee Home, and how to accommodate the guests for anniversary luncheons, thousands of WI members at branch level were not part of the Lee Homestead project, nor

To celebrate the seventy-fifth anniversary of the WI, the Ayr Women's Institute dressed in their centennial costumes and gathered around a portrait of Adelaide Hoodless in the home of one of their members. — UG, FWIO Collection

Over 1,600 attended the banquet at the Royal York Hotel to celebrate the seventy-fifth anniversary of the Women's Institutes.
— UG, FWIO Collection; *Home and Country*, winter 1972

While some members celebrated the WI's important birthday with feasting at the Royal York, others put their stitchery talents to work. The South River WI created this stunning commemorative quilt to mark the occasion. Pictured here are Mrs. R. Millar, the Provincial Board Director representing South River WI, and Mrs. Gordon Wilson, the Branch President.
— UG, FWIO Collection; *Home and Country*, winter 1973

Gracing the head table at the seventy-fifth anniversary banquet was a model of the newly acquired historic site, the Erland Lee Home near Stoney Creek. The remarkable thing about this model, however, is the fact that it was also the anniversary cake, created by Mrs. Willard Gingerich of Baden, Ontario.
— UG, FWIO Collection; *Home and Country*, winter 1972

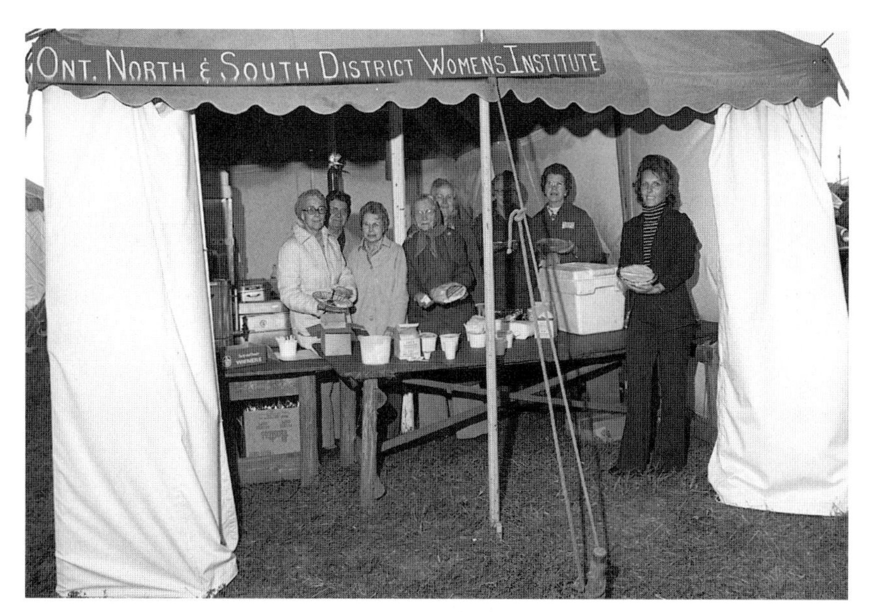

In the tented city at the 1975 International Plowing Match, held in Ontario County, Institute members served what was proclaimed as "the best homemade pie." — UG, FWIO Collection; *Home and Country*, fall 1975

were they present at the special anniverary luncheon. Instead, they organized their own local celebrations to mark the seventy-fifth anniversary closer to home and involve as many members as possible.

Members in Northwestern Ontario, for example, were isolated from the celebrations and the sites in Southern Ontario by the problems of distance. "We were supporting some of the things that we cannot take advantage of," a WI member in Thunder Bay told me during an interview. "Just drop by for tea some afternoon [they say]. That's stupid, in my opinion, get real! I'll tell you something that happened when I was on provincial board. This was when they started to talk about the Erland Lee Home, they wondered why [we objected]. I said, well, we would never be able to take advantage of it as you people do . . . we just can't go to those places and see them. A lot of our women would never see them . . . they can't."[18]

For the majority of WI members, involvement at branch level was the main attraction. For some women, it was the craft classes or other instruction that really attracted them to the Institute and kept them involved. The educational component was very important. For others, the experience was more social. A member of the Stanley WI in Thunder Bay District recalled that her mother-in-law encouraged her to join. "I was [at home] alone with three small boys and she said, 'You can't stay home with those three kids all the time. You've got to do something else.' So she brought me to the meeting and that's when I joined and I haven't been sorry, that's my female outlet."[19]

Christine Jacobson from the McIntyre branch emphasized the female connections too. "I joined in October 1974 and I joined because my mother and my grandmother and my aunts and my grandmothers and their daughters all encouraged me to join. I think the first year I joined they nominated me secretary treasurer. I tended to be really shy at the time, I had little kids and I was happy just to participate but they very much encouraged me to become active. They introduced me to 4-H and I got very active there, for a number of years, was a leader. Very much enjoyed that. They sent me out to conferences all by my lonesome where I met some wonderful ladies. . . It's really got me out and involved."[20] The increased confidence was an experience shared by countless other women. Another member told a similar tale about joining the WI to

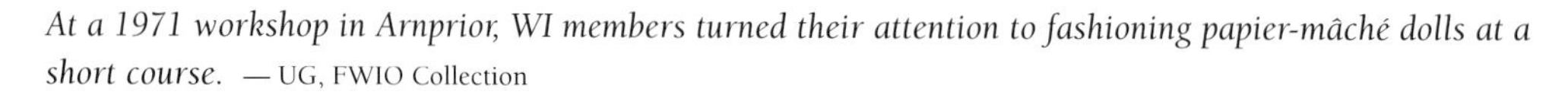

At a 1971 workshop in Arnprior, WI members turned their attention to fashioning papier-mâché dolls at a short course. — UG, FWIO Collection

meet a personal need for relationships. "We moved out from the city in 1969," Rose MacDonald of the O'Connor WI recalled. "I was impressed by the calibre of the women that I met both at the district and the area conventions and I thought it was the best thing that I have ever done and I have never regretted it. My kids were teenagers by then and I felt I needed something on my own and I found it in the Institute."[21]

The ever-popular idea of meeting other women in the community also continued to attract newcomers in the 1970s, as it had done for eighty years. Jeanne Davies was a housewife with young children when she joined the South River WI. "The reason I picked WI (I knew nothing at all about them) but they had sent me two birth congratulations when my babies were born and I thought, well this is an interesting group, they're interested enough to send me a card and I didn't even know the women. So anyway, I thought I would find out who they were and that was the reason I joined."[22] For the majority of WI members, Institute work continued to revolve around those relationships forged in their local branches.

Dedication to the local community was, after all, one of the most enduring themes of Institute experience. According to one estimate, less than five percent of WI members ever move on to involvement in the highest levels of the organization. One former provincial president, remarking about local branch composition, commented, "I would say three-quarters of our members really aren't interested in moving up to even the district level."[23] Recognizing that most members did not aspire to progress beyond branch involvement, the FWIO leadership concentrated on the importance of developing leadership at the branch level through training sessions known as Officers' Conferences. At these events, branch executive members from across the province came together to learn effective leadership methods. In the 1970s, those conferences were usually held on the campus of the University of Waterloo. Margaret Zoeller reminded delegates to the 1976 Officers' Conference about the importance of local activity in a talk entitled "Women in Our

On the move, these women travelled to the University of Waterloo campus in 1976 to attend the annual Officers' Conference. Under a creative cost-sharing scheme, officers throughout Ontario could all attend for the same price because travel costs were divided equally among the delegates. LEFT TO RIGHT: *Mrs. Orval Jordon, Mrs. Norman Tuck, Mrs. E. Urstadt, Mrs. Rebecca Johnson.* — UG, FWIO Collection

Simcoe County members Mrs. Don Hennessy and Mrs. Donald Jacobs displayed some of the work of local women in creating "House Logs." Not only did these books make fascinating genealogical studies of the former occupants of a home, they also served as a practical reference tool. Current owners were able to trace the renovation history of the structure and the finer points of the electrical and plumbing systems. — UG, FWIO Collection; *Home and Country,* fall 1977.

"Never again — twenty back seat drivers."

— *McIrvine WI Tweedsmuir History*

World." She urged the members to think about the roles of women, but "not about the great women whose names are recorded in history, nor the group that are household names, but the women of today that form part of our society. You and I. . . . The democracy in which we live gives us women a certain liberty."[24]

Women's roles in society were receiving a lot of attention in the 1970s inside WI circles and beyond. When she took office in 1975, the new FWIO president from Chesley, Mrs. Herbert (Verna) Maluske, was introduced as a woman with many interests including her church work and her local historical society. She suggested that the most appropriate way to mark the occasion of International Women's Year would be to focus attention on women's roles in history. "We could learn the history of the women in our own communities, those who have made contributions in the past and the present time. Or we could study the image of women at various times in history and in different cultures. We could even focus on the history of women's struggle for emancipation. . . . How about doing a study of women's role, past and present, in local, regional, provincial or national affairs? Better still, why not apply that to a study of the women who have served us so well at every level of our great organization through all the seventy-eight years of its existence."[25] It was a worthy idea, but in some members' minds, the association between WI and history was altogether too strong.

"I personally worry about the future of the WI, and so do others that I have talked to from time to time," wrote Mary E. James from Union Hall WI in Lanark North District. "I don't think it can survive long as an organization that teaches handicrafts, yet that is how many outsiders see it. I'm not sure that it is fulfilling the vision of Adelaide Hoodless, whom I perceive as a true feminist — free, loving and responsible; but we need to talk about that. So far, in *Home and Country*, I see all kinds of anniversaries being celebrated, but I also want to see the NOW celebrated. Adelaide Hoodless lived NOW, and her NOW was 1897; ours is 1979. In *Home and Country* please." In response, the editor agreed that there was much more to the WI than the celebration of the past. She pointed out the volunteerism, the social stimulus, the resolutions, the international projects, and its role as "mouthpiece in government and industry" to emphasize that the WI was alive and well, and much more than just a teacher of handicrafts. Without using the word "feminist," the editor, Margaret Zoeller, even seemed to concur with the writer when she said "there will always be a need, regardless of the decade, to encourage women to have confidence in themselves and stand on their own feet."[26]

Indeed, despite opinions to the contrary, the Institutes were devoted to empowering women. This was not an organization that was locked in the past, nor was it devoted solely to commemorating past achievements. The images that were imprinted on many people's minds because of the historical celebrations of the Canadian centennial and the Institutes' seventy-fifth anniversary did not tell the full story. The Institutes were very much a part of current concerns as well. For example, when the Royal Commission on the Status of Women in Canada was collecting briefs for their report, the Women's Institutes were a part of that process. Represented by their national body, the Institutes submitted a brief to the Status of Women Ad

Hoc Committee. While they continued to emphasize the importance of women's roles as homemakers, the Women's Institutes did not do so to the exclusion of all other issues. The Women's Institutes were concerned about much more than historical costumes and craft classes. The leadership was not caught in a trap of outdated ideas.

Their submission on the Status of Women was a combination of traditional notions and some surprisingly progressive ideas. In the FWIC brief, they asked for

> Adult Education Courses where they do not exist; for daycare facilities for working mothers; for Home Economics Courses in High Schools where they are not available; for compulsory pre-marital health certificates; for Family Centres to be established across Canada. They asked that abortion be taken out of the Criminal Code and be acceptable when carried out by a recognized doctor; that grounds for divorce be extended to include cruelty, incurable insanity and desertion; and that government enforce maintenance by husbands of their deserted wives and children. In the field of women in the labour force, they asked for equality of sex where ability and experience are equal; for a $2,000.00 exemption for the individual taxpayer; exemption for household help where there are dependent children and for a wage for farm women commensurate with their labours.

Helen McKercher and Margaret Zoeller enjoy the calf club competition at the Royal Winter Fair in Toronto. — UG, FWIO Collection

Bernice Noblitt, FWIO President from 1971 to 1974, reported with some pride that "Many of these submissions were included in the final report of [the Royal Commission on] the Status of Women."

The sometimes conflicting wish to celebrate the past and the need to face the future continued to present a dilemma for the Institutes. A report in a local newspaper, the *Listowel Banner*, reprinted in *Home and Country* in 1976, addressed some of the stereotypical images of the WI, and the writer of the column, herself an outsider to the WI organization, was surprised by what she observed after attending the Guelph Area Convention the previous fall. "Traditionally a rural organization, to the outsider at least, the WI has appeared to be little more than an afternoon get-together for farm wives. What the women actually did at their meetings seemed to be something of a mystery, but whatever it was, it always appeared to be secondary to the fun and games portion of the programme. After attending the Guelph Area WI Convention in Atwood early this month, however, we can assure you that apple pie-

At the 1977 Officers' Conference there were opportunities for members to put their feet up and to put their thinking caps on as they met in small groups to discuss their leadership roles at the branch level. Pictured here are Mrs. Audrey McGill, Model WI; Mrs. Agnes Hutchinson, Mount Brydges WI; Mrs. Helen Falkner, Goderich; Mrs. Audrey Young, Long Sault; Mrs. Mary Werden, Aughrim WI; and Mrs. Eleanor McGugan, Melbourne WI. — UG, FWIO Collection; *Home and Country*, fall 1977

checkered apron image of the WI is downright misleading." Familiar with the activity of Institutes in documenting local history, the journalist was surprised to find that there was much more to the WI than that. "These women know where it's at and WI units are as vital a force in their communities today as when they first formed over half a century ago," the reporter said. "WI branches are concerned with such issues as pay for farm wives, the Bail Reform Act, patient care in hospital and the relationship between the patient and the doctor and television violence. All of these issues were discussed and discussed intelligently — in the form of resolutions before the convention. . . . Besides their concern for current conditions, we learned WI branches also contribute substantial amounts of money to organizations dedicated to improving education and nutrition in the world and to assisting those with eyesight difficulties."

The range of activity came as a surprise to the Listowel journalist. Given the scope of WI activities and involvements, it was logical to associate the Institutes with the contemporary women's movement. The reporter continued, referring to "a phrase we'd heard often this year, 'From Adam's rib to Women's Lib, baby you've come a long way.' That 'baby' bit is condescending, but the message is there and organizations like the Women's Institute have got it loud and clear."[27] It was intended as a compliment, but the association with "women's lib" was not something with which all WI members were comfortable. The progressive activities of the WI and more traditional roles for women were held in constant tension throughout the 1970s, not only in the minds of outsiders looking in, but also by members of the WI themselves. While some members adamantly denied any connection between themselves and the feminist movement, others were eager to highlight what the WI had done and to see it as a step forward for rural women. Asked whether or not they considered themselves feminists, one member told me that she found that term problematic. "I think there is a bit of a problem maybe with that word, feminist, they've maybe gone a little, the extreme I mean, has gone a little too far maybe, but I don't see any reason why not. . . . We'd all be proud to be feminists."[28]

Just as perceptions about the WI were changing, so too were the organizational aspects of the Institutes' relationship with the provincial government. In October 1976, Helen McKercher retired after serving for twenty years as the Director of the Home Economics Service of the Extension Branch of the Department of Agriculture. During her tenure, Miss McKercher had maintained a very effective link between the WI and the Department of Agriculture. In part, her own rural background helped her to understand rural people. "Helen's upbringing on a farm in Huron county . . . gave her the knowledge and understanding of rural families and their problems, which was helpful in arranging programmes designed for small towns or rural areas." It was also her personality, which gave her many fond ties to the WI membership. In a tribute to her, Ilda Holder, a former provincial secretary-treasurer, recalled, "Everywhere she travels the comment is the same: 'Isn't she wonderful!' She has the gift of making friends wherever she goes and of inspiring people to reach for and achieve goals they never dreamed possible. . . . She will never be forgotten by the many thousands whose paths she has crossed."

As was customary, McKercher became an honorary president of the FWIO, and over the years, she provided a real source of continuity as provincial presidents came and went. Margaret Zoeller remarked, "She knew all about the workings of the Women's Institute and would take time to tell about the background of FWIO, the scholarships, investments, anything to help a Provincial President, with an interchange of ideas. She personally knew all the FWIC Presidents, ACWW's Mrs. Drage (the instigator of Pennies for Friendship) and Mrs. Alfred Watt, so it was little wonder that she was a tower of strength to me as President." Bernice Noblitt echoed those sentiments: "Presidents and secretaries have come and gone but she was there — a unifying presence, helping, directing, and making it possible to get things done. Throughout her years as Director, she has always had the interests of the WI uppermost in her mind and all her efforts on behalf of the members are reflected in the warmth and affection she holds in the hearts of all."

Perhaps the most important ingredient in McKercher's ability to get things done was her influence with the provincial government's Department of Agriculture. "Her management of relations with the provincial government has been such as to permit the flowering of the WI into the strong and responsible organization it is today." That rapport with the Ontario government would never again be the same. Over the following twenty years, it was understandable that members would lament the fact that things were not the way they used to be on that front.

In March 1977, Molly McGhee became the new director and she filled the post for the next five years. McGhee was born in Belfast, grew up in London, England, and received her university training at Edinburgh, where she studied dietetics in the Department of Medicine. She came to Canada to work at Mount Allison University, then later at Brockville Hospital, Rideau Regional Children's Centre, and later as associate principal at Centralia College. She obtained a B.Sc. in nutrition from University of Ottawa, and later studied psychology at McGill and completed a Master's degree at Carleton.

The Women's Institutes were entering a period of transition because of changing values and changing structures within the provincial government. While the editor of *Home and Country* emphasized in the spring 1977 issue the role of the WI in providing stability and strengthening family life during a time of transition in societal values, McGhee gave a different message in her first address to the organization at the Officers' Conference in May that same year. "Many believe there is no such thing as the family today," she began. "This may be very distressing news to members of FWIO whose motto is "For Home and Country," [however] we must be realistic in 1977 and recognize that there are many types of families, apart from the nuclear family; communal, unmarried females with children, unmarried couples living together, and divorced, separated or single parents with children. Marriage is much less permanent today, and statistics show every fourth marriage will break up. Then there is a new breed of parent today, born out of changing values at the universities since the '60s, the formation of the women's liberation movement, and a much greater affluence in the post-war years." Whether or not one accepted McGhee's assertions about the cause of the changes, there was no denying that she was absolutely right in one thing: societal values were shifting.

This was not the folksy pastoral outlook that members were used to when they thought about the meaning of their motto. Nor was it the familiar message of old-fashioned morality and traditional values that many people affectionately associated with rural living. McGhee was reflecting her academic training about societal trends, and the advice she gave to the delegates was that they needed to somehow change their programming to meet those new challenges. It was not an optimistic prognosis. The director continued by telling the young women at the Girls' Conference in Guelph that year that "she had no crystal ball to point the way to the future." Speaking about the changes that were on the way, Miss McGhee referred to the impending demise of the familiar family farm, the implications of the energy crisis, and the advent of a cashless society, where "electronic signals" would become the means of exchange "instead of cash, cheques or charge slips." Whereas delegates in previous years had heard about the limitless possibilities that awaited them as young women, McGhee's audience was told that "the choice of career will become increasingly difficult." Her advice was to "research all the avenues open to you before you make your final career choice and make sure you have an opportunity to up-grade your skills or learn new skills along the way."[29] The times were changing, and McGhee did not mince words when she prophesied pessimistically about the future.

When Florence Diamond from New Hamburg became the new FWIO president (1977–1980) she commented in her first column in *Home and Country* that she was very aware of the historical significance of the WI entering its ninth decade after the celebrations of the eightieth anniversary the previous year. Acknowledging that the WI could not afford to stand still or focus on past accomplishments, she reiterated the importance of recruiting new members. "I would like to challenge that we have not tried hard enough to involve nor invited our neighbours to participate in our monthly meetings. Let us take this as a personal member blitz as we sit down and think about our own communities." The fact was, however, that the communities had changed. No amount of thinking or trying harder or blitzing could reverse the trends that had fundamentally changed rural Ontario in the preceding years.

Mrs. Diamond was realistic about some aspects of those changes, acknowledging that "there is now no such thing as the isolation of most rural people from city influence or urban people from the country way of living. Six years ago the subjects under our Convenorships were changed to suggest more appealing avenues for women no matter where they lived. Not all patterns of living are good or bad but each of us needs to discuss and understand each other's viewpoint. If we are truly programming with current new ideas under our objectives, then we will meet the needs of ALL women in our individual districts." Urban sprawl was beginning to encroach on a number of rural communities, highway transportation made travel much more accessible, and it was quite true that WI members were not isolated from the effects of those changes.

Ironically, the real threat to the WI in terms of competition would come from a group of women who did consider themselves "rural," namely younger, activist farm women who were concerned that they needed a forum to represent the voices of women in agriculture. When those women looked at the WI, and even at the changes that Mrs. Diamond was proud to announce, they decided that the Institute was not for them. Women for the Survival of Agriculture was founded by Diane Harkin in 1975 to voice the concerns of farm women and to call for economic and political reform to recognize the particular needs of women who made their living from farming.[30] The challenges and criticisms that these new organizations raised about the Women's

Institutes forced the issue to come to a head over the next few years.

"As your Honourary President," Molly McGhee told the WI members in her annual report for 1978, "I feel I would be remiss if I did not speak frankly about matters that bother me. Eight or ten years ago WI's seemed to receive good coverage in the large daily papers, why not today? . . . [W]hy is it so difficult for the nominating committee to raise a slate of officers? . . . Are the reports [at Area Conventions] useful and meaningful to the membership? Can you really justify this somewhat extravagant way of reporting?" These hard-hitting questions were difficult to answer; nevertheless, it was important to ask them.

McGhee continued in her criticisms for several more paragraphs, and ended her report by saying "These are a few of my concerns. I hope you will not feel I am being overly critical when I tell you I think it important they receive attention."[31] McGhee was wise to issue that warning, because the provincial government was no longer able or willing to sustain the support levels that the WI had been accustomed to receiving. Realizing that the future of the Women's Institutes was precarious, the Director tried to communicate her concerns to the provincial Board in the fall of 1981. Referring to the historic agreement struck between the Province of Ontario and the Women's Institutes in *The Agricultural and Arts Amendment Act of 1902*, McGhee reminded the Board members why they received financial aid from the province. "Today, you still receive financial support and services from the Ministry under this Act," she pointed out. "The only reason you receive this support is that you are supposed to be the official voice of farm women in Ontario. Can you truthfully say that you do represent farm women adequately today?" she asked. "If not, why should you receive substantial funding from public funds?"[32]

The answers to these questions were vitally important, as the Director pointed out. "These questions are asked by other, newer organizations when they pressure government for similar financial support." The kinds of concerns that she was highlighting were very real. So too were the criticisms made by the new rural women's organizations. "It disturbs me greatly," she continued, "that three new organizations have sprung up during the past three years. It disturbs me more that it was the President of Women for the Survival of Agriculture in Ontario who was asked to represent rural women on the Canadian Advisory Council on the Status of Women; to represent rural women at a rural women's conference in Washington, and last month to represent all farm women in Canada on a Cultural Exchange to China. A more logical choice perhaps would have been the WI Convenor of Agriculture and Canadian Industries. Why weren't FWIO asked to represent Ontario rural women, instead of W.S.A.?"[33]

Hoping that her musings would goad the Institutes into action, McGhee left them with one last question: "Have you forfeited your right to represent rural women in Ontario, due to inactivity in recent years?"[34] Fifteen years earlier, the Institutes had occupied a very prominent public role as the keepers of local history. When people went searching through their attics to prepare for Canada's centennial celebrations, they turned to the Institutes for help. Now the WI itself was in danger of being relegated to the storage closet. Rural Ontario had been through some significant changes, and new organizations for rural women were competing for government recognition and funds. It was time for the Women's Institutes of Ontario to take those changes into account and carve out new roles for themselves. Their very survival depended on it.

Branch, district and area presidents gathered outside of the Mountview Women's Institute hall for the final event of the day at the Centennial Prelude celebrations.
LEFT TO RIGHT: *Peggy Knapp, Associated Country Women of the World Area President for Canada; Donna Russett, Federated Women's Institutes of Ontario President; Charlotte Johnson, Federated Women's Institutes of Canada President.*
— *Home and Country*, fall 1995

CHAPTER NINE

Moving On: Organizational Changes 1982–1997

In April 1982 the Assistant Deputy Minister of Agriculture asked Molly McGhee to bring reassurances to the FWIO Board that despite major restructuring, the relationship between the Department of Agriculture and the Women's Institutes was secure. "Dr. Clare Rennie [Assistant Deputy Minister] has asked me to read two letters to you at this time, one from the Honourable Dennis Timbrell [Minister of Agriculture] and one from himself," McGhee reported. "He hopes that this information will allay any fears you may have about the level of support that FWIO will receive in the future."[1] No doubt Dr. Rennie was sincere in his sentiment, but in spite of the letters, there were many solid reasons for the fears the WI felt about future levels of government support. The assurances that Molly McGhee read to the FWIO Board that spring were premature promises. By the fall of the same year, McGhee herself had been reassigned, the branch of the ministry that she had directed no longer existed, and the offices of the Ontario Ministry of Agriculture and Food (OMAF) were being relocated from Toronto to Guelph. As the Institutes celebrated their eighty-fifth anniversary, the future relationship between the Institutes and the government was anything but secure.

The new organizational structure meant that now the Women's Institutes would be connected to the OMAF through an arm called the Rural Organizations and Services Branch. This new creation was headed by Ken Knox, a former assistant agricultural representative and extension worker, and his assistant, who was directly responsible for the Women's Institutes, was Joyce Canning. Although she revealed that she had fond childhood memories of the WI, recalling "proudly (but carefully) passing cream and sugar to the ladies during lunch when [her] mother hosted the monthly meetings," Canning's approach was not based entirely on sentiment.[2] Instead, she was committed to a critical review of the movement. That review, she repeatedly reminded the members of the Institutes, sprang from the conviction that "tomorrow's job cannot be done with yesterday's tools."[3] By implication, Ms Canning was suggesting that the WI might be an outdated tool for working among Ontario's rural women in the 1980s. Her relationship with the WI would prove to be a difficult one. Ten months after she had taken on her new job, she challenged the membership to help her justify the Institutes' continued existence. "Why does the Federated Women's Institutes of Ontario exist? What is their purpose? their objectives? What need do they fill today in the rural woman's life?" she wondered.

85th Anniversary Luncheon
in honour of
The Founding of the Women's Institute in Ontario
August 12, 1982 - 12 noon
Galaxy Ballroom - Constellation Hotel
900 Dixon Road, Rexdale, Toronto, Ontario
Guest Speaker - Mrs. Z. Westebring-Muller
President of A.C.W.W.
Luncheon ticket - $13.75

As the relationship between the FWIO and the Ministry of Agriculture was undergoing drastic changes, the FWIO continued to mark milestones with special events. The eighty-fifth anniversary was celebrated with a luncheon at which Mrs. Z. Westebring-Muller, the ACWW President, was guest speaker.
— UG, FWIO Collection, Eighty-fifth anniversary file.

"These are the kinds of questions that I seem to get on a regular basis." As though she was unsure about the answers, she asked the members, "What would you like me to be saying to people when they ask these questions?"[4]

Janet Hiepleh, the FWIO president who oversaw this transition time during her term in office from 1980 to 1983, had politely welcomed the new OMAF leadership and commented that Knox and Canning were "two concerned people . . . [who] really want to help and [who] show a dedicated concern about WI in Ontario."[5] Indeed, although sweeping changes were occurring, in fairness to Canning and to Knox, it should be pointed out that the pressure to justify the Ministry's support of the Institutes was not their own policy creation; the pressure was coming from outside the Rural Organizations and Services Branch. The new rural women's organizations, now united into the umbrella group called the Ontario Farm Women's Network, were very effective in pressing OMAF for recognition and financial support. They made a strong case suggesting that the WI did not represent their interests, and therefore it was not fair for the Ministry to support those old groups to the exclusion of the new ones. The new lobby groups were undoubtedly more specific in their focus on "agriculture," and their arguments about why they should receive funding and support were persuasive. Faced with these provocative questions about why the Women's Institutes enjoyed a special status with the Ministry of Agriculture and Food, the new staff of the Rural Organizations and Services Branch were hard-pressed to explain, let alone to continue to justify the old preferential arrangement.

With government restructuring and rationalization of services in the late 1980s and early 1990s, the relationship between the WI and the Ontario Ministry of Agriculture and Food finally ended. Although that relationship had been changing dramatically over the years, the WI had continued to draw tremendous benefits from its association with the provincial government. The Ministry underwrote the costs of producing and circulating the *Home and Country* magazine, and provided office space for the WI's downsized staff. However, by the 1980s, the days of a large Institute staff, a printed annual report (sometimes over a hundred pages in length), and posh conventions at the Royal York Hotel in Toronto, all at government expense, were only a distant memory of the most long-standing members. The final severing of ties seemed drastic then, but in hindsight one can see that the relationship had been evolving for some time.

Behind it all was the statistical reality that Ontario's demographics were changing. Throughout the first half of the twentieth century, rural voters held tremendous sway over public affairs in Ontario. By the end of the century, things were different. The rural portion of Ontario's residents had been steadily declining throughout the century. The 1901 census revealed that 57 percent of the population of Ontario lived in rural areas. By 1911 that number had slipped by 10 percent, so that rural residents represented less than half the total population. The trend continued, so that by 1981, only 18 percent of the people in Ontario lived in rural constituencies.[6] It should come as no surprise, then, that the political influence of Ontario's rural residents was correspondingly lower by the 1980s. Therefore, when the provincial government decided to restructure and relocate its ministries, there was little that the Women's Institutes could do about it but wait and wonder what their fate would be.

The move of the Ministry office from Toronto to Guelph in 1982–1983 posed severe challenges to the WI. Some of the problems were logistical, such as the task of transferring the bank accounts from one city to another and assuring that all the necessary paperwork was done.[7] But those details were minor in comparison to the changes that would follow the move itself. Designed to decentralize the operations of the provincial government departments to locations outside Toronto, the change in structure also became an opportunity for the various ministries to rethink their roles and their commitments. After that exercise was completed, the relationship between the OMAF and the WI would never again be the same.

The first phase of the battle was fought out in the pages of *Home and Country*. When Joyce Canning posed her tough questions to the members of the WI, she intended to stimulate their thinking and encourage new program initiatives. Pressing the members to plan their programs and to evaluate their activities, Canning hoped that the Institutes would adopt some of her assessment strategies. In 1984 she invited the branches to participate in an exercise called, "How are your vital signs?"[8] This was not about personal health and fitness, but rather, the well-being of the organization itself. She challenged the women to think about whether they were leading their groups effectively and whether their leadership was informed by contemporary management principles. Recognizing the seriousness of the challenge, Charlotte Johnson, FWIO President from 1983 to 1986, urged the members to take the exercises seriously and ask themselves, "[A]re we going along day by day without a vision, but just 'hanging in there'?"[9] Johnson was convinced that it was not enough to coast along, resting on past laurels. Faced with competition from other women's organizations vying for government resources, these exercises might have proven very effective for revamping the WI program. However, the tone of these articles could easily be misconstrued by members who were not aware of the politics or the urgency of justifying their continued existence in rural Ontario. Readers were not happy to see their beloved organization maligned in the pages of its own publication.

The changes were subtle at first. In the summer of 1986, Carol Stewart-Kirby, the editor of *Home and Country,* reported that the magazine might help to provide the solution to the competition between different groups of rural women. Promoting the idea of using it as a networking tool, Stewart-Kirby reported that *Home and Country* could effectively be used by all the various rural women's groups to help tie them together. The idea was discussed and approved at the April 1986 FWIO Board meeting. With guarantees that "in no way would the WI content of the magazine change,"[10] the Board accepted the notion that their publication would get a wider circulation, and might even help them to recruit new members.

What they had not bargained for was a drastic change in editorial policy and pressure to share the magazine with reports about competing rural groups. One early example of the challenge of the alternate new rural women's groups came in the fall of 1987 when the editorial committee of *Home and Country* replaced the publication information inside the front cover. Traditionally, a list of the FWIO executive and Board members' names and addresses had always appeared in that space as a reference for members wanting to make contact with the leadership. That was replaced by a list of the new farm women's organizations and the contact people for those groups. Information about FWIO officers was included in the list, but now they were only one of seven groups listed there, including Southwestern Ontario Women for the Support of Agriculture, Concerned Farm Women, Women for the Survival of Agriculture (Eastern Ontario), Norfolk Rural Women, and Simcoe County Farm Women.[11] A few months later, the magazine began to run a new masthead, purporting to be "A Magazine for Rural Women."[12] That same winter 1988 issue featured a profile of Maria von Bommel, "farmer, wife, mother, agricultural advocate and activist," Ontario's representative to the National Farm Women's Network.[13] Her successor, Rennie Feddema, was similarly featured the following year.[14]

Strategic planning to carry the Institutes into the next century has been an ongoing process for at least ten years. Leadership from each of the provincial presidents has been all-important in this process, and that role will continue to be central as new structures and programs evolve. Here are three of those officers: LEFT TO RIGHT *Arthena Hecker, President-Elect; Marg Harris, current FWIO President; Donna Russett, Past President.*
— Donna Russett

To a certain extent, the competition between WI members and members of the new farm women's groups was based on a false dichotomy. While it was certainly not true that all Institute members were directly involved in farm work, many of them were. Furthermore, it was not true that the Institutes had no interest in influencing policy on agricultural issues. For years they had had a standing committee devoted to those topics. The FWIO was trying to include agriculture on the list of topics about which it was concerned, but unlike the newly formed groups, the Institutes were not singleminded about one issue. Some individual members were very effective at combining their involvements. For example, the first woman to hold the title of "Canada's Outstanding Young Farmer" was Janet Parsons, a WI member from Veuve River Institute near North Bay who won the title in 1988. Janet, who also chaired the program committee for the WI's ninetieth anniversary celebrations, was recognized for "her management style and the emphasis she places on farming as a business."[15] Parsons was farming in partnership with her husband, but while he held an office job off the farm, she worked full-time on the farming operation; as she told *Home and Country* magazine, "I'm the farmer here." Yet she did not see women's increased recognition in agriculture as a woman's issue.[16] Janet Parsons's experiences in WI leadership and agricultural management illustrate that it was not incompatible for women to hold membership in the Institute and, at the same time, be active in a non-traditional role as farmer.

Many WI members were convinced that they were being misrepresented by the stereotypes that the new groups attributed to them. "Perhaps we are still seen as tea-drinking, quilt-making homebodies," the members of Bruce South District WI argued, but that image "is not to be put down." Neither was it complete. Responding to a news report in the *Kitchener–Waterloo Record* following the 1983 Officers' Conference in Waterloo that cast doubt on the value of the WI, these members wrote to explain that the reporter had not done her homework. A portion of the article was devoted "to the opinions of leaders of three other associations," namely, Gisele Ireland of Concerned Farm Women, Gerry Fortune of the Huron County Federation of Agriculture, and Valerie Bolton of Women Today (Huron County). In the rebuttal, the Bruce County members conceded that "our membership is becoming older," yet, they pointed out, so was society as a whole. And furthermore, they argued, "[O]lder does not mean useless. Most great achievements in history, philosophy, science, statecraft and the arts are made by persons between 40 and 70, when one has knowledge, understanding, wisdom and discernment." Concerned about the negative report, the letter continued, saying, "[I]f Hannon [the journalist] had researched she would know that the FWIO (FWIC and ACWW) has a much broader scope of interest than has any one of these more insular societies." The editorial continued, suggesting that Hannon should "delve into the background" of WI organization and activity in order to "discover just how advantageous [the Institutes] are to persons young and old, rural and urban, Ontarian, Canadian and foreign."[17] In the minds of most WI members, there was no comparison between the narrow focus of the new farm lobby groups and the wide-ranging scope of activities the Institutes performed.

Nevertheless the competition between the two types of women's organizations for Ministry resources was real. Responding to public pressure from the new lobby groups, the editorial policy of *Home and Country* magazine was rationalized this way: since the provincial government's OMAF was paying for the publication, it should strive to represent all women in rural Ontario, especially the members of the new farm women's groups. When they heard that argument, the Institutes reacted. Though they had been grateful for government assistance, they were not willing to relinquish control of their publication. Nor were they willing to share it with other rural organizations. In reality, the Institutes still boasted a membership of almost 30,000 while the new organizations had attracted several hundred women at most. If the Institutes lost control of their magazine, they would lose an important communication vehicle. Determined not to let that happen, the FWIO took steps to regain control of the publication and to keep it going, this time without help from the government. In April 1992 the FWIO hired Janine Roelens-Grant as editor for *Home and Country* and began to publish the magazine independently.[18]

Another development that occurred because of the changing relationship with OMAF concerned the issue of office space for the Institutes' headquarters. After the move from Toronto to Guelph, the provincial office of the FWIO was housed in space provided by the Ministry of Agriculture and Food and Rural Affairs. In 1993, OMAFRA served notice to the FWIO that its provincial headquarters would be relocated from the Ministry building on Royal Road in Guelph to another building on the edge of town. The notice was very short and arrangements for the move were made quickly. This abrupt relocation confirmed what the executive had known for some time, that the FWIO needed to seek a more satisfactory and more permanent arrangement for headquarters, independent of the Ministry's goodwill.

Anticipating this need, in 1991 the FWIO had created a "Space Task Force," whose mandate was to locate and negotiate the arrangements for moving the provincial office of the FWIO into its own space. On August 21, 1994, the Federated Women's Institutes hosted a grand opening to display

The search for a new home for the FWIO office ended when the Space Task Force Committee negotiated with Guelph Township for the renovation and lease of Park House on the Marden Road outside the city of Guelph.
— Donna Russett

Accepting the key to the new provincial office from Les Foote, Reeve of Guelph Township, are Donna Russett, FWIO President, and Maisie Lasby, of the Negotiating Committee. — Earl D. Evans, Guelph

Committees

NEGOTIATING
Maisie Lasby
Peggy Knapp

MOVING & FURNISHING
Glenna Smith (chair)
Millie Graham
Eve Martin

OPENING
Cindy Ashton
Ruth Halbert (chair)
Brenda Hallman
Peggy Knapp
Margaret Munro
Joan Playle
Donna Russett

VOLUNTEERS
Jo Heyden
Anna Jackson
Don Jackson
Wally Knapp
Bob Lasby
Wallace Lasby
Janine Roelens-Grant
Dale Smith
Doug Smith

FLOWERS
Erin Twp. JWI
Jean Scott JWI
Mosborough WI
Ponsonby WI
Riverside WI
West End WI

PLATFORM FLOWERS
Betty Clubine

— FWIO

Two important players in the transition years of the FWIO were Hilde Morden (left), the first Program Co-ordinator, and Anna Jackson, Executive Secretary from 1988–1995. They are pictured here at the new headquarters, in front of a quilted wall-hanging presented to the FWIO by the Crumlin WI, Middlesex East District. — Donna Russett

their beautiful new office space in a renovated farmhouse just outside the city of Guelph, in Guelph Township at RR 5, on the Marden Road. In a symbolic ceremony, Donna Russett (FWIO President from 1993 to 1995) accepted the key to the house from the Reeve of the Township. The restored country farmhouse seemed a perfect location for the rural women's movement, which was about to celebrate its one hundredth anniversary. Under an arrangement with Guelph Township, who assumed the costs of renovation and agreed to lease the space to the FWIO on a permanent basis, the FWIO now had a lovely new setting from which to plan its birthday celebrations and look to the next century.

The open-house celebration drew a crowd of several hundred people, mostly WI members, along with a gathering of local dignitaries and other curious well-wishers. None were more curious than the members themselves. Eager to celebrate this new phase of WI independence, and to explore the new home of FWIO, the membership was also ready to see how its money was being spent. From the outset, the project to relocate had been heavily financed by individual members through schemes such as the "metre of loonies" project. Each member was urged to collect thirty-nine one-dollar coins — a quantity that would measure approximately one metre when laid side by side. It was a substantial contribution to request. Nora Huyek, from Magnetawan, explained her reaction, saying, "At first I thought 'that is a lot of money to ask from members.' Then I realized all the benefits I have received from being a member of the FWIO — all the knowledge gained through the various courses . . . all the friendships made over those years and all the leadership training. My life has been greatly enriched through my activities with FWIO. So I am very happy to send my $39.00 so the organization may continue to help others."[19]

The campaign to raise funds introduced members to the new responsibilities they would have to assume now that they were truly leaving the OMAF nest. The goal was set at raising one million dollars, a sum that would be invested so that returns could finance the expenses of maintaining the new office. The members were enlisted to collect their loonies, hold fundraising drives and find creative ways of pooling their resources in order to support the headquarters fund.

A grass-roots activism was displayed in a variety of ways, demonstrating that the Institutes understood the new responsibilities that went along with independence. One of the most remarkable displays was a housewarming "shower," held in conjunction with the provincial Board meeting in the spring of 1994. Board members were invited to bring gifts from their areas to shower on the FWIO and to help stock the shelves of the new "home" with office supplies and lunchroom staples. The gifts, which were unwrapped by the provincial executive members and the executive secretary, Anna Jackson, ranged from boxes of pencils, staplers, paper punches, and computer diskettes, to teabags, small appliances (a coffee maker), and a set of monographed tea towels, each one representing a branch from the districts of Manitoulin Island. In keeping with the spirit of the 1990s, the givers were instructed to wrap their gifts in environmentally friendly ways. It was a festive occasion and everyone seemed very happy for the new headquarters.

Nora Huyck (second from the left) commented that the WI had done a lot for her over the years, but as this 1973 photo reveals, she has made some significant contributions herself. She is pictured here with her fellow members from Bogartown WI as they display the fruits of their labour after a pie-baking bee. They were baking for the Institute's annual bazaar, and the ladies report that while they made these fifty cherry pies, as many apple and raisin pies were prepared at two other homes. LEFT TO RIGHT: *Frances Walker, Nora Huyck (now of Magnetawan WI), Eva Cook, Gladys Ridley* — Bogartown WI

But all was not well at the branch level. There was a great deal of misunderstanding about issues that were directly related to the new headquarters specifically, and to the move toward independence generally. The most concrete effect of the end of government sponsorship was the rise in membership fees. In just over five years, the fees had increased from $3 in 1989 to $15 per year by 1994. Some members began to wonder why the increase was so dramatic. Just what was being done with the money in Guelph? Why did they need to keep increasing the fees every year? How were senior citizens on fixed incomes and farm women struggling against major economic recessions to come up with the extra money? Many members felt that the increase in fees accounted for the increasing number of disbanded branches, and they wondered how long their own branches would continue to operate in light of the increased fees.

Membership fees in the WI are still reasonable by many estimates. Yet one correspondent from Lambton North District explained to me, "Some older members are turned off by the large increase in membership fees. They think of the time when fees were $3.00 a year [some even remember paying 25 cents!] and fail to understand that a $15.00 fee is not out of line. Just think what it costs to play Bingo for an evening, go out to the Playhouse, go to see the Blue Jays or join the Golf Club."[20] But the reaction to the rising fee was based on historical precedent. The WI fee had always been extremely low, and had, for the first fifty years of the movement, remained unchanged at twenty-five cents per member. Even at

Fundraising takes many forms, and for members of Nesterville WI in Algoma, that includes garage sales. At this 1993 sale in Thessalon, Patsy Wardell, Vera Murray, Marg Bailey and Lou Bigras wait for customers and look over the merchandise. — Nesterville WI Tweedsmuir History

WHO PAYS MORE?

In answer to the controversy over membership rates, Arthena Hecker (FWIO President-elect), spoke at a 1996 Board meeting.

"In 1897 the fee was set at 25 cents a year — about one third of a man's daily wage," she pointed out. "Now, almost one hundred years later, the provincial fee is $15.00. If the same percentages were used, it would mean working for $45.00 a day, hardly a decent wage in 1996! So, I ask you, who pays more: our members now, or those in 1897?"

— Arthena Hecker, St. Joseph Island WI

that reasonable rate, members had enjoyed a whole variety of educational courses and other services at government expense. Therefore, in 1991, some members argued, it did not make sense to them that fees should be increased so substantially while the educational services no longer existed.

The strong negative reaction to the increases in the 1990s was based on lack of information and a lack of historical appreciation for the fact that the WI had been subsidized by the province for so many years. To those who understood that part of the WI story, there was no question that it was long overdue, in the 1990s, for the WI to strike out on its own, become independent, and learn to balance her own books and assume her own financial responsibilities. As total independence loomed closer on the horizon, it was critical that the Institutes come to grips with their membership revenues. Although the move away from OMAF support was obviously the biggest single factor behind all these changes, there were other problems to contend with as well.

In part, increased membership fees were made necessary in order to offset the lost revenues due to life memberships. This special membership category was created as a form of recognition for long-standing members. Under the regulations, those who qualified became exempt from paying annual dues. In the early 1990s, a study revealed that a full one-fifth of the members in Ontario had been honoured as life members, and although some of them continued to voluntarily pay the annual fees, most did not. After considering the situation, a recommendation came forward to replace life membership with a new category of "honourary life members for those too infirm to take part in their branches, those women who had spent a lifetime working to build the organization," and eventually to phase out life memberships altogether.[21]

Adjustment to the increased membership fees was undoubtedly one of the most visible outcomes of the changing times, but it was only one. The FWIO executive was proactive in facing the realities that independence would bring. Joyce Canning was the last person to play the role of liaison between the Ministry of Agriculture and the FWIO. From now on, the Institutes' provincial executive officers were very much on their own. A process of strategic planning was put in place to chart the path toward autonomy and lay out plans for future developments. A full report of that planning process appeared in *Home and Country* in 1993 for the members' information, but the membership itself had been presented with numerous opportunities to contribute their ideas over the previous five years. It

At the 1988 convention in Kingston, waste management became the focus for Institute projects. Four FWIO Board members helped to bring the theme to life: Mabel Logan as the plastic bottle; Isabelle Booker as the tin can ; Allan Bradley, the Minister of the Environment; Helen Burns as the recycled newspaper, and Joan Law as the glass bottle. — Provincial Tweedsmuir History

RECYCLING SONG

Recycling is the answer, friends, to many of our woes.
It isn't too much trouble, and this is how it goes.
Save everything re-usable, e'en skins of po-ta-toes,
And clean up the garbage mess.
Save oh save your old glass bottles, (3x)
And clean up Norfolk North.

When you're finished with the morning news, don't throw them in the trash,
Just put them out for the Boy Scouts so they can make some cash.
Tin cans recycle too you know – cut out the ends and smash,
And clean up the garbage mess.
Save your papers and tin cans, (3x)
And clean up Norfolk South.

Make a quilt top, braid a rug, hook a carpet for your floor,
Take all the cotton rags you have to mechanic men next door.
These are a few suggestions, friends, there's many, many more,
Take heed to the garbage mess.
Save your old rags and pop tins, (3x)
And clean up Ontario.

At the Norfolk North and South District Rally in 1989, the program emphasized waste management and recycling. Dorothy Skevington of Courtland WI composed this song, to the tune of "Battle Hymn of the Republic," for the occasion.
— Dorothy Skevington, Courtland WI; *Home and Country*, March 1989

seemed very apt to have that grass-roots participation, since the new mission statement of the organization declared that the FWIO was "an organization for personal development and community action."[22]

Beginning in the mandate of Margaret Munro, FWIO President from 1986 to 1989, significant changes to the WI constitution were introduced. These would stand the Institutes in good stead as they evolved toward greater autonomy. One of the most important new measures in the constitution was the creation of the office of president-elect in 1987. This allowed the incoming president of the FWIO to sit on the provincial executive for two years before she took office, all the while gaining valuable experience and increasing her familiarity with the issues of current concern. The first ever president-elect was Peggy Knapp, who came to the post with a resumé that was already impressive in its scope because of her past involvements with advisory boards and a variety of rural organizations. However, Peggy asserts that the new office offered her a very practical apprenticeship in Board affairs.[23]

Other important changes were also introduced at the same time. Ever mindful of their membership statistics, the WI appointed a New Branch Co-ordinator, with the mandate to encourage and facilitate the formation of new Institute branches. The creation of new branches had always been a priority for the FWIO, but even more so now that competition from other rural organizations existed. News of newly organized branches was always cause for celebration, as recorded in the Board minutes of 1983, when the FWIO President congratulated four new branches that had recently formed: Bloomfield in Parry Sound South, Otty Lake in Lanark South, Trillium in Simcoe South, and Veuve River in Nipissing.[24] With the creation of an officer to look after this important aspect of the organization's growth, the significance of new branches was further emphasized. The New Branch Co-ordinator was given the responsibility for exploring "the reasons why some groups of women in the province did not find their needs were being met in the existing WI groups."[25]

One big change for the branches was the end of government-sponsored educational opportunities. With the new distance between OMAFRA and FWIO, short courses and special Institute training were abolished. For educational opportunities, the onus was now on the Institutes themselves. Districts were encouraged to create their own learning experiences by establishing education committees and sponsoring local workshops. In a report reminiscent of those of earlier years, the Women's Institutes' Education Committee for Wellington and Halton described an event in the fall of 1994 where some of their members had made lampshades. But that home-decor class was only one of a multitude of offerings. The agenda for their workshops that year included "seminole quilting, tatting, photography, household appliance maintenance, self-defense, healthy eating and special needs diets, defensive driving and routine car maintenance, [and] twisted paper crafts."[26] Evidently, the end of government sponsorship did not mean the end of WI learning.

Another critical change was the abolition of standing committees and the accompanying offices, known as convenors. In their place, the office of Program Co-ordinator was introduced. This was an attempt to simplify the Institutes' structure and allow for more clearly focussed activity. Rather than taking up a whole variety of causes, the Institutes would focus on one theme, and concentrate their efforts. Although some people regretted the passing of the old standing committees and the familiar structure they provided, the new model proved to be very effective. Under the leadership of Hilde Morden, the first person to hold the new office of program co-ordinator, environmental concerns became the dominant theme.

In 1988 the Women's Institutes held a provincial conference at Queen's University in Kingston, and the conference theme, "Educate/Initiate," led them to focus their attention on environmental issues. At that gathering, "following a panel discussion featuring the Deputy Minister of the Environment, there was an overwhelming vote to set a goal of 100 new waste management and recycling projects across the province in the next year. The Deputy, with a smile, suggested that was a pretty lofty goal." The Institutes were used to achieving lofty goals, and this province-wide project provided an opportunity to promote one issue with some concerted effort. Recycling campaigns meant that "blue boxes" had already become a common sight in urban centres by the late 1980s, and the WI had its own program to raise awareness and promote good caretaking of the environment in rural communities as well. Concern for the environment was really nothing new to the WI. The Institutes had been promoting good stewardship of the environment for many years, even before it became fashionable to do so.[27] It was no surprise then, that Hilde Morden's proposal in Kingston captured the enthusiasm of Women's Institutes across Ontario. When she recalled the scepticism of observers who wondered whether the women could meet their goal of one hundred new waste management projects, Peggy Knapp exclaimed, "Imagine the Program Co-ordinator's delight when she could report 300 new projects!"[28]

At branch level, this emphasis on the environment was acted out in a variety of ways. Many local Institutes decided to plant trees to commemorate special occasions and improve the environment at the same time. For example, to mark the eightieth anniversary in 1991, the Burnstown WI in Renfrew South planted a tree at the site of their first district annual.[29] In Perth South District, the Carlingford WI planted a tree behind their WI hall to celebrate the 125th anniversary of Canada's confederation.[30] Other branches resolved to take a political stand on environmental issues. In Lambton North, for example, "some branches and individual members [became] members of the Warwick–Watford Landfill Committee to help in the fight against expansion." At the Aberarder branch in the same district, the politics were made very personal when the membership "passed several by-laws as a result of their concern for the environment. The members will not use styrofoam cups at meetings — each member will lug-a-mug."[31] In Grey County, at the August 1988 rally, "delegates decided to sell mugs with the WI logo as a county project. It is hoped that these will be used in place of styrofoam mugs to help the waste management reduction program."[32]

The members insisted that *Home and Country* should reflect their concerns over the environment, not just in editorial decisions over the content of the magazine, but in more practical ways. In her letter to the editor, Marilyn Engelke-Dubay, a member from Warsaw WI, commended the editor for a recent article on recycling. "Excellent coverage, but what about you as a publication?" she asked. "Your publication is printed on non-recyclable, glossy paper, bundled up together in plastic sheeting." After pointing out that her WI branch tried to make careful choices in their catering business, using biodegradable products, she ended her letter, "Here's hoping you will consider changing your ways."[33]

Raising awareness about the environment was not the only current issue that captured the Institutes' attention. One innovative branch, determined to continue the tradition of supporting the local schools, decided to do so with a gift of technology. In 1987, the Bloomfield WI donated two computers to their local elementary school.[34] Others took it upon themselves to become informed about health issues including AIDS awareness, anorexia nervosa and bulimia, and breast cancer.[35] Branches also continued activity in the area of community health projects by raising money for equipment purchases. Two examples include the donation by the Perth North District WI and Maple Keys Junior WI to purchase mammography X-ray equipment for the Listowel Memorial Hospital, and the Aberdeen Junior WI project to buy two wheelchairs for seniors homes in Durham.[36]

Many branches chose to plant trees to mark Canada's 125th birthday celebrations in 1992. Members of the Lee Valley WI and Kawartha Valley WI each made a contribution to the environment with the trees they planted. — Lee Valley WI Tweedsmuir History; Kawartha Valley WI Tweedsmuir History

Vera Knowles, a member of Langton WI, designed the centennial anniversary collector plate. The plate features a map of Ontario (in green to represent the Institutes' commitment to the environment), with a star indicating the location of Stoney Creek. Her design was chosen from among thirty submissions, and the limited-edition plate went on sale in June 1994. — *The Simcoe Reformer*, April 10, 1993

In answer to a difficult 1980s issue, several branches took up projects to help provide child care services in their rural communities. In Ontario North District, the Bethesda–Reach WI explained that this kind of project was important because it left "the parents free for farm and harvest responsibilities." Under this scheme, specially trained students were sent out to provide care for children in their own homes throughout the busy months when parents were preoccupied with the responsibilities of the farm harvest season. WI members felt that they were able to make an important community contribution in this way, and several reported that this was one of the most significant things their branch had done in recent years.[37] Similar projects existed in Kent County, near Ridgetown, and in Northumberland County, in the outlying areas around Cobourg. In Kent County, a daycare facility was established so that care was provided from one centre rather than sending caregivers into the children's own homes. Northumberland County's child-care project took a variety of forms, including in-home care and supervised playdays at locations throughout the county. In these cases, the WI members lent leadership to the projects, working in conjunction with the Ministry of Community and Social Services. The fact that WI branches took on this kind of work shows that the organization was willing to change with the times and to look for ways to meet contemporary needs. Marg Eberle, a member of Palmyra WI and a future FWIO president (1991–1993), was directly involved with the Kent County project. "Our lifestyles have changed so much," she explained, "saying that mothers should be home with their children is no longer realistic." Willing to share the expertise she had gained in helping to develop this project, Eberle added, "[W]e hope we are helping families of the 1980s with our child care centre."[38]

Venturing into the field of child care certainly meant that these Institutes were making an updated interpretation of the Institutes' motto, "For Home and Country." Traditionalists, committed to the idea that a woman's place is in the home, might have had trouble with the idea that the Institutes were helping to support women who found it necessary to work outside their homes. And yet by the 1980s, child-care issues were central to the concerns both of farm women and of rural women who worked for pay off the farm. It seemed logical, then, that the organization that was created to improve the conditions of rural life should take up this kind of work. Rural life had changed dramatically since the turn of the century, and so had the needs of rural women. The constant challenge facing the Institute, it seems, was to be true to its historical roots and still relevant to its contemporary context.

Occasions of celebration are times to look back to past accomplishments and to look forward to future challenges. The WI has used its important occasions to do both things. Reaching the milestone of one hundred years of continuous activity is certainly an opportune time both to look back and to look ahead. Appropriately, when the official celebration of the WI centennial occurs in Hamilton in June 1997, the convention theme will be "Indebted to the Past, Committed to the Future." It will be a time for reflection. Planning for that historic event is in the capable hands of the Convention '97 Committee chaired by Peggy Knapp. Their mission is to "stage a convention to celebrate 100 years of Women's Institute work," and in so doing, "to create a new awareness among members and others" about the impressive history of the organization and its promising future.

"What is our place in this changing world as a group? Are we still thinking back in the days of Adelaide Hoodless or have we grown up with the times?" Thus Mrs. Purcell mused in her president's opening remarks to the annual meeting in November 1953 at the Royal York Hotel in Toronto. "Has our WI degenerated into a social get-together or developed into a social service group? If women as a group are to keep the position they have gained, they must keep alert to changes in the community, they must use the vote intelligently, they must study. Adult education in homemaking arts, so as to insure the family better health, nutrition and living standards is important. But this is not the whole answer. There must be education of our membership by study groups, panel discussions, and every means possible to make them more conversant with the needs of our world today. It is time we made a new assessment of our groups to see if we are growing up." Those questions and remarks still seem relevant today, as the Institutes approach this important centenary celebration. Leaders and members alike agree that the occasion of the one-hundredth birthday might be an important turning point for the organization.

This WI design became very popular among members looking forward to the celebration of the Institutes' centenary. Emblazened on T-shirts and notecards, it was at once a nostalgic celebration of country life and a proud declaration of WI membership. — Katharine Garwood of Nassagawega WI, designer

Realizing the importance of the centennial and its potential to bring renewal to the movement, in 1988 the FWIO appointed a Centennial Committee to plan well in advance for the festivities. Margaret Zoeller, who had been so actively involved in the celebrations of the seventy-fifth anniversary, was chosen to serve as Chair. The mandate of her committee, she said, was "to involve as many members as possible in programs, projects, competitions and activities." There is no doubt that that goal is being accomplished, since "enthusiasm has been created and hundreds of members have contributed and feel a part of the celebration."[39] The committee has been involved in a variety of projects, including a competition for the design and production of a limited edition centennial plate. All kinds of souvenir items — T-shirts, mugs, poetry books, and a whole variety of other wares — were prepared by the various districts and areas, and these have proven to be effective fundraisers as well as special mementoes.

Many of those special souvenirs were made available prior to 1997 at the "Centennial Prelude" celebration hosted by the Centennial Committee on June 14, 1995, at the Ontario Agricultural Museum in Milton. The Gambrel Barn was gaily decorated with quilts from across the province entered in the quilt competition. Approximately 4,000 women attended the event; each receiving her own commemorative mug, and treated to coffee and muffins provided by the Hamilton Area Institutes, and later, a hot meal. Everyone agreed that the Prelude was a wonderful kick-off to the celebrations, and anticipation for the 1997 celebrations was definitely building.

PRELUDE FOOD FACTS

1/2 ton potato salad
360 heads of lettuce
1/2 ton barbequed turkey breast
60 flats strawberries
3,700 tea biscuits
40,000 ounces of coffee, tea and lemonade

Janet Horner of Whitfield Farms Country Catering Service reported on the quantity of food consumed on the occasion of the Centennial Prelude.
— *Home and Country*, fall 1995

Anticipating the official birthday celebrations of June 1997, about 4,000 WI members attended the Centennial Prelude. Members swarmed around the grounds of the Ontario Agricultural Museum in Milton, admiring the submissions to a quilt competition. — FWIO Centennial Committee
Enjoying a barbeque lunch, at bottom left, are Rhea Biggs, Lynnville WI and Hazel Goble, Villa Nova WI. — Helen Young

Two very special events are planned for 1997 to mark the anniversary. First, on February 19, the date when Adelaide Hoodless and Janet and Erland Lee held the organizational meeting at Stoney Creek, Institute members across the province will gather together in their own branches, and each group will use the same program to commemorate that historic occasion. This is a significant reminder that the real life of the WI movement is centred at that very local level, and that throughout its history, the Women's Institute movement has been built from those small units. The second event will be a larger demonstration of the collective life of the organization, as the Federated Women's Institutes of Ontario host Convention '97 at the Hamilton Convention Centre, a centennial celebration and the FWIC Triennial Convention, to be presided over by Ontario's Charlotte Johnson, FWIC President, 1994–1997. The theme of that convention, "Indebted to the Past, Committed to the Future," is a reminder that historic occasions are indeed a time both for reminiscing about past accomplishments and also for charting future direction.

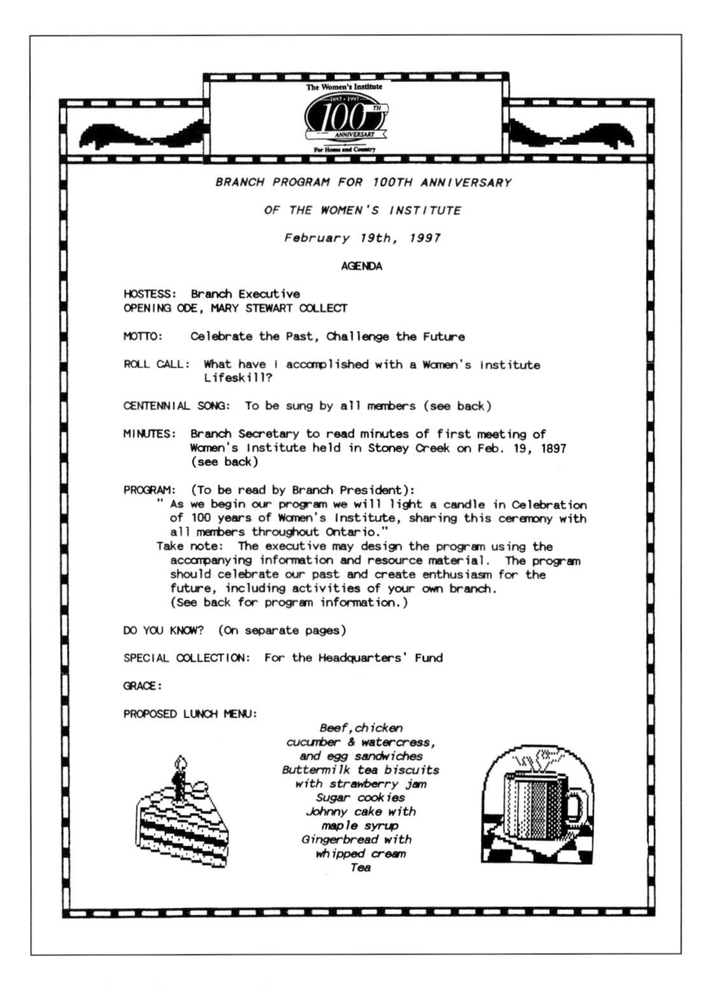

BRANCH PROGRAM FOR 100TH ANNIVERSARY

OF THE WOMEN'S INSTITUTE

February 19th, 1997

AGENDA

HOSTESS: Branch Executive
OPENING ODE, MARY STEWART COLLECT

MOTTO: Celebrate the Past, Challenge the Future

ROLL CALL: What have I accomplished with a Women's Institute Lifeskill?

CENTENNIAL SONG: To be sung by all members (see back)

MINUTES: Branch Secretary to read minutes of first meeting of Women's Institute held in Stoney Creek on Feb. 19, 1897 (see back)

PROGRAM: (To be read by Branch President):
" As we begin our program we will light a candle in Celebration of 100 years of Women's Institute, sharing this ceremony with all members throughout Ontario."
Take note: The executive may design the program using the accompanying information and resource material. The program should celebrate our past and create enthusiasm for the future, including activities of your own branch.
(See back for program information.)

DO YOU KNOW? (On separate pages)

SPECIAL COLLECTION: For the Headquarters' Fund

GRACE:

PROPOSED LUNCH MENU:
Beef, chicken
cucumber & watercress,
and egg sandwiches
Buttermilk tea biscuits
with strawberry jam
Sugar cookies
Johnny cake with
maple syrup
Gingerbread with
whipped cream
Tea

To commemorate the founding date of the Stoney Creek Women's Institute, all of the existing Women's Institutes throughout Ontario will follow this program at special meetings of their branches on exactly the same date, Feburary 19, 1997.

— FWIO Centennial Committee

Research for this book has involved both those exercises. Members shared their histories, but also their concerns, hopes and dreams for the Women's Institute as it faces the next century. The predictions ranged from undiluted pessimism to forecasts filled with optimism. Those who were pessimistic gave several reasons for their sentiments. They pointed to rising membership fees as prohibitive, yet that was only part of their concern for their branch's future. More commonly, members expressed concern over the fact that their membership was aging. Many members felt that they had not been successful in attracting younger women into the group, and therefore they worried about what that might mean for the future. One woman, a member for more than fifty years, said candidly, "I can't see any future as we can't get any new members and we are all getting older and will not be able to carry on."[40]

Pressed to explain why their average age was reaching seventy, the members gave varied explanations for lack of youthful involvement. Some pointed to their program and wondered if they were presenting programming that was relevant to the younger generation's concerns. But they found, when offering craft classes or special information sessions, that younger women would attend for special events but hesitated to become involved in long-term commitments and especially resisted assuming an office in the branch executive. "I do not feel the WI has a very good future," one member confided. "I do not like to say this as I really enjoy it, but all the younger girls are working and even if we get them to join they get a job and WI is secondary in their lifestyle."[41] But others explained that they did not blame the younger women. Looking at their own daughters, daughters-in-law and neighbours, older members understood that young women with families were often employed outside their homes and had little leisure time to give to the WI or any other volunteer organization. Several remarked on this as different from their own experiences in joining the WI as a new bride, and holding continuous membership over the next fifty years together with their friends, relatives and neighbours.

When younger women were not at work, they were busy with their children's activities. "Young women are so involved with their children in 4-H, sports, etc. that they have no time for WI," a member from Maple Grove WI in Durham West explained.[42] There is no doubt that childhood for rural children has changed dramatically over the past thirty years, since rural school consolidation. Social activities often centre around schools outside the rural community, and children in the country are commonly involved in sports leagues and lessons with their urban schoolmates. Invariably, for the mothers of those children, it means driving their kids to sports events and weekly meetings. Senior WI members observed that this too was a major lifestyle change for women in rural Ontario, and not something that they had experienced.

Many of the responses to the question of women's changing roles in rural life led members to reflect on broader changes to rural community organization in general. For example, remarks about children's social activities led to a discussion of the changes connected with the fact that rural schools across Ontario had consolidated by the mid-1960s. No longer was the little rural schoolhouse the centre of community life. Members reminisced fondly about the days of Christmas concerts held in the one-room school, where all the families in a community gathered to watch their children's performances. The WI members can still recite the contents of the treat bags that they often prepared for the schoolchildren on those occasions: an orange, a candy cane, hard striped candy and a few peanuts. How many thousands of such treat bags have WI members packed over the years for those occasions? Yet with the closure of rural schools, those days had ended.

Trends in organized sports marked a difference from days gone by as well. The days of the outdoor skating rink built and flooded by local families gave way to new arenas and sports complexes in the larger centres. Very often these were sponsored by government funding collected after the legalization of lotteries in Ontario, through programs such as Wintario. By the 1970s, most communities of even several hundred people could boast a new facility for skating lessons and hockey tournaments. For rural families, this had a positive impact because their children were able to enjoy facilities previously reserved for "town children." The members of the WI were pleased that their children and grandchildren had these improved facilities, but they fondly and wistfully recalled an earlier time when children's leisure did not cost mothers so much in energy, time and gas mileage.

Ease of travel had brought another reality to rural communities: commuters. For rural areas within driving distance of major urban centres, workers looking for a rural setting away from their urban "rat race" often chose rural communities for settling. This boosted the real estate values and accelerated the development of many urban fringe communities that were previously home to family farm operations. If that place was within a half hour to an hour's drive of a big city, it was a target for commuters looking to settle in a bedroom community. But in the minds of many WI members, these urban refugees did not make the kind of neighbours that longtime rural residents were used to. With their economic and social ties to the city, these new neighbours did not seem as interested in or committed to rural community life as the oldtimers might have hoped. Bringing with them their urban values of anonymity, the growing population of rural bedroom communities did not necessarily provide the WI with a larger potential membership base. City folk were not interested in the WI, it seemed, or maybe they did not have time for it.

Longtime members miss the short courses that were offered through the Ministry of Agriculture. "I am 81 years old," one Bruce County member told me, "and I would like to see the one or two week courses brought back. I took sewing, baking, home nursing, [it was] a great help for young mothers."[43] Yet now, educational opportunities are offered through continuing education programs at community colleges or high schools. Most Institutes do not see themselves competing with that level of formal education. "What is left for us to do?" they ask rhetorically. Indeed, for branches that have recently disbanded, all these reasons were cited — the aging members, the lack of young recruits, the competition with other groups and programs, and the rising costs of membership. The current trend is definitely one of decline, as the FWIO records reveal. From a list of over 900 branches when this project began in January 1993, the list has shrunk to under 800 active branches at the time this book went to press. That is a dramatic decrease over a three-year period.

Putting their support into the community means a variety of things for branches such as the Sunshine WI in Prescott District. Not only have these members served meals at the Riceville Agricultural Society's Fair for the past ten years, but in 1994, they also helped to paint and spruce up the facilities. LEFT TO RIGHT: *Lila Howard, Leah Bradley, Rita Lalonde, Pauline Ryan, Pat Bradley, Ruth Proudfoot, Erin McBride, Georgette Surch, Marie Wilkes and Ruby Proudfoot.*
— Ruth Proudfoot, Sunshine WI;
Home and Country, fall 1994

Several respondents were very frank in their predictions, based on the changing face of rural society. Given the consolidation of rural schools, the new focus of leisure activities, and the reality of commuting neighbours, some of the most pessimistic WI members clearly do not expect the WI to survive. "In twenty years," they predicted, with tears in their eyes, "it will all be over."

So, is it true then, that the WI movement is, as they say, "history"? Not according to its more enthusiastic promoters. Those gloomy predictions were not the only ones I heard. Many WI members vowed to do all that they could to keep the WI movement alive and well. For some of the most committed members, they could not imagine life without the WI. After all, they have been members for life, as were their mothers and grandmothers before them. "I'm doing all I can to keep it going, and my mother would roll over in her grave if we disband," a Renfrew North member said.[44] Many others like her vowed to do whatever it takes to keep the organization alive and thriving. What were their ideas?

For some, the necessary prescription is a change in focus, away from business-based meetings and too much attention to procedure and format, to issues that really interest women of all ages. They are ready to de-emphasize the preoccupation with parliamentary procedure and recapture the WI's educational mandate. A number of branches are actively searching for ways in which the WI might reach a new audience of members by offering a curriculum that is not widely available from other sources. This will undoubtedly be a key area of growth as the WI movement enters the next century.

Another area of opportunity will be for local groups to recapture their sense of community

Past, Present and Future . . . On the occasion of its ninetieth anniversary, the Moorefield WI presented a skit in three acts, using the occasion to look back to the past and forward to the future. Dora Smith highlighted scenes from the turn of the century, Irene Maurer represented the present-day WI member, and Kay Ayres delighted the audience with her projections about where the WI might be headed, ninety years into the twenty-first century!

— Margaret Olliff, Moorefield, Ontario

contributions. "I hope that we can be a community force once again," a member from Horton North WI declared. "We need more willing workers. I hope to see this come about in the next five years."[45] Under the current administration, the provincial government seems poised to turn responsibility for social programs and community services back to people at the local level. There may well be an increased new role for the Institutes to play as community-based programs are encouraged by the provincial government. The new theme for the Institutes, "Working for Safe and Healthy Communities" is in keeping with that emphasis.

The WI's most enthusiastic boosters are not discouraged by the declining membership statistics. They foresee a new type of organization. What may be history, they concede, is the small, very local branch that drew all of its members from the same rural concession or crossroads community. "We may have to amalgamate with a neighbouring WI," a Lanark County member conceded.[46] With the new realities of rural life, which include a greater ease of travel, the future of WI may be based on a new structure that sees members of dwindling branches consolidate their resources and group together with other branches in their district. This will not be an easy transition for many members and branches whose sense of identity is closely tied to a very small geographic radius where the members can recite the names of every family who has owned each property for the last several decades. But for many members, a changed Institute is preferable to no Institute at all.

Growth for the Institutes may come from a different age-group of members as well. Traditionally, the newest members of the WI were the youngest members of the community — typically, in the 1940s and '50s, new brides who took up membership in the postwar years as part of their role as farm wife and mother. Women in that younger group who are still busy with their childbearing responsibilities, careers outside the home, and financial burdens may not be the most likely recruits. Strategists predict that the new members of the WI may now come from women in an older age-bracket, perhaps in their forties and older. These women have a lighter load of family responsibilities, more financial freedom, and more leisure time to pursue activities outside their work and homes. As one member explained, she hopes to maintain contact with her WI branch, and in her retirement, maybe even do more than ever. "I am willing to work on goals of the WI . . . I am beginning the most carefree years of my life and will have time to help out."[47]

Not all the branches in the movement share a sense of gloom. As I travelled across the province, I could almost always count on meeting at least one branch in each district or area that was thriving — a branch with exciting programs, growing membership lists of various ages, interest in the provincial organization, and a healthy balance of a sense of pride in their history and flexibility for the future. I made a point of asking these groups what their secret was for growth and longevity. What is required, one member prescribed, is to "hold fast to the founding truths and roots but change and adapt to accommodate the needs of the generation of [the year] 2000."[48] A member from Craighurst WI in Simcoe Kempenfeldt explained, "We are still one of the largest branches in our district. I think the WI will continue as long as we have worthwhile objectives to work for. Branches fall apart when members feel their talents can be put to better use elsewhere." [49] Other testimonies echoed those sentiments. Myrtle Crawford from Appleton WI in Lanark North wrote about the personal benefits she gained from her membership.

Safe and Healthy Community logo.
— FWIO

> The WI has been a positive factor in my life for the past thirty-five years. When a neighbour asked me to join, I was a young, inexperienced farm housewife. Through the WI, I made friends with other farm wives, and learned from their experience. By taking courses, I learned new and better skills to enrich my life and that of my family.
>
> The WI has given me confidence in myself, to speak in front of others, to conduct meetings, and to interact with my fellow members. It has broadened my horizons as to what women can accomplish by working together. Through the WI I have engaged in activities around the community, which I would not have done otherwise. It has also created an interest in world affairs. I consider it most educational. I really enjoy the District Rallies and the Area Conventions. I feel a wonderful sense of pride to be part of a worldwide organization of women. It is my hope that the WI will continue for many years to come! Here's to a long and bright future![50]

Many of the women cited their own experiences from earlier in the century as possible models for the coming century. The story of Mrs. Jean Sadler is but one example. She wrote me a long letter telling of her girlhood contact with the WI, which stretched back to the days of Laura Rose Stephen, through the Depression and beyond. "When I was approximately ten years old, I travelled by train from Carleton Place to Smith's Falls to spend two months of the summer with an aunt who lived at Chantry, a little village near Westport, Ontario," she began. "It being my first time leaving home and travelling alone on the train, I was crying copiously when a lady left her seat, sat down with me and talked me out of my homesickness. She saw me off the train and on leaving, gave me her card to give to my aunt, who was an Institute member. On seeing the card, my aunt told me I had the honour of meeting Laura Rose Stephen, the first Women's Institute organizer and lecturer." In the following years, local WI officers encouraged Jean to use her artistic talents to make signs for WI events, and to compete in local fairs for prize money. With those funds and the money she earned working when a local WI member hired her for domestic help, Jean went on to pursue an education in nursing. Later, as a married woman, she joined a WI branch for a time and then became involved again after retiring. As for the future of the WI movement, Jean offers some advice. "There are many young people out there who, as in the Depression years, are in the position I was, attempting to meet school and university

Shown here in her nursing uniform, Jean Sadler recalls how much the WI helped her to set goals as a young woman, and work to achieve an education for herself. As a little girl, she had a chance meeting with Laura Rose and a great deal of support from local WI women. Now she is full of ideas about how the Institutes might once again play vital roles in the lives of young women throughout Ontario.

— Jean Sadler, Arnprior, Ontario

costs. Maybe this is where the WI can once again be an influence."[51] Based on her own story with WI, Jean suggests some possible roles that WI might play in the lives of Ontario's girls and women as we face another set of challenging circumstances under present government restructuring and financial cutbacks.

Members of the Blue Lake and Auburn WI busily preparing dinner for the St. George Lions Club. After their branch disbanded, members from this Institute joined with the nearby St. George WI. This monthly fundraising activity continues to bring in proceeds for the branch, putting them on a firm financial footing and allowing them, in turn, to make contributions to the community. — Blue Lake and Auburn WI Tweedsmuir History

The most active WI branches knew that they had a purpose, and they played an important role in their community. They were convinced that if they did not exist, their community would suffer. These were branches with strong links of sponsorship to youth organizations in the community, either Scouts, Guides or more typically, the local 4-H chapter. They felt that they made an important contribution to the young people in their community and they would be missed if they stopped doing so. Other groups made their community contributions in other ways. For example, the St. George WI in Brant County serves a meal once a month for a service club in town, and the community reaps a twofold benefit. The Lions Club is supported in its community work and doesn't have to go out of town to have their meal, and the proceeds from the catering itself are turned back over to community projects that the WI sponsors. This vibrant branch and others like it represent some of the trends that will probably become typical in the future. First, the St. George branch has recently welcomed several new members from the neighbouring Blue Lake and Auburn branch, which recently disbanded. This gave a real boost to their rolls, so that they now have sixty members and an average attendance of forty. Second, they have a reliable income, based on their thriving catering business. And third, they play an important role in their community because they are counted upon as active participants.

There are other factors too that can account for success. The branches with lots of enthusiasm are those in which members are friends with one another, and often, where members are daughters or relatives of long-standing members either in that same branch or some other. In other words, the members have strong relationships with one another, and also with the larger movement in terms of current involvement at upper levels of the organization, and they have, through their connection with senior members, a sense of the past. This historical basis is very important. Members are often surprised to learn what the WI has done in their local community, for example, that the WI was responsible for installing the street lights and sidewalks, inviting the first public health inspectors into their local school, lobbying for the improvement of roads, bridges and safety signs. New members of the movement may not initially realize these important roles their predecessors played in the life of the community.

In 1990, after the sale of their hall, the Scotch Block WI of Milton donated over $39,000 to the Milton District Hospital for arthroscope equipment, another worthy cause and part of the long WI tradition of supporting local projects.
— Edythe Davis, Scotch Block WI

Although many WI members can trace a long family tradition of involvement through their own mothers' and grandmothers' involvement, for others, the WI is something brand new. One member from Simcoe County explained her branch's situation. "[W]e are bordered by ski resorts with more and more housing developments," she said. "[W]e have two subdivisions on the outskirts of the village. From these have come several intelligent women who seem to enjoy our meetings and they are a breath of fresh air to our branch. We make them welcome and accept their input into our programmes."[52] A member from Queen's Line WI near Pembroke, Ontario, in North Renfrew District started out as one of those newcomers. "In 1977, my husband and I and our two children . . . bought some acreage on the Queen's Line in Ross Township and built a house. We moved to the area from Vancouver Island, and decided to live in this location because we liked the area. We liked the rolling land, and the farm land. We did not have any ties to the area. I was born and brought up in Toronto, and my husband is from Yorkshire, England. We are not farmers. I am a Speech Pathologist, and my husband, although a graduate Geologist, is now owner of a bicycle store in Pembroke." She explained that she joined in order to meet other women, and that she had started out by taking a course in needlework. "It takes a long time to make friends, especially when one is from a completely different background," she said, "but several of the members are women I can talk to and confide in. This has been very important to me."[53]

Would Adelaide Hoodless and Erland and Janet Lee recognize the WI as it exists now and celebrates its first centennial? They might be pleasantly surprised to know that the movement has been so successful in attracting such a large membership and playing such a variety of roles over time. No doubt they would take pride in the record of education, community action and personal development that the WI has provided to the women of Ontario over these past one hundred years. They could still recite the familiar motto, "For Home and Country," the ode and some of the Institute songs. Some parts of the movement, however, they would not recognize at all. The computerized office, the independence from government sponsorship, the urbanization of Ontario society, and the changes in homemaking, agriculture and

One Hundred Years Young . . . The Kemble Women's Institute in Grey County, founded the same year as the Stoney Creek Charter WI, has a special claim to fame. Of the other branches formed that year, Stoney Creek meets officially once a year, and Whitby has since disbanded. That makes Kemble WI the oldest active branch in the world! BACK ROW (LEFT TO RIGHT): *Ruth Crampton, Jean Judge, Helen Sinclair, Ruth Waite, Helen Davenport, Margery Taylor, Dorothy McLeod, Betty Dredge, Joan Davidson* MIDDLE ROW: *June Beckett, Marie Davidson, Jean Davenport, Sally Cappelletto, Gladys Coxon, Joyce Robinson, Nora Jones* FRONT ROW: *Florence Edmonstone, Eileen Danard, Jane Lundy, Mary Mackenzie, Nelda Shade, Elizabeth Graham, Cathy Dewar, Grace Sutherland, Bernice Hurlbut* ABSENT: *Ted Sutherland, Reta Scott, Lois Glidden, Corey McQuigge* — Kemble WI family life would be most unfamiliar to them. In keeping with their founding goals, though, they would no doubt want to know about the roles that the women of Ontario now occupy and the needs they have. Above all, they would want to know what the Women's Institutes could do to meet those needs. When the founders met together originally in 1897, they took the risk of proposing something deemed to be quite radical, a new organization for women. Now the Women's Institutes are celebrating one hundred years of activity, and it is time to make proposals for the future. With a century of experience behind them, there is no doubt that members will have a wide variety of ideas. As the convention theme for 1997 suggests, the Women's Institutes are indebted to the past, and, at the same time, committed to the future. Decisions about how to act out that commitment will shape the developments and characteristics of the WI in the years to come. Here's to the next hundred years!

Notes

AO Archives of Ontario
AR Annual Report of the Institutes Branch of the Ontario Department of Agriculture
FWIO Federated Women's Institutes of Ontario
H&C *Home and Country*
UG University of Guelph Archives and Special Collections

CHAPTER ONE

1. Mrs. J.B. Shrigley, AR 1916, p.115. The original poem is eight verses long. This is only a portion of it.
2. Cheryl MacDonald, *Adelaide Hoodless: Domestic Crusader* (Toronto: Dundurn Press, 1986), p. 16.
3. *The Hamilton Daily Spectator*, Saturday, Aug. 10, 1889, p. 1.
4. MacDonald, *Domestic Crusader*.
5. AO, "The Origins of the Women's Institute," *Stoney Creek Women's Institute Tweedsmuir History*, Book One, p. 14.
6. MacDonald, *Domestic Crusader*.
7. Bernard Hoodless, cited in *Ontario Women's Institute Story* (Toronto: FWIO, 1972), p. 7.
8. *Ontario Women's Institute Story*, p. 6.
9. AO, *Stoney Creek Tweedsmuir History*, p. 16.
10. Ibid., p. 17.
11. *"When the Women's Institute Started Jennie Was There," The Hamilton Spectator*, n.d., cited in AO, *Stoney Creek Tweedsmuir History*, Book Two.
12. AO, *Stoney Creek Tweedsmuir History*, p. 17.
13. The branch now operates quite differently than the regular branches, since it meets only once a year. It is governed by a body of six FWIO officers. AO, "Yearly Summary for 1978," *Stoney Creek Tweedsmuir History*, Book Two.
14. AO, Verna Rowena S. Conant, "Mrs. Ernest D. Smith (nee Christina Ann Armstrong)," *Stoney Creek Tweedsmuir History*. Mrs. Conant was the Smith's third child.
15. AR 1899, p.16.
16. Viola M. Powell, *Forty Years Agrowing: A History of Ontario Women's Institutes* (*The Port Perry Star*, 1941), p. 21.
17. Ibid., p. 85.
18. Ibid., p. 21.
19. The earliest records for the Whitby WI have been lost, but the minute books from 1912 and the *Whitby WI Tweedsmuir History* are housed at the Town of Whitby Archives, Whitby, Ontario.
20. UG, *Kemble Women's Institute Tweedsmuir History*.
21. *Chronicles of Kemble*, p. 22. This commemorative booklet prepared by the Kemble Women's Institute documents the history of the WI and the local area up to 1967.
22. AO, Marjorie Lee,"The Founding of the Women's Institute," *Stoney Creek Tweedsmuir History*.
23. *Ontario Women's Institute Story*, p. 15. This section of the seventy-fifth anniversary account is based almost word for word on "The Origin of the Women's Institutes," in AO, *Stoney Creek Tweedsmuir History*, Book One, p. 19–20.
24. *An Act to Further Improve the Agriculture and Arts Act, 1895, Statutes of the Province of Ontario*, 59 Victoria, 1896, Chapter 14, assented to Apr. 7, 1896, clause 10, section 29a.
25. AR 1899, p. 16.
26. AO, Farmers' Institutes of Ontario, Annual Reports 1887, alphabetic by county, RG 16, 85, Box 1.
27. AO, Farmers' Institutes of Ontario 1888, Annual Report, South Renfrew Farmers' Institute.
28. AO, Letterbooks, Oct. 11, 1894, Hodson to Mr. M. Moyer, Dec. 14, 1894.
29. AO, Letterbooks, 1895–1896, Hodson to Arch. McColl, Alboro, Jan. 9, 1996.
30. AO, Letterbooks, F.W. Hodson to George H. Greig, Winnipeg, n.d. letter; RG 16, 85, Box 3.
31. AO, Letterbooks, Hodson to Prof. J.W. Roberston, June 3, 1895.
32. AO, Letterbooks, Hodson to Mrs. H.M. Edwards, Ottawa, June 24, 1895, RG 16, 85 Box 3.
33. AO, Letterbooks, Hodson to Bessie Livingston, Superintendent, Ottawa School of Cooking, Aug. 19, 1895.
34. AO, Letterbooks, Hodson to Livingston, Oct. 19, 1895.
35. AR 1900, p. 9.
36. AR 1901, p. 7.
37. AR 1900, p. 135.
38. Several of these papers were reprinted in the WI Annual Reports, in the Ontario Sessional Papers.
39. Alice Hollingworth diary, cited by Helen Black burn in unpublished student paper, OISE. I wish to thank Helen Blackburn, the granddaughter of Alice Hollingworth, for the information she shared with me.
40. Alice Hollingworth Webster, "History of the Creemore Women's Institute," *Creemore Tweedsmuir History*, cited by Blackburn.
41. *The Agriculture and Arts Amendment Acts, 1902, Statutes of the Province of Ontario*.
42. *Ontario Women's Institute Story*, p. 23.
43. Powell, p. 22.
44. *Ontario Women's Institute Story*, p. 128.
45. Annie Walker, Edith M. Collins, and M. McIntyre Hood, *Fifty Years of Achievement* (FWIO, 1948), p. 15

CHAPTER TWO

1. George Putnam, AR 1905, p. 17.
2. Ibid.
3. Adelaide Hoodless, AR 1905, p. 38.
4. MacDonald, *Domestic Crusader*. The phrase "gospel of homemaking" comes from AR 1912, p. 12.
5. Rev. Canon Cody, Toronto, AR 1912, p. 13.
6. *Ontario Women's Institute Story*, p. 7.
7. Powell, p. 83.
8. Mrs. William Bacon, Orillia, "Reply to Address of Welcome," AR 1912, p. 11.
9. Mrs. D. McTavish, Port Elgin, AR 1912, p. 28.
10. Chairman, AR 1911, p. 13.
11. C.C. James, "Address," AR 1912, p. 86.
12. Ibid., p. 87.
13. Mrs. (Dr.) McPhail, Manilla, AR 1912, p. 18.
14. Putnam, AR 1912, p. 15.
15. Mrs. McTavish, Port Elgin, AR 1912, p. 28.
16. Putnam, AR 1912, p. 99.
17. Putnam, AR 1906, p. 5.
18. Mrs. McTavish, AR 1912, p. 28.
19. Chairman, AR 1912, p. 90.
20. Ibid.
21. "Question Box," AR 1912, p. 42.
22. Mrs. John Darling, Lansdowne, AR 1912, p. 22–23.
23. AR 1912, p. 89.
24. McTavish, AR 1912, p. 28–29.
25. Linda M. Ambrose, "The Women's Institutes of Northern Ontario, 1905–1930: Imitators or Innovators?" in *Changing Lives: Women and the Northern Ontario Experience* (Toronto: Dundurn Press, forthcoming).
26. AR 1905, 1906.
27. Margaret McAlpine, Toronto, "Women's Institutes in Northern Ontario," AR 1912, p. 33.
28. Ibid.
29. Ibid., p. 34.
30. AR 1912, p. 36. See also AR 1905 for Gray's travel itinerary in June and July for the purpose of organizing.
31. Putnam, AR 1911, p. 14–15.
32. Linda M. Ambrose, "What Are the Good of Those Meetings Anyway?: Early Popularity of the Ontario Women's Institutes," *Ontario History*, Vol. LXXXVII, No. 1, Mar. 1995, p. 1–20.
33. Putnam, AR 1907, p. 5.
34. UG, Macdonald Institute Collection, Director (1903–1920: Watson). General Correspondence, Box 4, file correspondence U–Z, Mary Urie Watson to William Weld, Sept. 23, 1904.
35.Mary Urie Watson, "What the Macdonald Institute is Prepared to Do for the Institutes," AR 1911, p. 59.
36. Ibid.
37. The letters are collected and preserved at the Archives of Ontario. Records of the Federated Women's Institutes of Ontario, RG 16, 87, Box 3, Early Correspondence 1909–1910. These were previously catalogued as part of the Records of the Farmers' Institutes Branch, RG 16, 85, Box 4. Some other samples of these letters are scattered throughout Mary Urie Watson's correspondence in the collection at the University of Guelph, Archival and Special Collections. Macdonald Institute Director's Correspondence, RE1 MAC A0145.
38. AO, FWIO, Box FF 1, Lizzie G. Diamond (Mrs. Harry), Bluevale Ontario to Mary Urie Watson, Nov. 2, 1909.
39. Ibid., Mrs. Otto Damm, Ayton to Mary Urie Watson, May 29, 1909.
40. Ibid., Mrs. J.W. Mills, Wingham Ontario to Mary Urie Watson, Oct. 21, 1909.
41. Putnam, AR 1912, p. 17.
42. Terry Crowley, "The Origins of Continuing Education for Women: the Ontario Women's Institute," *Canadian Woman Studies*, Vol. 7, No. 3, fall 1986, p. 78–81.
43. Mary Urie Watson, AR 1912, p. 65.
44. Watson, AR 1912, p. 66.
45. Author correspondence with the Canfield WI, printed material enclosed with survey response.
46. Mrs. E. Richmond, "Lonely Women," AR 1907, p. 128.
47. Ibid.
48. Mrs. D. McTavish, AR 1911, p. 23.
49. Miss E.L. Nie, Fenelon Falls, AR 1911, p. 33.

50. Mrs. Bacon, Orillia, AR 1911, p. 32.
51. Putnam, AR 1912, p. 18.
52. Mrs. Brethour, Burford, AR 1912, p. 85.
53. Mrs. H. Quinlan, Damascus, East Wellington, AR 1911, p. 34–35.
54. Putnam, AR 1912, p. 18.
55. Mrs. A. Brown Sr., Winterbourne, North Waterloo, AR 1911, p. 33.
56. Putnam, AR 1912, p. 16.
57. Mrs. Brethour, AR 1912, p. 86.
58. Mrs. Johnston, Agincourt, "Procuring and Expending Institute Funds," AR 1912, p. 66–67.
59. Burgessville Representative, AR 1912, p. 70.
60. Richard's Landing Public Library, Kentvale WI, *Minute Book*, Aug. 31, 1916.
61. Mrs. C.H. Emerson, Halton Branch, AR 1911, p. 28.
62. Miss S. Campbell, Brampton, AR 1912, p. 84; AR 1911, p. 18.
63. Mrs. W. Bacon, AR 1911, p. 31.
64. Putnam, AR 1911, p. 18.
65. Mrs. Wilson, Parkhill WI, AR 1911, p. 30.
66. Bloomfield Representative, AR 1912, p. 68.
67. Mrs. Wilson, AR 1911, p. 31.

CHAPTER THREE

1. W.B. Roadhouse, Toronto, AR 1916, p. 116.
2. Mrs. E. McGee, Chesterville, AR 1917, p. 14.
3. Mrs. I.A. Ashton, Morrisburg, AR 1916, p. 12.
4. AR 1917, p. 96. An interesting note here about Native women's involvement. "Besides this knitting we are helping the Indian women. As perhaps you all know the 114th Haldimand Battalion is almost half made up of Indians. Now the Indian women cannot afford to buy the yarn, so we are helping them by supplying the yarn and they are knitting the socks." Reported by Mrs. Lindsay, Caledonia.
5. Miss M.E. Pearson, Merrickville, AR 1917, p. 13.
6. Putnam, AR 1918, p. 9.
7. Mrs. McPhedran, Toronto, AR 1916, p. 166.
8. Dr. Margaret Patterson, Toronto, AR 1917, p. 43.
9. Noel Marshall, AR 1916, p. 162.
10. Mrs. H.W. Parsons, Cochrane, "Women and War," AR 1915, p. 165.
11. Mrs. R. Condie, Beachburg, AR 1915, p. 48.
12. Mrs. H.W. Parsons, AR 1915, p. 165.
13. Mrs. J. Wilson, Ottawa, "Red Cross and Methods," AR 1916, p. 31.
14. Premier W.H. Hearst, Toronto, AR 1915, p. 106.
15. Mrs. J.A. Wilson, AR 1916, p. 31.
16. Mrs. H.W. Wilson, Wardsville, AR 1917, p. 34.
17. Margaret Scott, York County District Officers' Reports, AR 1917, p. 108.
18. E.J. Guest, Toronto, "Chairman's Address," AR 1915, p. 102.
19. Margaret Scott, AR 1917, p. 108.
20. Gore Bay Public Library, *Barrie Island Tweedsmuir History*.
21. Mrs. Parsons, AR 1915, p. 166–167.
22. Mrs. Plumptre, Toronto, "Questions on the Work of the Red Cross," AR 1916, p. 185.
23. Dr. Margaret Patterson, "Red Cross Work," AR 1917, p. 45.
24. Mrs. Plumptre, AR 1916, p. 185–186.
25. Ibid.
26. Dr. Margaret Patterson, AR 1917, p. 45.
27. Noel Marshall, AR 1917, p. 104.
28. Mrs. Somerville, London, "Red Cross and Other Patriotic Work," AR 1916, p. 104.
29. Ibid., p. 107.
30. Ibid.
31. Mrs. McPhedran, AR 1916, p. 166.
32. Noel Marshall, "The Work of the Red Cross Society," AR 1915, p. 77–78.
33. AR 1916, p. 28.
34. Mrs. Donald McLean, "Address of Welcome," AR 1918, p. 52–53.
35. AR 1916, p. 27.
36. Miss M.E. Pearson, Merrickville, "How to Extend the Institute Work and Maintain Interest," AR 1915, p. 40–42.
37. Putnam, "Report of Superintendent," AR 1916, p. 117.
38. Dr. Jas. Robertson, Ottawa, "Red Cross Work and Our Allies," AR 1916, p. 33.
39. "Business Methods in District Work," Eastern Ontario WI Convention, 1917, AR 1918, p. 41.
40. Mrs. W.H. Edwards, Pakenham Institute Report to Eastern Ontario WI Convention, 1914, AR 1915, p. 47.
41. Mrs Parsons, AR 1915, p. 166.
42. Putnam, AR 1915, p. 19.
43. Dr. Jas. W. Robertson, AR 1916, p. 32.
44. Major Stethune, Ottawa, Address, AR 1916, p. 43.
45. Mrs. Robert McDiarmid, "Carleton Place Women's Institute," AR 1916, p. 13.
46. Major Stethune, AR 1916, p. 42.
47. Mrs. Plumptre, AR 1916, p. 185.
48. Dr. Annie Backus, "Why Conserve?" AR 1918, p. 67.
49. Dr. Jas. W. Robertson, "War Service by Women," AR 1918, p. 34–35.
50. Mrs. Shortt, AR 1918, p. 19.
51. Putnam, AR 1918, p. 56.
52. Ibid., p. 10.
53. Mrs. A.H. Robertson, Maxville WI, AR 1916, p. 13.
54. Putnam, AR 1918, p. 10.
55. Putnam, AR 1917, p. 10.
56. Condensed Reports from Branch Institutes, AR 1918, p. 15.
57. Mrs. H.W. Dummert, Carleton Place, "Reports of Carleton Place Institute and Bonnechere Valley," AR 1918, p. 26.
58. Dr. Margaret Patterson, AR 1917, p. 45.
59. Mrs. A.M. Huestis, "Address of Welcome," AR 1915, p. 76.
60. Athens Women's Institute Report, AR 1917, p. 18.
61. Dr. Annie Backus, "A Mother and Her Child," AR 1915, p. 56–57.
62. *Barrie Island Tweedsmuir History.*
63. AR 1916, p. 14
64. Mrs. W.R. Munroe, Demorestville, "Social Life in the Rural District," AR 1916, p. 163.
65. Mrs. V. Stock, Tavistock, AR 1917, p. 32.
66. Mrs. J.G. Edwards, "Our Girls in the Institute," AR 1916, p. 107–108.
67. Putnam, AR 1915, p. 13.
68. Putnam, "Question Box," AR 1916, p. 29.
69. AR 1916, p. 61-70.
70. Putnam, AR 1917, p. 88.
71. Mrs. Amos, Exeter, "How to Maintain Interest in the Institute," AR 1915, p. 68.
72. Putnam, AR 1916, p. 9–10.
73. Mrs. R.V. Fowler, South Lanark District, AR 1915, p. 45.
74. Putnam, AR 1915, p. 32.
75. *Barrie Island Tweedsmuir History*.
76. AR 1916, p. 13.
77. Mrs. W.R. Munroe, "Social Life in the Rural District," AR 1916, p. 164.
78. Mrs. D.O. White, Mapleton, AR 1916, p. 61.

CHAPTER FOUR

1. Mrs. W. Buchanan, Ravenna, AR 1916, p. 166.
2. Putnam, AR 1917, p. 89.
3. Dr. Margaret Patterson, "Patriotic Work," AR 1918, p. 27.
4. Mrs. V. Stock, Tavistock, AR 1917, p. 32.
5. Ven. Archdeacon Cody, Toronto, "Children's Rights," AR 1915, p. 123.
6. Mrs. D.O. White, Mapleton, AR 1916, p. 61.
7. Mrs. W. R. Lang, Toronto, "What Women in Other Countries Have Done Along Patriotic Lines," AR 1916, p. 167.
8. Putnam, "Question Box," AR 1916, p. 179–180.
9. Putnam, AR 1917, p. 61.
10. Richard's Landing Public Library, Kentvale WI, *Minute Book*, Sept. 28, 1916; Nov. 2, 1916; Dec. 7, 1916.
11. Miss Mildred McMillen, Lee Valley WI, AR 1917, p. 113.
12. G.C. Creelman, "Rural Leadership," AR 1916, p. 44.
13. Putnam, AR 1916, p. 72.
14. Putnam, AR 1917, p. 88.
15. Putnam, AR 1918, p. 21.
16. Putnam, AR 1915, p. 32.
17. Dr. C.C. James, AR 1916, p. 152.
18. AR 1919, p. 4; Kentvale WI, *Minute Book*, Mar. 28, 1919.
19. AR 1923, p. 42.
20. AR 1925, p. 43-44.
21. Private Collection, Hoyle WI, *Minute Book*, Nov.-Dec. 1947.
22. AR 1923, p. 42.
23. AR 1924, p. 31.
24. Kenora District WI, *Minute Book*, 1935.
25. Powell, p. 42-43.
26. "Waterloo South District WI, 1903–1978, Seventy-five Years of Achievement," p. 26.
27. AR 1925, p. 43.
28. AR 1927, p. 29.
29. AR 1923, p. 42.
30. Powell, p. 39.
31. AR 1928, p. 39.
32. Kentvale WI, *Minute Book*, June 21, 1917.
33. AR 1919, p. 40.
34. Powell, p. 40.
35. UG, FWIO Collection, *Handbook*, 1926. p. 5.
36. A district officer [anonymous] report to George Putnam, AR 1915, p. 30.
37. Mrs. Wm. Todd, Orillia, "Reply to Address of Welcome," AR 1917, p. 70.
38. AR 1915, p. 113.
39. Putnam, AR 1916, p. 78.
40. AR 1925, p. 38–39.
41. AR 1926, p. 34.
42. Ibid., p. 35.
43. Ibid.

CHAPTER FIVE

1. *H&C*, July 1933, p. 4.
2. *H&C*, Supplement to Feb. 1934, p. 2.
3. Putnam, "Essentials for Success in the Institutes," *H&C*, Sept. 1933, p. 2.
4. "Membership Fees and Collections," *H&C*, Nov.–Dec. 1933, p. 4.
5. Ibid.
6. *H&C*, Mar.–Apr. 1934, p. 3.

7. *H&C*, Nov.–Dec. 1933, p. 4.
8. Kenora District WI, *Minute Book*,1932.
9. "Waterloo South District Women's Institute, 1903-1978, 75 Years of Achievement," p. 22.
10. *H&C*, summer 1937, p.4
11. Paipoonge Museum Collection, Thunder Bay District, Stanley WI, *Scrapbook*, May 18, 1939.
12. "News Flashes from the Branches," *H&C*, Jan. 1935, p. 4.
13. Ibid., p. 4.
14. AR 1932.
15. AR 1934, p. 60.
16. AR 1933, p. 37.
17. Ibid., p. 34.
18. Resolutions about Mothers' Allowance were still being discussed in the 1950s, when both the FWIO and District Institutes passed resolutions to suggest reforms to the system that would provide better levels of support for women. See FWIO, *Board Minutes*, Nov. 1952, Nov. 1953, and Nov. 1956; also Kenora District WI, *Minute Book*,1950 and 1951.
19. Englehart and Area Museum Collection, Dane WI, *Minute Book*, Feb. 2, 1932. See also Jan. 13, 1933. "A letter of thanks to Wexford Institute for their kindness, in sending the Christmas gifts of 28 stockings."
20. Ontario Agricultural Museum, Sheffield WI, *Minute Book*, Jan. 31, 1923.
21. AO, Thornhill WI, *Minute Book*, June 19, 1919 and Sept. 18, 1919, microfilm MS 687, reel 1.
22. Ambrose, "The Women's Institutes of Northern Ontario ..."
23. AR 1935, p. 29.
24. FWIO, *Board Minutes*, May 9–11, 1955.
25. AR 1938, p. 72.
26. *H&C*, fall 1937, p. 1.
27. AR 1935, p. 68.
28. *H&C*, Oct. 1935, p. 4.
29. Stanley WI, *Scrapbook*.
30. *Gore Bay WI Tweedsmuir History*.
31. AR 1934, p. 60.
32. Maple Grove WI, "Waterloo County District WI, 1903–1978, 75 Years of Achievement," p. 23.
33. AR 1934, p. 64.
34. AR 1937, p. 65.
35. UG, Watson Correspondence, Mrs. Robt. Minorgan, Sundridge to M.U. Watson, Feb. 18, 1920.
36. *Stratton WI Tweedsmuir History*.
37. Finch WI, Tweedsmuir History Collection, *Scrapbooks*. The contractor who built the hall was a French Canadian from nearby Casselman, Ontario and the bilingual correspondence with him is preserved in the scrapbook collection. Sixty-two years later, the Finch WI continues to meet in the hall, free of charge, as the agreement stated.
38. *H&C*, Apr. 1936, p. 4.
39. *Stratton WI Tweedsmuir History*.
40. *H&C*, July 1935, p. 3.
41. *H&C*, Apr. 1936, p. 4.
42. Dorothy M. Seymour, District Secretary of North Bruce, *H&C*, fall 1937, p. 3–4.
43. Fort Frances Museum Collection, East Rainy River District WI, *Minute Book*, 1937 and 1938.
44. *H&C*, Dec. 1936, p. 4.
45. Putnam, "Essentials for Success in the Institute," *H&C*, Sept. 1933, p. 2.
46. *H&C*, Nov.–Dec. 1933, p. 4.
47. AR 1934, p. 63.
48. AR 1933, p. 38.
49. Putnam, "Essentials for Success in the Institute," *H&C*, Sept. 1933, p. 2.
50. Mrs. R.B. Colloton, "Special Message," *H&C*, Sept. 1934, p. 8.
51. Ibid.
52. *H&C*, Dec. 1936, p. 1.
53. *H&C*, July 1936, p. 2.
54. AR 1935, p. 71.
55. AR 1937, p. 65.
56. Fort Frances Museum Collection, East Rainy River District WI, *Minute Book*, 1937.
57. AR 1936, p. 68.
58. AR 1937, p. 66.
59. Ibid., p. 67.
60. AR 1936, p. 71.
61. Ibid.
62. AR 1937, p. 67.
63. AR 1932, 1933, 1935.
64. *H&C*, Jan. 1936, p. 4.
65. AR 1935, p. 71, p. 69.
66. Ibid.
67. AR 1936, p. 72.
68. See *Head Heart Hands Health: A History of 4H in Ontario* by John R. Lee, for a reference to the myths and American roots associated with these four terms, and also for references to Florence Eadie's role in preserving the Homemaking clubs.
69. *H&C*, May 1937, p. 1.
70. Ibid.
71. *H&C*, 1933, p. 1.
72. *H&C*, Sept. 1934.
73. Annie Ross, "Health Exercises for Every Day," *H&C*, Aug. 1934, p. 4.
74. *H&C*, fall 1937, p. 1.
75. "Mary Wright Untangles the Amendment," *H&C*, fall 1938, p. 2. No more columns on Mary Wright ever appeared. Mary's true identity is not known; it may have been either Colloton or Bess McDermand.
76. "Special Notice," *H&C*, Mar.–Apr. 1934, p. 8.
77. *H&C*, Apr. 1936, p. 1.
78. *H&C*, spring 1939, p. 1.
79. AR 1935, p. 64.

CHAPTER SIX

1. *H&C*, winter 1939–1940, p. 1.
2. *H&C*, winter 1941–1942, p. 1.
3. *H&C*, summer 1944, p. 1.
4. *H&C*, winter 1940–1941, p. 1.
5. *H&C*, spring 1941, p. 3.
6. *H&C*, winter 1940–1941, p. 1.
7. *H&C*, spring 1941, p. 3.
8. *H&C*, spring 1943, p. 1.
9. *H&C*, winter 1941–1942, p. 1.
10. *H&C*, summer 1942, p. 2.
11. *H&C*, winter 1941–1942, p. 1.
12. *H&C*, fall 1942, p. 1.
13. *H&C*, spring 1943, p. 1.
14. *H&C*, summer 1944, p. 1.
15. *H&C*, fall 1943, p. 4.
16. *H&C*, spring 1941, p. 3.
17. *H&C*, summer 1941, p. 1.
18. *H&C*, fall 1941, p. 1.
19. Ibid., p. 4.
20. Ibid.
21. *H&C*, summer 1941, p. 1, 3.
22. *H&C*, winter 1941–1942, p. 1.
23. *H&C*, summer 1942, p. 2.
24. Paipoonge Museum, Thunder Bay District, Stanley Park WI, *Scrapbook*, n.d.
25. *H&C*, spring 1941, p. 1.
26. Noreen Desjardins, Westmeath Branch WI, Renfrew North, Ambrose Centennial History Book Personal Survey, 1994.
27. Wabis Valley WI, *Minute Book*, Jan. 8, 1941.
28. Kenora District WI, *Minute Book*, 1943.
29. AR 1946, 1947.
30. AR 1945, p. 67.
31. AR 1927, p. 31.

CHAPTER SEVEN

1. Helen Redman, member of Scugog Island WI, R.R. 3, Port Perry, reply to Centennial Survey, 1994.
2. I conducted interviews with over 500 WI members from 1993 to 1995, and I asked each one to recount the story of her earliest connections with the WI. Invariably, women told about enthusiastic recruiters who encouraged them to become members.
3. Membership rose from 37,500 in 1947 to 47,000 in 1950. UG, FWIO, *Board Minutes*, May 1–3, 1950.
4. Ambrose, FWIO Centennial Survey, personal reminiscences by Dorothy Walton, RR 2, Englehart, 1994.
5. Milberta WI, *Minute Book*, Sept. 1953.
6. Hunta WI, *Minute Book*, Aug. 1954.
7. Kenora District WI, *Minute Book*, 1951.
8. *Ilderton WI Tweedsmuir History*.
9. Waterloo South District WI, "75 Years of Achievement," p. 18–19; UG, FWIO, *Board Minutes*, Nov. 1954.
10. *H&C*, 1949–1950, p. 8.
11. Although the number of branches was at its highest level ever in 1953, the membership statistics were somewhat lower, with 45,457 members. Statistics compiled by the author from AR, 1947–1953.
12. Statistics compiled by the author from AR, 1947–1953. For further membership statistics, see Appendix.
13. Marguerite Young, interview, Ambrose, Oral History Tape # 1, 1994.
14. See for example, Hoyle WI, *Minute Book*, Oct. 1948; AO, Thornhill WI, *Minute Book*, 1949.
15. UG, FWIO, *Board Minutes*, May 1950.
16. *H&C*, Nov. 1949, p. 8.
17. UG, FWIO, *Board Minutes*, Nov. 1950.
18. UG, FWIO, *Board Minutes*, May 1951.
19. UG, FWIO, *Board Minutes*, May 1953.
20. UG, FWIO, *Board Minutes*, Nov. 1953.
21. "Gleanings from Convention Area Meetings," *H&C*, fall 1950, p. 4.
22. *H&C*, Summary Issue 1950–1951, p. 8.
23. *H&C*, Feb. 1952, p. 12.
24. AR 1948, p. 151.
25. *H&C*, winter 1949–1950.
26. UG, FWIO, *Board Minutes*, Nov. 1954.
27. *H&C*, fall and winter 1949–1950, p. 8.
28. Ibid., p. 13.
29. *H&C*, Summary Issue 1950–1951, p. 4.
30. *H&C*, fall and winter 1949–1950, p. 14.
31. *H&C*, Summary Issue 1950–1951, p. 7.

32. AR 1951, p. 190.
33. *H&C*, Summary Issue 1950–1951, p. 8.
34. AR 1950, p. 160.
35. UG, FWIO, *Board Minutes*, Nov. 1951, May 1952, and Nov. 1952.
36. UG, FWIO, *Board Minutes*, Nov. 1952.
37. UG, FWIO, *Board Minutes*, Nov. 1951.
38. UG, FWIO, *Board Minutes*, Nov. 1952.
39. UG, FWIO, *Board Minutes*, May 1954.
40. UG, FWIO, *Board Minutes*, Nov. 1954.
41. AR 1948.
42. AR 1952, p. 182. No longer published as part of the Sessional Papers, the Annual Reports were now "The Women's Institute Branch and Home Economics Service."
43. Fort Frances Museum Collection, *Barnhart WI Tweedsmuir History.*
44. Ambrose, Oral History Tape # 92 and # 95, 1993.
45. *H&C*, Summary Issue 1950–1951, p. 6.
46. Clair White, interview, Ambrose, Oral History Tape #26, 1994.
47. Ruth Burkholder, interview, Ambrose, Oral History Tape # 42, 1994.
48. UG, FWIO, *Board Minutes*, Nov. 1959.
49. Helen Anderson, interview, Ambrose, Oral History Tape # 27, 1994.
50. AR 1952, p. 180. In 1954, 1,600 participants were again reported at Guelph, and 50 at Kemptville, AR 1954, p. 176.
51. *H&C*, Feb. 1, 1952, p. 12.
52. UG, FWIO, *Board Minutes*, May 1951.
53. UG, FWIO, *Board Minutes*, May 1959.
54. UG, FWIO, *Board Minutes*, Jan. 1962.
55. Jean Brumpton WI, Elgin East District, Ambrose, Oral History Tape # 2, 1994.
56. UG, FWIO, *Board Minutes*, Nov. 1964.
57. UG, FWIO, *Board Minutes*, Nov. 1956.
58. UG, FWIO, *Board Minutes*, Nov. 1964.

CHAPTER EIGHT

1. *H&C*, summer 1967, p. 24.
2. *H&C*, winter 1968, p. 13.
3. Ethel M. Demaine, "The Individual's Centennial Plans," *H&C*, winter 1967, p. 26.
4. *H&C*, winter 1968, p. 27.
5. *H&C*, summer 1967, p. 24.
6. *H&C*, spring 1974, p. 20.
7. *H&C*, winter 1973, p. 10.
8. *H&C*, fall 1973, p. 22; *H&C*, fall 1974, p. 31.
9. *H&C*, winter 1968, p. 23.
10. Interview, Ambrose, Oral History Tape # 68, 1994.
11. Margaret Penning, interview, Ambrose, Oral History Tape # 16, 1993.
12. *H&C*, fall 1973.
13. Ibid., p. 7.
14. Ibid., p. 5–6.
15. "Purchase of Home From Estate of Katherine I. Lee," draft deed, June 1972, FWIO files loaned to the author.
16. UG, FWIO, *Board Minutes*, Nov. 1968.
17. UG, FWIO, *Board Minutes*, Apr. 1972.
18. Ibid.
19. Interview, Ambrose, Oral History Tape # 68, 1994.
20. Ibid.
21. Christine Jacobson, interview, Ambrose, Oral History Tape # 69, 1994.
22. Rose MacDonald, interview, Ambrose, Oral History Tape # 69, 1994.
23. Jeanne Davies, interview, Ambrose, Oral History Tape # 69, 1994.
24. Margaret Zoeller, interview, Ambrose, Oral History Tape # 49, 1994.
25. *H&C*, spring 1976, p. 12.
26. *H&C*, spring 1975, p. 4.
27. *H&C*, winter 1979, p. 3.
28. *H&C*, winter 1976, p. 27.
29. Lorraine Gillette, interview, Ambrose, Oral History Tape # 16, 1993.
30. *H&C*, summer 1977.
31. For a discussion of the impact of these new organizations for farm women, see E.A. (Nora) Cebotarev, "From Domesticity to the Public Sphere: Farm Women, 1945–86," in Joy Parr (ed.), *A Diversity of Women: Ontario 1945–1980* Toronto: (University of Toronto Press, 1995), p. 214.
32. *H&C*, winter 1978, p. 9.
33. UG, FWIO, *Board Minutes*, Apr. 1981.
34. Ibid.
35. Ibid.

CHAPTER NINE

1. UG, FWIO, *Board Minutes*, Apr. 1982.
2. *H&C*, winter 1983, p. 3.
3. Ibid.; UG, FWIO, *Board Minutes*, Nov. 1982, p. 6.
4. *H&C*, fall 1983, p. 5.
5. UG, FWIO, *Board Minutes*, Nov. 1982.
6. Statistics Canada, cited by Randall White in *Ontario 1610–1985: A Political and Economic History* (Toronto: Dundurn Press, 1985), p. 340.
7. UG, FWIO, *Board Minutes*, Apr. 1983.
8. *H&C*, spring 1984, p. 5–7.
9. Ibid., p. 4.
10. *H&C*, July–Aug.–Sept. 1986, p. 3.
11. *H&C*, Oct.–Nov.–Dec. 1987, p. 2.
12. This new phrase first appeared in the Feb.–Mar. 1988 issue, and the cover was a composite of four historical photographs about services that OMAF had provided to the WI over the years. The issue was also intended to mark the centenary of the Ministry of Agriculture.
13. *H&C*, Feb.–Mar. 1988, p. 4.
14. *H&C*, Oct.–Nov. 1989, p. 4.
15. *H&C*, Feb.–Mar. 1989, p. 5.
16. Ibid.
17. Letter to the editor, *H&C*, fall 1983, p. 6. Reprinted from the *Kitchener–Waterloo Record* in response to the article by Sheila Hannon, May 6, 1983.
18. Janine Roelens-Grant had been employed by the Ministry as editor from January 1991 to March 1992. Starting in April 1992, she was employed by the FWIO instead.
19. Nora Huyck, FWIO "Make a Difference" Headquarters Campaign Fund Flyer, n.d.
20. Edna M. Steadman to the author, Ambrose Centennial Survey, Bear Creek Women's Institute file, 1993.
21. Peggy Knapp, correspondence with the author, Jan. 27, 1996.
22. *H&C*, winter 1993, p. 6–7.
23. Peggy Knapp, correspondence with the author, Jan. 27, 1996.
24. UG, FWIO, *Board Minutes*, Nov. 1983.
25. Ibid.
26. *H&C*, fall 1994, p. 22.
27. UG, FWIO, *Board Minutes*. See for example, Apr. 1980, on disposal of nuclear waste. Earlier examples include May 1955, on pollution of St. Clair River near Sarnia; Nov.1959, on need for tree planting along provincial highways.
28. Peggy Knapp, correspondence with the author, Jan. 27, 1996.
29. Irene Robillard, Ambrose Centennial History Book Personal Survey, 1994.
30. Carlingford WI, Ambrose Centennial Survey, 1993.
31. *H&C*, Nov. 1989, p.12.
32. *H&C*, Oct.–Nov. 1988, p. 14.
33. *H&C*, Feb.–Mar. 1989, p. 3.
34. *H&C*, Oct.–Nov.–Dec. 1987, p. 16.
35. See for example, Ibid., p. 16–17.
36. Ibid., p. 16; *H&C*, Oct.–Nov. 1989, p. 12.
37. *H&C*, Oct.–Nov. 1988, p. 7; Bethesda–Reach WI Members, Ambrose Centennial History Book Personal Survey, 1994.
38. "Rural Child Care in Ontario — Service Meets Local Needs," *H&C*, Apr.–May 1988, p. 14–15
39. Margaret Zoeller, correspondence with the author, Apr. 29, 1996.
40. Bertha Trew, Elizabethville WI, Durham East, Ambrose Centennial History Book Personal Survey, 1994.
41. Lois Winton, Bury's Green WI, Victoria East, ibid.
42. Marjorie Prescott, Maple Grove WI, Durham West, ibid.
43. Sadie Fitzsimmons, Pinkerton WI, Bruce East, ibid.
44. Noreen Desjardins, Westmeath WI, Renfrew North, ibid.
45. Dorothy Cobus, Horton North WI, Renfrew South, ibid.
46. Blanche Dezell, Innisville WI, Lanark County, ibid.
47. Jane Mottershead, Pembroke Ontario, Queen's Line WI, correspondence with the author, Aug. 15, 1994.
48. Barbara Evans, Bethesda–Reach WI, Ontario North, Ambrose Centennial History Book Personal Survey, 1994.
49. M.E. Fay Craig, Craighurst WI, Simcoe Kempenfeldt, ibid.
50. Myrtle Crawford, Appleton WI, North Lanark, correspondence with the author, 1994.
51. Mrs. Jean [Nelson] Sadler, Arnprior Ontario, correspondence with the author, 1994; telephone conversation, Dec. 1995.
52. Craig, Craighurst WI, Simcoe Kempenfeldt, Ambrose Centennial History Book Personal Survey, 1994.
53. Mottershead, Pembroke Ontario, Queen's Line WI, correspondence with the author, Aug. 15, 1994.

Appendices

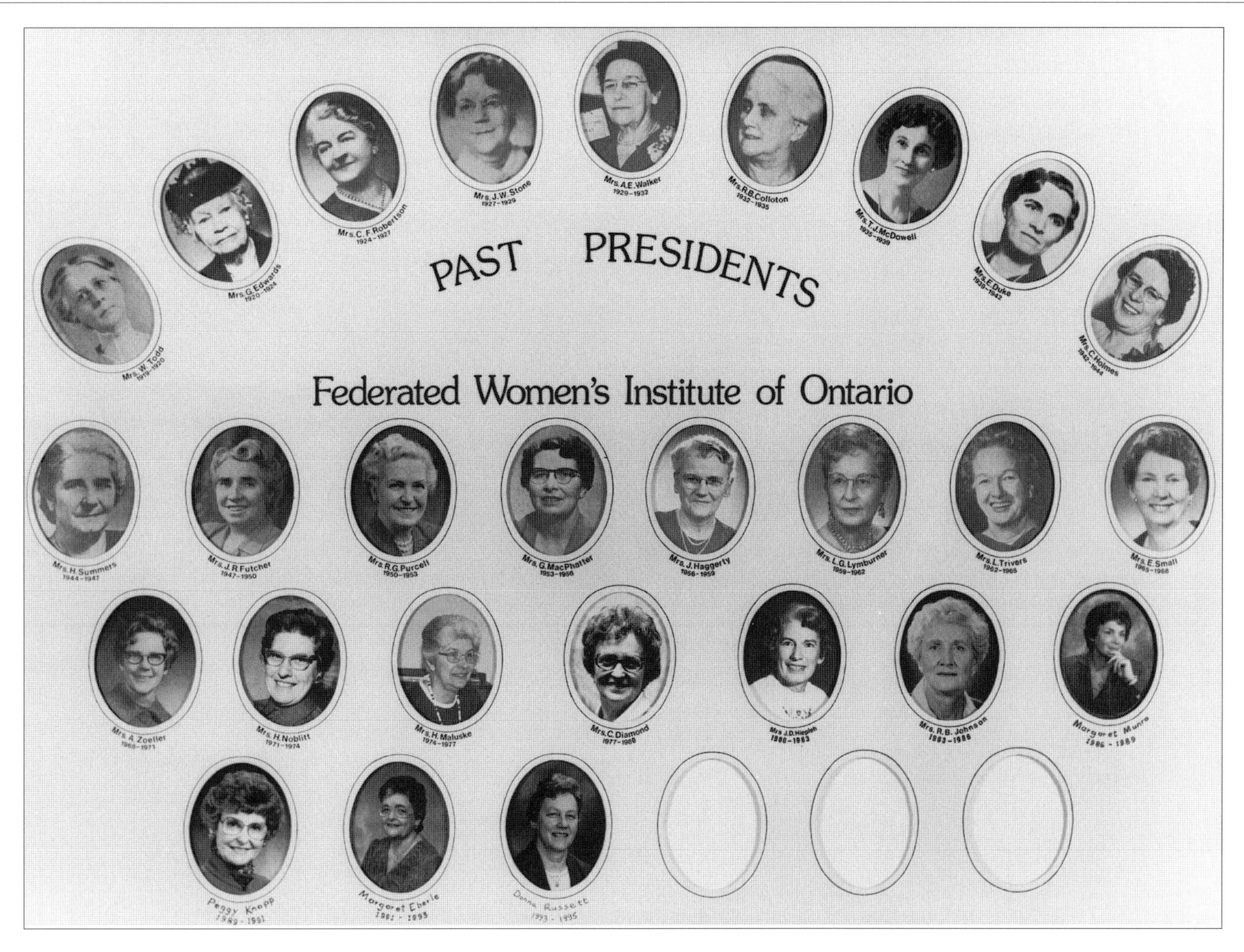

PAST PRESIDENTS FEDERATED WOMEN'S INSTITUTES OF ONTARIO: *Mrs W. Todd, 1919–1920; Mrs G. Edwards, 1920–1924; Mrs. C.F. Robinson, 1924–1927; Mrs. J.W. Stone, 1927–1929; Mrs. A.E. Walker, 1929–1932; Mrs. R.B. Colloton, 1932–1935; Mrs. T.J. McDowell, 1935–1939; Mrs. E. Duke, 1939–1942; Mrs. C. Holmes, 1942–1944; Mrs. H. Summers, 1944–1947; Mrs. F.R. Futcher, 1947–1950; Mrs. R.G. Purcell, 1950–1953; Mrs. G. MacPhatter, 1953–1956; Mrs. J. Haggerty, 1956–1959; Mrs. L.G. Lymburner, 1959–1962; Mrs. L. Trivers, 1962–1965; Mrs. E. Small, 1965–1968; Mrs. A. Zoeller, 1968–1971; Mrs. H. Nobblitt, 1971–1974; Mrs. H. Maluske, 1974–1977; Mrs. C. Diamond, 1977–1980; Mrs. J.D. Hiepleh, 1980–1983; Mrs. R.B. Johnson, 1983–1986; Margaret Munro, 1986–1989; Peggy Knapp, 1989–1991; Margaret Eberle, 1991–1993; Donna Russett, 1993–1995* — FWIO

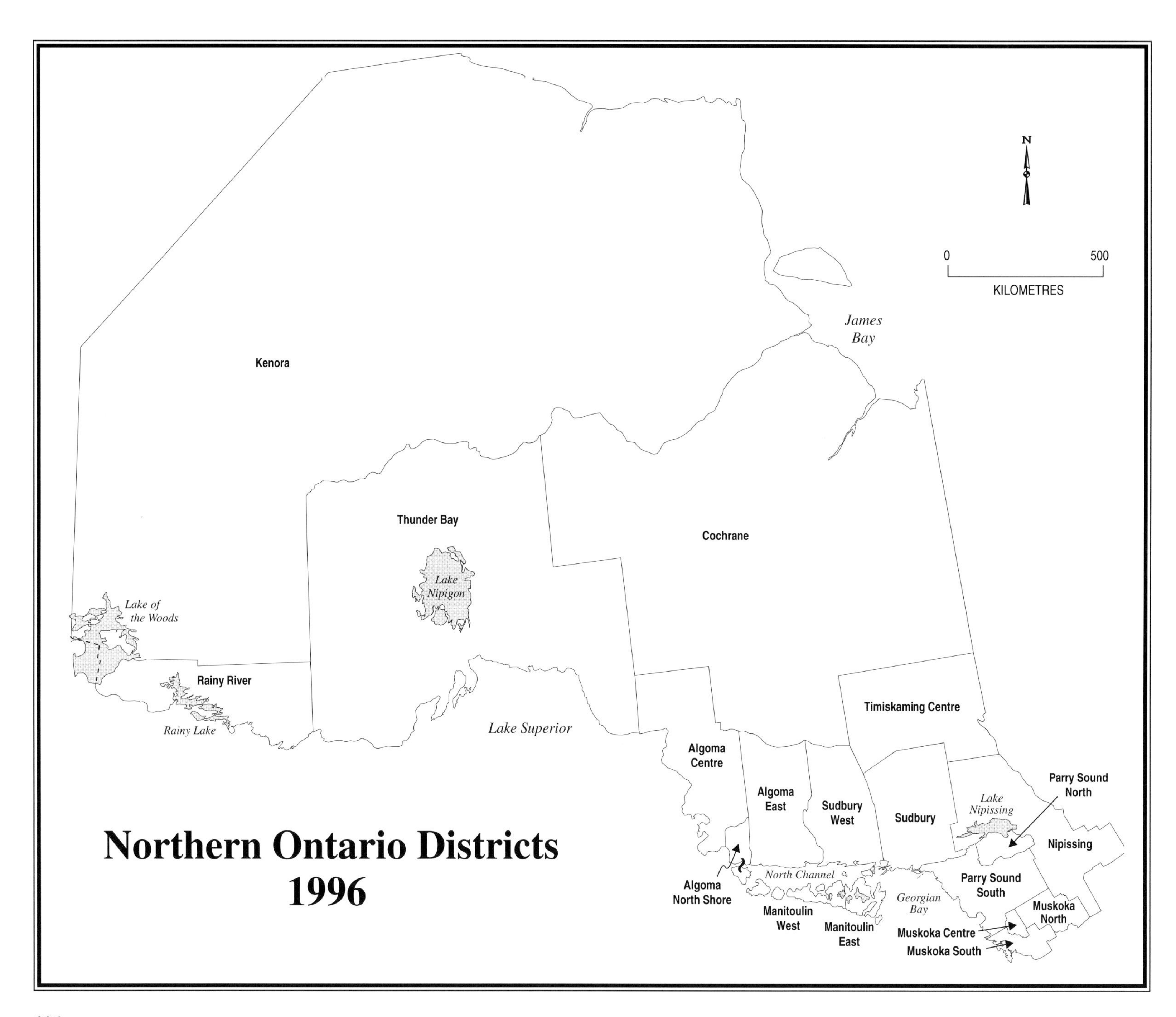
N
0
500
KILOMETRES
James Bay
Kenora
Thunder Bay
Cochrane
Lake Nipigon
Lake of the Woods
Rainy River
Rainy Lake
Lake Superior
Timiskaming Centre
Algoma Centre
Algoma East
Sudbury West
Sudbury
Lake Nipissing
Parry Sound North
Nipissing
Northern Ontario Districts
1996
Algoma North Shore
North Channel
Manitoulin West
Manitoulin East
Georgian Bay
Parry Sound South
Muskoka North
Muskoka Centre
Muskoka South

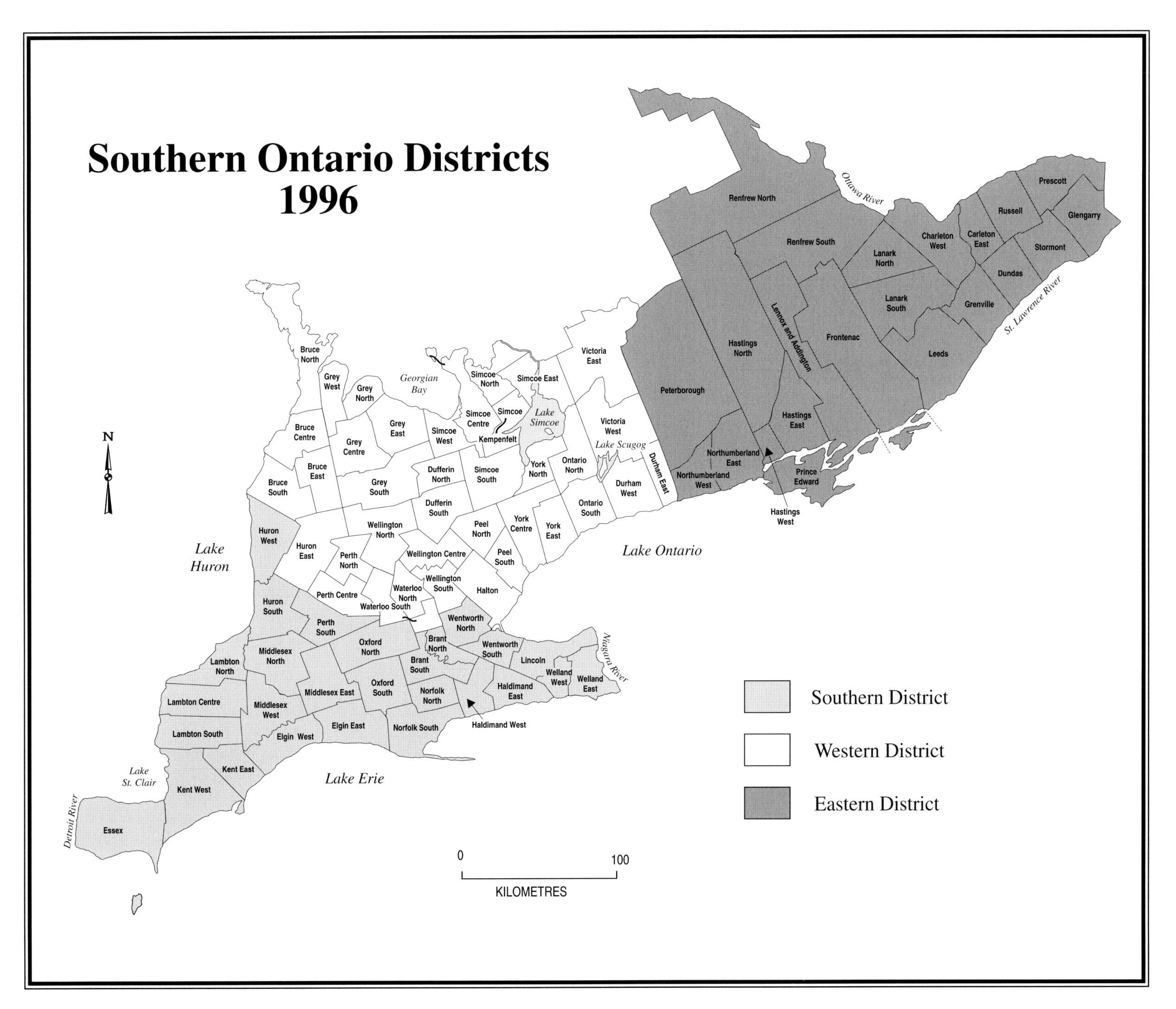
Southern Ontario Districts
1996
N
Renfrew North
Ottawa River
Prescott
Russell
Glengarry
Charleton West
Carleton East
Renfrew South
Lanark North
Stormont
Dundas
Lanark South
Grenville
St. Lawrence River
Frontenac
Lennox and Addington
Hastings North
Leeds
Peterborough
Hastings East
Northumberland East
Northumberland West
Prince Edward
Hastings West
Victoria East
Victoria West
Lake Scugog
Durham East
Durham West
Ontario North
Ontario South
York North
York Centre
York East
Simcoe North
Simcoe East
Simcoe Centre
Simcoe
Lake Simcoe
Kempenfelt
Simcoe West
Simcoe South
Georgian Bay
Bruce North
Grey West
Grey North
Grey East
Bruce Centre
Grey Centre
Bruce East
Bruce South
Grey South
Dufferin North
Dufferin South
Peel North
Peel South
Halton
Wellington North
Wellington Centre
Wellington South
Waterloo North
Waterloo South
Huron West
Huron East
Perth North
Perth Centre
Huron South
Perth South
Lake Huron
Lake Ontario
Wentworth North
Wentworth South
Brant North
Brant South
Oxford North
Oxford South
Lincoln
Welland West
Welland East
Niagara River
Haldimand East
Haldimand West
Norfolk North
Norfolk South
Middlesex North
Middlesex East
Middlesex West
Lambton North
Lambton Centre
Lambton South
Elgin East
Elgin West
Kent East
Kent West
Lake Erie
Lake St. Clair
Detroit River
Essex
0
100
KILOMETRES
Southern District
Western District
Eastern District

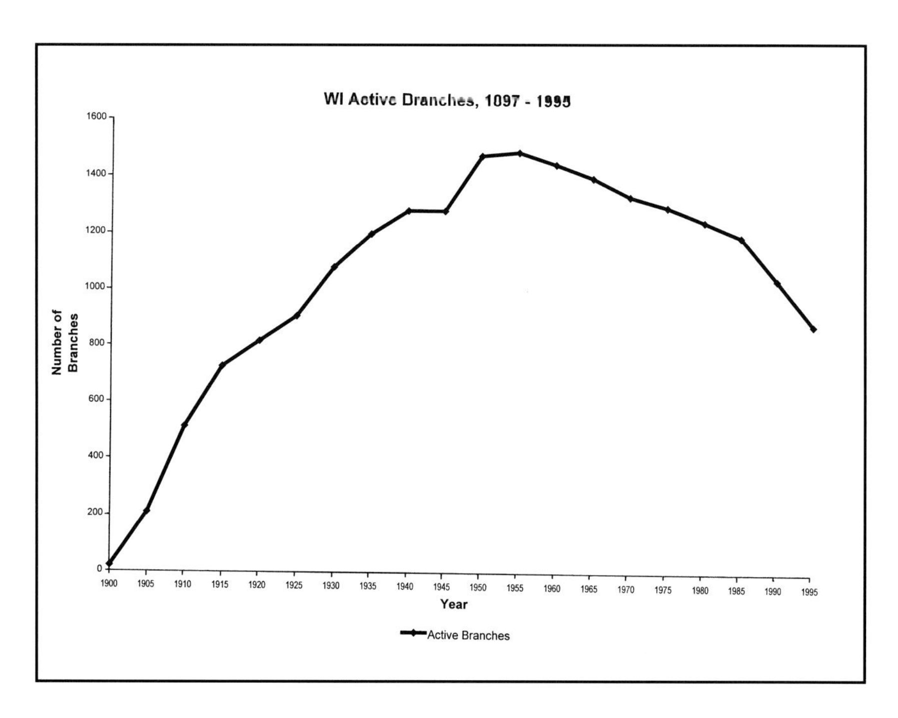
WI Active Branches, 1897 - 1995
Number of Branches
1600
1400
1200
1000
800
600
400
200
0
1900
1905
1910
1915
1920
1925
1930
1935
1940
1945
1950
1955
1960
1965
1970
1975
1980
1985
1990
1995
Year
Active Branches

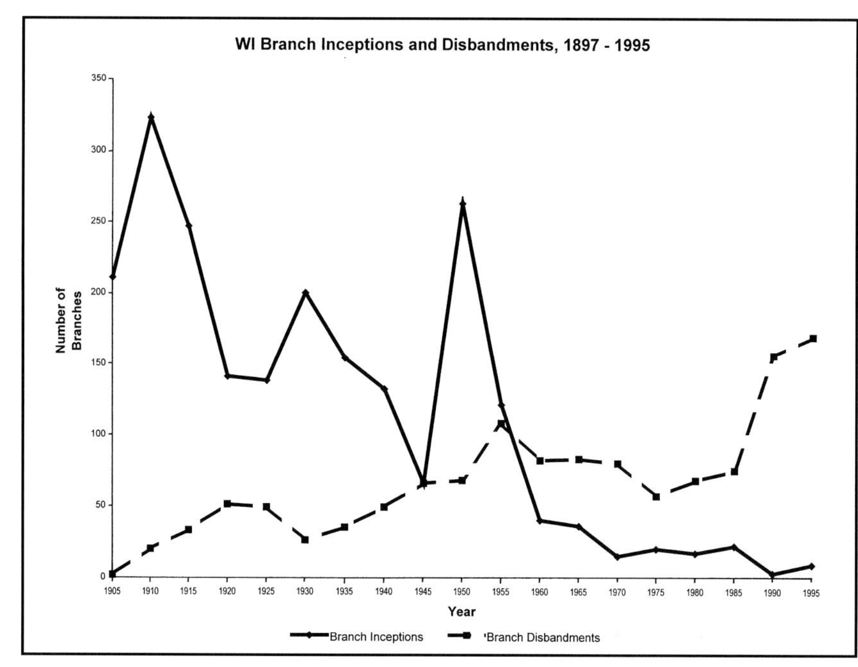
WI Branch Inceptions and Disbandments, 1897 - 1995
Number of Branches
350
300
250
200
150
100
50
0
1905
1910
1915
1920
1925
1930
1935
1940
1945
1950
1955
1960
1965
1970
1975
1980
1985
1990
1995
Year
Branch Inceptions
Branch Disbandments

List of Branches, 1897–1995

Notes:

1. This list of branches has been compiled from a variety of sources, including local branches, districts, local histories and provincial FWIO records.
2. Data shown for branches is current to to the end of 1995. Every possible effort has been made to ensure the accuracy of dates.

EASTERN CONVENTION AREA

PRESCOTT

	Inception	Disbandment
Cassburn	1947	still active
Everready	1933	1988
Greenlane	1938	still active
Hill View	1955	still active
Lemieux	1940	1956
Lookout Bay	1954	still active
Pendleton	1934	1979
Plantagenet	1952	still active
Stardale	1947	still active
Sunshine	1938	still active

RUSSELL

	Inception	Disbandment
Cumberland	1937	still active
Grant	1937	1946
Leonard	1945	still active
Navan	1931	still active
North Russell	1930	still active
Rockland–Clarence	1954	1967
Russell Village	1936	still active
Vars	1927	1971

STORMONT

	Inception	Disbandment
Aultsville	1914	1921
Aultsville (reorganized)*	1951	1957
Avonmore	1924	still active
Berwick	1915	1993
Chrysler	1940	1968
Cornwall Centre	1912	1989
Dixon	1929	1980
Elm Branch Jrs	1975	disbanded
Farran's Point*	1927	1957
Finch	1910	still active
Goldfield Jrs	1922	1925
Ingleside	1957	still active
Long Sault	1975	1978
Lunnenburg	1928	1987
Milles Roches	1931	1957
Moose Creek	1915	still active
Newington Cedar Brae	1922	still active
Osnabruck Centre	1929	1994
Wales*	1924	1957

* to Ingleside

DUNDAS

	Inception	Disbandment
Brinston	1908	1911
Chesterville	1902	still active
Colquhoun	1949	1965
Elma	1947	1991
Inkerman	1908	1910
Iroquois	1912	still active
Matilda	1930	still active

DUNDAS *continued*

	Inception	Disbandment
Morewood	1905	still active
Morrisburg	1908	still active
Mount Hall	1938	1942
Mountain	1951	1991
Riverside Heights	1958	still active
South Mountain	1906	1988
Williamsburg	1906	still active
Winchester	1919	still active
Winchester Springs	1910	1913

GLENGARRY

	Inception	Disbandment
Bainsville	1929	still active
Dunvegan	1935	still active
MacCrimmon	1915	still active
Martintown	1910	still active
Maxville	1909	1986
Maxville-Rainbow	1995	still active
Picnic Grove	1916	still active
St. Lawrence	1951	1992
Summerstown	1946	1975
The Tweedsmuir	1942	1951
Williamstown	1915	1956

CARLETON EAST

	Inception	Disbandment
Bowesville	1914	1938
Bowesville (reorganized)	1943	1951
Carlsbad Springs	1934	1963
Carsonby	1923	1927
Cedardale	1959	1968
Dalmeny	1920	1926
Glen Ogilvie	1919	1990
Gloucester Glenn	1952	1987
Goodwood	1924	1925
Greely–Manotick Station 1957	still active	
Greely (later Greely–Manotick)	1945	1946
Hawthorne	1921	1966
Hazeldeen	1920	1932
Hurdman's Bridge	1925	1965
Kars	1912	still active
Kenmore	1935	still active
Leitrum	1919	still active
Malakoff	1929	1944
Metcalfe	1928	still active
Osgoode	1932	still active
Overbrook	1930	1938
Quarries	1926	1941
Ramsayville (Carlsbad Springs)	1963	still active
Ridge	1936	1966
Ridgemont	1946	1953
Vernon	1912	still active

CARLETON WEST

	Inception	Disbandment
Antrim	1910	1987
Britannia	1948	1984
City View and Merivale	1910	1985
Dunrobin	1918	still active
Fitzroy Harbour	1929	1941
Fitzroy Harbour (reorganized)	1948	1950
Galetta	1910	1924
Galetta (reorganized)	1932	1976
Huntley (Carp)	1911	still active
Johnston–May	1951	still active
Kinburn	1911	1915
Kinburn (reorganized)	1924	1955
Lorne Sutherland	1919	still active
Manotick	1909	still active
North Gower	1907	1994
Richmond	1927	still active
South March	1939	still active
Stittsville	1908	1993
Torbolton	1917	1993

GRENVILLE

	Inception	Disbandment
Algonquin	1926	1937
Bishop's Mills	1985	still active
Blue Church	1922	1958
Brouseville	1902	1918
Burritt's Rapids	1912	1989
Cardinal	1924	1976
Heckston	1946	1956
Jasper	1931	still active
Kemptville	1916	still active
Maitland	1924	still active
Mainsville (Third Line)	1946	1988
Maynard	1909	still active
Merrickville	1910	1988
North Augusta	1920	1984
Oxford Mills	1914	still active
Oxford Mills Jrs	1946	1948
Prescott	1923	1954
Roebuck	1926	still active
South Augusta	1920	1985
Spencerville	1925	1960
St. Lawrence	1932	1992
Third Line	1932	1946
Ventnor	1931	1969

LANARK NORTH

	Inception	Disbandment
Almonte	1909	still active
Appleton	1944	still active
Beckwith	1945	still active
Carleton Place	1913	1924
Cedar Hill	1913	still active
Clayton	1910	still active
Galbraith	1916	1925
Hopetown	1914	still active
Janey Canuck Jr	1918	1924

LANARK NORTH *continued*

	Inception	Disbandment
Middleville	1910	1923
Pakenham	1913	1919
Pakenham (reorganized)	1926	still active
Pine Grove	1939	1961
Ramsay	1944	still active
Rocky Ridge	1945	still active
Rosetta	1938	still active
Union Hall	1932	still active
Watson's Corners	1913	1938

LANARK SOUTH

	Inception	Disbandment
Balderson	1938	still active
Bethel (Maberly Sr & Jr)	1937	still active
Clarendon	1954	1993
Drummond (2nd Line)	1960	still active
Drummond Centre	1913	still active
Elphin	1913	1961
Fallbrooke	1919	still active
Ferguson's Falls	1928	still active
Franktown–Numogate	1982	still active
Harper	1929	1934
Harper (reorganized)	1960	still active
Innisville	1913	1918
Innisville (reorganized)	1938	still active
Lanark	1908	1987
Lavant Station	1915	1920
Maberly	1912	1928
Maberly (Sr & Jr)	1929	1937
McDonald's Corners	1915	still active
McIlquham's	1952	still active
Mississippi	1931	1992
Otty Lake	1983	still active
Perth	1912	1929
Poland	1914	1935
Port Elmsley	1939	still active
Rideau	1950	still active
Rosedale	1935	1956
Snow Road	1935	still active
Watson's Corners	1913	1938
Zealand (from Frontenac)	1963	still active

RENFREW NORTH

	Inception	Disbandment
Alice	1938	still active
Beachburg	1904	still active
Bromley	1906	1918
Bromley (reorganized)	1934	still active
Cobden	1911	1987
Cobden Jr	1946	1948
Forester's Falls	1905	still active
Germanicus	1969	1983
Golden Lake	1934	still active
Greenwood	1985	still active
Killaloe	1967	1979
Lake Dore	1934	1946
Lake Dore (reorganized)	1948	still active
Laurentian View	1951	still active
Locksley Rankin	1930	still active
Mackey's	1949	1953
Micksburg	1925	1991
Pembroke	1931	1979
Pleasant View	1951	still active
Point Alexander	1947	1975
Queen's Line	1907	still active
Roche Fondu	1947	1983

RENFREW NORTH *continued*

	Inception	Disbandment
Snake River	1932	still active
Stafford	1909	1915
Westmeath	1905	still active
Zion Line	1919	still active

RENFREW SOUTH

	Inception	Disbandment
Arnprior	1932	still active
Balsam Hill	1946	still active
Bonnechere Valley	1914	still active
Braeside	1927	1983
Burnstown	1911	still active
Calabogie	1934	still active
Castleford	1913	still active
Clay Bank	1917	1989
Combermere	1934	still active
Dacre–Hyndford	1964	1983
Dewars	1941	still active
Glasgow Station	1913	1918
Glasgow Station (reorganized)	1945	still active
Goshen	1914	1994
Horton North	1915	still active
Horton South	1914	still active
Lockwinnoch	1913	still active
Madawaska Valley	1973	1975
Palmer Rapids	1937	1940
Pine Grove	1914	still active
Rosebank	1943	still active
Stewartsville	1949	still active
White Lake	1915	still active

KINGSTON CONVENTION AREA

FRONTENAC

	Inception	Disbandment
Battersea	1923	still active
Crystal Springs	1963	still active
Fernleigh	1938	1950
Fort Henry	1947	1950
Glenburnie	1925	still active
Godfrey	1916	still active
Harrowsmith	1924	still active
Inverary	1910	1992
Joyceville	1935	still active
Jubilee	1935	1988
Kingston Jr	1923	1932
Kingston Jr (reorganized)	1947	1959
Mountain Grove	1917	1941
Murvale	1927	still active
Parham	1923	still active
Perth Road	1927	1948
Pittsburg	1924	still active
Sharbot Lake	1934	1943
South Frontenac Jr	1947	1951
St. Lawrence	1927	still active
Sunbury	1923	1985
Sydenham	1919	still active
Verona	1927	1976
Westbrooke	1910	1991
Westside	1993	still active
Wolfe Island	1927	still active

LEEDS

	Inception	Disbandment
Alonna Lea	1940	1978
Athens	1911	1940
Athens (reorganized)	1955	still active
Brick School	1948	1976
Chaffey's Locks	1924	1995
Crosby	1917	1961
Delta	1910	1989
Elgin	1912	1953
Fairfield East	1924	still active
Fairgrove	1947	still active
Frankville	1928	still active
Junetown	1942	still active
Landsdowne	1909	still active
Lombardy	1936	1943
Lombardy (reorganized)	1951	still active
Lyn	1925	still active
Lyndhurst	1919	1948
Mallorytown	1920	1993
New Dublin	1924	1987
Newboro	1909	1967
Phillipsville	1919	still active
Portland	1918	1969
Rockport	1920	1980
Seeley's Bay	1949	1965
Shanes	1962	still active
Tincap	1929	still active
Westport	1911	1965

ADDINGTON (WITH LENNOX)

	Inception	Disbandment
Camden East	1927	still active
Centreville	1951	1954
Cloyne	1935	1983
Croyden	1923	1944
Denbigh Dames	1951	1986
Enterprise	1914	1930
Fifth Lake	1935	1936
Moscow	1923	1991
Newburgh	1929	1946
Reidville	1928	still active
Tamworth	1921	still active
Yarker Colebrook	1927	1959

LENNOX (WITH ADDINGTON)

	Inception	Disbandment
Adolphustown	1901	1995
Amherst Island	1900	still active
Bay View	1913	1974
Centennial	1967	still active
Conway	1910	1942
Ernestown	1926	1974
Grandview	1951	still active
Hawley	1967	still active
Hay Bay	1960	still active
Maple Leaf	1914	still active
Maple Ridge	1933	still active
Millhaven	1955	1994
Mount Pleasant JWI	1983	1993
Mount Pleasant Pioneer	1933	1978
Napanee	1921	1989
Napanee Jr	1949	1953
Odessa	1926	1981
Roblin	1931	still active
Victoria II Sharp's Corners	1936	still active
Violet Switzerville	1926	1942
Wilton	1925	still active

TRENT VALLEY CONVENTION AREA

PRINCE EDWARD

	Inception	Disbandment
Big Island	1916	1919
Bloomfield	1908	still active
Cherry Valley	1908	still active
Consecon	1913	still active
Demorestville (Big Island)	1919	still active
Elmbrook	1974	1984
Gilbert's Mills	1908	still active
Glenora	1919	1933
Greenbush	1919	1984
Hillier	1914	still active
Milford	1908	1923
Mountain View	1908	still active
Picton	1908	1919
Picton (reorganized)	1963	1979
Prince Edward Jr	1946	1972
Rednersville	1909	still active
Waupoos	1916	1931
Wellington	1908	still active
West Lake	1908	1920

HASTINGS EAST

	Inception	Disbandment
Belleville East	1912	1918
Belleville West	1913	1921
Bethany	1913	1919
Bethel Zion	1912	still active
Cannifton Corbyville	1950	1988
Carmel	1949	still active
Chapman	1950	still active
Foxboro	1901	1969
Halston	1913	1919
Lonsdale	1968	still active
Marysville	1915	1919
Marlbank	1994	still active
Melrose	1902	still active
Mohawk	1935	1942
Moira (Huntingdon East)	1946	1967
Park Dale	1953	disbanded
Plainfield	1910	still active
Queen Alexander School	1914	1917
Quinte	1907	disbanded
Read	1914	1917
Roslin	1908	1919
Roslin (reorganized)	1924	still active
Shannonville	1916	disbanded
Spencers	1901	1906
Thomasburg	1913	1919
Thurlow Jrs	1948	1960
Tweed	1901	1921
Tyendinaga East	1929	still active

HASTINGS NORTH

	Inception	Disbandment
Bannockburn & Eldorado	1908	still active
Beltistas	1954	1957
Carlow	uncertain	still active
Cooper & Remington	1928	still active
Detlor & L'amable	1950	disbanded
Gilmour	1940	1952
Harts Riggs	1955	still active
Hastings County Jr	1976	still active
Hungerford Jr	1950	1956
Ivanhoe	1910	still active

HASTINGS NORTH *continued*

	Inception	Disbandment
Madoc	1910	1994
Madoc Jr	1946	1957
Marmora	1910	still active
McArthur's Mills	1947	disbanded
Mont Eagle	1976	disbanded
Paudash	1947	disbanded
Queensboro	1948	still active
Rawdon Jr	1947	1953
Rylstone	1924	still active
Springbrook	1901	still active
Wellman's	1905	still active

HASTINGS WEST

	Inception	Disbandment
Bay of Quinte	1921	still active
Bayside	1915	1924
Chatterton	1906	1979
Pine Grove	1940	still active
River Valley	1910	still active
Sidney Jr	1947	1957
Sidney South	1961	still active
Stirling	1912	still active
Uniondale	1928	still active
Wallbridge	1907	1991

NORTHUMBERLAND EAST

	Inception	Disbandment
Brighton	1903	1918
Castleton	1905	still active
Codrington	1900	still active
Colborne	1932	disbanded
Colbridge	uncertain	1993
Community	1944	still active
Lakeview	1937	disbanded
Mapleview	1970	still active
Percy	uncertain	disbanded
Seymour East	1907	still active
Seymour West	1912	still active
White School	1946	still active
Wooler	1901	still active
York Road	1901	still active

NORTHUMBERLAND WEST

	Inception	Disbandment
Baltimore	1912	still active
Cobourg	1906	1995
Coldsprings	1912	still active
Elmview	1905	still active
Fenella	1905	1988
Grafton	1902	still active
Harwood	1919	still active
Precious Corners	1979	1993
Roseneath	1907	still active
Wicklow & Vernonville	1914	1981

PETERBOROUGH

	Inception	Disbandment
Apsley	1928	still active
Belmont	1907	still active
Brookdale	uncertain	1951
Buckhorn	1931	disbanded
Chandos	1947	still active
Hall's Glen	1940	1970
Havelock	1928	still active
Keene	1951	still active

PETERBOROUGH *continued*

	Inception	Disbandment
Lakefield	1927	1988
Lakefield Jr	1929	1945
Mount Pleasant	1905	still active
Nephton	1952	1968
North Shore	1993	still active
Norwood	1910	still active
Otanabee West	1964	1993
Selwyn	1950	still active
South Smith	1951	1988
Trent River	1929	still active
Warsaw	1927	still active
Westwood	1932	still active
Young's Point	1929	1938

CENTRAL CONVENTION AREA

DURHAM EAST

	Inception	Disbandment
Bailieboro	1905	still active
Bethany	1914	still active
Bewdley	1910	1915
Canton	1912	1914
Cavan	1914	still active
Charlecote	1909	1933
Elizabethville	1911	still active
Fairmount	1909	1919
Garden Hill	1902	1994
Hope Township Jr	1949	1951
Lifford	1911	1914
Manvers Station	1910	1920
Millbrook	1901	still active
Morrish (formerly Charlecote)	1933	still active
Pontypool	1915	1919
Port Hope	1910	1919
Rossmount	1953	1968

DURHAM WEST

	Inception	Disbandment
Blackstock Victorian	1915	still active
Bowmanville	1900	still active
Hampton	1903	still active
Kendal	1937	1993
Maple Grove	1946	still active
Nestleton	1906	1995
Newtonville	1912	1994
Orono	1909	1955
Providence–Shaw's	1981	still active
Solina	1903	still active
Starkville	1906	1913
Starkville (reorganized)	1916	1923
Tyrone	1914	1958
Village People Jrs	1982	1992

VICTORIA EAST

	Inception	Disbandment
Blythe	1926	still active
Bobcaygeon	1900	1993
Burnt River	1908	still active
Bury's Green	1953	still active
Cameron	1909	1987
Coboconk	1912	disbanded
Fenelon Falls	1905	still active
Haliburton	uncertain	1947

VICTORIA EAST *continued*

	Inception	Disbandment
Lakeview of Fenelon Falls	1938	still active
Minden	1907	still active
Norland	1929	still active
Omemee	1904	disbanded
Pleasant Valley	1909	still active
Powel's Corners	1915	still active

VICTORIA WEST

	Inception	Disbandment
Bolsover	1949	still active
Cambray	1905	still active
Grasshill	1946	still active
Islay Zion	1908	still active
Janetville	1916	1989
Kawartha Valley	1929	still active
Linden Valley	1904	1917
Lindsay	1904	1987
Little Britain	1903	1988
Lorneville Argyle	1909	still active
Manilla	1910	1990
North Emily	1958	still active
North Ops	1944	still active
Oakwood	1903	1989
Reaboro	1913	still active
Sonya	1910	1911
South Ops	1951	1963
South Verulam	1952	still active
The Glen	1946	1972
Valentia	1909	1920
Victoria County Jr.	1987	1994
Victoria West	1903	1953
West Ops	1912	still active
Woodville	1903	still active

ONTARIO NORTH

	Inception	Disbandment
Atherley	1950	1975
Beaverton	1913	still active
Beaverton Jrs	1950	1958
Bethesda-Reach	1956	still active
Brechin Jr	1946	1949
Brechin Senior	1949	1951
Brock Jr	1945	1949
Gamebridge	1909	still active
Goodwood	1909	1956
Goodwood (reorganized)	1964	still active
Quaker Hill	1951	1991
Sandford	1903	still active
Sunderland	1911	still active
Udney	1931	1975
Uxbridge Jr	1945	1958
Zephyr	1910	still active

YORK CENTRE

	Inception	Disbandment
Aurora	1911	still active
Bogarttown	1946	still active
Elder's Mills	1949	still active
Gormley	1930	1990
Kettleby	1911	1981
King (reorganized from King East)	1939	still active
King East	1909	1919
King Ridge	1951	1964
Kleinburg & Nashville	1900	still active

YORK CENTRE *continued*

	Inception	Disbandment
Laskay	1900	1989
Nobleton	1908	still active
Pine Orchard	1913	still active
Schomberg	1911	1990
Schomberg Jr	1948	1951
Snowball	1926	1971
Temperanceville	1934	1970
Vandorf	1907	still active

YORK EAST

	Inception	Disbandment
Agincourt	1900	1970
Bethesda	1935	still active
Buttonville	1932	1986
Buttonville Jr	1927	1928
Dawes Road	1930	1977
East Toronto	1911	1918
Elmhurst	1930	1943
Fairglen	1952	1955
First Toronto	1994	still active
Glen Elm	1957	1958
Highland Creek	1908	still active
Highland Creek Jr	1933	1946
Lakeview	1914	1993
Langstaff Jr	1949	1976
Malvern	1947	1956
Mark–Vaun	1951	1976
Markham	1904	1967
Markham Jrs	1921	1929
Mary H Graves	1932	still active
Richmond Hill	1913	1964
Scarboro Jrs	1935	1936
Scarboro Junction	1909	1976
Stouffville	1905	1995
Stouffville Club	1936	1938
Stouffville Jrs	1927	1940
Thornhill	1902	still active
Unionville	1902	1968
Victoria Square	1913	1914
Victoria Square Jr	1927	1989
West Hill	1914	1925
Wexford	1924	1989

YORK NORTH

	Inception	Disbandment
Belhaven	1928	still active
Egypt	1960	1990
Elm Grove	1939	1972
Elmhurst Beach	1930	1960
Glenpark	uncertain	1947
Islington	1912	1945
Lakeside	1938	disbanded
Mount Albert	1907	still active
Newmarket	1906	1971
Nobleton Jrs	1945	1947
Pefferlaw	1933	disbanded
Queensville	1908	1988
Roche's Point	1938	still active
Sharon	1926	still active
Union Street	1941	still active
Virginia Jr	1947	1948

YORK WEST (now disbanded)

	Inception	Disbandment
Burwick	1925	1995
Eatonville	1921	1959
Edgeley	1913	1993
Elder's Mills (to York Centre)	1949	still active
Elia	1908	1931
Kleinburg & Nashville (to York Centre)	1900	still active
Lambton Mills	1907	1978
Maple	1898	1991
Richview	1914	disbanded
Thistletown	1908	1955
Vellore	1915	1988
Vellore Jr	1930	1965
Woodbridge	1904	1964

ONTARIO SOUTH

	Inception	Disbandment
Ajax	1946	1981
Altona	1910	still active
Audley	1938	disbanded
Brooklin	1910	still active
Brooklin Jr	1945	1953
Brougham	1910	1982
Claremont	1909	still active
Greenbank	1903	1923
Greenbank (reorganized)	1962	still active
Honeydale	1935	still active
Kinsale	1897	1990
Myrtle	1955	1985
Pickering	1908	1966
Port Perry Jr	1950	1958
Scugog Island	1972	still active
Shirley	1910	still active
Whitby	1899	1988
Whitevale	1909	1948

PEEL NORTH

	Inception	Disbandment
Alloa Jr	1947	1958
Alton	1903	still active
Belfountain Rockside	1904	1990
Bolton–Coronation	uncertain	1984
Bolton Jr	1937	1944
Bolton Jr (reorganized)	1947	1958
Caledon	1906	still active
Caledon Jr	1948	1966
Campbell's Cross	1935	still active
Cheltenham	1905	1986
Inglewood	1906	1993
Mono Road	1926	still active
Rosehill	1946	still active
Sandhill	1915	1993
Snelgrove	1912	1988
Terra Cotta	1931	1993

PEEL SOUTH

	Inception	Disbandment
Brampton (Brampton West)	1936	still active
Brampton East	1933	1988
Castlemore	1910	still active
Clarkson–Lorne Park	uncertain	1948
Derry West	1929	still active
Dixie	1919	1950
Ebenezer Jr	1945	1952

PEEL SOUTH

	Inception	Disbandment
Erindale	1914	1988
Flower Town	1947	1979
Malton	1906	1957
Malton (reorganized)	1975	1976
Meadowvale	1910	1993
Port Credit	1910	1956
Streetsville	1905	still active
Streetsville Jr	1945	1954
Trixie Jr	1946	1953
Tullamore Jr	1945	1956

DUFFERIN NORTH

	Inception	Disbandment
Back Line	1946	still active
Corbetton	1907	1956
Elba	1913	still active
Honeywood	1904	1994
Hornings Mill	1902	still active
Keldon	1909	1911
Kilgorie	1928	1956
Lavender	1945	1970
Mansfield	1946	still active
Melancthon (to Back Line)	1936	1972
Perm	1902	1904
Redickville	1902	1930
Rosemont	1944	still active
Ruskview	1914	still active
Shelburne	1902	1994
Silk's Ruth Sayre	1950	still active
Violet Hill	1911	still active
Whitfield	1944	still active

DUFFERIN SOUTH

	Inception	Disbandment
Black Bank	1914	1921
Blount	1907	1978
Bowling Green	1909	1990
Camilla	1902	still active
Campania	1947	still active
Colbeck & Monticello	1909	still active
Coleridge Union	1948	still active
Hereward	1929	still active
Hockley Valley	1949	still active
Laurel	1904	1920
Laurel (reorganized)	1952	still active
Marsville	1905	still active
Mono Centre	1912	1922
Mono College	1913	1922
Orangeville	1905	1994
Relessey	1902	1907
Salem	1927	still active
The Maples	1914	still active
Waldemar	1918	still active
Whittington	1908	1921

GUELPH CONVENTION AREA

WATERLOO NORTH

	Inception	Disbandment
Bloomingdale	1949	still active
Bridgeport	1946	still active
Centreville	1936	1978
Conestogo	1908	disbanded
Dorking	1946	1977
Elmdale	1951	1986

WATERLOO NORTH *continued*

	Inception	Disbandment
Helena Feasby	1948	still active
Lexington	1962	still active
Linwood	1907	1988
Rummelhardt	1962	1994
St Jacobs Friendly	1939	still active
Sunnyside	1941	1949
Wellesley	1903	still active
West Montrose	1908	1928
West Montrose (reorganized)	1950	disbanded
Winterbourne	1902	still active
Woolwich Ever Faithful	1950	still active

WATERLOO SOUTH

	Inception	Disbandment
Ayr	1908	1989
Branchton	1904	still active
Central Dumfries	1909	still active
Galt	1906	1980
Grand River	1947	1978
Haysville	1914	still active
Hespeler	1906	1992
Jubilee	1947	1988
Laura Rose	1942	still active
Little's Corners	1927	still active
Little's Corners Jr	1942	disbanded
Maple Grove	1930	still active
Mill Creek	1931	1970
New Dundee	1907	still active
New Dundee Jr	1933	1940
New Hamburg	1909	1909
New Hamburg (reorganized)	1921	still active
Preston	1906	still active

WELLINGTON NORTH

	Inception	Disbandment
Arthur Centennial	1972	still active
Beehive	1949	still active
Carry On	1938	still active
Clifford	1900	disbanded
Conn	1905	1978
Damascus	1968	still active
Drayton	1903	1995
Drew	1908	disbanded
Erin Township Jrs	1948	1957
Farewell	1948	1994
Greenbush	1925	still active
Little Ireland	1926	still active
Maryborough	uncertain	disbanded
Maryborough Jr	1948	1954
Moorefield	1904	still active
Mount Forest	uncertain	disbanded
North Gate	1951	1995
Palmerston	1903	1988
Rothsay	1908	still active
Teviotdale	1954	still active

HURON EAST

	Inception	Disbandment
Bluevale	1903	still active
Brussels	1910	1941
Cranbrook	1950	1991
Ethel	1903	1992
Fordwich	1903	still active
Gorrie	1902	still active

HURON EAST *continued*

	Inception	Disbandment
Howick Jr	1970	still active
Howick Near Gorrie	1950	1969
Jameston	1909	1941
Lakelet	1918	1941
Lakelet (reorganized)	1952	still active
Majestic	1939	still active
Molesworth	1903	1931
Molesworth (reorganized)	1948	still active
Moncrieff	1957	1991
Ruth Pirt	1921	1922
Rutnam Girls	1926	1946
Walton	1913	1925
Walton (reorganized)	1956	still active
Wroxeter	1919	1984

PERTH CENTRE

	Inception	Disbandment
Athlone	1945	still active
Avon	1926	1976
Bornholm	1950	still active
Brunner	1939	1991
Classic	1927	1993
Elmhurst	1926	still active
Gadshill	1923	still active
Gravelridge	1946	still active
Hampstead	1903	still active
Kuhryville	1933	still active
Lily Dempsey	1960	still active
North Easthope Jr	1922	1983
Shakespeare	1913	1995
Stratford Jr	1943	1983
Wartburg	1934	1979

PERTH NORTH

	Inception	Disbandment
Britton	1932	still active
Donegal	1949	still active
Elma Centre	1932	1992
Evergreen Jr	1982	1986
Gowanstown	1938	still active
Listowel East	1907	still active
Listowel Jr	1949	1968
Listowel West	1913	still active
Maitland	1936	1994
Maple Keys Jr	1979	still active
Maple Leaf	1921	still active
Mary Wallace	1949	still active
Millbank	uncertain	1995
Milverton	uncertain	1945
Monkton	1929	still active
North Mornington	1962	still active
Peace	1936	still active
Tralee	1947	still active
Wallace Goodwill	1950	still active

WELLINGTON SOUTH

	Inception	Disbandment
Arkell	1909	still active
Badenoch	1934	still active
Bethany	1906	1907
Brock Road	1948	still active
Downey	1939	1962
Eden Crest	1950	1967
Eden Mills	1907	1909
Eden Mills (reorganized)	1924	1969
Eramosa	1931	1974

WELLINGTON SOUTH *continued*

	Inception	Disbandment
Eramosa Jr	1923	1933
Erin Jr (reorganized)	1984	still active
Everton	1908	1952
Guelph Jr	1948	1951
Jean Scott Jrs	1975	still active
Killean	1905	1908
Marden	1903	1915
Marden (reorganized)	1924	1927
Morriston	1956	still active
Mosborough	1947	still active
Paisley Block	1905	1923
Ponsonby	1971	still active
Puslinch	1903	still active
Puslinch Lake	1948	1964
Riverside	1915	still active
Riverside Jrs	1978	1988
Rock a Long	1936	1995
Rockwood	1903	1955
Rockwood Jr	1932	1936
Royals	1927	1993
Utoka	1924	1988
West End	1915	still active
West End Jrs	1979	1989

HALTON

	Inception	Disbandment
Acton	1903	1980
Acton Junior	1943	1970
Appleby	uncertain	1908
Ashgrove	1926	still active
Ballinafad	1906	1921
Ballinafad (reorganized)	1952	still active
Bannockburn	1918	still active
Brookville Jr	1950	1954
Burlington	1903	1963
Busy Bees	1947	1963
Campbellville	1902	1908
Campbellville (reorganized)	1937	still active
Cedar Grove	1916	disbanded
Drumquin	1946	1973
Dublin	1925	still active
Esquesing	1912	1980
Georgetown	1903	1978
Hornby	1906	1911
Hornby (reorganized)	1914	1990
Kilbride	1908	1914
Kilbride (reorganized)	1930	1939
Limehouse	1921	still active
Milton	1903	1908
Milton Jrs	1937	1963
Moffat	1908	1912
Mountain Union	1924	1982
Nassagaweya	1913	1921
Nassagaweya (reorganized)	1934	still active
Nelson	1907	1907
Nelson (reorganized)	1931	still active
Norval	1906	still active
Norval Jr	1933	1979
Omagh	1917	1958
Palermo	1903	1957
Palermo Jrs	1936	1968
Postville (Trafalgar)	1905	1947
Scotch Block	1933	still active
Sheridan	1906	1919
Silverwood	1951	still active
Allardice Nicol	1955	1986

WELLINGTON CENTRE

	Inception	Disbandment
Alma	1973	still active
Belwood	1927	still active
Belwood Belles Jr	1951	1953
Brisbane	1921	1931
Cedarville	1932	1938
Coningsby	1905	still active
Cummoch	1947	1967
Elora	1931	still active
Ennotville	1914	still active
Erin	1926	1962
Erin Jr	1927	1956
Fergus	1921	still active
Greenock	1948	still active
Hillsburg Auxiliary	1922	still active
Hillsburg Junior	1922	1948
Hillsburg Senior	1904	1967
Living Springs	1925	1995
Mimosa	1918	1993
Nichol Jr	1949	1953
Ospringe	1926	1986
Speedside	1915	still active

SIMCOE CONVENTION AREA

SIMCOE CENTRE

	Inception	Disbandment
Allenwood	1907	still active
Barrie	1917	1965
Birch	1914	1919
Central Flos	1953	still active
Centre Vespra	1929	1992
Christian Island	1930	1954
Crossland	1910	still active
Cundles	1929	1960
Edenvale	1908	still active
Elmvale	1906	1955
Minesing	1904	still active
New Flos	1903	still active
Phelpston	1903	1915
Pine Ridge	1961	still active
Saurin	1947	still active
Silver Maple	1917	1942
Silver Maple (reorganized)	1950	still active
Van Vlack	1930	1990
Waverley	1955	still active
Wyebridge	1901	still active

SIMCOE EAST

	Inception	Disbandment
Argyle	1954	1989
Atherley	1976	1990
Hampshire–Ardtrea	1958	still active
Harvie Settlement	1908	still active
Hydro Glen	1933	1951
Lake St George	1923	1987
Orillia	1907	1978
Pine Grove	1946	still active
Prices Corners	1916	1985
Rugby	1920	still active
Severn Bridge	1919	still active
Sparrow Lake	1917	still active
Udney	1976	1992
Victoria Crescent	1957	1992
Washago	1913	still active

SIMCOE EAST *continued*

	Inception	Disbandment
West Ward Evening	1937	1967
Westmount	1956	still active

SIMCOE NORTH

	Inception	Disbandment
Big Chute	uncertain	1951
Coldwater	1952	1981
Coldwater Huronia	1961	1981
Coldwater Jr	1926	1952
Coulson	1927	still active
Creighton & Jarrett	1929	still active
Eady	1916	1988
Eady–Grenard	1988	still active
Ebenezer	1938	still active
Hillsdale	1950	1985
Hobart Carley	1921	1986
Melduf	1930	1962
Moonstone	1933	1964
North River	1915	still active
Penetanguishene	1906	disbanded
Vasey	1928	still active
Warminster	1949	1995
Waubaushene	1911	1989

SIMCOE SOUTH

	Inception	Disbandment
Alliston	1914	1989
Beeton	1920	still active
Belle Ewart	1927	1964
Bond Head	1920	still active
Bond Head Jr (to Tec-We-Gill Jr)	1921	1947
Bradford	1925	1990
Chilli Willi Jr	1950	1955
Churchill	1903	still active
Cookstown	1901	still active
Coulson's Hill	1911	1953
Coulson's Hill Jr	1934	1952
Deerhurst Sr (Coulson's Hill)	1953	1955
Everett	1908	1989
Fisher's Corners	1921	still active
Gilford	1934	1988
South Adjala	1961	1964
Tec-We-Gill Sr	1953	still active
Tec-We-Gill Jr	1947	1953
The Hollows	1946	1967
The Ridge	1938	1975
Tottenham	1920	still active
Tottenham Jr.	1939	1942
Trillium	1983	1989

SIMCOE WEST

	Inception	Disbandment
Avening	1907	still active
Cain's Corners	1948	still active
Clearview	1943	1992
Clover Lea	1937	1990
Creemore	1902	1989
Crown	1953	1954
Duntroon	1902	still active
Georgian	1937	1988
Jack's Lake	1922	1980
Maple Valley	1914	still active
Mrs Alfred Watt Memorial (Crown)	1953	still active

SIMCOE WEST *continued*

	Inception	Disbandment
New Lowell	1903	still active
Pine Tree	1922	1989
Singhampton	1902	1988
Stayner	1912	still active
Sunnidale Corners	1904	still active
Sunniwood	1960	1990
Zion Jubilee	1935	still active

SIMCOE KEMPENFELDT

	Inception	Disbandment
Edgar	1913	1970
Clowes	1924	still active
Craighurst	1928	still active
Crown Hill	1911	still active
Dalston	1910	still active
Guthrie	1913	still active
Hawkestone	1910	still active
Holly	1930	1953
Ivy	1910	1987
Lefroy	1903	disbanded
Little's Hill Coronation (Holly)	1953	still active
Mitchell Square	1913	still active
Painswich	1924	1989
Shanty Bay	1910	1980
Sparkling Waters	1977	1979
Stroud	1909	still active
Thornton	1902	still active

GREY-BRUCE CONVENTION AREA

All Grey Districts were reorganized in 1959.

GREY CENTRE

	Inception	Disbandment
Cherry Grove	1920	1940
Balaclava Jr	1945	1946
Centreville	1950	still active
Desboro	1920	still active
Dornoch	1912	still active
Dundalk	1908	1991
Elmwood	1903	still active
Golden Valley	1946	still active
Holland Centre	1950	still active
Hopeville Swinton	1906	1987
Lamlash	1913	still active
Louise	1911	still active
Louise & Crawford Jr	1945	1947
Marmion	1952	still active
Moggie	1948	1960
Osprey Jr	1951	1954
Proton Jrs	1950	disbanded
Proton Station	1939	1961
Saugeen Jr.	1984	1993
Thornbury	1926	1958
Williamsford	1906	1990
Willow Run	1948	1974
Zion	1914	still active

GREY EAST

	Inception	Disbandment
Blantyre	1949	1994
Cherry Dale	1953	1962
Clarksburg	1910	1977
Flesherton	1901	1978

GREY EAST *continued*

	Inception	Disbandment
Goring	1947	1991
Heathcote	1911	still active
Kimberley	1897	still active
Markdale	1952	1992
Maxwell	1904	1990
Millcreek	1902	1988
New England	1916	1982
Osprey	1988	still active
Ravenna	1904	1992
Rocklyn	1917	still active
Third Line West Mountain	1932	still active
Vandeleur	1903	1992
Walter's Falls	1908	still active
Walter's Falls Jrs	1978	1984

GREY NORTH

	Inception	Disbandment
Annan	1903	still active
Arnott	1925	1967
Balaclava	1926	1949
Bognor	1901	1910
Bognor (reorganized)	1912	still active
Bothwell Corners	1937	still active
Briar Hill	1949	1973
Dinna Weary	1947	1964
Hillview Fifth Line	1942	1969
Hoath Head & Grey	1920	1966
Kent	1949	disbanded
Kiowana	1930	1975
Massie	1903	still active
Meaford	1902	1964
North Grey Jrs	1973	still active
Pleasant View	1930	1992
Riverside	1947	still active
St Vincent	1918	still active
Woodford	1929	still active

GREY SOUTH

	Inception	Disbandment
Aberdeen	1926	1973
Aberdeen Jr	1983	1993
Allan Park Jr	1945	1950
Ayton	1908	still active
Ayton Jr	1951	1952
Campbell's Corners	1925	still active
Cedarville	1907	1993
Dromore	1907	still active
Durham	1902	1991
Gleneden	1919	still active
Hampden	1949	still active
Hanover	1907	1989
Holstein	1903	still active
Neustadt	1929	1945
Neustadt (reorganized)	1952	still active
Priceville	1904	1925
Priceville (reorganized)	1935	disbanded
Royaltide	1939	1963
South Glenelg	1935	1979
Sunnyview	1938	still active
Victory	1941	1995
Woodland Springs	1992	still active

GREY WEST

	Inception	Disbandment
Bluewater	1964	still active
Clavering	1908	still active

GREY WEST *continued*

	Inception	Disbandment
Grimston	1947	1967
Kemble	1897	still active
Keward	1925	still active
Kilsyth	1902	still active
North Derby	1958	still active
Owen Sound	1906	still active
Owen Sound Jr	1949	1963
Oxenden & Lake Charles	uncertain	still active
Pine Corner	1948	1988
Rockford	1919	1982
Rockview	uncertain	1952
Salem	1914	1990
Sarawak	1944	1995
Shallow Lake	1925	1991
South Sarawak & Keppel	1944	1964
Springmount	1921	still active
Sunny Valley	1930	1985
Zion & Wolsely	1954	1993

BRUCE CENTRE

	Inception	Disbandment
Allenford	1903	still active
Arkwright	1908	still active
Brucedale	1949	still active
Burgoyne	1921	1925
Burgoyne (reorganized)	1939	still active
Elsinore	1946	disbanded
Mount Hope	1956	still active
Port Elgin	1898	disbanded
Saugeen Jr.	1984	1993
Southampton	1939	disbanded
South Saugeen	1947	still active
Tara	1902	still active
Tara Jr	1925	disbanded
Underwood	1919	1929
Underwood (reorganized)	1952	still active
West Arran	1946	still active
White School	1920	1995

BRUCE EAST

	Inception	Disbandment
Bradley	1952	1990
Brant Greenock	1964	still active
Chesley	1910	still active
Chesley Jr	1948	1954
Dobbington	1951	1959
Eden Grove-Cargill	1961	still active
Elora Road North	1948	1962
Gillies Hill	1959	still active
Jackson	1963	still active
Malcolm	1954	still active
Mildmay	1949	1994
Mildmay Jr	1949	1957
Paisley	1900	1992
Paisley Jr	1953	disbanded
Pinkerton	1912	still active
Port Elgin Jr	1927	disbanded
Solway	1951	still active
South Line Brant	1934	still active
Walkerton Saugeen Jr	1953	disbanded
Walkerton Evening	1901	still active
Walkerton Young Women's Evening	1947	disbanded
Williscroft	1909	1920
Williscroft (reorganized)	1949	still active

BRUCE NORTH

	Inception	Disbandment
Adamsville	1934	still active
Bluebell	1954	still active
Colpoy's Bay	1910	still active
Edenhurst	1924	1964
Ferndale Swan Lake	1935	still active
Hepworth	1908	1988
Hope Bay	1910	1914
Hope Bay & Hope Ness	1916	1973
Limberlost	uncertain	disbanded
Lindsay	1926	1973
Lion's Head	1904	1954
Mar	1905	still active
Miller Lake & Dyer's Bay	1936	1948
Oliphant	1917	still active
Park Head	1910	still active
Purple Valley	1934	still active
Skipness	1951	disbanded
Spry	1914	1976
Stokes Bay	1956	still active
Wiarton	1907	1989
Zion Amabel	1936	still active

BRUCE SOUTH

	Inception	Disbandment
Armow	1950	1994
Belmore	1904	still active
Bervie	1908	1945
Bervie (reorganized)	1946	still active
Holyrood	1903	still active
Kincardine	1902	1989
Kincardine Jr	1950	1960
Kinloss–Kairshea	1947	still active
Lisburn	1957	1972
Lucknow	1908	still active
Lucknow Jrs	1974	still active
Paramount	1939	1962
Purple Grove	1947	still active
Reid's Corners	1913	still active
Ripley	1904	1994
Ripley Jr	1948	disbanded
Silver Lake	1957	still active
Teeswater	1908	still active
Teeswater Jr	1949	disbanded
Tiverton	1912	still active
Tiverton Jr	1950	1957
Whitechurch	1928	still active

HAMILTON CONVENTION AREA

LINCOLN

	Inception	Disbandment
Abingdon	1915	1983
Beamsville	1905	still active
Beamsville Jr	1936	disbanded
Caistorville	1914	1995
Community Builders	1949	still active
Fulton & Grassies	1917	1945
Grace Community	1948	1963
Grantham	1914	disbanded
Grimsby	1905	1971
Grimsby Beach	1949	1983
Jordan Station Jr	1926	disbanded
Louth	1916	still active
Louth Jr	1932	disbanded
McNab	1926	1940

LINCOLN *continued*

	Inception	Disbandment
Niagara Jr	1936	disbanded
Niagara Jr (reorganized)	1968	1992
Niagara on the Lake	1911	disbanded
Port Dalhousie	1919	1979
Queenston St Davids	1908	1994
Rosedene	1909	still active
Smithville	1904	1968
St Anns	1925	disbanded
St Anns Jr	1925	disbanded
Union Branch	1900	1991
Victory	1945	disbanded
Vineland	1940	still active
Virgil	1916	still active
Wellandport	1918	still active
Wellandport Jr	1936	disbanded
West Lincoln Jrs	1971	disbanded

WENTWORTH NORTH

	Inception	Disbandment
Aldershot	1930	1962
Beverly Young Jr (to Rockton)	1942	1960
Carlisle	uncertain	disbanded
Clyde & Scott's Corners	1923	still active
Copetown	1921	still active
Dundas	1916	1968
Freelton	1909	1925
Greensville	1925	1980
Ira Brock	1933	1955
Kirkwall & Valens	1909	1989
Lynden	1902	still active
Millgrove	1908	still active
Mountsberg	1952	still active
Orkney	1908	still active
Rockton	1902	still active
Sheffield	1908	1993
Strabane (Ira Brock)	1933	still active
Troy	1947	still active
Union "A"	1925	1972
Waterdown	1897	1974
West Flamboro	1903	1995
Westover	1903	still active

WENTWORTH SOUTH

	Inception	Disbandment
Adelaide Hoodless	1921	1982
Alexandra	1906	1974
Ancaster Jr	1949	1952
Binbrook	1903	still active
Binbrook Jr	uncertain	1951
Blackheath	1905	1987
Carluke	1901	still active
Community Beach	1948	1961
Fairfield	1919	1963
Glanford	1904	1968
Hannon	1906	1918
Jerseyville	1903	1916
Jubilee	1927	1970
King's Forest	1955	1974
Maggie Johnson	1961	still active
Mount Albion	1948	1979
Mount Hamilton	1910	1965
Mount Royal	1928	1965
Patricia	1925	still active
Queen Mary	1927	1963
Saltfleet Jr	1926	1936

WENTWORTH SOUTH *continued*

	Inception	Disbandment
Saltfleet Sr (formerly Saltfleet Jr)	1936	1983
South Wentworth Jr	1947	1949
Southcote	1922	1961
Stoney Creek (Charter Branch)	1897	still active
Tapleytown	1906	1925
Upper Hamilton	1915	1970
Vinemount	1926	still active
West Hamilton	1918	1963
Winona	1905	1982
Woodburn	1945	still active

HALDIMAND EAST

	Inception	Disbandment
Bethel	1923	1941
Bingham	1912	1938
Canboro	1909	1921
Canboro (reorganized)	1928	still active
Canfield	1902	still active
Cayuga	1907	still active
Cayuga Jr	1926	1937
Diltz & Robinson Road	1926	1983
Dunn	1918	still active
Dunnville	1911	1960
Dunnville Jr	1926	1929
Fisherville	1907	1967
Franconia	1936	1941
Grand River	1916	1993
Haldimand Jr	1947	1963
Haldimand Jr (reorganized)	1982	1986
Inman Road	1928	still active
Kohler	1927	still active
Nelles Corners	1906	1992
Oswego Friendship	1993	still active
Rainham Centre	1909	still active
South Cayuga	1906	1986

HALDIMAND WEST

	Inception	Disbandment
Caledonia	1906	still active
Caledonia Jr	1926	1946
Cheapside	1905	1919
Cheapside (reorganized)	1926	1945
Clanbrassil	1904	still active
Decewsville	1910	1912
Erie	1910	1912
Garnet	1911	1917
Garnet (reorganized)	1950	1994
Hagersville	1906	1993
Haldimand Jr	1981	1994
Holmes	1929	1989
Jarvis	1906	1990
Lamb's Corners	1954	still active
Mount Healey	1932	1988
Nanticoke	1905	1958
Nober	1927	1972
Oneida Jr	uncertain	disbanded
Sandusk	1904	1974
Selkirk	1902	still active
Sim's Locks	1931	still active
Springvale	1905	still active
Varency	1913	1966
Willow Grove	1926	still active
York	1902	1922
York (reorganized)	1971	1972

WELLAND EAST

	Inception	Disbandment
Allanburg	1903	1916
Allanburg (reorganized)	1932	still active
Black Creek	1960	1995
Bowen Road	1908	still active
Burnaby	1931	1956
Chippawa	1918	1987
Crowland	1910	still active
Crystal Beach	1933	1970
DeCew Falls	1932	still active
Ever Ready	uncertain	disbanded
Humberstone	1909	1965
Mildred Summers	1965	1975
Montrose	1925	1964
Niagara Falls (Stamford Evening)	1947	still active
Peace Bridge	1930	1983
Port Robinson	1944	disbanded
Quarryville	1940	1957
Ridgeway	1900	1940
Stamford	1911	still active
The Old Fort	1953	1954
Willoughby	1907	1991

WELLAND WEST

	Inception	Disbandment
Bethel	1914	1968
Fenwick	1909	1984
Fonthill	1913	still active
O'Reillys Bridge	1926	still active
Pelham	1934	still active
Port Colborne	1914	still active
Quaker Road	1910	1963
Ridgeville	1937	1975
Singers Corners	1954	still active
Wainfleet Jrs	1973	still active
Welland	1901	1914
Welland (reorganized)	1923	1983
Winger Wainfleet	1902	still active

BRANT NORTH

	Inception	Disbandment
Alford & Park Road	1914	still active
Blue Lake & Auburn	1917	1992
Brant County Jr	1978	1987
Cainsville	1907	1985
Echo Place	1913	1955
Glen Morris	1907	still active
Grandview & Terrace Hill	1913	1976
Langford	1911	1989
Middleport	1911	1942
Moyle Tranquility	1903	still active
Onondaga	1906	still active
Paris	1905	1946
Paris Plains	1948	1968
Riverside	1945	still active
St George	1903	still active
Tranquility Fairview	1950	1985
Tutela	1911	1965

BRANT SOUTH

	Inception	Disbandment
Burford	1899	still active
Burtch	1922	1994
Cathcart	1903	still active
Oakland (East Oakland)	1913	still active
Falkland	1909	still active

BRANT SOUTH *continued*

	Inception	Disbandment
Maple Grove	1921	still active
Mount Pleasant	1903	1992
Mount Vernon	1903	1955
New Credit	1927	1962
Newport	1925	still active
Oak Hill	1916	1993
Ohsweken	1921	1925
Ohsweken (reorganized)	1976	1981
Pleasant Ridge	1921	1981
Princeton & Woodbury	1919	still active
Scotland	1906	1908
Scotland (reorganized)	1910	1988
Sour Springs	1920	1987
Sour Springs Jr	1954	1960
Tansley	1915	still active
Whiteman's Creek	1911	still active

NORFOLK NORTH

	Inception	Disbandment
Bealton	1914	still active
Boston	1928	1945
Boston Jr	1933	1938
Courtland	1906	1989
Delhi	1908	still active
Friendly Corner	1952	1988
Goshen	1914	1942
Lynnville	1911	still active
Norfolk Jr	1927	1929
Norfolk Jr (reorganized)	1948	1954
Simcoe	1902	1974
Teeterville	1928	1989
Tyrrell	1913	1987
Tyrrell Jr	1931	1933
Union	1941	1985
Villa Nova	1915	still active
Villa Nova Jr	1983	still active
Waterford	1903	1939
Waterford Jr	1927	1929
Wilvancrest	1953	still active
Windham Centre	1914	1928

NORFOLK SOUTH

	Inception	Disbandment
Atherton	1932	1986
Carholme	1913	disbanded
Fairground	1913	1914
Forestville	1915	1979
Houghton	1946	1947
Lake Shore	1933	still active
Langton	1934	still active
Long Point	1952	1994
Lynedoch	1914	still active
Lynn Valley	1925	still active
Marburg	1920	still active
Norfolk Jr (reorganized)	1978	still active
Normandale	1914	1915
Oakcrest	1933	still active
Port Dover	1903	1914
Port Dover (reorganized)	1918	1984
Port Rowan	1923	1972
Port Rowan Auxiliary	1952	1982
Port Ryerse	1955	1986
Renton	1936	still active
St Williams	1914	still active
Vittoria	1939	still active
Walsh	1913	1971

NORFOLK SOUTH *continued*

	Inception	Disbandment
Walsingham	1939	still active
Woodhouse	1918	still active

LONDON CONVENTION AREA

MIDDLESEX EAST

	Inception	Disbandment
Belmont	1912	1978
Birr	1911	still active
Bryanston	1931	1968
Byron	1922	1968
Crumlin	1924	still active
Dorchester	1919	1968
Dorchester Jr	1933	1947
Dorchester Jr (reorganized)	1951	1954
Harrietsville	1908	still active
Harrietsville Jr	1938	1952
Hyde Park	1910	still active
Lambeth Jr	1951	1957
Mossley	1954	1991
Reynold's Creek	1991	still active
Salem Nilestown	1916	still active
St Andrews	1935	still active
Thorndale	1908	still active
Thorndale Jr	1933	1955
Wellburn	1912	1918
Wellburn (reorganized)	1949	still active
Wilton Grove	1909	still active

MIDDLESEX NORTH

	Inception	Disbandment
Ailsa Craig Jr	1945	1955
Beechwood	1904	still active
Clandeboye	1907	still active
Cloverdale	1948	1992
Coldstream	1903	1995
Edgewood Jr	1947	1958
Granton	1914	still active
Ilderton	1923	still active
Ilderton Jr	1927	1956
Keyser	1916	1985
Komoka	1913	1995
Lobo North	1926	still active
Lobo South	1904	still active
Lucan	1909	1989
Lucan Jr	1949	1957
McGillivray	1935	1973
Mooresville (Clandeboye)	1907	1913
O'Dell's	1922	disbanded
Parkhill Jr	1945	1954
Prospect Hill	1923	1993
Riverview	1938	still active

MIDDLESEX WEST

	Inception	Disbandment
Appin	1903	1977
Delaware	1914	1967
Glen Oak	1916	1973
Glencoe Jr	1949	1958
Kerwood	1910	still active
Melbourne	1926	still active
Middlemiss	1914	1972
Model	1934	still active

MIDDLESEX WEST *continued*

	Inception	Disbandment
Mosa No 9	1919	1988
Mount Brydges	1903	1904
Mount Brydges (reorganized)	1911	still active
Mount Brydges Jr	1947	1954
Muncey	1927	1953
Napier	1907	still active
Newbury Mosa	1912	1968
Strathroy	1902	1979
Strathroy Jr	1922	1945
Tait's Corners	1935	1947
Wordsville	1912	1972

ELGIN EAST

	Inception	Disbandment
Aylmer	1902	1987
Bayham	1907	1981
Calton	1952	still active
Central Elgin Jr	1945	disbanded
Central Yarmouth	1948	1969
Copenhagen	1910	1910
Corinth	1926	still active
Eden	1952	1995
Elgin East Jr	1946	1960
Kingsmill Mapleton	1907	still active
Lakeview	1919	1975
Luton	1908	1955
Lyons	1908	1978
North Yarmouth	1930	still active
Port Burwell	1907	1910
Port Stanley	1909	1957
South Yarmouth	1920	1984
Sparta Sorosis	1907	1908
Sparta Sorosis (reorganized)	1930	still active
Springfield	1904	still active
St Thomas Jrs	1976	1988
Straffordville	1915	1920
Yarmouth Glen	1959	still active

ELGIN WEST

	Inception	Disbandment
Boxall	1941	still active
Clachan	1914	still active
Cowal	1925	still active
Crinan	1919	still active
Dutton	1905	1914
Dutton (reorganized)	1925	1988
Dutton 75	1975	1977
Elgin Jr	1976	1988
Iona	1909	1989
Iona Station	1928	1991
Middlemarch	1918	still active
Paynes Mills	1927	still active
River Road	1921	still active
Rodney	1906	1977
Shedden	1913	still active
Talbotville	1927	1966
Tyrconnell	1947	still active
Wallacetown	1912	still active
West Elgin Jr	1946	1969
West Lorne	1913	still active

OXFORD SOUTH

	Inception	Disbandment
Brownsville Jr	1947	1949
Brownsville Sr	1949	still active
Burgessville	1903	1987
Cornell	1925	still active
Culloden	1949	1993
East Oxford	1967	still active
Jean Brumpton	1936	still active
Maple Park	1918	1992
Mount Elgin	1903	still active
Norwich	1907	1988
Ostrander	1944	still active
Ostrander Jr	1944	1955
Otterville	1905	1988
Pleasant Valley	1930	1974
Salford	1933	still active
Springford	1903	still active
Summerville	1929	still active
Tillsonburg	1903	1985
Tillsonburg Jr	1936	1948
Verschoyle	1936	1983
West Oxford	1929	still active
Zenda	1933	1991

PERTH SOUTH

	Inception	Disbandment
Avonton	1924	still active
Carlingford	1930	still active
Dublin	1956	1981
Elm Grove	1946	still active
Fullarton	1903	still active
Glen Gourie	1952	still active
Goulds	1919	still active
Hillcrest	1923	1991
Kirkton	1908	still active
Mitchell	1909	1954
Mitchell Jrs	1948	1962
Motherwell	1950	still active
Rannoch Jr.	1931	1943
Sebringville	1907	still active
St Marys & Queen Alexander	1909	1981
St Mary's Jr	1948	1962
St Pauls	1911	still active
Staffa	1903	still active
Staffa Jr	1929	1945

HURON SOUTH

	Inception	Disbandment
Crediton	1919	still active
Dashwood	1953	still active
Elimville	1948	still active
Exeter Jrs.	1947	disbanded
Grand Bend	1914	1916
Grand Bend (reorganized)	1945	still active
Hensall	uncertain	disbanded
Hurondale	1919	still active
Kippen East	1934	still active
Seaforth	1941	still active
Seaforth Jr	1928	1957
Zurich	1914	still active

HURON WEST

	Inception	Disbandment
Auburn	1922	still active
Belgrave	1911	still active

HURON WEST *continued*

	Inception	Disbandment
Belgrave Jr	1950	1991
Blyth	1910	1991
Blyth Jr	1945	1949
Clinton	1905	1985
Clinton Jr	1945	1960
Colwanash Jr	1948	1962
Dungannon	1914	still active
Dungannon Jr	1932	1939
Goderich	1901	1984
Godwich Township	1972	1989
Kintail	1911	1965
Londesboro	1909	1941
Londesboro (reorganized)	1950	still active
Maitland	1975	still active
North Huron Junior	1950	1967
St Augustine	1916	1943
St Helen's	1905	still active
Tiger Dunlop	1948	1990
Wingham	1903	1988

OXFORD NORTH

	Inception	Disbandment
Anna P. Lewis	1946	still active
Braemar	1907	still active
Bright	1904	1915
Brooksdale	1922	still active
Brown's (Nissouri?)	1936	still active
Cassel	1906	1915
Drumbo	1904	1985
East Missouri Jr	1950	1957
Embro & W Zorra	1908	still active
Harrington Community	1915	disbanded
Harrington Community (reorganized)	1955	1986
Hickson	1904	1915
Hickson (reorganized)	1919	still active
Innerkip	1906	1907
Innerkip (reorganized)	1953	1994
Innerkip Jr	1937	1946
Kintore	1903	1991
Lakeside	1911	1915
Lakeside (reorganized)	1921	still active
Plattsville	1904	1987
Princess Elizabeth	1947	still active
Tavistock	1902	1993
Thamesford	1904	1945
The Grace Patterson	1945	1989
Uniondale	1941	still active
Woodstock North	1928	1993

SOUTHWESTERN CONVENTION AREA

ESSEX

	Inception	Disbandment
Allouette	1954	1956
Anderdon-Malden	1926	still active
Anderton and Sandwich Jr	1947	1948
Colchester North	1962	1994
Combe	1908	1984
Cottam	1909	1991
Cottam Jrs	1945	1949
Elford Community	1909	still active

ESSEX *continued*

	Inception	Disbandment
Erie View	1969	1987
Essex	1905	1978
Essex County Jr	1954	1962
Essex Jr	1984	1994
Good Luck	1952	1992
Good Neighbours	1948	1986
Harrow	1908	still active
Kingsville	1969	still active
Maidstone	1907	disbanded
Malden (joined Anderdon)	1918	1990
Maple Leaf	1909	1988
Old Castle	1950	1983
Olinda	1909	1974
Puce	1951	1985
Roseland	1906	still active
Ruscom	1962	1994
South Woodslee	1903	1981
Windfall Community	1952	still active

KENT EAST

	Inception	Disbandment
Beechwood	1930	still active
Blenheim Ridgetown Jr	1949	1950
Bothwell	1912	still active
Clachan Jr	1949	1951
Green Ridge	uncertain	1994
Highgate	1905	1921
Highgate (reorganized)	1928	still active
Moravian	uncertain	1952
Morpeth	1908	1978
Muirkirk	1919	1987
North Thamesville	1919	still active
Palmyra	1949	still active
Rural Ridgetown Jr	1947	1949
Rural Ridgetown Workers	1937	1994
Wabash	1947	still active
Zone Centre	1922	1993

KENT WEST

	Inception	Disbandment
Balmoral	1953	still active
Bear Creek	1906	disbanded
Cedar Springs South Harwich	1905	1942
Charing Cross	1915	1960
Coatsworth	1906	disbanded
Dover	1913	disbanded
Fletcher & Valetta	1903	1924
Fletcher Friendship	1947	1994
Harwich Centre	1915	1947
Irwin	1905	1989
Kent Bridge	1907	still active
Kent Centre (Harwich Centre)	1947	still active
McKay's Corners	1958	still active
Molly Creek	1947	1991
Port Alma	1903	1921
Port Alma & Glenwood	1930	still active
Quinn	1907	1994
Romney	1927	still active
Rondeau	1915	disbanded
South Raleigh	1961	still active
Sydenham River	1918	1991
Thames River	1913	1992
Thorncliffe	1930	1978

KENT WEST *continued*

	Inception	Disbandment
Tilbury	1905	1919
Wallaceburg	1913	disbanded
Wheatley	1903	1907

LAMBTON CENTRE

	Inception	Disbandment
Adanac	1920	still active
Alvinston	1909	1987
Birk Hall	1946	still active
Brigden	1939	still active
Brooke	1912	still active
Brooke Jr	1950	1963
Corunna	1914	still active
Courtright	uncertain	1955
Enniskillen (Central Enniskillen)	1929	still active
Enniskillen	1951	disbanded
Enniskillen Jr	1951	1956
Froomfield	1949	1969
Inwood	1909	1994
Moore Centre	1920	still active
Moore Township Jr	1948	1960
Providence	1918	1993
Sunny Brooke	1982	still active

LAMBTON NORTH

	Inception	Disbandment
Aberarder	1910	still active
Arkona	1909	1976
Bear Creek	1929	still active
Blackwell	1913	1981
Bosanquet Jr	1948	1954
Clover Leaf (Union)	1953	1968
Forest	1906	1985
Lucasville	1910	1990
Maple Leaf	1907	1993
Plympton Township Jr	1949	1954
Point Edward	1930	1960
Ravenswood	1938	still active
Sarnia Township Jr	1949	disbanded
Union	1913	1953
Uttoxeter	1913	still active
Warwick	1909	still active
Warwick Jr	1946	1950
Watford	uncertain	1950

LAMBTON SOUTH

	Inception	Disbandment
Aughrim	1907	still active
Becher	1910	still active
Bentpath	1913	still active
Dawn Jr	uncertain	1960
Do R Best	1933	still active
Edy's Mills	1946	still active
Euphemia	uncertain	1955
Euphemia Jr	1950	1954
Florence	1912	1989
Oakdale	1910	1919
Oakdale (reorganized)	1949	1993
Oil Springs	1929	1988
Plum Creek	1946	1962
Port Lambton	1928	1980
Rutherford	1913	1932
Rutherford (reorganized)	1947	still active
Shetland	1907	still active
Sombra	1917	disbanded

LAMBTON SOUTH *continued*

	Inception	Disbandment
Sombra (reorganized)	1954	1976
Sombra Township Jrs	1952	1960
Thornyhurst	1911	still active
Wilkesport	1910	1961

NORTHERN CONVENTION AREA

MUSKOKA CENTRE

	Inception	Disbandment
Allensville	1951	1952
Beatrice	1919	1991
Bent River	1927	still active
Raymond	1915	1954
Rosseau	1921	still active
Ufford	1947	1991
Ullswater	1930	1991
Utterson	1918	1979

MUSKOKA NORTH

	Inception	Disbandment
Ashworth	1907	1967
Aspdin	1907	still active
Bayside (formerly Portage)	1981	1985
Birkendale	1907	1947
Brunel	1910	1925
Chaffey	1959	1963
Dorset	1913	1966
Dwight	1910	still active
Fox Point	1910	disbanded
Haystack Bay	1939	1963
Hekkla	1949	1955
Huntsville	1921	1971
Huntsville North	1913	still active
Ilfracombe	1943	1949
Portage	1920	1981
Ravenscliffe	1910	1920
Silverdale	1910	1944
The Locks	1915	1921
Yearley	1915	1919

MUSKOKA SOUTH

	Inception	Disbandment
Bala	1915	1980
Bardsville	1907	disbanded
Barkway	1946	still active
Baysville	1904	1931
Baysville (reorganized)	1946	disbanded
Bracebridge	1903	1992
Draper-Macaulay	1921	1956
Falkenburg	1928	1994
Footes Bay	1924	1966
Germania	1907	disbanded
Glen Orchard	1946	still active
Gravenhurst	1911	disbanded
Gravenhurst (reorganized)	1946	1986
Housey's Rapids	1946	1964
Monck	1911	1942
Penninsula	1947	1972
Reay	1907	1965
Sanford	1903	still active
South Macaulay	1900	still active
Torrance	1934	1966
Windermere	1912	still active

PARRY SOUND NORTH

	Inception	Disbandment
Callander	1931	1988
Chisholm	1926	still active
Golden Gate	1938	still active
Golden Valley	1906	still active
Lakeview	1935	1995
Loring	1911	1921
Maple Hill	1930	still active
Restoule	1906	1988
Silver Crescent	1948	1995
Trout Creek	1906	1988

PARRY SOUND SOUTH

	Inception	Disbandment
Balsam Creek	1939	1951
Bloomfield	1983	still active
Burks Falls	1908	1994
Chalmers	1941	1986
Christie (formerly Orrville)	1927	1966
Doe Lake	1906	1920
Dunchurch	1914	still active
Eagle Lake	1950	1964
Emsdale Scotia	1910	still active
Falding	uncertain	1915
Haldane Hill	1941	1944
Hemacville	1951	1957
Kearney	1926	1988
Magnetawan	1909	still active
Maple Island	1949	1951
McKellar	1933	1960
Mecunoma	1910	1923
Midlothian	1909	1938
Orrville	1915	1926
Parry Sound	1995	still active
South Christie	1937	1973
South River	1906	1931
South River (reorganized)	1935	still active
Sprucedale	1918	1973
Starratt	1922	disbanded
Sundridge	1910	still active
Sunny Slope	1938	1954
Whitney's Corners	1939	1942
Wiseman's Corners	1929	1939

NIPISSING

	Inception	Disbandment
Balsam Creek	1955	1966
Bonfield Jr	uncertain	1952
Calvin	1910	still active
Calvin Jr	1950	1953
Chisholm Jr	1949	1950
Feronia	1912	disbanded
Gateway	1959	1964
Kipling	1953	still active
Mattawa	1908	still active
Nipissing Jct	1930	disbanded
North Star	1946	1967
Phelps	1939	still active
Phelps Northern Jrs	1971	disbanded
Rutherglen	1950	still active
Songis	1929	disbanded
Temagami	1950	disbanded
Thibeault Hill	1958	1985
Trout Mills	1947	still active
Veuve River	1983	1994
Widdifield Station	1939	disbanded

COCHRANE-TEMISKAMING CONVENTION AREA

COCHRANE

	Inception	Disbandment
Beaver	1935	1940
Brower (to Dunning)	1930	1938
Capell	1938	disbanded
Clute	1924	still active
Cochrane	1913	1929
Cochrane (reorganized)	1929	disbanded
Dunning	1930	disbanded
Dunning (reorganized)	1947	1968
Eastford	1935	1935
Florida	1939	1945
Fraserdale	uncertain	1936
Frederickhouse	1929	1959
Friendship Circle	1935	1965
Golden Star	1939	1951
Hanna Township	1934	1944
Hearst	1917	1949
Holtyre	1939	1969
Homer	1917	1920
Hoyle	1946	1951
Hunta	1949	still active
Island Falls	1931	1959
Kapuskasing	1938	1944
Kelsa	1927	1931
Kitigan	uncertain	1938
Makina	1926	disbanded
Margaret Rose	uncertain	1944
Matheson	1914	disbanded
Monteith	1913	still active
Northern Star	1936	1971
Porquois Jct.	1915	1975
Scotty Springs	1930	1931
Shillington	1936	disbanded
Valgagne	1917	1921
Wild Rose	1954	1981

TEMISKAMING CENTRE (DISBANDED)

	Inception	Disbandment
Bailey's Corners	uncertain	disbanded
Boston Creek	1929	1935
Bourkes	1940	1963
Charlton	1910	1954
Dack	1936	1981
Dane	1930	1935
Dane (reorganized)	1964	1965
Earlton	1910	1968
Englehart	1913	1956
Heaslip	1911	1935
Hill's Lake	1930	1937
Ingram # 1	1934	1950
Leeville	1933	1941
Marter	1914	1920
Riverside (Marter)	1939	1950
Robillard	1935	1941
Savard	1926	1992
Sunday Creek	1934	1942
Swastika	uncertain	1946
Tarzwell	1961	1963
West Chamberlain	1930	1945
West Channel	1930	1945
Whitewood Grove	uncertain	disbanded

TEMISKAMING SOUTH

	Inception	Disbandment
Blanche River	1935	disbanded
Cane	1924	still active
Dymond	1937	disbanded
Elk Lake	1914	1924
Elk Lake (reorganized)	1924	1991
Elk Pitt	1938	1954
Englehart (formerly Dack)	1981	still active
Haileybury (formerly Clover Valley)	1906	disbanded
Hanbury	1905	disbanded
Henwood	1930	1953
Hillview	1907	1940
Hudson	1964	still active
Leesville	uncertain	disbanded
Matabitchuan	uncertain	disbanded
McCool	uncertain	1948
Milberta	1906	still active
New Liskeard	1910	1988
North Sunshine (North Cobalt)	1938	still active
Rockley	1929	1994
Silver Nugget	1955	1986
Sunday Creek (reorganized)	1950	still active
Sunshine	1913	disbanded
Sutton Bay	1933	1985
Thornloe	1911	1995
Wabi Valley	1929	1954

NORTH CENTRAL CONVENTION AREA

MANITOULIN EAST

	Inception	Disbandment
Assiginack	1934	1955
Big Lake	1906	still active
Green Bay	1905	disbanded
Little Current	1907	disbanded
Mindemoya	1907	still active
No. 1 Howland	1918	disbanded
Providence Bay (Carnarvon)	1909	disbanded
Rockville	1913	still active
Sandfield	1937	still active
Sheguiandah	1908	still active
Tekhummah	1905	disbanded
Tekhumman Jr	uncertain	1944

MANITOULIN WEST

	Inception	Disbandment
Barrie Island	1906	still active
Billings	1905	1972
Burpee Evansville	1935	1953
Cockburn Island	1905	1947
Elizabeth Bay	1914	1921
Gordon	1910	still active
Gore Bay	1915	1917
Grimsthorpe	1905	1920
Ice Lake	1905	still active
Meldrum Bay	1905	1951
Poplar	1905	1990
Silver Water	1905	still active
Spring Bay	1905	1920
Spring Bay (reorganized)	1927	still active

SUDBURY

	Inception	Disbandment
Azilda	1954	1974
Capreol	1920	1927
Capreol (reorganized)	1932	1969
Chelmsford	1949	1960
Falconbridge	1936	1945
Garson	1937	1967
Lebel	1957	1961
Markstay	1947	still active
Mary Louise	1948	1951
McVittie	1939	1941
Minnow Lake	1936	1939
Naughton	1961	1975
Norman	1937	1990
North Star (Star of the North)	1949	still active
Penage Road	1948	still active
Skead Road	1943	still active
Wahnapitae	1951	1951
Waters	1936	still active
Westree	1936	1938
Westree (reorganized)	1939	1953

SUDBURY WEST

	Inception	Disbandment
Espanola	1980	still active
Lee Valley	1910	still active
Massey	1941	still active
Spanish River	1948	still active
Walford (joined Massey, 1995)	1915	1995

ALGOMA CENTRE

	Inception	Disbandment
Batchewana	1941	1942
East Korah	1907	still active
Garden River	1947	1956
Goodwill	1960	1963
Goulais Bay	1905	1964
Highland Park	1948	still active
Margaret Marshall Memorial	1950	1988
North Tarentorus	1934	still active
Prince	1909	still active
Prince of Wales	1939	1982
Princess Anne	1953	disbanded
Searchmount	1920	1922
South Tarentorus	1905	1987
Wesley	1962	1967
West Korah	1905	1965
West Korah Jr	1934	1950
West Tarentorus	1951	1968

ALGOMA EAST

	Inception	Disbandment
Black Creek	1949	1954
Bright	1920	1961
Community	1947	1964
Coronation	1937	1950
Dayton	1961	still active
Elliot Lake	1965	1987
Harmony	1930	1982
Iron Bridge	1914	still active
Lee Valley*	1910	1988
Little Rapids	1954	1983
Massey*	1941	1988
Nesterville	1948	still active
Patricia	1919	1984
Patricia Evening	1963	1987
Princess Elizabeth	1948	1953
Princess Margaret Jr	1949	1956
Queen Elizabeth	1953	still active
Royal	1939	1957
Soweby	1912	1920
Soweby (reorganized)	1947	1987
Spanish River*	1948	1988
Sunnyside (Ansonia)	1929	still active
Thessalon	1965	1975
Victoria	1927	1962
Walford*	1914	1988
Wharncliffe	1952	1977

* to Sudbury West, 1988

ALGOMA NORTH SHORE

	Inception	Disbandment
A Line Sailors Encampment	1917	1920
A Line Sailors Encampment* (reorganized)	1925	1968
Bar River	1931	still active
Caterton (The Mountain)	1932	disbanded
Clover Valley*	1948	still active
Desbarats	1906	1923
Desbarats (reorganized)	1924	still active
Echo Bay	1906	1992
Echo Bay Evening	1960	still active
Echo Valley	1949	1993
Five Lakes	uncertain	disbanded
Gordon Lake	1916	1987
Hilton Beach*	1920	1991
Johnson	uncertain	disbanded
Kentvale*	1905	1953
Laird	1934	1968
McLennan	1905	still active
MacLennan North Shore	1935	1956
Richard's Landing*	1905	still active
Royal (Portlock)	1939	1992
Sunnyside	1935	1957
Sylvan Valley	1936	1953
Temby Bay	1919	disbanded
The Mountain*	1902	1924

* formerly in St. Joseph's Island District

NORTHWESTERN CONVENTION AREA

THUNDER BAY

	Inception	Disbandment
Beardmore (Leitch Gold Mines)	1938	1942
Blake	1919	1921
Carter's (School)	1913	1930
Cascades	1936	1939
Cloud Bay	1924	1926
Conmee	1909	disbanded
Coronation	1937	1947
Dorion	1906	1935
East End Junior	uncertain	disbanded
Finmark	1926	1943
Fort William East	1910	1995
Fort William West (Westfort)	1919	still active
Harstone	1924	1955
Hornepayne	1919	1932
Hydro	1927	disbanded
Hydro (reorganized)	1935	1939
Hymers	1906	1969
Jarvis River (Cloud Bay)	1935	1938
Jumbo Gardens	1931	still active
Kakabeka Falls	1945	still active
Macdiarmid	1950	1951
McIntyre	1913	still active
Moose Hill (Blake)	1921	1934
Murillo	1906	1928
Murillo (reorganized)	1934	1935
Nipigon	1927	1935
Nipigon (reorganized)	1935	1937
Nipigon (reorganized)	1969	1979
North Blake (reorganized)	1935	still active
North Neebing	1952	1954
O'Connor	1909	still active
O'Connor Junior	1927	1928
Ouimet	1906	1936
Ouimet-Dorion	1936	1972
Pass Lake	1930	1942
Pass Lake - Pearl	1966	still active
Pearson Pardee	1935	still active
Pearson West	1935	1939
Piper Park	1936	1939
Port Arthur	1911	1945
Princess Elizabeth	1947	1954
Raith	1935	1938
Red Rock	1950	1967
Rosslyn	1924	still active
Rossport	1925	1963
Schreiber	1927	1980
Scoble-Gillies	1925	1935
Scoble West	1920	1925
Scoble West	1935	1941
Silver Mountain	1935	1936
Slate River	1906	1946
Slate River (reorganized)	1958	still active
South Gillies	1909	1925
South Gillies	1909	1929
South Gillies	1935	1980
South Neebing	1918	1995
Stanley	1925	still active
Stanley Park	1936	1943
Stanley Park (reorganized)	1951	1954
Stepstone	1973	1979
Stirling Lyons	1923	1972
Sunshine	1928	1934
Terrace Bay	1948	1951
The McGregor	1949	1967
Thunder Bay Jr (Port Arthur Jr)	1935	1940
Upsala	1935	1977
Vicker's Heights	1935	1953
Vicker's Heights (reorganized)	1968	still active
Wamsley	1925	1927
Wamsley Pearson & Pardee	1927	1934

RAINY RIVER

	Inception	Disbandment
Atikokan	1922	1979
Atwood	1927	still active
Atwood Jr.	1932	1934
Aylsworth	1921	1945
Aylsworth (reorganized)	1947	1992
Aylsworth Jr (Lash Jr)	1923	1931
Barnhart	1906	1988
Barwick	1906	1970
Beaver	1919	1943
Berglund	1925	1947
Big Fork	1911	1914
Big Fork (reorganized as Big Fork & Aylsworth)		
	1919	1947
Black Hawke	1910	1913
Black Hawke (reorganized)		
	1934	1951
Box Alder	1918	1925
Burriss	1907	still active
Carpenter	1921	still active
Chapple	1918	still active
Crozier	1914	1960
Dance	1939	1970
Dearlock	1932	1946
Devlin	1918	1980
Devlin–La Vallee	1916	1925
Dobie	1957	1971
Emo	1905	1989
Emo Jrs	1978	disbanded
Finland	1964	1969
Forest	1934	still active

RAINY RIVER *continued*

	Inception	Disbandment
Fort Frances	1907	1909
Fort Frances (reorganized)		
	1919	1987
Four Seasons Jr	1963	1967
Harris Hill	1940	1949
Kingsford	uncertain	1935
Kingsford East	1917	1934
La Vallee	1915	1916
La Vallee Jr	1925	1926
Lake of the Woods	1952	still active
Lash	1919	1983
Lash Jr	1923	1931
Matherford	1913	disbanded
McIrvine	1920	still active
Minahico	1920	1945
Mine Centre	1937	1946
Miss Campbell	1922	1927
Miss Campbell (reorganized)		
	1957	1983
Morson	1953	still active
North Branch	1936	1952
Pinewood	1915	1937
Pinewood Jr	1930	1933
Rapid River	1906	1907
Roddick	1935	1938
Roddick (reorganized)	1938	1939
Shenston	1909	1968
Stratton	1906	1993

KENORA

	Inception	Disbandment
Amesdale	1929	1966
Barclay	1909	1914
Barclay (reorganized)	1962	still active
Britton Pioneers	1955	1995
Camp Robinson	1949	1952
Dryden	1906	1948
Dyment	1928	1962
Eagle River	1906	1945
Ear Falls	1928	1962
Ignace	1921	1962
Jaffray	1938	1992
Keewatin	1920	1964
Keewatin Jr	uncertain	1941
Kenora	1912	1944
Laclu	1955	1955
Minnitaki	1933	1991
New Prospect	1960	still active
Osaquau	1933	disbanded
Ostersund	1934	1940
Oxdrift	1906	still active
Oxford	uncertain	disbanded
Pellatt–Laclu	1955	1962
Pine Portage	1948	disbanded
Quibell	1919	1965
Redditt	1938	1961
Richan	1926	1993
Rideout	1928	still active
Sioux Lookout	1953	1956
Wabigoon	1924	1961
Wabigoon Jr	1924	disbanded

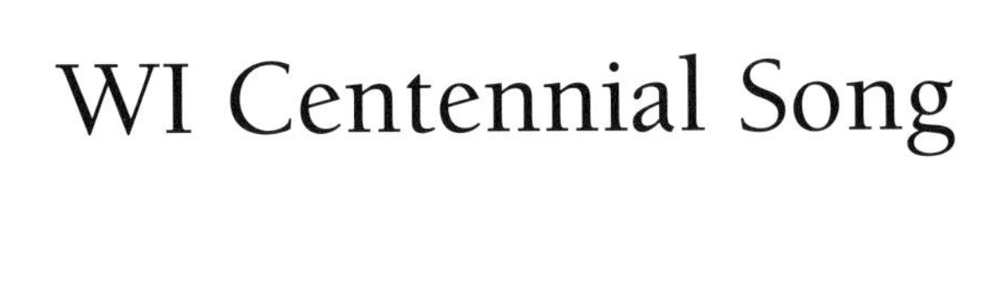

WI CENTENNIAL SONG

It's a hundred years since
Adelaide Hoodless was convinced
That milk should be pasteurized.
Then Janet and Erland Lee
Found it easy to see
That women should organize.

For Mrs. Hoodless knew
That informed women grew,
So they did mobilize.
Hundred and one women came
And things were ne'er the same
And they formed the WIs.

So this idea spread,
Round the world it shed
Its light. Things modernized.
Then women's homes improved,
And country's laws were moved,
Their knowledge exercised.

To encourage, help and share,
Build a better world with care
Is the work of the WIs
Now a hundred years young,
Still there's work to be done.
Women's lives to be vitalized.

Now it's time to celebrate:
Achievements commemorate
With honour and with pride.
This Centennial salute
Of the Women's Institute.
Women of the world, Arise!

Verse 2
ize For Mrs. Hoodless knew that in----formed women grew. So they did mo----bi-
For Mrs. Hoodless knew that in—formed women grew. So they did mo——bi-
lize. Hundred and one wo-men came And things were n'er the same For they formed the W.
lize. Hundred and one wo-men came And things were n'er the same For they formed the W.
Verse 3
I's. So this i---dea spread, Round the world it shed Its Light, Things mod------ern
I's. So this i---dea spread, Round the world it shed Its Light, Things mod------ern

ized. Then wo-men's homes im-proved, And country's laws were moved, Their know----ledge ex-------er-
ized. Then wo--men's homes im--proved, And country's laws were moved, Their know----ledge ex--------er-
Verse 4
cised. To en----courage, help, and share, Build a better world with care Is the work of the W.
cised. To en---courage, help, and share, Build a better world with care Is the work of the W.
I's. Now a hundred years young, Still there's work to be done. Women's lives to be vi--------tal
I's. Now a hundred years young, Still there's work to be done. Women's lives to be vi---------tal

Verse 5 - unison with descant
ized. Now it's time to celebrate A-----chievements commemorate. With ho-------nour and with
ized.
pride. This Cen--tennial salute Of the Women's Institute. Women of the world, a----------rise!
This Cen--tennial salute Of the Women's Institute. Women of the world, a----------rise!
poco rit.
8va
— Marie F. Harris

The Women's Institute Ode

A goodly thing it is to meet
In Friendship's circle bright,
Where nothing stains the pleasure sweet
Nor dims the radiant light.
No unkind word our lips shall pass,
No envy sour the mind,
But each shall seek the common weal,
The good of all mankind.

The first official reports of the Ode occurred between 1910 and 1915.
It is sung to the tune of "Auld Lang Syne."

The Women's Institute Grace

We thank Thee, Father for Thy care,
Food, friends and kindliness we share;
May we forever mindful be
Of "Home and Country" and of Thee.

In 1950 the Women's Institute Grace, composed by Mrs. Clara Lintell Deakin of Ottawa Area, was accepted by the provincial Board.
It is sung to the tune of "Old Hundred."

The Mary Stewart Collect

Keep us O Lord from pettiness;
let us be large in thought, in word and deed.
Let us be done with fault finding
and leave off self seeking.
May we put away all pretence and meet
each other face to face, without self-pity
and without prejudice.
May we never be hasty in judgement
and always generous.
Let us take time for all things;
make us grow calm, serene, gentle.
Teach us to put into action our better
impulses straight forward and unafraid.
Grant that we may realize that it is
the little things that create differences;
that in the big things in life we are one.
And may we strive to touch and know the
great human heart common to us all, and
O Lord God let us not forget to be kind.

Miss Mary Stewart wrote the Collect as a prayer for the day. It was adopted as a "Collect for Club Women."

A Note About Sources

Published writing on the Women's Institutes is not plentiful. Three earlier commemorative histories have been written about the WI in Ontario, and they are a good starting point for those interested in earlier versions of the history. Three official histories of the WI movement have been written to date: Viola M. Powell, *Forty Years Agrowing: A History of Ontario Women's Institutes* (Port Perry: The Port Perry Star, 1941); Walker et. al., *Fifty Years of Achievement* (Toronto: Federated Women's Institutes of Ontario, 1947); and *Ontario Women's Institute Story: In Commemoration of the 75th Anniversary of the Founding of the Ontario Women's Institutes of Ontario* (Federated Women's Institutes of Ontario, 1972).

Among academic authors, Terry Crowley's work is the most widely cited to date. Specifically, his article, "The Origins of Continuing Education for Women: The Ontario Women's Institutes," *Canadian Woman Studies* 7, 3 (fall 1986): 78–81 focusses on the educational side of the WI. Robert Stamp takes up related themes in "Teaching Girls Their 'God-Given Place in Life': The Introduction of Home Economics in the Schools," *Atlantis*, 2, 2 (1977): 18–34. On Adelaide Hoodless, see Cheryl MacDonald, *Adelaide Hoodless: Domestic Crusader* (Toronto: Dundurn Press, 1986), and Terry Crowley, "Madonnas Before Magdalens: Adelaide Hoodless and the Making of the Canadian Gibson Girl," *Canadian Historical Review*, 67, 4 (1986): 520–547. Professor Crowley gave an illustrated talk on Hoodless at the Ontario Women's History Network Conference in Guelph, October 1993. A recent doctoral dissertation by Margaret Kechnie looks at the early years of the WI, before federation in 1919, and emphasizes the organizers' agenda of reinforcing traditional roles for women. "Keeping Things Tidy for Home and Country: The Early Years of the Ontario Women's Institutes," Ph.D. thesis, OISE, 1995. I take a different view, emphasizing branch autonomy and local directives in Linda M. Ambrose, "What Are the Good of Those Meetings Anyway?: The Early Popularity of the Ontario Women's Institutes," *Ontario History* (March 1995):1–20; and also in my essay on the WI in Northern Ontario, "Imitators or Innovators?: The Women's Institutes of Northern Ontario, 1905–1930," in Margaret Kechnie and Marj Reitsma-Street (eds.), *Changing Women, Changing Lives: Women and the Northern Ontario Experience*, Dundurn Press, forthcoming. Nora Cebotarev has written about some of the newer organizations for rural women in "From Domesticity to the Public Sphere: Farm Women, 1945–1986," in Joy Parr (ed.), *A Diversity of Women: Ontario 1945–1980*, University of Toronto Press, 1995. To put the history of the Women's Institutes into a broader context, some readers might enjoy the synthesis of Canadian women's history, now in its second edition: Alison Prentice et al., *Canadian Women: A History*, Harcourt, Brace, Jovanovich, 1996.

Because of the link between the Women's Institutes and the Department of Agriculture of the Province of Ontario, government records provide an important source of information. In particular, the *Sessional Papers* of Ontario (containing the published annual reports of various government departments) are helpful for the period up to 1948. University libraries and larger public libraries usually hold fairly complete collections of these reports. For the early years of the WI in Ontario, the Annual Report of the Women's Institutes was contained in the Annual Report of the Department of Agriculture. Sometimes these reports were over a hundred pages long, and they contain a wealth of both quantitative material (membership statistics and financial records) and qualitative reports of various conferences, officials and guest speakers. For the provincial overview, these records are the definitive source on the WI. There is also a surprising amount of local information hidden in those same reports since area conventions were covered in great detail, and individual branches were well represented. After 1948, the *Sessional Papers* ceased being published in that comprehensive format, and one must turn to the published *Reports of the Department of Agriculture,* which were no longer bound together with all the other government departments. The record is much more sparse for the later period. The reporting style changed, no doubt as a cost-cutting measure, and the reports no longer contained the full detail of the organization's activity. Though they are still useful for limited statistical and financial records, the reports are only sketchy and very short on detail. Again, these reports are available in many places, but I found the collection at the University of Guelph Library to be the most complete.

The official organ of the Women's Institutes from 1933 to the present is the magazine *Home and Country*. First published in tabloid form, the magazine has evolved through several different formats and publishing schedules. Currently published quarterly by the FWIO from its headquarters outside Guelph, the magazine was previously funded and underwritten by funds from the Ministry (previously the Department) of Agriculture. Complete collections of the magazine are available on microfilm at the University of Guelph Library, and perhaps at a number of other locations as well. Broken collections of paper copies of the magazine undoubtedly exist in countless attics or basements across the province, held by interested members who have preserved their personal copies. The FWIO headquarters owns a complete set. Prior to 1933, the Women's Institutes had an arrangement with the *Canadian Home Journal* to devote several pages of that women's monthly magazine to news of the Women's Institutes. Very few copies of that magazine exist for the early years of the century. I was able to locate only two issues at the Archives of Ontario.

The Tweedsmuir Histories are probably the most well known historical source that documents not only the local branches of the WI, but also local communities throughout Ontario. The idea of collecting local history dates back to the 1920s in some branches, when a Historical Research Committee was established by the FWIO Board. Serious attention to the creation of local histories was renewed in the 1940s as the fiftieth anniversary of the WI approached, and Lady Susan Tweedsmuir gave her approval to have the books named after her late husband, the former governor general of Canada. These books are held by the curator of each local branch during her term of office. Various arrangements are made, but the books sometimes reside in the curator's home, or in a public place such as the local library, museum or municipal office. Some branches have had the foresight to arrange for fireproof storage of the volumes, and have had the original volumes microfilmed or photocopied, both to preserve the originals and to allow for greater circulation of the books. In the case of disbanded branches, it is more difficult to locate the Tweedsmuir history books. Some remain in private hands, others have been turned over to district or area officials of the WI. In most cases, members have arranged for the deposit of these books in libraries or museums. I discovered in my travels, though, that archival, museum and library holdings are not always fully catalogued. It pays to ask lots of questions. There are several impressive and extensive collections of Tweedsmuir history books in the province. The most complete is undoubtedly at the Archives of Ontario, where hundreds of these volumes have been microfilmed. The University of Guelph Library owns a complete set of those microfilms too. The Ontario Agricultural Museum at Milton has an extensive collection of records including several Tweedsmuir history books. In Northwestern Ontario, the Rainy River District WI Museum at Emo has a very impressive collection as well. For local research, one must be thorough in scouting throughout the regional, county and township museums and archives.

Local record books are also important, in particular, the branch, district and area minute books. Access to these records is usually granted through contact with WI members. Often, the current secretary has the complete set of minute books in her possession. In some cases, these are stored for safekeeping in fireproof vaults or cupboards in the community. Branch records vary in quality and in detail, depending on the secretaries who have kept those minutes over the years. In altogether too many cases, branches report with regret that early books were lost in fires, usually in individual members' homes but sometimes in fires in the community buildings. Again, in the case of disbanded branches, the books may be held in private hands, though WI policy dictates that the records are to be turned over to district officials. Local quarrels sometimes mean that this protocol has not been followed. The problem of storage space is a real one. The bulky collections are sometimes not given a place of honour, and the dilemma of what to do with them is real. At one point in the recent past, the FWIO passed a resolution that the record books of disbanded branches should be deposited in the Ontario Agricultural Museum in

Milton. That provided a good solution for some branches in that part of the province who found that their local museum or library was not able to house the collection. Again though, the wish to keep the records in the community where they were created is a real concern. Milton is a long way from Kingston or Chatham or Kenora. Nevertheless, the Agricultural museum has an impressive collection. At the time of writing, the future of that museum is in jeopardy because of the cutbacks of the provincial government.

In the course of this project, a new archival collection was created, which is housed at the University of Guelph. When the FWIO was relocating to its new headquarters at RR 5, Guelph, dozens of boxes of material were salvaged and deposited in the University Archives at the University of Guelph. That collection, known as the Federated Women's Institutes of Ontario Collection, contains a variety of materials including FWIO Board minutes, correspondence and memorabilia. One of the most significant parts of that collection is several hundred photographs, some of which appear in this book. As well, the materials that were given to me for this project are being processed for archival deposit. In response to my inquiries, members of WI branches across the province gave or sent materials that pertain to their local organizations and complement the provincial record.

Oral history helped to inform this study as hundreds of women shared their experiences and stories. For this project, I chose to interview women in groups rather than individually. This was a deliberate decision, allowing for more women to share in that part of the project. Group discussions drew more women into the experience than individual interviews would have permitted. Researchers interested in pursuing more local studies will find many willing informers who might agree to answer questions about their adventures in the Institute.

Local newspapers are a helpful source of information because most community newspapers across the province have carried news of the local Institutes' activities. This sometimes took the form of a regular column by the public relations officer for the branch, and at other times involved coverage of special events sponsored by the Institute or celebrations of anniversaries and milestones. From time to time, newspapers have issued special commemorative editions to mark WI occasions. For example, in 1947, the *London Free Press* published a special issue to celebrate the fiftieth anniversary of the WI in Ontario; so did the *Brantford Expositor* on the occasion of the provincial seventy-fifth. Researchers will find such accounts very helpful in tracing local and district Institute activity. Other local sources include published versions of township or county histories that highlight WI branches in that area. Sometimes the local Institute itself spearheaded the publication as they turned their Tweedsmuir volumes into more accessible format by releasing a book of local history.

A wealth of sources is available, some in public collections, and others in private hands. Whether one is interested in researching Women's Institute history at a local level or looking beyond that to a larger synthesis, the sources I have mentioned will provide a good starting point. There is no shortage of sources and no shortage of resource people. In most cases, the study of one branch or district could provide an interesting case study of the larger trends that are traced in this book. I would suggest that as part of the centennial festivities, branch members should consider undertaking that kind of study (or encouraging local students to do so) in order to see how their local group's experiences compare with the version of the provincial history that is presented here.

Acknowledgments

My first debt is to the members of the Women's Institutes themselves, who have been unwavering in their enthusiasm from the start. Countless individuals have welcomed me into their homes and their halls, fed me, met my train or bus, directed me or driven me, as I toured across the province. Thank you for welcoming a non-member and sharing your books, your records, your photographs, your communities and your stories. Over six hundred women agreed to be interviewed, some reluctantly at first, and your voices have helped to shape my understanding of the WI movement. The staff of the FWIO provincial office and Janine Roelens-Grant, editor of *Home and Country*, were always prompt and efficient in answering all my queries and requests for help. The members of the FWIO Centennial Book Committee (Jane Croft, Margaret Atkins and Lynn Campbell) have been supportive throughout the process. Jane Croft has done an expert job as administrator, fundraiser, booster and research assistant. Thank you for your drive, your curiosity and your patience. This has been a wonderful experience.

Over the life of this project, I have been associated with three different university history departments. At the University of Waterloo, Wendy Mitchinson, John English, Heather MacDougall, and friends in the Women's History Discussion Group first encouraged me to apply for the position of researcher and writer, and their initial enthusiasm remained as an important inspiration throughout the project. In 1993–1994 I was awarded a SSHRC postdoctoral fellowship at the University of Guelph where Terry Crowley, Jamie Snell, Donna Andrew and Eric Reiche made me most welcome. Nancy Sadek and the staff of the University of Guelph Archives and Special Collections went out of their way to help me, especially Gloria Troyer, who oversaw the processing of the FWIO collection that we deposited there. In the fall of 1994, when I accepted a position in the history department of Laurentian University in Sudbury, I met another group of wonderfully supportive colleagues who have made my first years of full-time teaching most enjoyable. Matt Bray, Janice Liedl, Carl Wallace, Rose May Démoré, Ashley Thomson and Margaret Kechnie each took a personal interest in me and my project, and I wish to thank them for creating a warm, welcoming and productive atmosphere for research and writing. Research assistants, including Tricia Leduc, Tracy Penny Light and Margaret Boyd, provided capable support at critical stages, and I thank them for their careful work, probing questions and delightful friendships.

Funding for the project came from a variety of sources, and I want to acknowledge the Ontario Heritage Foundation, the Social Sciences and Humanities Research Council of Canada (SSHRC), the Institute for Northern Ontario Research and Development (INORD), and the Laurentian University Research Fund (LURF). A list of corporate sponsors appears elsewhere.

In true grass-roots fashion, the Federated Women's Institutes of Ontario have backed the project all the way, supported in large part by contributions from individual members, local branches and district officers who believed in the project and paid for the work through their pre-orders and donations.

Several people read the manuscript in part or in whole, and they have offered a variety of helpful advice: Rosemary Ambrose, Jane Croft, Terry Crowley, Jenna Kennedy, Peggy Knapp, and Wendy Mitchinson. Joan Schlotzhauer and Claudette Larcher efficiently transcribed the interview tapes. Rob Ambrose provided the technical expertise to manage large databases of research material, and helped to collate the list of branches that appears in the appendix. Janine Roelens-Grant suggested the inclusion of a map showing WI districts, and then took the initiative to research and create it.

Good friends in Waterloo and Sudbury and our two families have cheered me on in this work and their support kept me going. Thanks for your interest and encouragement, and for the support you showed in so many different ways. In Rosemary and Gordon Ambrose, I have a wonderful set of second parents and a home away from home. My mother, Doreen McGuire, is a continuing inspiration to me; she makes me appreciate roots and wings. My daughters, Meredith and Meghan, know that history is important to me, but they help me focus on the here and now, on being and becoming. Rob always believes and he is still the one.

Linda M. Ambrose
May 1996,
Sudbury, Ontario.

Index